BRITAIN AT THE CROSSROADS

BRITAIN AT THE CROSSROADS

Russell Wood

The Book Guild Ltd
Sussex, England

The Book Guild Ltd.
25 High Street,
Lewes, Sussex

First published 1997
© Russell Wood, 1997

Set in Times
Typesetting by Acorn Bookwork, Salisbury, Wiltshire

Printed in Great Britain by
Bookcraft (Bath) Ltd, Avon

A catalogue record for this book is
available from the British Library

ISBN 1 85776 211 8

This book is dedicated to
Margaret Hilda Thatcher
who has the qualities of the
great Queen Elizabeth I – strength of character
and intellect and the political gift and strength of being
in harmony with her times.

CONTENTS

PREFACE

The original object of this book was to question the desirability of the post-war consensus and to comment favourably on the way in which Margaret Thatcher succeeded in breaking it. On finding that this had been done before, I widened my horizon to give a much broader view of our history in the belief that a knowledge of the past helps immeasurably to understand the present. The pre-war appeasement policy is a well-known example of this but there are many others such as the pre-war vested interests of the owners of the old staple manufacturing industries and the trade unions to see that these industries were protected in every way, to the detriment of the new and dynamic industries that were rising in the southern part of the country. There have been many opportunities to point to the unsatisfactory policies and attitudes which Margaret Thatcher was to reform after 1979 (30 times in all) but as this book finishes at the General Election of 1964 the greater part of this massive achievement is not here recorded.

The second object of the book is to provide a concise and, hopefully, easily readable explanation of our constitutional, political, economic and social history. There must be many people whose training, qualifications and experience are in other fields but who would like to be able to improve their knowledge in these subjects. How many people who are non-specialist historians, for example, really know about the decline of the Liberal Party or, for that matter, the rise of the Labour Party, or of the significance of our Common Law or the meaning of the Rule of Law or the shadowy place in Britain's legal structure of Administrative Law. There have been weighty tomes written on all these topics but the people who, hopefully, will read my book would have neither the time nor inclination to read them. I have done it for them – and my book would be a convenient source of reference ready to hand.

In my reading and thoughts in almost fifty years I have come to a number of conclusions which should, at the very least, be interesting to the readers of this book. The chief of these is that the greatest achievement of the English, and their main and significant contribution to civilization, is their development of political liberalism, namely political and legal freedom before the law – parliamentary democracy and the rule of law. This has arisen partly because of geographical advantages whereby the English Channel has enabled the English people to get on with their lives with the minimum of foreign incursions, unlike the Continental countries of Europe. But the main factor has been the unusual, if not unique, facility of the English of combining to a high degree, the paradoxical qualities of conservatism and radicalism. Finally, the book is slightly autobiographical which, hopefully, will add to its interest.

FOREWORD BY
LORD HARRIS OF HIGH CROSS

Towards recovery of national self-confidence

Part of the joy of reading these crowded but well-written pages is the impression that the author embarked on this conspectus of what I would call the maturing of our English polity and society less for any didactic purpose than for his own evident enjoyment in such a voyage of discovery. True, Russell Wood put in a stint as teacher of history and economics at Shrewsbury School. But academics too often pride themselves on a narrow specialism and seek to impress colleagues by advertising their expertise with endless pernickety flourishes that distract the average reader from a strong grasp of the unfolding story.

Mr Wood's special contribution to our illumination no doubt owes much to his remarkable decision to abandon schoolteaching and take up – of all things – stockbroking in the City. Although his purpose was to play an active part in local and national politics, a by-product of becoming an investment analyst was at once to intensify his fascination with the origins of the post-war 'Butskellite' consensus and to sharpen his doubts about its viability. The result is a powerful antidote to that catastrophic collapse in national self-confidence which lies at the root of our multiplying contemporary anxieties.

In his exploration of the genesis of the welfare state, trade union power, mounting taxation, and the imperial retreat that led to our European imbroglio, Russell Wood is led to recount the principal political, economic and social developments since the Glorious Revolution that shaped Britain's inglorious post-war decline. Although his present account ends with the 1964 General Election, he reviews the problems culminating in 1979, thereby setting the stage for what Richard Cockett in *Thinking the Unthinkable* has recently described as 'the economic counter-revolution' which others have vulgarised as 'Thatcherism'. In so doing, he throws light on one of the most dramatic political tragedies in our history, namely the failure of the Liberal party either to preserve the historic tenets of liberalism or to attract the support of 19th century working-class protest, thereby opening the way for its replacement by an ideological Labour Party supported by middle-class intellectuals opposed to capitalism.

The breezy optimism that pervades even the gloomiest chronicles of errors in policy on housing, education, local government, stems from the author's overriding admiration for what he has called the greatest contribution of the English to civilisation, namely their development of parliamentary democracy and the rule of law – on the uniqueness of which he has much to say. With the objectivity of a New Zealander, boasting English, Scottish and Irish antecedents. Mr Wood credits this great contribution, firstly to the national independence fostered by geographical separation from undue Continent involvements and, most importantly of all, to the facility the English have of paradoxically combining in rare measure the qualities of conservatism and radicalism. It is only when they are lulled into acceptance of consensus that this natural defence is stultified, as with the pre-war appeasement of Hitler or the neglect of technical schools which prevented the 1944 Butler reforms ever becoming truly tripartite.

The full story is clearly and powerfully told, with a vigour drawn partly from its charming autobiographical flavour. It is an unashamed celebration of the long-maturing background to the crossroads at which Britain was to arrive in 1979. When we rediscover our national self-confidence and finally commit ourselves to taking the right turning, this book may be seen to provide a large part of the essential bones of the much-debated school history curriculum.

ACKNOWLEDGEMENTS

As Lord Harris has implied, this book is a labour of love and although it is not the result of years of original research, it is, as I have said, the result of reading and thoughts in almost fifty years. Soon after I began writing it on my retirement in mid-1990, I contacted Lord Harris out of the blue, and he could not have given me more encouragement if he had known me for many years, as an established authority. One of the bonuses of my embarking on this book is to have been able to know the warmth of his personality and to benefit from his sagacity. Typically, he volunteered to write his flattering Foreword, which I had not even thought of asking him to do.

I have always said that pursuing such activities as collecting for charity and canvassing for a political party restores ones faith in human nature for, on the whole people are kindly disposed, for a variety of reasons, including the fact that they probably feel as though they should be doing it themselves. Similarly, I was impressed by the response of the many people to whom I spoke in organizations such as the House of Commons Library, the Glasgow Mitchell Library, the Conservative Central Office Library, the Labour Party Research Department and the museum of Labour Party History, the Essex County Library, the Law Society and the Law Chancellor's Office, and various Government Departments and Embassies. In particular, Messers Paul Pollack and David Young, archivists of the King's School, Canterbury and Christ's Hospital, respectively, have been very helpful as also has my accountant Mr Victor Coles, who provided some useful information on the introduction of investment allowances in the 1954 budget.

I was fortunate that Dr David Ibbetson, of Magdelen College Oxford, kindly undertook to read the first chapter and the main one on law, for they have benefited greatly from his legal expertise. My greatest debt, however, is to Christopher Thompson of the Open University, who has answered particular queries and read the script critically. It may be objected that the book contains too many generalizations but its quality has undoubtedly been much enhanced by his scholarly interjections.

As one of the few remaining authors not to use a word processor, I have to thank Debbie Teare, not only for the quality of her work but for her unfailing cheerfulness and support. My wife, also, has played an important part, for she has had to put up with many hours of solitude and has uncomplainingly done many of the day to day tasks that should fall in the province of the man of the family. I am indeed grateful to her.

Finally I should like to record my appreciation of the fact that my original agent, Patrick Walsh, took me on as an unknown 'amateur' author and, although we were unable to gain the support of a publisher, he was always helpful and encouraging. Through the good offices of my son Antony, I was able to enlist the help of Robert Vaughan Williams, whose years of experience in the public relations field have seen to it that the project has proceeded to a successful conclusion. I am also grateful for the active support of my son Christopher.

1

The Background

Although the book is entitled *Britain at the Crossroads*, I suspect that it will be more about England and the English than our 'Celtic' cousins, the Scottish, Welsh and Irish. I am sure that anthropologists have written, and will write, learned treatises debunking the notion of national characteristics but they will not overcome the doubts of the silent majority whose unrecorded views are presented in this book. The left wing and ultra-left wing are the most vociferous of the chattering classes, the latter most of all, in spite of the fact that they represent a minuscule proportion (probably less than one per cent) of the population but the most effective and insidious of the unrepresentative minority opinion is the so-called liberal establishment, ensconced as they are throughout the media, schools and universities and various pressure groups. One of the characteristics of our times is the tyranny of the minority (pressure groups) over the majority of citizens who do not share their usually exaggerated and twisted views. Traditionally, we have led the way in encouraging and protecting people who wish to espouse unpopular or untraditional views (such as conscientious objectors) but we now have the unsatisfactory situation when these views are pressed with verbal and even physical violence. In none of the above minority categories would I place the typical post-war Liberal Party activist who is characterized by his intense and effective interest in local affairs and politics, and by his woolly thinking and bleeding heart in national and international politics. Unlike so many other political and quasi-political gatherings, pictures of Liberal party conferences show the metaphorically bearded, bespectacled and 'sandalled' Liberal faithful to be the thoroughly decent although slightly dotty people who they undoubtedly are.

But, to return to the subject of national characteristics, I must hasten to declare a position of comparative neutrality for I was born and bred a third generation New Zealander and came to England (sorry, the United Kingdom) in 1943 to be trained for a wartime commission in the Royal Navy (RNZNVR as opposed to the RNVR) with about 60 other New Zealand ex-army officers (from Colonel down to Second Lieutenant) who had become redundant in view of the fact that the New Zealand Army had been suddenly and superficially expanded to deal with the threat of a Japanese invasion which was stopped decisively in its tracks by the great US Navy air-sea battle victories of the Coral Sea and Midway Island in May 1942.

However, be that as it may, my father was of a generation who called England 'Home' and he was the son of a Londoner, from the City of London, (cockney, I expect) who emigrated and married the daughter of an Irish Protestant from Tipperary[1], called Blackwell, who emigrated in 1864 to the Great Barrier Island in the Auckland Gulf and who, single-handed, carved out a home from the bush and brought up eleven healthy children – in spite of the fact that, before he arrived in New Zealand, he had lost a leg in an accident. His eldest child had died on the voyage out to New Zealand through an acute shortage of fresh water. If my father came from tough working-class stock, my mother, according to my completely biased grandmother, was almost on a par with royalty. Her father, Edward Russell, was the son of a Scottish emigrant from Inverness, John Russell, who sailed with his family from Glasgow to Auckland in the ship *St Michael* in 1849 for a cost of £105 (a considerable sum at the time) 'being passage money agreed for yourself, lady and child in the chief cabin of the *St Michael* to Auckland, New Zealand. To include provisions but not to include wine, beer or spirits.'[2]

The Russells in Scotland were descended from Huguenots called Roussel while the Russells in Auckland gave themselves 'airs and graces' without the material means to support such superiority except that the female members of this good-looking family usually managed to marry reasonably affluent men who were made to feel that they were privileged to strike such an alliance. It was the opposite with my mother's mother who revelled in the social superiority and amazing historical claims of the Russell family. My grandmother's name was Ellen Slater and she was the daughter of John Slater, a cabinet-maker and singer from Manchester who met and married Mary Anne McGrath (from Limerick in County Cork) in Australia before moving to Waikato in New Zealand. Thus I am half-English and a quarter Scottish and a quarter Irish although slightly more Irish than Scottish; truly British in fact!

---

[1]See note on page 6.
[2]See my book *From Plymouth to the New Plymouth* (A.H. & A.W. Reed, 1959) for an account of the experiences of the early New Zealand pioneers both on their way to and after their arrival at the colony.

My book is dedicated to the proposition that the English have two main and decisive qualities. On the one hand, they exhibit radical, even revolutionary, qualities and on the other hand, their conservatism is notorious. The notable, possibly unique, quality of the English is the way in which these qualities are intermingled in their history. Many nations are revolutionary on the one hand and conservative on the other but very few, if any, have succeeded in combining the two qualities so outstandingly.

For example, the French were essentially conservative until 1789 but it is questionable whether they have ever recovered from the excesses of their revolution. For many years, they had the greatest difficulty in reconciling freedom and authority, for it seemed that at any one time they could only have one without the other. In the years leading up to and at the beginning of the last World War, the French had all the qualities of a nation which had lost its soul, or its way, for it was leaderless and morally decadent. For a nation that had been so brilliant under authoritative leadership for centuries and was able to be so again under Napoleon, this failure after the fall of Napoleon was notable. It took the authority and leadership of De Gaulle to restore French confidence. All seems to be well in prosperous France now but the jury will not be able to make a final judgment until France comes under very real pressure once again. Membership of the European Union, however integrated and even federated, will not absolve France or any other European nation from the need and responsibility to preserve and foster the qualities of its own distinctive nationhood. Anything else would spell failure both for those nations and the Union. One thing for sure is that united Germany will not be found wanting in this respect. This brilliant but dogged nation will plot its allotted course, come what may.

The second great quality of the English is their outstanding political maturity. In my view, neither the Scottish, the Welsh nor the Irish possess these two qualities in any marked degree, neither together nor even separately. It is my contention that they are politically immature, in that the first two consist of border areas, beyond the limits of the Roman Empire, the 'Celtic Fringe', where the remaining embers of the historic Liberal Party smoulder without any likelihood of the flames ever being fanned into any meaningful force. What is worse, they continued to vote by a majority for Labour at a time when the English had correctly decided that this party was unelectable because of its mindless prejudice and of its failure to learn from the past and to bring itself up to date. The Irish, both the Roman Catholic and Protestant (Tudor, Stuart and

3

Cromwellian English and Scottish 'settlers' must be among the most politically immature people in the developed world for otherwise they would not remain in a seventeenth-century time warp.

That is not to say that these three great peoples do not have other invaluable qualities the English lack. The Scottish have, historically, created an educational system far superior to the more narrowly based one of the English while the legal system, partly influenced by Rome through the historic Scottish connection with France, has long been respected throughout the world. The rather forbidding Church of Scotland, Calvin's legacy, suits the Scottish character while the absence of the subtle, and sometimes not so subtle, class distinctions of England has made the Scottish a compact and effective nation who have excelled as entrepreneurs, bankers and engineers and, above all, as emigrants. In fact, leave one Scotsman and three Englishmen on a desert island and the Scotsman will almost certainly dominate the scene, if for the only reason that Englishmen prefer a quiet life until, that is, someone begins to push them around. Then look out for the fireworks! One certain fact, in my experience, is that the concept of the 'dour Scot' is the biggest myth of all time – unless the breed prospers in the northern Highlands and Hebrides. Wherever one goes in the English-speaking world, one is likely to hear a Glaswegian trade unionist 'sounding-off' if one turns on the radio or television while, in general, the Scots appear to be extremely voluble.

In regard to the Welsh, I am prejudiced for I cannot help being biased by the historic and awesome rivalry in the glorious game of Rugby Football by our two small nations whose national game it is. Furthermore, as an Oxford Boxing Blue for three hectic years, I regard Cambridge as enemy territory so that I can hardly bear to contemplate, without a shudder, that long line of distinguished Welsh Rugger Blues wearing those hideously beautiful light blue and white jerseys, set off by the menacing red lion.

However, enough of such uncontrolled prejudice. As I have already indicated, I have no Welsh blood and, prejudice apart, I cannot help feeling, like, I suspect, most English people, that the Welsh are really a foreign and mysterious people in our island. In fact, one of the wonders of our British world is that four such distinct nations could exist and co-exist in such a small area without losing their distinctive identities. To help me understand the Welsh I have to turn to my wife whose first husband was Welsh and in whose eyes the Welsh are 'absolute darlings', a sentiment which one would not normally associate with the typical Welsh rugger forward but I can assure them, and you, that the expression is meant as a great compliment. She does make the point though that the Welsh are really two

4

peoples, the northern and southern. The northern Welsh are those who actually speak Welsh and who therefore are better qualified than our other 'Celtic' nationalists to press for a separate identity, but who are a hard and unforgiving lot who, among other activities, burn down the holiday cottages of the English. On the other hand, she maintains that the southern Welsh are the soul of kindness and friendliness. Further evidence of this is that when I lived in Virginia Water, Surrey, a place of great beauty with many amenities, some neighbours moved regretfully to Cardiff owing to a job change and after several years, such was the friendliness and hospitality which they enjoyed, they returned to leafy Surrey with some reluctance.

In my assessment of the Welsh I shall disregard my wife's distinction, leaving it to the experts to agree or disagree, and deal with them as one group characterized by qualities that are European and Continental (Celtic) compared with the English with their Teutonic, Anglo-Saxon and Danish backgrounds. The physical characteristics of the Welsh, essentially Mediterranean in type, accord with the theory, unfortunately long since discounted, that many years ago, their country was occupied by people from the Iberian Peninsula, some of whom dropped off in what is now Cornwall, where the same physical type also exists. The Welsh are also 'Mediterranean' in their temperament for with them there is none of the traditional English restraint and 'stiff-upper-lip' but rather spontaneity and emotional highs and lows which fit in well with the remarkable national gift for song. Even more than the Scottish, the Welsh have refused to allow their homogeneity to be sullied by the English class system, notwithstanding the existence of sharp social distinctions between owners and managers and the workforce in the coal, iron and steel industries in the nineteenth and early twentieth centuries. For example, there is the dominance and importance of 'the Chapel', which is an aggressively classless institution, in their society, in spite of the traditional Church of Wales, supported by a local squirearchy.

Whereas aggressive nationalism has been the scourge of the modern world since the French Revolution which, paradoxically, invented the phenomenon, the development of any form of internationalism (the League of nations, the United Nations, the European Union, and the like) is conventionally regarded as desirable but, on the other hand, a tremendous tribute to nationalism in the sense of the pride and psyche of a homogeneous race of people identifying themselves as a nation, is the failure of the English, after hundreds of years of occupation and domination, to stifle the national identities of their three neighbours. The English, on the other hand, would say that they have no wish to do any such thing for, being the pragmatists that they are, would expect a compromise situation whereby national pride and tradition would not stand in the way of the common political and economic good.

Even more than the Scottish and Welsh, the Irish have retained their national identity doggedly in the face of English incursions and influence but, unlike the other two, have turned the tables by largely absorbing the English aristocratic land-owning class who were foisted on them, by their becoming 'more Irish than the Irish', in spite of the fact that the latter regarded them as alien exploiters of their lands, an attitude that was maintained regardless of a series of Land Acts by both Liberal and Conservative governments between 1881 and 1903 (admittedly interspersed by draconian Coercion Acts) in an attempt to alleviate the wrongs suffered by the Irish tenant farmers and peasants. It is interesting further to record that many of the Irish patriots and leaders who opposed the Tudors, Stuarts and Cromwell were the descendants of the Normans who were allotted Irish lands after the Conquest of 1066.

Of course, I am now speaking of the southern Irish and not of Ulster and Ulstermen who were mainly sent from Scotland around 350 or more years ago with the precise aim of subjecting the recalcitrant Irish.[1] If the latter had succeeded in absorbing these alien Scots in the same way as they did the English aristocracy, Irish history would have been very much less troubled and the apparently insoluble Irish problem would still not be with us but, owing to intense national and religious differences, this was not to be. The Northern Irish must of course be regarded as an entirely distinct entity from the historical Ireland and Irish. Their national characteristics are very similar to those of their Scottish cousins and it is only owing to a trick of history that their main political aim is to remain independent of Eire by preclaiming as a permanent feature their loyalty to and union with England, at a time when the majority of the Scots in Scotland are determined to weaken, if not sever, their ties with England. On the other hand, they have something in common in wanting to put the political clock back, both exhibiting a political naivety which the English find difficult to comprehend for in

---

[1]The Tudors and Cromwell established English settlers, often soldiers, in Ireland but the main exercise of colonization was the Plantation of Ulster in 1610 when 150,000 acres were given to English and (mainly) Scottish settlers and the recalcitrant landowners of Ulster were not only deprived of their land but expelled from the area. It will be remembered that the King at the time, James I, was King of Scotland as well as King of England.

similar circumstances their approach would be much more pragmatic and effective.

On the question of the integration in Ireland of the non-aristocratic and non-Catholic 'settlers' from England and Scotland, my own family history shows that where these people were not concentrated in the north-eastern area, it was done successfully. Years after the Wesleyan George Blackwell left Tipperary for Great Barrier Island, he was followed by what appeared to me as a child by a number of 'wild' Irishmen from the same part of Ireland, by name Cavanagh, Williams and Armitage. Unfortunately, I never knew my paternal grandmother, Charlotte, for she died in childbirth at the age of twenty-four but I remember her sisters, Jennie and Harriet, well. Jennie married 'Charlie' Cavanagh who had been successful as one of the main New Zealand representatives of the Good Year tyre company and who lived in some style on the outskirts of Auckland. Harriet married a fine Scotsman, Gerald Nairn, and they had a beautiful 400-acre dairy farm about 40 miles south of Auckland. From the age of nine or ten I spent my school holidays on that farm for a number of years and the point of this diversion is to note that my Aunt Harriet was an extremely religious person of the Methodist persuasion. Grace was said before every meal and no work was done on Sunday when the neighbours would congregate at the farmhouse, 'Hilcroft', and there would be Bible-readings, prayers and hymn singing – and once a month an itinerant Methodist minister would preach. Although George Blackwell was a Protestant the cause of his act of emigration would not necessarily have been religious intolerance for economic hardship, and the desire to find a better living led to massive emigration from Ireland from the time of the great potato famine of the 1840s and subsequently. A final point on family history is that the household of the Cavanaghs was famous in the family for prodigious hospitality, for my Aunt Jennie was a brilliant cook and I well remember her dining table groaning with food for Sunday lunch and tea. Here there was no evidence of any religious fervour other than pheasant shooting which was pursued by Charlie Cavanagh and Jim Williams, who had married one of his daughters, with fanaticism but with none of the finesse that is associated with field sport in England. Those two, and the other emigrants from Tipperary, all spoke with broad Irish accents, 'Bejabbers' being every second word. To me, as a child, they seemed to be extremely boisterous – almost frightening. Unlike their counterparts in the north-east, these descendants of the earlier 'settlers' had been completely integrated for they were indistinguishable from the native Irish.

Boisterousness is certainly a trait of the Southern Irish but so is effortless charm and verbal dexterity. One has only to think of such people as Val Doonigan, Eamonn Andrews and Terry Wogan to appreciate these facets. The expression 'Irish blarney' is not only a cynical comment on these gifts but is also an expression of frustration by those people (mainly English) who feel themselves to be socially awkward and tongue-tied in comparison. I can only ask the question, for I cannot properly answer it, why such brilliant people have so singularly failed to manage their own affairs owing to their capacity for perpetually looking back, never forgetting, indulging in self-pity and never seeming to learn from their mistakes as well as those of others? In other words, the Irish are politically inept. Of course, they will answer that the English have fouled-up their history and their lives but this is no excuse, for nations as well as individuals have, if they want to achieve any kind of contentment in life, to make the most of the cards that life has dealt them. The Irish spend their time bemoaning the hand with which they have been dealt instead of pragmatically making the most of that hand, however bad it may appear to be. In saying this, I am not overlooking the heartlessly cruel treatment of the Irish peasantry by the English for centuries, especially by Oliver Cromwell, until the previously mentioned land reforms after 1881. There are many examples in history, ancient and modern of peoples surviving such cruelty with dignity and honour, such as the people in central Europe, and elsewhere, cruelly subjected for so long by the Turks and which led to Gladstone's famous campaign in 1876 against the 'Bulgarian atrocities' perpetrated by the Turks, to the embarrassment of Disraeli's Conservative Government. (This was in the process of propping up, diplomatically, the remnants of the Ottoman Empire because of the vacuum that would be otherwise created, leading to massive encroachments by Germany, Austria and Russia – a situation making a striking parallel with the recent break-up of the Soviet Union.) Perhaps this section on Ireland and the Irish can best be concluded by quoting the words of the Irish poet, Yeats:

Out of Ireland we have come.
Great hatred, little room
Maimed us at the start,
I carry from my mother's womb
A fanatic heart.

How different are the English. Having lost an empire in the American War of Independence, they acquired a second maritime

8

empire in, as has been said, 'A fit of absence of mind' but, by the end of the nineteenth century, all the colonies peopled by European white settlers had been granted self-government – the Dominion status of the early twentieth century. After the Second World War, non-European remnants of this empire were given up with almost indecent haste, a purely pragmatic and successful decision, for throughout history, ancient and modern, all imperial nations have relinquished their vassal states with supreme reluctance which history has shown to be the wrong decision both for themselves and their colonial territories. Admittedly, Winston Churchill, being a romantic traditionalist, like myself, would have clung to the Empire as long as he was in power but, whereas Clement Attlee had none of the gargantuan powers of intellect, imagination and character that enabled Churchill to be one of the greatest, if not the greatest, war leader in the history of the world, the prosaic Attlee was much better equipped to take such a typically English pragmatic decision. In regard to Ireland, the 1920/21 settlement granting virtual independence to Southern Ireland and giving Ulster its separate independent status with constitutional union with Britain, in accordance with the wishes of both, was the only practicable decision, although it must be said, it was the work of the great Welsh Prime Minister, Lloyd George. In addition to the other negative qualities mentioned at the beginning of this paragraph, is the failure of the Southern Irish to accept and make the most of the 1920/21 settlement not also due in great part to the capacity for violence in the Irish character?

Before I say more about the success of the English in combining radicalism with conservatism and about their political maturity – all of which amounts to pragmatism – I should like to emphasize that the English character and characteristics are in no way superior to those of their neighbouring nations. If anything, one could argue to the contrary. Even making allowance for the fact that they were enemies for a thousand years, the French expression, 'la perfide Albion' is very damning. For the greater part, this probably arose from the exasperation of the French in the eighteenth century in dealing with the early party system of the Tories and Whigs. The important researches of Professor Sir Lewis Namier have indicated that it is fallacious to compare our eighteenth-century political parties with those of the twentieth for the main characteristic of the eighteenth-century member of the House of Commons was his political independence as the voting records showed that he supported different parties at different times. However, the two parties had become identified and political power did change hands so that the French, and other foreigners, interpreted a change in policy due to a change of the party in power as national deviousness. Aiding and abetting this problem was the fact that the English virtue of pragmatism could also be interpreted as deviousness.

Again, although the cool, calm and collected aspect of the English character obviously has its virtues and uses, the lack of human warmth and spontaneity compares unfavourably with the Welsh and Irish as also, with the more direct and less inhibited Scots. For example, in the last two world wars, servicemen from the Dominions found that the further north they went in Britain the more friendly they found the people. But, as a cynical friend of mine has commented: 'Unlike the Americans, the English have never lost any sleep over whether other people liked them but they have been more concerned at gaining their respect.' Again, this attitude can be interpreted both as a virtue, from the political point of view, and as a defect from the human point of view.

Perhaps the most notable feature of the English and the English character is the aspect that has produced the famous, or should one say, infamous, English class system. All societies have the rich, the not-so-rich and the poor so that they all have different social structures and attitudes emanating from material differences as Marx so rightly pointed out in his materialist interpretation of history, but as the vulgar but apt modern expression puts it, the English class system is 'something else', with its unnatural coldness, ruthlessness and infinite gradation of class and class-consciousness. From my own experience, many years ago, taking my young family on holidays to Brittany, on the one hand, in the summer, and Austria, on the other, in the winter, I noted that in both cases, wealthy French and Austrians (or possibly German) guests of many years standing would be welcomed on arrival and farewelled on departure by the staff of the respective establishments by kisses and hugs that were very much more than a formality on both sides. In the English middle-upper-class world such an attitude would be impossible from either side of the social divide. In its place, there would be much artificial bonhomie from both sides but the arm's-length aspect of the social barrier would remain intact. All of which, as always, has its virtues and defects.

Such social discipline and rigidities are invaluable in the field of practical endeavours such as winning wars, carving out empires and administering them or in achieving political order and economic wealth at home, but the obverse defect is not so much the ignominy of those at the bottom end of the social scale as the arrogance of those at the top end. It is difficult to appreciate now that those true-

10

to-life characters in Jane Austen's novels really did believe that the poor (even the genteel poor) were in every way inferior to the rich and 'well-born' who consequently had every right to patronize the former, at the best, and, at the worst, to treat them harshly and cruelly. In the nineteenth century matters became even worse for in addition to cruelty the Victorians added hypocrisy for the smug superiority of the rich was re-enforced by the assiduous support of and liaison with the established Church (of England) to give thanks for the good things life (blessed are the rich) and to set an example to 'the lower orders'. A more enlightened manifestation 'was the influence of Evangelicalism on the British aristocracy in the nineteenth century which enabled the country to surmount the worst excesses of the industrial evolution and the revolutionary forces that plagued the other countries of Europe – except Belgium' (p. 315). Additionally, English class-distinction was given another decisive twist in the nineteenth century for the Victorian grandees and industrial barons were among the richest people whom the world has ever seen, especially when adjusted for the fall in the value of money. Furthermore, the British nineteenth century was one of the few eras in world history when the value of money was higher at the end than at the beginning of the century. When one thinks of the ravages and insecurities of inflation in the course of world history it is not surprising that the Victorians should have developed qualities of arrogance and pomposity the like of which has not been seen before or since, which included the general attitude that all foreigners were innately inferior to the English. In the light of our miserable post-war history (until 1979) there is nothing more ridiculous or pathetic than when one encounters odd pockets of this attitude today.

Having dealt with the English defects, although remembering that these partially helped to explain the virtues and successes, it is necessary to look more closely at the two qualities which have made English political history such a success story, namely the combination of radicalism and conservatism, on the one hand, and political maturity on the other. It is these pragmatic qualities which have made possible the constructive political changes that the English have enjoyed over the centuries and, at their behest, the other British in these islands and English-speaking peoples overseas – the USA and the old Dominions. The particular tenor of the English polity is something that has developed from the earliest times. This is, of course, true of any society or nation but the English, through good management and good luck, have been fortunate in the political fecundity and continuity of their story.

With the collapse of the Roman Empire in the fourth century AD

11

the Celtic Britons were subjected to raids by the Teutonic Angles and Saxons from Denmark and the north German coastlands who by around the middle of the fifth century began to settle in the land that they found more hospitable than their own. However, unlike the Teutonic peoples who invaded southern Europe (the modern France, Spain and Italy), they had not come under the civilizing influence of the Roman Empire which had by this time accepted Christianity. Thus, by the end of the sixth century, England had reverted to paganism and, unlike the Continent, contact was mainly lost with Roman civilization and the Roman language except between south-eastern England and Gaul. However, during the seventh and eighth centuries, the Anglo-Saxons produced a dynamic culture of their own. Christianity was introduced to Kent and the south and east via Rome in AD 597 and in the north via Celtic Ireland and Scotland (the later 'Celtic-fringe') where Christianity and civilization had never died. There were eventually three dominant English kingdoms, Northumbria, Mercia and Wessex and by the early ninth century Wessex gained ascendancy under Egbert, the first of a line of extremely able and effective kings of England. Once again, England was subjected to barbarous raids by hard and cruel non-Christian men from the North Sea, the Scandinavian Vikings who scoured Europe for many years to come – Norsemen, Danes and Swedes – but it was mainly the Danes who came to England, at first on annual raids which grew longer and longer and eventually as armies of occupation. It was due to King Egbert and his descendants, of whom the greatest was Alfred (AD 871–900), who ruled England for two and a half centuries, that the Danes were held at bay and eventually integrated into English society, and although they affected the development of the national character, such as love of the sea, and introduced new institutions, they adopted the Anglo-Saxon language and were eventually absorbed by Saxon England.

By the ninth century England was the prime example in Europe of a country to be loosely united into a single state with a supreme King whose witan or council consisted of his leading followers. The Church was organized in bishoprics, parishes were well developed and learning was pursued in religious houses. There were a number of freemen owing allegiance to the King and meeting and deliberating in the moots of the hundred (the earliest and smallest agricultural and administrative unit over and above the earliest kindred or village) and the shire was governed by an earldorman, the highest rank among the thegns. However, there was the beginning of a form of feudalism in the estates allotted by the King to the thegns and leading churchmen, the former in return for military service and support, and the latter in order to ensure a place in heaven, and whose 'freemen' owed allegiance to bishop, abbot or a nobleman. When the House of Egbert at last produced a weak King (the infamous Ethelred the Redeless or Unready) at the end of the tenth century, the Danish invasions began again and the Danish conquerors' king became King of England as well as the greater part of Scandinavia. However, Canute (1014–35) completely identified himself with England and did much to strengthen the monarchy and the Anglo-Saxon institutions that he inherited. The weak reign of the last of Egbert's descendants, Edward the Confessor (1042–66), was followed by the Norman conquest of 1066.

This was probably the most dynamic 'event' in English history. William, Duke of Normandy, was descended from Northmen who had conquered that part of France, but the combination of their own abilities with the culture that they absorbed produced an outstanding breed of people who stood out even against the other communities in France. By 1066 they were French-speaking, builders in stone and fighters on horse-back, the knight on horseback being the greatest and most successful military innovation in history to that date. Duke William had long coveted the throne of Edward the Confessor, his weak English cousin for the Normans despised the unimaginative and isolated English, with their 'backward' Church and illiterate priesthood although, in fact, the English Church was noted for its patronage of the arts and of music while English book-production, embroidery, metalwork and coinage enjoyed an international reputation, and English vernacular literature was without parallel in contemporary Europe. Also, the English state had much more sophisticated financial and administrative arrangements than the Duchy of Normandy. However, the Normans regarded their feudalism as inadequate for it lacked legal definition and their armies did not fight on horseback but on foot and were supported by poorly armed and organized peasants. In the event, Harold, the new English King, a distant member of the Wessex royal family, was a good and great man and soldier but the well-known story of his untimely death, together with that of his two brothers, at the Battle of Hastings, led to an unexpectedly quick and decisive victory for William.

In spite of dogged Saxon resistance in the North and East Anglia (where the legendary Hereward the Wake was not defeated until 1071), and because there was no Saxon leader of the position and stature to take Harold's place and, above all, because of William's terrifying brutality in putting down any resistance, his victory was one of the most complete in history, so that he did not have to compromise with the Saxon leaders over their lands and customs. As the Domesday Survey of 1086 showed, the Saxon earls had vanished and the thegnhood had almost ceased to exist. In their place were Norman barons and knights while the bishoprics and abbeys were bestowed upon the clergy from France and Italy as well as from Normandy. The final outcome was the replacement of the haphazard and unsystematic Anglo-Saxon feudalism by one which was completely systematic and uniform whereby conditions of military service were attached to most grants of lands. At the pinnacle was the King who granted every acre of land, at first to the barons who in turn granted land to knights and they in turn to under-knights – all in return for conditions of military service, strictly defined in regard to the numbers of men to be supplied and length of service. Similarly, the English Church was systematically reformed and disciplined in common with the movement that was sweeping Europe at the time.

In a sense, this could be called a revolution leading to the obliteration of the Anglo-Saxon culture, but this was not so, for as early as this the conservative English had developed the capacity to absorb these revolutionary changes with the result that the society and culture that emerged was much more dynamic than that in pre-1066 but which nevertheless retained the inherent English strengths, especially and including the love of individual freedom. It must be remembered that 'Norman England' consisted of around 2 million Anglo-Saxons and roughly 20,000 Norman and French soldiers and clerics, and eventually the greater element absorbed the lesser; the instincts, habits, traditions and folk-memory that comprised the English nationality continued. Even though the French language remained the language of the Court well into the Middle Ages it was never spoken by the populace and eventually faded away entirely. As would be expected, the Norman feudal system had its legal counterparts. From the King's Court (Curia Regis) downwards every lord of the land held his court which all his dependents were bound to attend. However, this feudal system of justice never supplanted the rival system of the shire and hundred moots. The shire moots survived as the county courts under officers appointed by the King and gradually they encroached upon the feudal jurisdictions and supplanted them. In parallel, the whole system of Saxon local government – the counties, the sheriffs and, of course, the courts survived and were used by the King to maintain his contacts throughout the country, by the use of the new breed of trained officials – lawyers and educated men from the clergy (the compilers of the Domesday Book). Finally, there are two extremely important factors. First, the strength and ability of William the Conqueror, William I of England and Duke of Normandy, continued the work of Canute in making the English King the strongest in Europe, in his own land. Indeed, in comparison with England, the other historic countries of Europe were then merely 'geographical expressions'. Secondly, the English peasantry never lost the memory of the kindred and the moot and the concept of freemen. Thus, although in the twelfth and thirteenth centuries nearly all peasants became villeins, in the fourteenth century they made great steps to regain their freedom and completed the process in the fifteenth century. On the other hand, in Latin Europe although the cities, with traditions going back to the Roman Empire, achieved their liberty, the peasants remained unfree for centuries. In England, the townsmen were granted charters and their liberty by William so that by the fourteenth and fifteenth centuries the English townsmen and peasants, now the yeoman-farmer, free craftsman or labourer, comprised a nation of freemen. The concept of combining authority with freedom took early root in England.

Before moving to the fifteenth century we need to enquire more deeply into the importance of the twelfth and thirteenth centuries in explaining how England was in the process of developing her own unique legal and political institutions. In the twelfth century the two men responsible were William's son, Henry I (1100–35) succeeding his older brother, William Rufus, William II (1087–1100), and then Henry's grandson, Henry II (1154–89). Both came to the throne after weak kings when there had been years of baronial anarchy and trouble with the Church which revived the claim, earlier disallowed by William I, that the Church's spiritual authority (claimed by Archbishops of Canterbury on behalf of the Pope) was superior to the King's temporal authority. Both were men of great strength of intellect and character, like their respective father and great-grandfather and, like him, both had a passion for order. After many trials and tribulations both successfully resisted the Church's claims, failure to have done which would have been disastrous for England's future political development. Henry II's tragic differences with his friend, Archbishop Thomas Becket, is one of the best known episodes in our history.

Throughout his long and successful reign, Henry I re-established the King's authority and justice by fully utilizing his Court, the Curia Regis, to which he summoned as many or as few as he chose and where he made laws, levied taxes and tried disputes. It was, however, in the last respect that he made such an important contribution to the future for whereas the feudal baronial courts were under the control of the local lords who pocketed the fines, Henry strengthened the shire courts which met under the King's officer, the sheriff. This was the beginning of the important process whereby the King's national law was to take the place of local feudal law. By the time of his death Henry had fully earned the title, 'The Lion of Justice', and it was England's good fortune that after nineteen years of social and political disintegration under his nephew, Stephen, Henry's grandson, Duke of Anjou, the son of his daughter Matilda, whom he had hoped would succeed him but for Stephen's usurpation, began one of the most important and decisive reigns in English history. This is doubly impressive when one considers that Henry Plantaganet was a Frenchman and that as well as England he also ruled half of France.

Building on the foundations laid by Henry I, Henry II transformed the English monarchy, its legal system and government administration. The Anglo-Saxon system of self-government was further strengthened under royal command in the shires and boroughs, the powers and duties of feudal magnates being transferred to trained civil servants. He relaid the foundation of central government by greatly extending the power and responsibility of the Curia Regis. Permanent members specialized in trying suits between subjects and others in conducting financial business. Thus were sewn the seeds of the great courts later to be known as the King's Bench, Common Pleas and Exchequer. Even more radical, was his extension of the authority of the Curia to places where the King could not be in person. Judges from the central court travelled round the country as itinerant justices: the 'assizes' have continued from that day until they were abolished in both civil and criminal cases under the terms of the Courts Act 1971 (pp. 307 and 308). Where the itinerant judges required local evidence they were empowered to summon a jury of 'twelve good men and true' and could swear to local facts for the benefit of the judge. Later on they became judges of the facts themselves. Henry did not invent the jury for it was an ancient Frankish device which, for example, William I used in compiling the Domesday Book, but with great astuteness he offered it to litigants in the royal courts. Even before William's time, in the reign of the aforementioned Ethelred the Unready, Ethelred II (978–1013), an ordinance instructed '12 senior thegns in every wapentake' to search out and present on oath anyone they believed to have committed crimes. Certainly, trial by jury was much more acceptable than the Norman devices of trial by ordeal, and trial by battle, and the important point was that only the King had the right to summon a jury, and he restricted that right to the royal courts. If trial by jury was the jewel in the crown of Henry's legal achievements, his crowning achievement is that he is credited with laying the foundations of the English Common Law.

In fact, this can be traced back to King Alfred's Book of Laws, or Dooms.

> The Laws of Alfred, continually amplified by his successors, grew into that body of customary law administered by the shire and hundred courts which, under the name of the Laws of St Edward (the Confessor), the Norman Kings undertook to respect, and out of which, with much manipulation by feudal lawyers, the Common Law was founded.[1]

The twelfth century saw the rise of lawyers as a specialized profession (to rival the clergy) and it is they who collected and recorded the legal decisions of generations of judges and drew principles from them to produce a national or Common Law existing alongside the law enacted in statutes. As Winston Churchill writes, referring to Henry II:

> A modern lawyer, transported to the England of Henry's predecessors, would find himself in strange surroundings; with the system that Henry bequeathed to his son he would feel almost at home. That is the measure of the great King's achievement.[2]

The significance of the Common Law in our history is profound for it lies at the root of many of our national habits and ways of thoughts. It is the reason why we are not burdened with the limitations of a written constitution or of a Bill of Rights, as advocated by the Liberal Democratic party, and it is part and parcel of the jury system which, sad to say, has been emasculated by 'progressive' and unwise modern developments. But, above all, it is innately superior to the legal systems in France and elsewhere in Europe deriving from the more centralized, logical and codified system inherited from Rome. These systems are basically inquisitorial whereby the judge determines and controls the entire proceedings, including interrogation of the suspect and of witnesses, after all of which the charge is formulated. On the other hand, under our Common Law,

---

[1] *A History of the English Speaking Peoples*, (Volume I), by Winston S. Churchill, p. 95.
[2] Ibid, p. 175.

A man can only be accused of a civil or criminal offence which is clearly defined and known to the law. The judge is an umpire. He adjudicates on such evidence as the parties choose to produce. Witnesses must testify in public and on oath. They are examined and cross-examined, not by the judge, but by the litigants themselves or their legally qualified and privately hired representatives. The truth of their testimony is weighed not by the judge but by twelve men 'good and true', and it is only when the jury has determined the facts that the judge is empowered to impose sentence, punishment, or penalty accordingly to the law.[1]

In more general terms, the Common Law places its emphasis on the freedom and rights of the individual as opposed to the Roman concept of the rights of the state, whereby the rights of the individual only make sense as a citizen or member of the state. There is no difference between the good man and the good citizen, a concept which ultimately denies the freedom of the individual. It is no coincidence that in the course of the last thousand years England has been notable, with the exception of the Stuart period, for avoiding the excesses of absolutism, on the one hand, and revolutionary reaction, on the other. This is well illustrated by the important milestone of Magna Carta (the Great Charter) in 1215. John (1199–1216) was an erratic individual who clashed seriously with a strong Pope and the King of France as well as with the barons, a combination to which he succumbed and as a result was forced to accept and sign the famous document on the meadow at Runnymede, near Windsor. The significance of Magna Carta is that whereas William I, Henry I and Henry II had ensured that the barons obeyed the law, the barons, in turn, were now ensuring that the law was to bind the Crown and vassals alike. This was a recipe for the antithesis of absolutism – strong government and freemen both subject to the law of the land.

It was the development of this concept that led in turn to the rise of Parliament where once again the English led the world. John's son, Henry III (1216–72), was a weak and feckless monarch whose main fault was financial ineptitude and extravagance so that there was a notable increase in the financial demands that were made on his subjects. This was especially so in that the population and wealth of England were expanding rapidly in the thirteenth century with the growth of wool production and cloth manufacture

---

[1]*A History of the English Speaking Peoples*, (Volume I), by Winston S. Churchill, p. 175.

by the 'cottage system' and its export to the Low Countries. Not only the King but the distant Pope could not resist the temptation to exploit this new-found source of wealth. Barons, knights, citizens and the clergy were all affected and grew increasingly restive as the years went by. After thirty years the explosion took place, the lead being taken by the barons who as members of the Great Council were being continuously assembled by the King to consult them regarding his excessive demands for money. Instead of weakly acceding to these demands the barons began to insist on a 'redress of grievances' and in 1246 the importance of these deliberations was recognized by their being called to Parliament for the first time. In 1254 the barons strengthened their position by including in their assembly four knights elected from every shire to represent the interests of the smaller landowners. However, the King continually failed to keep his promise to 'redress grievances' and in 1258 the Parliament, meeting at Oxford, took the governing power out of the King's hands by virtue of the Provisions of Oxford. In 1261 the King repudiated the Provisions and civil war broke out, the barons' leader, Simon de Montfort, defeating the King at Lewes in 1264, after which he summoned a new Parliament in 1265. The reason why every schoolboy (by which I unashamedly include schoolgirls) knows of Simon de Montfort as the founder of Parliament, is that in 1265, for the first time, commoners from town and city were called in addition to the barons and knights of the shire.

Once again the situation was saved by a strong leader in the person of Henry III's son, Prince Edward, later Edward I (1272–1307), who beat and killed Simon de Montfort, who had grown unpopular and had split the barons, at Evesham in 1265. Edward virtually took over from Henry III until his death in 1272, and for the rest of his outstanding reign there was no more trouble from the barons for Edward did not abuse the system. Instead, he developed it. Under Henry III both the meetings of the King, alone with his barons, the old Great Council, and those including the knights of the shire and the burgesses of the towns, were called Parliament, and Edward continued to call both assemblies as the best means of governing the country; as always, the knights' and burgesses' attendance was necessary when extra taxes were required for the King's wars. These full Parliaments continued 'humbly' to present petitions for the redress of grievances, local and national, and to draw the attention of the King and his Council to urgent matters. When the King granted the petition it became the law of the land: thus began Statute Law, as we know it. In the later years of Edward I the two kinds of Parliament merged into the body

although there was no division into Houses as yet. The disputation was done by the lords and prelates, and the knights and burgesses were summoned only to stand (while the former sat) to hear the decisions about their petitions or to consent to the grant of taxes. The origins of the Speaker of the House of Commons arose from the fact that the Commons were not empowered to speak in Parliament so that they had preliminary meetings among themselves to discuss taxes and petitions and elected a Speaker to report to Parliament.

It was during the reign of Edward III (1327–77) that Parliament finally developed its modern structure owing to his need to ask for more money to finance his dreaded war with France (the beginning of the Hundred Years' War, 1337–1453) during the course of which he exhausted both himself and his country. The fact that the Commons presented their petitions as a body in a formal way, through their Speaker, distinguished the Lower House from the rest of Parliament, while the Lords regarded themselves as the natural counsellers of the Crown with the right to separate consultation. The separation of the Houses of Parliament first appeared in 1343 which is also the first time that the Speaker is mentioned. Thus, by the end of the reign of Edward III, although the Commons stood in awe of the Crown, which in the last resort asserted its Royal Prerogative, the stage was set for it to play the decisive part in opposing and defeating royal absolutism in the seventeenth century. Until 1485 the political history of the fifteenth century was negative for it was mainly concerned with pursuing the unprofitable war against France and when the magnates, captains and soldiers returned from France after 1450 they were virtually professional soldiers who had lost the art of living in peace. Under the weak Henry VI (1422–61), the magnates inevitably quarrelled and the veterans of the French wars plunged into the Wars of the Roses in 1455 which lasted for thirty long years, although 'many of the battles of the Wars of the Roses whose names still resound in history were mere skirmishes in military terms' (p. 185).

In the above account of the development of English legal and political institutions the combination of conservatism and radicalism, deriving from and further developing political maturity, is a never-ending kaleidoscope. The fusing of the new (radical) concept of Statute Law with the old (conservative) concept of Common Law is only one, although perhaps the best, example. Again, the original and conservative notion of the royal prerogative did not prevent the rise of the new notion of Parliament, both of which were eventually to fuse into the mature notion of constitutional monarchy. It is necessary to refer again briefly to the thirteenth and fourteenth centuries to complete our identification of new instruments which were eventually to become integral factors in the machinery of government, although, be it noted, they were derivatives from the old system.

It has already been noted that the Curia Regis of the Norman Kings had developed into three distinct branches, judicial in the Court of King's Bench and Common Pleas, financial in the Exchequer, and political in the King's Council. However, the Crown never relinquished its function as the supreme law-giver and its natural adviser in this respect was the Lord Chancellor, the head of the legal profession, around whom developed under Edward III the Court of Chancery which dealt with cases which were beyond the scope of the regular courts, especially in dealing with disputes over land and property among the richest in the land. Also, successive kings had long selected councillors to hear the petitions of men too poor to sue at Common Law which developed into the Court of Requests, the formal history of which can be traced back to 1493, in the reign of Henry VII, and by the end of the 1520s the Court of Requests was an established entity. However, apart from the above, the Council continued to act as judges in matters that could not be left safely, even to the Chancellor's Court; for example, those that affected the safety of the throne – what came to be called, 'matters of state'. When it was sitting in this capacity, the Council became known as the Star Chamber and during the dynamic reign of Henry VII (1485–1509) it was strengthened and regularized but, unlike the other courts, it was given Parliamentary authority to dispense with the usual laws or rules and to flout the Common Law by examining people without oath, to condemn them on written evidence alone, and the like. Under the Tudors the Star Chamber was a source of summary tyranny and was accordingly abolished. However, it has been argued that we now need its modern equivalent to deal summarily and cheaply with the myriad of cases, whereby the ordinary citizen clashes with one of the many functionaries of government, on the grounds that the complex and cumbersome machinery of the Common Law is not really suited for this purpose.

Lastly, in the field of local government there was an extremely important new development which can be traced back to the reign of Edward I but which was regularized by statute by Edward III – the creation of Justices of the Peace. Henry II and Edward I had already encroached on the duties of the sheriffs, the King's officer in every shire, by appointing itinerant justices, later Justices of the Assizes, to travel round fixed circuits at regular intervals. The Justices of the

Peace represented yet another diminution of the sheriff's duties. They were chosen in large numbers for each county from members of the local gentry. Their initial function, according to statutes of Edward III in 1327 and 1330, was 'to keep the peace' by proclaiming and enforcing the law, arresting evildoers and committing them for trial at the assizes. At that time they were more correctly known as conservators of the peace but after a statute of 1360 empowered them not merely to receive indictments but to try the indicted, they became known as Justices of the Peace. In 1388 they were further directed by statute to hold their sessions four times a year, the origin of the Quarter Sessions of the justices of the peace and an integral part of our legal system in the subsequent centuries. A respected constitutional historian comments:

> The whole jurisdiction was an extraordinary experiment in justice which was at once anti-feudal and a reversal of the hitherto universal trend towards centralization. It was typical of the day, in that it conformed to the rise of the county community and to the growth of a county interest neither feudal nor royal.[1]

Throughout the subsequent centuries when the Justices of the Peace became increasingly important – the veritable backbone of the state – their hallmark was that of voluntary, part-time but, above all, unpaid, local government officers. Their example was respected and followed in many other voluntary activities which were not necessarily political. However, in the political field, when the Labour Government in April 1974 introduced payment for the services of local councillors, in accordance with the Conservative Government's Local Government Act of 1972, the subsequent drastic reduction in the standards of responsibility and the abuse of authority were predictable. I, for one, predicted it.

All but our present deprived generation of schoolchildren will have heard of or read the general outline, or key dates, of the above early history of our political, constitutional and legal development. They will also have learnt how Henry Tudor (Henry VII), partly by marriage but mainly by battle at Bosworth in 1485, ended the long drawn-out late medieval conflict between the Lancastrians and Yorkists, and by so-doing ushered in 'modern times' in England and cleverly laid the foundations for the two subsequent outstanding Tudor monarchs. Henry VIII (1509–1547) and Elizabeth I (1558–

---

[1] *The Constitutional History of Medieval England*, by J.E.A. Jolliffe, p. 413.

1603) were famous for being brilliant and ruthless leaders of an aggressive young nation which was flowering in many respects – increases in wealth and population, intellectual endeavour and military strength. But above all, the Tudors were notable for being in 'harmony' with their times which was an important ingredient in the success of the golden Elizabethan Age.

It was not so with the Stuarts, who ruled between 1603 and 1688, with the republican interregnum (1649–1660) in between. The key to the early Stuarts' failure was the fact that, as foreigners, 'Frenchified Scotsmen', they were completely out of sympathy and harmony with their people, the English, and their times. True, they were in tune with contemporary developments in Europe but in mid-seventeenth century England the attempt to put the clock back by insisting on the Royal prerogative in the form of the Divine Rights of Kings, was hopeless and disastrous, even though for many years it looked as though Charles I was going to succeed in his admittedly sincere efforts – so much so that he was lulled into a false sense of security. The English reply was to perpetrate one of the most revolutionary acts in modern history, the beheading of Charles I (1625–1649) in 1649 and the setting up of a republic under the leadership of Cromwell, in the defence of the rights of the House of Commons which by now had become the lynchpin of the constitution – a revolutionary act in support of a conservative institution. However, more successfully than the French, after their revolution, the English turned their back on the authoritarian anarchy of the republic and restored the much-chastened monarchy in 1660 in the person of Charles II (1660–1685) who, although a Stuart, was a brilliant and effective man of the world who managed to survive and surmount the many crises during his reign, but on his death in 1685 his Roman Catholic brother, James II, reverted to type and was sent packing in 1688. The so-called 'Bloodless Revolution' of those years installed the monarchy in the form of Mary (1689–1694) (James II's elder and Protestant daughter) and her Dutch husband, William (1689–1702), Prince of Orange, under the terms of the Bill of Rights of 1689 which, as the Whig-inspired history textbook would say, ushered in constitutional monarchy – an English invention – the supreme example of pragmatic compromise, and of actions at the same time both radical, even revolutionary, and conservative. The Whig historians who, like myself, regarded this as a unique achievement leading to the most satisfactory system of government ever devised by man, are not to be gainsaid in spite of the subsequent 'nit-picking' of their twentieth-century critics. The rest of the story is well-known (apart, once again, from our unfortunate, ill-educated and semi-

23

literature present-day state schoolchildren),[1] of how the Monarchy and the House of Lords have been retained, although their form has been radically altered until the British Prime Minister, with an ample majority in the House of Commons, is relatively and constitutionally the most powerful political leader in the world.

In all, whereas the ancient civilizations such as the Egyptian, Persian, Chinese and Indian all made important contributions to civilization and, more recently, the Greeks have been associated with political developments, culture and humanism (the flowering of the human spirit), the Romans with the more earthly concepts of empire-building and law and order, and Judaism with the ethical disciplines imposed by religion, the English have given to the world their great nineteenth-century concept of political liberalism with all that this implies, including the Rule of Law. That is to say, all men shall be free before the law which, in addition to the Common Law, shall be enacted by a sovereign assembly or Parliament of which the electorate by 1884 included artisan voters, and by 1928 there was universal suffrage, including women,[2] while in 1911 the House of Lords finally became subject to the veto of the House of Commons because of the former's non-representative composition – and as everyone, from the Crown and the Government down, is subject to that law.

I make no excuse for my historical excursions in explaining English political, constitutional and legal achievements because, as our 'progressive' modern educationalists will no doubt learn one day, or, if they do not learn they will be replaced, nothing can be understood about anything without recourse to its history while, although one cannot be expected to know all history, the mere fact of understanding a particular history or particular histories is itself a civilizing and mind-training influence which matures the judgment and gives one the mental discipline to turn one's attention to other subjects.[3] I have also taken the trouble to summarize our national political history because, in my view, the period between the end of the last war and the coming of Margaret Thatcher was one in which we had largely lost our way.

Earlier on, I mentioned that both nations and individuals have to make the most of the hand of cards with which they have been dealt

---

[1]Written in 1990.

[2]The New Reform Act of 1918 extended the franchise to women over the age of 30 who were not subject to any legal incapacity and who were qualified as local government electors. By the Representation of the People (Equal Franchise) Act 1928 women were placed on the same footing as men in respect of the franchise.

[3]Written in July 1990.

by 'life'. In this respect, England has been fortunate for the geographical position of a small island separated from the amorphous Continental land mass and protected from invaders by the North Sea has been invaluable. It was partly because of this advantageous location that, as we have already seen, England was the first country in Europe to enjoy unitary government by a king as far back as Alfred the Great in the ninth century. France was the next European country to achieve this distinction but not until her people had finally rid themselves in the middle of the fifteenth century of their unwelcome English invaders who since the time of William, Duke or Normandy, had extended their hold on France to around half the country. The Spanish had to share around half their country with Moslem invaders between the early eighth and mid-fifteenth centuries. Poland, which never really ceased to be feudal, was entirely partitioned away between Prussia, Russia and Austria by the end of the eighteenth century. 'Germany' and 'Italy' were mere 'geographical expressions' until 1870, for it was not until that year that both these nations officially came into being as a result of the unification of historically separate provinces. It must be admitted therefore that England's more advanced political development derives partly from these fortuitous circumstances, but the more important point probably remains that the English, typically, turned this good fortune to the best advantage and did not squander their splendid opportunity. For example, whereas one of the main causes of the French Revolution was the enormous and unbridgeable gulf between the mass of the people and the aristocracy who were the arch-proponents of absentee-landlordism, the English aristocracy did take an interest in their estates and their tenants, even though this was fairly detached, while the squirearchy, the under-aristocracy, were full-time country gentlemen, even speaking the local dialect in many cases. The pub, the cricket match and country pursuits, including hunting, were all activities where fraternization took place. Again, with Belgium, which only suffered from riots, Britain was the only Western European country not to have a revolution of sorts in the year of revolutions – 1848. In both cases, an urban middle class with 'a stake in the land' were growing fast while Britain was well on the way to developing that political liberalism which was to be so important to her and to the rest of the world.

Finally, although I have mainly confined myself to the political implications and manifestations of the English character, its complex mixture of the conservative and radical has been and is an enormously potent force in English society. How else could it be that the English, socially, apparently go from one extreme to another?

There are many examples in the social field but the one that I find to be the most striking is the pre- and post-war comparison between the middle-class Englishwoman's fashions and attitudes. The typical pre-war *Country Life* magazine covergirl with her twin-set and pearls and infinitely correct, subdued and low (sexual) profile was the model followed without question throughout Britain and the Dominions overseas. Yet, it was the daughters and grand-daughters of these pre-war conventional paragons who in the 'Swinging Sixties' pioneered the mini-skirt and bra-less freedom both in regard to fashion and morals, and in so-doing influenced the rest of the world. Admittedly, the 'Swinging Sixties' was essentially a working-class revolution in that the songs, language and dress of the mass entertainers, which were adopted wholesale by the masses, overwhelmed our society. This was the time when one would collect one's son from Eton College at the end of term to find that he had taken the trouble to change into the uniform of jeans and T-shirt which had been adopted by the masses. Before the war and throughout the fifties and early sixties a middle-class son would instinctively dress like his father: sports jacket, cavalry twill trousers, country shirt and club tie so as to differentiate himself from those of a lower social order who could be easily identified by their less 'gentlemanly' dress. Once again, we have a striking example of how the English middle and upper classes went along with an essentially working-class revolution, the many ramifications of which have virtually abolished important aspects of the traditional English class distinction. It has been a typically English revolution. The pre-war expression, 'the Old School Tie', which was so meaningful, has not only fallen into entire disuse but today's younger generation would not even begin to understand its meaning. Historically, the Labour Party has advocated the abolition of the private Public Schools as a major means of eliminating class distinction. The fact that they still believe indirectly, through threatened tax penalties, in this retrogressive and self-defeating step, emphasizes not only their dismal doctrinaire fixations but also their political and social blindness.

It is well-known that wars usher in great social changes and much, although by no means all, of the above developments can be explained partly by the war. In that respect, post-war Britain can be said to have been representative of any country that had suffered from the effects of a long and painful war but to my mind, the English (and through them, the British) implemented their own striking adaptation to these changes, and nowhere more so than in the political field. It will be remembered that pre-war Britain was an entirely class-ridden society with 'one-tenth of the people owning

26

nine-tenths of the wealth', although it must be noted that in the second half of the nineteenth century the 'real' wages of the 'average' British worker increased significantly so that at that time he enjoyed the highest standard of living among European workers. More accurately, in 1922:

> one per cent of the population owned two thirds of the national wealth; 0.1 per cent owned one third. Three-quarters of the population owned less than £100. Even this was an improvement on pre-war when 88 per cent owned nothing. Put differently, 2½ per cent of occupied persons over the age of 20 owned two-thirds of the national wealth, and 0.25 per cent owned one-third.[1]

Again 'in 1910 1.1 per cent of the population took 30 per cent of the income: in 1929 1.5 per cent took 23 per cent of the income',[2] indicating a slight decrease in inequality after the First World War but leaving a marked division of income and wealth. However, in 1938 the average wage was around three pounds and ten shillings per week[3] and although money went very much further in those days there was a great deal of poverty and hardship among those who fell below this level, especially because of unemployment, as was attested by the researches of Charles Booth in the East End of London and of Seebohm Rowntree in York. In our day we have learnt that a country such as the USSR had managed to become the world's second military power in spite of the failure and weakness of its economy by making the positive decision to use its limited wealth to buy 'guns' instead of 'butter' – up to at least 25 per cent of its Gross Domestic Product. This was essentially the British position in 1939, in spite of the disastrous rundown in arms as a result of the appeasement of the 1930s, for how else could she afford a navy, which, along with that of the United States, was the largest in the world, with 118,167 men and 400 ships, including a dozen battleships of which she cannot afford one today, even if she wanted one. In 1914, when the disparities in wealth were even greater, the Royal Navy was by far the largest in the world, with 151,000 men and around 600 ships, including 72 capital ships.[4] When one remembers

---

[1] *English History, 1914–1945*, by A.J.P. Taylor, p. 171.
[2] *Britain in the Century of Total War*, by Arthur Marwick, p. 169.
[3] *Ibid.* p. 418.
[4] In 1993 it had around 100 ships, including 3 Invincible class carriers, 4 nuclear submarines with missiles, 17 other nuclear submarines, 13 destroyers and 35 frigates, compared with 665 ships at the end of World War II.

that in pre-war Britain the working class consisted of about 75 per cent of the population and that the much smaller middle and professional class had much higher economic security, incomes and standard of living, the answer is that, in the absence of its redistribution, British wealth was going into 'guns' instead of 'butter' and towards the maintenance of an Imperial status which she could no longer afford.[1] In other words, and the war was to prove it, Britain was really in no economic position to adopt the position of the world's leading political and military power but it was as well for the world that she did and that the pre-war hardships of the British working class were not suffered in vain. Besides, as we shall see, the harsh economic and social regime produced a disciplined, well-balanced and happy breed which not only fought a brilliant war at home and abroad but whose lost qualities are mourned by all and sundry in these days of affluence, welfare dependency and decadence.

In any event, by the end of the war, there had been another major although extremely subtle English political revolution, namely the quiet determination of the English artisan class and middle class to vote Labour in the 1945 post-war election, in spite of all that Winston Churchill had done for the country and the world during the war. Then, as now, for Labour to win a British majority it was necessary to gain a good slice of the vote of the English better-off working class and middle class, especially in the South-East. It has been said, and written, that in the war years there was a cryptic socialist plot to infiltrate the Army Bureau of Current Affairs, and the like, to poison the minds of the people to think socialist and vote socialist in the July 1945 election. In my view, and in the immortal words of Henry Ford I, this is 'all bunk'. Undoubtedly there were dedicated socialists hard at work such as Michael Foot and his colleagues who wrote pamphlets (disguised as books) in 1944, called 'Guilty Men' and 'Your MP', respectively, which set out in detail what is now called the 'Establishment' and business connections of Tory MPs, such as Public Schools and Oxford and Cambridge educations, as well as the many examples of nepotism in the form of directorships, and the like. In retrospect, this does not appear to be highly inflammatory material but it did make an impression, especially on the middle classes who, as I have said, were quietly determined to support a radical change in post-war Britain, namely a

---

[1] The middle class comprised around 20 per cent of the population and the upper class around 5 per cent. See *Britain in the Century of Total War*, by Arthur Marwick, pp. 231–2.

major redistribution of wealth leading to a much fairer society. This spirit of idealism for the post-war era permeated thought at all levels so that it was only natural that Army Current Affairs and Education lecturers, and the like, should have been affected by it. Referring to the period between the two World Wars, Harold MacMillan wrote:

> Throughout the whole of the post-war period there had been growing an uneasy consciousness of something radically wrong with the economic system; and this uneasiness had been overshadowed by political controversy both within and between all the political parties for many years. One of the consequences of the crisis was to confirm these suspicions and liberate men's minds from a continued subservience to the economic orthodoxy of the pre-war world.[1]

The Government, and remember that Churchill's Government, formed on the fall of Neville Chamberlain in May 1940, was a coalition government with the leading Labour politicians occupying important positions, led the way by commissioning the Liberal, Sir William Beveridge, to write his famous report which appeared in December 1942 under the title, 'Social Insurance and Allied Services'. It is well-known that the Beveridge Report was the blueprint for the post-war 'Welfare State', the lynchpins of which were to be full employment, universal social security and the National Health Service, which was put into effect by the 1945 Labour Government of Clement Attlee. It has been said that this government was elected with the help of the votes of admirals and generals, and people of that ilk, who had never voted Labour before and have never voted Labour since.

---

[1]Quoted in *Britain in the Century of Total War*, by Arthur Marwick, p. 244.

2

The Decline of the Liberal Party, 1886–1945

Before moving on to the post-war years, I want to deal with, and demolish, the insidious and non-cerebral myth (which even has supporters among a minority of Tories) that our traditional electoral system of one-man, one-vote in single-member constituencies is unfair, in the sense of producing a political outcome that is inferior to the alternative system of proportional representation in multi-member constituencies. Apart from the obviously superior satisfaction of single-member as opposed to multi-member constituencies, proportional representation also produces a multiplicity of parties and has to resort to government by coalition (that is by different parties having different outlooks and objectives) which is a byword for weak government. Pre and post-war Europe has many examples of this unsatisfactory state of affairs which compares so unfavourably with the ideal set forth by the Whig, and later, great Tory philosopher, Edmund Burke, when he wrote in 1770 that a political party should be 'a body of men united for promoting by their joint endeavours the national interest, upon some particular principle in which they are all agreed'.

And yet, the Liberal Democrats (and the now defunct Social Democrats) have as the main plank of their policies the introduction of proportional representation whereby their percentage of the vote, say 20 per cent, in a good year, would be mathematically reflected in the number of seats won – say, well over 100 seats in the House of Commons, instead of the derisory 20 or so which has been their lot, even in a good electoral year. The argument is that our electoral system is so constructed as to militate against the smaller third party, and other parties, and to favour the two larger parties. And this is correct, but far from this being an undesirable situation it is one that is entirely desirable – brilliant in fact – for the object is to have two major parties each of which agrees on its own policies and sets of principles while the party in opposition is in a position to oppose effectively and to take over the government at a moment's notice if needs be. In recognition of this fact, the Leader of the Opposition has been paid a salary since 1937. It is no use left-wingers and 'trendy-lefties' (different varieties of the same species) wringing their hands about the excessive power of the British executive or cabinet, even taking into account the ramifications of such developments as Orders in Council and Enabling Legislation. The brutal truth is that the British system of combining its version of democratic government with wholly authoritative government is more than one of the wonders of the political world: it is THE wonder of the political world. A wholesale change to proportional representation would therefore be a completely retrograde step and could only be advocated by political illiterates or by people who have a vested interest in gaining more votes for a third or whatever party, against the general interest of the nation as a whole. It is significant that Italy which, in the post-war years, has suffered from a bewildering series of weak coalition governments owing to a system of proportional representation, has recently moved to one based on single member constituencies. That is not to say that there should not be changes in the machinery of day-to-day government if it is felt that they are beneficial. A good example is the development of the Select Committee system (strengthened after May 1979) whereby committees comprising a mixed membership of members of the House have the right to call ministers and members of the government to account and report on their findings, a procedure borrowed from the United States's political system, as also were the concepts of the party caucus and election mandate. But in regard to third, and other minor, parties our system is purposely hard on these parties for the very good reason that they really should have something of supreme importance to contribute as opposed to a mixture of unrelated and incoherent ideas, and that the third party is such that it is fitted to replace the weaker of the two main parties. For the glory of our system is that although it favours the two main parties, neither of these can take it for granted that its place is guaranteed for ever and that one or other of the main parties can decline in public estimation until it eventually finds itself supplanted by what has previously been the third party. An excellent example of this factor is the decline of the historic Liberal party and the rise of the Labour Party.

To deal with the decline of the Liberal party first, it is a remarkable fact that the last time the Liberal Party gained a majority in 'England', in January 1906, it was a 'landslide' victory, with the Liberals winning 377 seats and a majority of 84 over all other parties combined; that is to say, (Conservative) Unionists with 132, Liberal Unionists with 25, the Irish Nationalists with 83 and, significantly,

31

from our point of view, Labour with 53. Of the Labour members, 29 were returned under the independent Labour Representation Committee and, of the other 24, a few were 'Lib-Labs' of the old school, but most were miners' unions officials who were not yet affiliated to the LRC – but Labour nonetheless. Thus the 1906 election forms a watershed in our history, but to deal with the 'decline and fall of Liberalism' the word 'Union' affords the main clue, for the supremely great statesman, William Gladstone, sowed the seeds of the destruction of the historic Liberal Party by his mission to solve the 'Irish Problem' by granting Home Rule to Ireland. His rejected Home Rule Bill of 1886 split the Liberal Party in a way from which it never recovered, for 93 Liberal MPs voted against the measure which was lost by 30 votes – 313 for, 343 against. Not only did Liberal members of the House of Commons effectively join the Conservative and Unionist Party, as the above voting figures indicate, including such major figures as Neville Chamberlain's father, Joseph Chamberlain, but the great Whig grandees, such as the Dukes of Bedford, Devonshire, Westminster and Argyll who, socially and territorially, were just as powerful as their Tory counterparts, and virtually the whole Whig peerage and the large majority of Gladstone's upper-class and upper-middle-class supporters, eventually left the Liberal Party over Home Rule. In fact, apart from Gladstone's brief and final fourth ministry between 1892– 94, followed by that of the Earl of Rosebery in 1894–95, the Liberals were out of power for the years between 1886 and 1906.

This development led to a dramatic change in British politics in general and party politics in particular. In mid-Victorian England, the apogee of the gladiatorial political contests between Disraeli and Gladstone – who, by the way, was a Peelite or ex-Tory (p. 74) – there was absolutely no class distinction in British politics. As both great parties passed their reform bills, gradually widening the franchise to include more and more working men, the assumption on behalf of both the party leaders and the broadened electorate was that 'the people' would vote for one or other of the groups of patrician leaders to govern them. It was unthinkable that the ordinary man would want to exercise political power in his own right. In retrospect, it can be seen that after 1886 this assumption could no longer be held. Radical, and even socialist, ideas and activities began to stir and initially it was to the Liberal Party that the early adherents of working-class solidarity looked for support but as we shall see, it was an outstanding opportunity that the Liberal Party failed to grasp in spite of the extension of their Government following their electoral victory in 1910.

In 1891, Gladstone had enunciated his 'Newcastle Programme' which, apart from Home Rule, was criticized as being a 'hotch-potch' of ideas which appealed to minorities such as those people who lived in the 'Celtic-fringe' which has already been mentioned (p. 5). Admittedly, some of those ideas can be said to have inspired the great Liberal reforming ministries of 1906–11, with David Lloyd George's controversial budget of 1909 leading to the emasculation of the House of Lords by the Parliament Act of 1911 for, especially since 1886, the Tory peers had been taking advantage of their built-in majority to negate any radical and controversial legislation which threatened their patrician interests, powers and prejudices. However, among other measures foreshadowing the post-1945 Welfare State legislation, the Liberals of this period made modest beginnings with (non-contributory) Old Age Pensions, Children's Allowances to income tax payers and the inception of Labour Exchanges. But, above all, the most important, ambitious and significant measure was Lloyd George's great National Insurance Bill of 1911 which would never have been passed by the House of Lords but for the passing of the Parliament Bill. The National Insurance Bill introduced compulsory contributions from both employers and employees so as to insure the whole working population against sickness and, to a lesser extent, unemployment. It is significant that Lloyd George, a Welsh orphan from an extremely humble, working-class background, should have entered Parliament at a by-election in 1890 as a Liberal and through the offices of the great Liberal Party.

Yet in the years and months preceding the outbreak of war in 1914 the Liberal Prime Minister, the intellectually brilliant Herbert Asquith, appeared to be bedevilled and overwhelmed by three major problems: the Irish question, women's emancipation and the suffragettes and, thirdly, militant trade unionism – syndicalism. The first was an old problem but the latter two were new. What the three had in common was the fact that their advocates were prepared to resort to illegal means (force) to attain their ends. However, the Liberal Government, after a shaky beginning, eventually succeeded in guiding the country to victory in the war, although the real improvement did not come about until Asquith was forced to accept a coalition with the Unionists (and with initially one Labour member of the Cabinet) in May 1915. So ended the last Liberal Government in British history. In December 1916 Asquith resigned and Lloyd George, who had effectively been running the war for some time, succeeded as Prime Minister in circumstances that led to the final and disastrous split of the Liberal Party between the followers of these two men. In the post-war election of 1918 Lloyd George succeeded in clinging to power by maintaining his coalition with the Conservatives although significantly Labour refused to join as they were now beginning to flex their muscles as a national party in their own right. The 150 Lloyd George Liberals (National Liberals) were not opposed by the Conservatives while the 229 Asquithians (Independent Liberals), who were opposed, were so decimated that only 26 were returned, compared to 136 Coalition Lloyd George Liberals, 339 Coalition Unionists and, significantly, 59 Labour, all but one of whom had been nominated by a trade union. In October 1922 Lloyd George's Coalition Government collapsed and he resigned never to hold office again. The Conservatives, under Bonar Law, won the subsequent election but there were two more (in December 1923 and October 1924) owing to the temporary break-up of the two-party system. Labour had become the main party presenting a radical alternative based on the working-class vote but the Liberal Party, split two ways, had finally to die as a major party before the great two-party system reasserted itself. By this time, the Liberal Party had become the weak third party against which our political system militates.

3

The Rise of the Labour Party, 1893–1945

It is well-known that the earliest seeds of the Labour Party were sown in the rise of trade unions and it was not until much later in the nineteenth century that the actual doctrine of socialism played an important part. The beginnings of the Industrial Revolution, the use of machines, driven by power, in factories, can be dated to about 1760 by which time improvements were being made to textile machinery and in Coalbrookdale, in Shropshire, Abraham Darby and his son perfected the process of smelting iron with coal by converting it into coke and eliminating its sulphur impurity. The Darby family succeeded in building the world's first cast-iron structure, the Iron Bridge, which can still be seen next to Coalbrookdale on the River Severn. Because of the original dependence on water-power the earliest factories were based somewhat picturesquely on riverbanks in the countryside. But, with vast supplies of coal and iron in close proximity to each other and to the coast and with the availability of iron for the construction of machinery and steam engines, the workers moved to the 'dark, satanic mills' in the grim industrial towns in the midlands and north of England and in the Clyde region of Scotland as well as to the coal-mining areas of England, Scotland and Wales. With workers congregating in the new factories, mills and mines it was inevitable that they banded together to form trade unions in order to further and protect their interests, although the way had been shown earlier in the shipping and ship-building industries. It was only natural that the earliest trade unions were influenced by the medieval craft guilds but it has proved to be a great disadvantage that British trade unions developed in the main, as craft unions, so that there have been a number of unions operating in one industry or even in one factory. The main exceptions occur in industries that have been nationalized such as the railways and the coal-mining industry.

Trade Unions were recognized much earlier in Britain than in France and Germany, enjoying a measure of liberty in the former since 1824, with the repeal of the Combination Laws of 1799–1800

35

(p. 324). The trade unions made too much of their new freedom and a return of the restrictions was demanded but the new Act of 1825 imposed some limitations on the unions, yet in general the reform was maintained, although it was not afforded in the latter two countries until 1884 and 1892 respectively. However, it was not until legislation by Gladstone in 1871, following the report of the Royal Commission on Trade Unions of 1867, and by Disraeli in 1875 and 1876, that British trade unions won recognition for peaceful picketing and collective bargaining, namely that a combination of persons engaged in a trade dispute might lawfully commit any act which was not punishable if committed by one person. After a period of legal confusion, the situation was regularized by the Trades Disputes Act of 1906, following the disastrous legal decision against the union after the Taff Vale Railway Company strike of 1900. However, a number of unions in the engineering industry had united in 1851 to form the Amalgamated Society of Engineers. Although it was on an informal basis, the first meeting of the Trades Union Congress was held in 1865 and in 1871 it elected the 'Parliamentary Committee' which became effectively the political executive of the movement which was still confined to skilled workmen (or craftsmen). In 1871 and 1872 there were several successful strikes by the comparatively prosperous engineering workers for shorter hours or higher wages. But, with the onset of depression after 1873, strikes by the old craft unions were severely defeated so that their younger members looked at and were influenced by the revival of socialism (which had been enunciated in the early part of the century) in the early eighties. In 1881 the Democratic (later the Social Democratic) Federation was founded, it being the first modern English socialist organization. One of its early members was William Morris, of poetic and artistic fame, and in 1884 he founded the Socialist league. The same year saw the foundation of the Fabian Society which eventually became the intellectual inspiration of the later Labour party. In the depressed winter of 1885–86, the Social Democratic Federation organized meetings and marches of the unemployed which culminated in a somewhat violent gathering in Trafalgar Square. To date, the few working-class or Labour parliamentary aspirants were trade-union officials who were elected as Liberals, under the so-called 'Lib-Lab' pact. However, with the further widening of the franchise in 1884, to include unskilled workers such as the miners, these latter began to think in terms of putting up their own candidates which, as we have already noted, was an entirely new and significant development. We shall see that, partly through snobbery and partly through lack of foresight (for example, a failure to deal with the problem that working-class parliamentary candidates would need to be financed by someone or other) the Liberal Party missed the outstanding opportunity to channel the emerging working-class political aspirations through its own organization – thus ensuring its eventual demise as one of the two great British Parliamentary parties.

As a result of the development of working-class solidarity after 1884, several socialists were elected to Parliament in the 1892 election, including the Scottish ex-coalminer, J. Keir Hardie, 'the Father of the British Labour Party', who did not endear himself to the Liberals, who should have cultivated him, by wearing a brown suit, hat and shoes in the House of Commons, as opposed to the statutory black tails and top hat. In 1893 Keir Hardie was the guiding light in founding the Independent Labour Party (ILP) which was an extremely important step in that it was the first popular socialist party in England, giving vent to working-class opinions and aims which had already been formed in the trade unions and non-conformist chapels. However, in spite of the enthusiasm and devotion of the ILP members, the most dynamic, popular and radical development of the day was the rise of aggressive imperialism, culminating in the election of the Tories in 1895 and 1900 and in a wave of militaristic enthusiasm, ending in the Boer War. The main exponent of this development, opposed by the Liberals, was the Liberal renegade, Joseph Chamberlain, who, after 1903, bracketed it with a crusade for the adoption of the extremely controversial policy of Imperial Preference, clean against the Free Trade ethic which had dominated Britain since 1846.

Nevertheless, although the ILP was 'little more than a socialist propaganda society although christened a "party"'[1] and a Parliamentary Representation Committee had been formed in 1893–94, enough progress had been made for the Trades Union Congress in 1899 to decide to call a conference of delegates from 'Co-Operative, Socialist, Trade Union and other working-class organizations' to 'devise ways and means for the securing of an increased number of Labour members in the next Parliament'.[2] This led to the creation of the 'Labour Representation Committee' in 1900, the secretary of which was an ILP delegate, J. Ramsay MacDonald, while it was greatly significant that the unions agreed to a small levy of '10s per annum for every 1000 members or fraction

---

[1]*England, 1870–1914*, by R.C.K. Ensor, p. 265. Further facts and figures in this chapter are attributable to this authority.
[2]Ibid, p. 265.

thereof'.[1] In view of the support of middle-class socialists, such as the Fabians, there was an important stipulation that parliamentary candidates need not be working men provided that they were 'sympathetic with the needs and demands of the Labour movements'.[2] An amendment to the original constitution was successfully carried by Keir Hardie establishing that the LRC was to be:

> a distinct Labour group in Parliament, who shall have their own Whips and agree upon their policy, which must embrace a readiness to co-operate with any party which for the time being may be engaged in promoting legislation in the direct interest of Labour and be equally ready to associate themselves with any party in opposing measures having an opposite tendency.[3]

This was a definition of 'party' in pursuing the Labour interest in the same tradition as Burke's earlier definition of 'party', while serving notice on the Unionist and Liberal Parties that they were quite distinct from them and in future would be only and wholly dedicated to pursuing the 'direct interest of Labour'[4] Keir Hardie had lost his seat in 1895 but regained it in the 1900 election in spite of the 'Imperialist hubbub'.

As we have already seen, between 1900 and the election of January 1906 enough progress had been made for the return of 53 Labour members in that election following the reaction against the Conservative and Unionist imperialism and protectionism. In this pursuit, Chamberlain had split the Conservative Party. For example, Winston Churchill had gone over to the Liberals on the issue of Free Trade and became a minister (President of the Board of Trade) in Campbell-Bannerman's reforming Liberal Government in 1908. At this stage, it is important to analyze the composition of the 53 Labour members who were elected in 1906:

> 29 were returned under the Labour Representation Committee to sit as an independent party. Of the other 24 a few were ordinary 'Lib-Labs', but most were the officials of the miners' unions who although not yet affiliated to the LRC, were elected like them on a decided class basis.[5]

---

[1] *Ibid.*, p. 266.
[2] *Ibid.*, p. 266.
[3] *Ibid.*, p. 266.
[4] *Ibid.*, p. 266.
[5] *Ibid.*, p. 386.

The fact that the Labour Representation Committee named itself the Labour Party in 1906 was supremely important and significant while in 1911 the second of the two essential developments to make the creation of the Labour party even possible, occurred. The first was Disraeli's Reform Act of 1867, which widened the franchise from the narrow middle-class basis of the original 1832 Reform Act to include the artisan class, the (secret) Ballot Act of 1872 and the Reform Act of 1884 which extended the vote to the rural areas and to the unskilled labourers. The second requirement was the passing of an Act of Parliament in 1911, enacting the payment of Members of Parliament (£400 a year), significantly, on the day on which the House of Lords passed the Parliament Bill. Thus Labour were indebted to the Liberal Party, for this measure had been a part of Liberal policy since it was first mentioned in Gladstone's Newcastle Programme of 1891 – but, typically, the Liberal Party did not benefit from this act of enlightenment.

At this time, and it was not foreseen by someone as politically astute as Lloyd George, the steps by which Labour superseded the Liberals, must have appeared slow and uncertain. But, in retrospect, they appear to be decisive and inevitable as indeed the Fabian, Sidney Webb, actually believed when he coined the phrase 'the inevitability of gradualness'. For example, the Kerensky Revolution in Russia in March 1917 inspired working-class, socialist and Labour aspirations. In May, Arthur Henderson, returned from Russia and resigned his seat in the war cabinet and determined as leader of the Labour Party not only to further those claims for independence made earlier by Keir Hardie but for it to become a national party with the requisite party and constituency organizations. Accordingly, Labour refused to fight the 1918 election as a member of Lloyd George's Coalition and independently increased its parliamentary members from 39 to 59, some of the 53 seats won in 1906 having been lost in the meantime. It is significant that between 1918 and 1922 Labour won 14 by-elections and lost only one, and that the Conservative electoral victory in November 1922, under Bonar Law, ushered in three-party politics, as the rise of Labour and the fall of the Liberals was played out in the further two elections of December 1923 and October 1924. The voting in the November 1922 election illustrates how our brilliant system was beginning to decimate the party on the decline.

Five and a half million voted Conservative; just over 4 million voted Liberal (Asquithians 2.5 million, National 1.6 million); 4.2 million voted Labour. The Conservatives held almost precisely their numbers at the dissolution: with 345 seats they had a majority of 77 over the other parties combined. Labour won 142 seats; the Liberals, with almost exactly the same vote (but about 70 more candidates), only 117.[1]

Labour can also be seen to be developing as even more of a national party in that whereas in previous parliaments Labour members had virtually all been trade unionists, these were now little more than half and their numbers included middle-class and even upper-class men for the first time. For example, Clement Attlee was elected at this election. By this time, Ramsay MacDonald had established himself as the dominant figure in the Labour movement and he was elected leader of the party by the Labour MPs.

In May 1923, the extremely ill Bonar Law resigned the premiership and he was succeeded by Stanley Baldwin, the very shrewd businessman and country gentleman who, with Ramsay MacDonald and Neville Chamberlain, was to dominate British politics until the outbreak of war, although Ramsay MacDonald was a spent force by 1935. Uncharacteristically, the usually cautious Baldwin called an election in December 1923, to seek a mandate to introduce Protection in order to fight unemployment. The Tory flirtation with Protection had always been disastrous in the past, and so it proved to be once again, leading to a final act of resuscitation by the dying Liberal Party, both wings of which united, under Asquith, in defence of their historic policy of Free Trade. Once again, we note the exquisite exaggeration of our voting system.

> Though the overall vote remained much the same – the Conservatives received about 100,000 less, the Liberals 200,000 (less) and Labour 100,000 more – the results were startlingly different. The Conservatives lost over ninety seats (258), the Liberals gained forty (159) and Labour fifty (191). The dominant groups of 1918 were further depleted, relatively in one case, absolutely in the other. The trade unionists, once all-powerful, were now a bare majority in the Labour Party (98 out of 191). The National (Lloyd George) Liberals, already halved in 1922, were now halved again, despite Liberal gains. There were only twenty-six of them. Their former seats nearly all went to Labour, evidence that they had formed the Liberal left wing. The outcome was a tangle: No single party with a majority, yet the Liberals barred

---

[1]*English History, 1914–1945*, by A.J.P. Taylor, pp. 197–8. Further facts and figures in this chapter are attributable to this authority.

from coalition by their dislike of Protection on the one side, of socialism on the other.[1]

When Parliament met in January the Conservative Government was voted out of office and Ramsay MacDonald formed the first Labour Government. Although this 'no-hope' minority government fell, as it was destined to do, in September of that year (1924) on a middle-class, anti-socialistic panic based on largely groundless and superficial evidence of the Government being involved with the Communists, both at home and abroad, this first Labour Government is notable for the moderation of its policies and its members which included ex-Liberal converts from the upper class such as Lord Haldane (Lord Chancellor), C.P. Trevelyan (later Sir Charles Trevelyan, Bart.) at the Board of Education, and Arthur Ponsonby, the son of Lord Posonby, Queen Victoria's Private Secretary, at the Foreign Office. However, it must be said that working men made up the majority of the Government – a social revolution.

In the ensuing election in October 1924, Baldwin acted with the sure-footedness for which he eventually became famous, having renounced Protection in June, thereby dishing the Liberals and, more important from the point of view of the future, winning Winston Churchill back to the Conservative party, after over 20 years with the Liberals. The result was that the Liberals lost 100 seats, with the remaining 40 members being led by Lloyd George as Asquith, having lost his seat, went to the Lords while Labour, despite losing 64 seats and winning 24 was, with 151 seats, established unquestionably as the second party. With 419 members out of 615 and with 48.3 per cent of the vote, Baldwin established the Conservative Party as the other main party, in case there had been any doubt about it previously.

From this time, there can also be traced another factor which was to be so important in the years after 1945 – political consensus. This was an interesting development in view of the fact that whereas the Liberal Party and its members were the social equals of the Conservatives, the Labour Party, which was superseding it, was essentially a working-class party which should have led to class conflict and a stalemate, in and out of Parliament. This, however did not happen and the serious General Strike in 1926 was conducted with great moderation by the leaders on both sides. Although the

---

[1]*English History, 1914–1945*, by A.J.P. Taylor, p. 208.

Trade Disputes and Trade Union Act of 1927 occupies an important place in Labour Party 'demonology' its provisions, making sympathetic strike action illegal and introducing 'contracting-in' for the payment of the political levy to the Labour party, were enlightened, and foreshadowed Mrs Thatcher's reforms of the 1980s. The point was that although they were very different kinds of people, Baldwin and MacDonald could each conceivably have been leader of their opponent's party, while in social legislation both MacDonald's administrations of 1924 and 1929–31 and Baldwin's of 1923–24 and 1924–29 carried on improving and adding to the enlightened efforts of the Liberals of 1906–11, from which the 'welfare state' was the natural concomitant. Among the Conservative leaders in 1922–23 and subsequent administrations, by far the most able and 'caring' administrator in the field of social legislation was the ill-fated Neville Chamberlain who eventually became Prime Minister in 1937, after a long apprenticeship.

The one aspect that all pre-war governments failed to understand and therefore cope with was the phenomenon of mass unemployment in the towns built on the historic staple industries – iron and steel, shipbuilding, cotton textiles and coal mining. It is now easy for us to see (although there are still people in the Labour Party and trade unions who do not see it) that those industries were in relative decline, in view of competition from Germany and the USA, a process which can be dated back to around 1875 when 'invisible' exports, in the banking, insurance and allied fields, began to make up for the shortfall in our visible exports of manufactured goods. It was very much a case of 'poverty amidst plenty' for at the same time as the old industries were declining, new ones, such as the motor, electrical and chemical industries were mushrooming in other parts of the country, notably the South-East, and were paying higher wages. Also, those in employment, especially the comparatively small middle-class and higher paid artisan, were experiencing an increasingly high standard of living owing to rising 'real incomes', as well as to higher wages. However, the fact remains that this was relative and that the 'poverty amidst plenty' syndrome was the one that counted when the British people went to the polls in 1945. Also, as A.J.P. Taylor brilliantly points out:

> In the Second World War the British people came of age. This was a people's war. Not only were their needs considered. They themselves wanted to win. Future historians may see the war as a last struggle for the European balance of power or for the

42

maintenance of Empire. This was not how it appeared to those who lived through it.[1]

The political consensus was even more marked, and eventually disastrous, in foreign policy and defence. Ramsay MacDonald was totally against the First World War and was a founder member in 1914 of the Union of Democratic Control which was virtually a pacifist organization and which was probably the initial and main influence in the pacifist streak in the Labour Party which eventually led to its adoption of unilateralism. Although many Conservatives were distrustful of such impractical idealism as that embodied in the League of Nations of 1918 and its Covenant, outlawing war as a means of settling national disputes, these ideals were accepted immediately by all three parties. The Liberals, under Gladstone, had, of course, been dedicated to keeping out of war by reducing foreign 'adventures' to a minimum. Thus in the twenties the belief in the maintenance of peace by 'collective security' and by disarmament was paramount. This is the form of idealism which still exists in the modern Liberal Party which has tended to assume that the mere identification and definition of a problem leads to its solution. The concept of enforcing collective security by the fact of armed strength (which we know to be the only way) was regarded as a contradiction in terms for the belief was that if there were armaments, there would be war. Thus the logical conclusion was to disarm: ergo there would be no war. Appeasement is now such a dirty word in the context of pre-1939 (although we have seen its modern equivalent in the form of unilateralism which has proved to be so wrong, once again) that one has to make a conscious effort to try to understand honest and intelligent men espousing such an impractical and hopelessly wrong view.[2] But the strength of the 'consensus' was like a powerful drug which had the effect of numbing the brain. A good example is Lord Robert Cecil who played a major part, while in the Foreign Office, in drafting the Covenant of the League of Nations and who showed that he was not an impractical idealist when, with other Conservatives, he was extremely hostile to the idea of a negotiated peace with Germany when it was suggested in late 1916. Yet so far had he partaken of the drug of this particular consensus that in September 1931, he told the League of Nations Assembly that 'there

---

[1]*English History, 1914–1945*, by A.J.P. Taylor, p. 600.
[2]This was written well before the Gulf War where, once again, the pacifist and anti-war influence has been so wrong and wrong-headed.

43

has scarcely been a period in the world's history when war seems less likely than it does at present.'[1] A week later Japanese troops invaded Manchuria which was nominally Chinese territory and the Chinese appeal to the League of Nations was of no avail. The weaker had to give way to the stronger, a process which was disguised by a mirage of words in the accompanying diplomatic statements. And so it happened on literally every occasion (and I should be happy to be proved wrong on this point) between the wars – and there were many of them. Manchuria, Abyssinia, and all Hitler's re-occupations and annexations, up until Neville Chamberlain at Munich in 1938, were only the main crises but on these and every other occasion 'collective security' through the Covenant and Non-aggression and Disarmament pacts such as Locarno and Kellog proved to be absolutely worthless and a manifest failure. The same can be said of economic sanctions as applied against Italy and elsewhere but it did not stop the naive idealists continuing to have faith in them.

The most consistent and famous critic of this MacDonald-Baldwin-Chamberlain consensus was Winston Churchill who had resigned from the shadow cabinet in January 1931 and did not hold office again until the outbreak of war in 1939. These have been described as Churchill's years of being 'in the wilderness' and of unpopularity for daring to challenge the sacrosanct 'consensus'. He had a reputation for eccentricity and poor judgment arising from the failure of the Antwerp expedition in 1914 and the Dardanelles operation in 1915 and other endeavours. He can be regarded as naturally aggressive and hostile to the working class as when he instigated the 'Siege of Sidney Street' in 1911, sent troops to Tonypandy in 1912, broke the strike in Coventry ruthlessly in 1918 and referred to the strikers in 1926 as 'the enemy'. His eventual resignation in 1931 over the subject of granting India Dominion status to the disadvantage of the princes, whereas he would have preferred to work with the princes, can be described as the posturing of a romantic reactionary, as also when he led the opposition to Baldwin in the crisis leading to the abdication of Edward VIII, and when he stated in 1951 that he had not become Prime Minister in order 'to preside over the dissolution of the British Empire'. All these criticisms pale into insignificance and irrelevance when one considers his many years of preparation through the reading and writing of history until he was absolutely immersed in it and able to see clearly through the futility of the League of Nations and its Covenant, 'Collective Security', Non-Aggression and Disarmament

[1] *English History, 1914–1945*, by A.J.P. Taylor, pp. 298–9.

Pacts – the whole hypocritical humbug of Appeasement as it was expounded so forcefully and consistently in that pre-war organ of the 'Establishment', *The Times*. Nor can the description of Churchill as a mere romantic reactionary be sustained when one considers the awesome prescience of his American Fulton Speech in 1946 when he emphasized the need to maintain and build on the political links with and in Europe, so that he has been credited as the intellectual precursor of the concept of the European institutions that have thrived since the war. Similarly, in home affairs, his unconventionality and freedom of spirit led him to espouse radical and enlightened ideas such as a school-leaving age of seventeen (in 1908!), a federal structure for Britain, like post-war Germany, and 'a big slice of Bismarckianism over the whole underside of our industrial system'. In other words, his radical vision was to raise the educational standards and status of our working class. But above all, and leaving his magnificent war leadership out of account, his pre-war political life stands as a warning for all time against the dangers of consensus in politics.

This diversion to discuss consensus politics has left us at the time of the massive Conservative victory in 1924 under Baldwin who 'went to the country' in May 1929, the duration of Parliament having been reduced from seven years to five by the Parliament Act of 1911. Another important change had been the Act of 1928 reducing the voting age for women from 30 to 21, the so-called 'flapper vote', which, incidentally, was opposed by Churchill. As we are still concerned to study the relationship between our electoral system and the rise of the Labour Party – and the fall of the Liberal Party – it is necessary to continue to look at the voting figures in some detail until we reach the 1945 general election. A.J.P. Taylor says that,

> The general election of May 1929 was the only fully three-cornered contest in British history. For the first and last time, three parties – Conservative, Liberal and Labour – fought on something like equal terms ... Both Conservative and Labour polled over eight million votes, the Conservatives 300,000 more than Labour. The distribution of seats, however, being based on the consensus of 1911, was already antiquated: it did not allow for the steady shift of population from Scotland and the north of England to the south, and from the centre of towns, including London, to the suburbs.[1] As the result, Labour won 288 seats; Conservatives 260.

---

[1] The Boundary Commission was first set up in 1945 which, independent of government, is responsible for altering the boundaries of constituencies following population changes and in accordance with an agreed formula.

Thus Labour, supposedly the party of the people, owed its success to comparatively rotten boroughs. The Liberals increased their vote by over two million – from under three million to over five. This was entirely due to the increased number of their candidates; their percentage of votes in contested seats actually declined (from 30.9% to 27.7%). The increased vote brought to the Liberals only 19 extra seats – 59 instead of 40.[1]

Thus Ramsay MacDonald formed his second minority Government. Once again, on home affairs, democratic moderation was the order of the day and short-shrift was given to the ILP and other left-wing pressure groups, such as the communists, who advocated 'red-blooded' socialism. As before, the capitalist system was taken for granted and if there was any intention to move towards a socialist society it was to do so by parliamentary control and manipulation of the existing system, a process which could be said to have been foreshadowed during the 1914–18 war. Thus, in 1926 a public corporation was set up (or rather restored, for it had already been formed during the war and abolished after) for the distribution of electricity in the form of the Central Electricity Board, and Herbert Morris laid the foundations for running London Transport by a public corporation, the later London Passenger Transport Board. In housing and education the reforming policies of 1924 were continued although, being a minority government, some legislations was rebuffed by the other two parties but in general the Government enjoyed Liberal support. As a quid pro quo, the Liberals asked for an act to bring in proportional representation. The Government agreed to bring in the single alternative vote, a watered-down version of PR, but the bill made slow progress and probably would have needed to utilize the machinery of the 1911 Parliament Act to become law. Fortunately, in this respect, the Government fell before the necessary two-year period expired and we were saved from taking the backward step envisaged by this particular form of political naivety. Above all, the greatest continuity or consensus in home affairs was in the person of Philip Snowden, Chancellor of the Exchequer in both governments, for his financial policy was purely Gladstonian in that he wholly accepted the traditional 'laissez-faire' system and the necessity for balanced budgets – come what may. Thus his explanation for the perpetual problem of the decline in the exports of the staple industries was that their costs were too high and his prescription was the traditional one of reducing wages which, in

---

[1]*English History, 1914–1945*, by A.J.P. Taylor, pp. 262 and 270.

addition to the increases in taxes in the attempt to balance the budget, were irrelevant in the first case, and the opposite to what should have happened in the second. In foreign affairs, Ramsay MacDonald and his Foreign Secretary, Arthur Henderson, were extremely busy implementing the policies which they developed in 1924 and which by now had become bipartisan – the consensus in fact. The finishing touches were made to the alleviation of German reparations and allied controls, and the acceptance of Germany into the comity of nations, which was part and parcel of the thinking of all the post-war idealists, together with the attainment of collective security by disarmament on which Henderson devoted a great deal of time and attention. I have already mentioned that steps were taken to grant Dominion status to India but these did not bear fruit initially, for Gandhi and the Indian Congress were agitating for independence. It was inevitable that it was to be the post-war Labour Government which would finally bring about this momentous event.

However, Ramsay MacDonald's second administration was destined to be overwhelmed by a worldwide development over which it had no control before or after it happened, and which was to change the very nature of the Labour Party and the political consensus which had existed up until 1931 – the Great Depression. When the Government came to office, although there was the usual unemployment of around one million (under 10 per cent) mostly in the staple industries, the country was still enjoying a measure of prosperity, but unfortunately this was being financed worldwide by an unsoundly based American financial expansion. Already there was an intense agricultural depression in the United States which had spread throughout the world and in October 1929 the collapse on Wall Street led to a world financial and business collapse. Although the United States and other European countries, especially Germany, were more adversely affected, there was a disastrous fall in the exports of our staple industries with the volume almost halving between 1929 and 1931. Unemployment rose to 2.5 million by the end of 1931 and there was a panic over the consequent deterioration in our balance of payments (which, anyway, had not balanced for over half a century without the help of invisible exports in the way of financial services, and the like, but on this occasion the worrying thing was that these collapsed also) and a threatened budget deficit. We now know that this was precisely what was required but when a brilliant young junior minister, Sir Oswald Moseley, suggested that this, as well as further left-wing (or totalitarian) remedies such as the public direction of industry and the planning of foreign trade, he was rebuffed. His subsequent resignation from the Labour Party and ventures up various blind alleys was a tragedy in that perhaps the best intellect in the Labour Party was lost both to it and to the service of the country.

Instead, for a solution of the problem, we have a classic example of the working of the consensus. At the end of Lloyd Georges's post-war ministry in 1922, the post-war boom collapsed and following the recommendation of Sir Edward Geddes's Committee (the Geddes Axe) there was a drastic retrenchment of public expenditure, not only in the army and navy but throughout all government departments, especially in education and public health, including reductions in salaries. Another committee, on this occasion, the May Committee, reported at the end of July 1931 in such a manner as to exaggerate Britain's economic and financial problems and to recommend the old, hopeless remedy of the need to balance the budget by government retrenchment, but especially by a 20 per cent reduction in unemployment relief. In August, there was a run on the pound which had been vulnerable since 1925 when Winston Churchill, an unwilling and unknowledgeable Chancellor of the Exchequer, returned to the Gold (exchange) Standard at the pre-war parity, which was completely uncompetitive for our exports and which was a last-ditch and vain effort to enable the City of London to return to its former glory and power. In the event, it was decided to reduce the unemployment relief by 10 per cent instead of the original proposal of 20 per cent, but although the Cabinet agreed to this by a majority, it was only a narrow majority and the Trade Union Congress, led by the powerful Ernest Bevin, was wholly opposed. In view of this fact and of his failure to carry his cabinet with him, MacDonald formed a National Government in August: 'To deal with the national emergency that now exists'. Of the small cabinet of ten members, four were Conservatives, four Labour and two Liberal. Snowden's emergency budget increased taxes and all government salaries from the top (cabinet ministers) to the bottom (the unemployed) were reduced by ten per cent. In September, the sailors of the Atlantic fleet 'mutinied' at Invergordon by refusing to man their posts following the cuts in their pay. There was such a heavy run on the pound that the foreign credits were exhausted and on 21 September the Gold Standard was suspended. The pound fell by over a quarter to around $3.40 and as the Gold Exchange Standard only applied to international operations and as the gold currency was not restored in 1925, the man in the street was not affected, while after the suspension people wondered what the crisis was all about. The Gold Standard was yet another consensus that had outlived its time although it at least had the merit of acting independently of politicians and even central banks. However, in its nineteenth-century classical period, the adjustment to balance of payments or inflationary pressures was made automatically and far too harshly in the form of wage reductions and unemployment – which men like Geddes and May were trying to emulate.

In a sense, though, things were never the same again. Ramsay MacDonald and the 'traitors' who followed him into the National Government were expelled from the Labour Party which from then on became much more class-conscious and critical of the pre-1931 consensus. But this latter development was not confined to the Labour Party. For example, rightly or wrongly, the consensus of balanced budgets and the thinking behind the Geddes and May reports, ceased to apply after 1945. Therefore we can ask the question: did the political crisis, leading to the fall of Ramsay MacDonald's Government, emanating from the extraneous economic and financial forces unleashed by the Great Depression, rob Great Britain of the boon of having as one of its two great parties, a Labour Party which was both radical and a defender of working-class interests, as well as being strictly democratic, in the sense of abiding by both the sovereignty of and the laws enacted by Parliament, and also not being infected by unacceptable doctrines such as communism. My answer is: yes. It will be remembered that the minority Labour governments were impeccable in their efforts to abide by 'the constitution' and that they were completely ruthless in outlawing extremist influences, whether from the ILP or the Communist Party. It can be said that one result was to drive these influences underground so that they have appeared in the post-war Labour party in disguise, as it were. Extremists, including Communists, have joined the Labour Party so that it can be infiltrated and hopefully turned into something very different from a social democratic and non-extremist party. Admittedly, one reason for this is our splendid voting system which has ensured that the Communist Party in this country has never held more than two parliamentary seats. However, the outcome is that we ended up with a Labour Party which has not been radical but reactionary, which, through ignorance, has acted against and not for working-class interests, and which has been suspect as a social democratic and non-extremist party. The Kinnockian desperate attempts to reform the Labour Party and the cultivation of the Red Rose image virtually admitted these deficiencies, an endeavour which has been carried on by his successors.

However, more of that anon. Ramsay MacDonald's National Government called for a general election in October on the grounds that it wanted a 'Doctor's Mandate' to continue to deal with the national economic crisis even though it had failed to save the pound in its earlier manifestation. The main prescription advocated by this Conservative-dominated Government was to impose Protection, which was embarrassing for their National Liberal allies and as the Labour opposition immediately espoused Free Trade, MacDonald and his ex-Labour rump should have been embarrassed, but such difficulties and differences never perturbed this non-pragmatic man with the golden tongue whose lifelong belief was that even the most radical differences in belief could be overcome by talk and patient negotiation; certainly in his view such differences should not prevent people from working together who were united in achieving a higher end. It is once again important and interesting to look at the voting figures in detail. For this, as well as the study of the pre-war decline of the Liberal Party and rise of the Labour Party, I make no apology, for it is only by looking carefully at our voting system that one can appreciate that it is a 'system' and that it works. That is to say, over a period of years the political complexion of our parties is changed, not in a haphazard or superficial way as with Proportional Representation but ineluctably and in line with the wishes of the people – the general will, as Rousseau would have said. A detailed study of pre-war history is extremely useful, if not essential, for understanding post-war attitudes, problems and solutions – right or wrong. Pre-war history has already identified for us the concept of political 'consensus' and that it is not all that it seems to be.

But back to the election results:

> Some three million Liberals, who had no longer a candidate of their own, presumably voted solid for Conservatives. MacDonald, not Lloyd George had caught the right tune: National emergency eclipsed Free Trade. Labour polled nearly two million votes less than in 1929. About half a million of these voted 'National'; they are said to have been mainly women. The rest merely did not vote. Thus even in the most decisive election of modern times, the swing of the pendulum was less than 2 per cent, so far as the essential question, Labour versus the rest, was concerned. Workers lost faith in the Labour Party; they did not get it in anyone else. Even so, the results were dramatic enough. The Conservatives, with their inseparable allies, National Labour (the MacDonaldites) and National Liberals (the Simonites), received slightly over sixty per cent of the vote – the only victors ever to top this mark – or with their less inseparable allies, the 'pure' Liberals, 67 per cent. The system, as often, exaggerated the effects of the voting. The Conservatives and their allies won 521 seats, (Conservatives 473;

National Liberal 35; National Labour 13). Labour, with a third of the total vote, held only 52. All the members of the former Labour cabinet lost their seats except George Lansbury. The Liberals got their deserts: 33 seats, which was about right for their vote.[1]

It might be thought that this was an insuperable set-back for the Labour party and that it was quite literally back to the position it occupied in 1906. This was not necessarily so. As has already been said, the traumas of 1931 brought about a decisive break between the 1920s and 1930s. The MacDonald-Baldwin consensus was dead and the Labour Party, for good or for ill, went along the road that made it the party to win victory finally in 1945. The new leader was George Lansbury who had been around for years and who, although a virtual pacifist like MacDonald, had been kept out of Labour cabinets by the latter because of his extremist views. Although extremely well-liked on a wide front, including King George V, who took to his personality, Lansbury was very much a 'class' politician and, unlike Ramsay MacDonald, would not be interested in flirting with the aristocracy, in more ways than one. For example, he had been very much involved in local politics in the East End and could be said to have pioneered the practice of Labour councils spending more on wages and relief than that allocated by the government and to do so by borrowing. It is not surprising that under his leadership,

> according to the resolution passed at the annual conference in 1932, the next Labour government must introduce 'definite socialist legislation immediately', whether it had a majority or not.[2]

Two junior shadow ministers promoted by him were Stafford Cripps and Clement Attlee, the former being such an ardent Marxist that he was temporarily expelled from the party in 1938. Clement Attlee was an enthusiastic believer in the League of Nations and all that it stood for and right up to the outbreak of war in 1939 he not only advocated disarmament but opposed re-armament which by this time was also the official policy of the Labour Party – shades of unilateralism! Attlee could be described as a middle-class intellectual who became a socialist through the dictates of his conscience in view of the social inequalities of the Britain of his day. In the 1930s this became a common breed of Labour supporter, most of whom were extremely left-wing, if not Marxist. Professor Harold Laski is the best

---

[1]*English History, 1914–1945*, by A.J.P. Taylor, pp. 325–6.
[2]Ibid, p. 346.

example. Following the break of the ILP with the Labour Party in 1932 because it refused to be bound any longer by Labour Party discipline, Aneurin Bevan and other dissidents formed the Socialist League which set about attempting to influence the Labour Party with its crypto-Marxist views. In those days, of course, intellectuals of this type were very excited by the manifestation of Soviet Russia, especially after the Five Year Plan began in 1928. In retrospect, the many idealistic books written in the early days about Russia, such as those by the Webbs, appear to be pathetically naive and one is tempted to suggest automatic disqualification from political office for anyone with a high degree of idealism in their veins – if such a measurement could be taken!

The Communists also infiltrated working-class movements such as 'The National Unemployed Workers Movement' and it was through them that the well-known protest marches of workers from the depressed areas to London were organized with such telling effects on the middle-class conscience. It is significant that these were not organized by the trade unions whose relationship with the Labour Party changed significantly as a result of the events of 1931. The traditional practice of trade unions, through their officials as Members of Parliament, playing a direct part in Parliamentary affairs, received a decisive blow for in the new Parliament only a little more than half the Labour MPs were union officials – and minor ones at that. Whereas union secretaries and leaders previously aspired to be and became MPs, apart from the wartime exception of Ernest Bevin, the practice ceased and, having lost confidence in the Labour Party, the trade union movement and its leaders from henceforth took an independent line in negotiating with employers and in making policy decisions on pragmatic grounds which sometimes were to the Left of the Party and sometimes to the Right. However, whereas traditionally the unions were the protagonists of class war and the Labour Party exercised a moderate influence, the roles were now reversed. Of course, the unions continued to have an indirect parliamentary influence through the sponsoring of MPs and through the block vote at party conferences. As the post-1945 years went by this indirect influence came to be excessive and it was mainly due to the public's revulsion at these trade union excesses that Labour fell from power in 1979 and Margaret Thatcher formed her first government with a mandate, among other things, to reform the trade unions.

4

The Rise and Rise of the Conservative Party, 1660–

We are also concerned with the rise and nature of the Conservative Party and it is necessary to make the obvious point that the National Government of 1931–35 was, in fact, if not in name, a Conservative Government, and that Baldwin, the Conservative Party leader, was, in fact, if not in name, Prime Minister which he actually became in June 1935, just after King George V's Jubilee, when MacDonald stepped down owing to ill-health. That Conservative workhorse, Neville Chamberlain, as Chancellor of the Exchequer, was once again the dynamic force in the administrative field. His budgets were framed along the traditional lines of his Labour predecessor, Snowden, curbing expenditure with a view to balancing the budget, although in the event he failed to do this which reminds us of the post-war situation. However, in his initial budget of April 1932 his arms estimates were the lowest between the wars. Although there was much idealistic espousing of disarmament in the period by the Labour and Liberal Parties, and others, the more pragmatic Conservatives were inclined to utilize the situation as a means of reducing expenditure. It will be remembered, however, that the National Government came into being in order to deal with a financial and economic crisis. How did it set about this task? Its policy had:

> three principal branches: devaluation and a managed currency; cheap money; tariffs. The British Government had arrived at the first unwillingly; at the second by accident; at the third with determination.[1]

Although each of these policies was decisive and had important effects, one feels that they were as uninspired as the foreign policy which ended so disastrously in 1939 as one also feels that the same

---

[1] *English History, 1914–45*, by A.J.P. Taylor, p. 336. Further facts and figures in this chapter are attributable to this authority.

lack of inspiration plagued post-war Conservative Governments until 1979.

Devaluation, of course, followed from abandoning the Gold Standard, and the pound settled down at about two-thirds of its earlier value, as also did the managed currency for which purpose the Exchange Equalization Fund was set up in 1932. Although the National Government had fought to keep the sterling exchange rate up, as did post-war governments, once it had fallen it was regarded as a brilliant opportunity to help the exports of the ever-ailing traditional industries. Thus conscious efforts were made to keep the pound down in the course of which larger quantities of gold were accumulated which was very useful after 1939. However, as always, devaluation was only a short-term expedient for it turned the terms of trade against the foreign customer exporting to Britain and led to competitive devaluations such as that of the United States to 59 per cent of its gold parity, in 1933, which sent the pound up to $5 again.

Cheap money was the consequence of the conversion of 5 per cent War Loan (over £2,000 million which was an enormous amount of money in those days) to 3½ per cent which had been projected by Snowden so that this was pure consensus. The appeal was to the rentier class to make this sacrifice and there was an immediate saving to the Exchequer of £23 million which by 1936 had increased to at least £86 million a year. On the other hand, owing to the yield from the tariffs the middle class was benefiting from a sharp reduction in direct taxation from 82 per cent of government revenue in 1917–18 to two-thirds in 1932 and 55 per cent in 1935. In any event, Bank Rate was reduced to 2 per cent in 1932 as part of the conversion plan and, apart from a short period on the outbreak of war in 1939, it did not change until 1951. The main benefit of this policy was the saving in government expenditure and although it was claimed at the time that it would also help to stimulate industry there is no real evidence that it did so although as has been mentioned before and will be again, there were two economies at the time – one which was beyond help and one which did not need any help.

It was the imposition of protective tariffs that was the distinctive Conservative contribution to the policies of the National Government and they were applied in spite of the dissent of ex-Labour and Liberal members of the Government and, of course, of that of the Labour and Liberal Parliamentary Opposition. The terminal decline of the British staple industries can be accounted for by the process which has been going on ever since 1875, or thereabouts, namely the failure to keep up-to-date with technological developments once the old-style Victorian industrialist had disappeared from the scene (for his Oxford and Cambridge-educated progeny were entirely concerned with more gentlemanly professional pursuits either at home or abroad in the Empire although they did not object to the incomes from the inherited wealth), and the ossification of the labour force owing to poor education in general and a virtual absence of technical education in particular, as well as to the earlier manifestations of trade union restrictive practices and economic illiteracy. However, the rise of our successful overseas competitors (who did not share the above disadvantages) appeared to result from the protective tariffs which they imposed in the early days of their industrialization. Thus that dynamic man, Joseph Chamberlain, father of Neville, led the process of retaliation by which a section of the Conservative Party became convinced Protectionists. As well as his earlier experiences of municipalization in local government, he was also father of that strain in the Conservative Party which is interventionist, for the main object of Protection was to 'protect' British (traditional) industry from this 'unfair' competition which was, of course, a hopeless cause. But, especially when accompanied by the quota system whereby the productive capacity of industries such as ship-building and cotton manufacture was significantly reduced voluntarily the Protectionists regarded themselves as planners, even more than interventionists. Like Protection, the quota system was a failure for it was simply tampering with the symptoms of the problem and not attacking the problem itself. Conservative governments continued to do this until 1979.

But, back to 1932: Chamberlain's Import Duties Bill in February imposed a general tariff of 10 per cent on imports except Empire goods, raw materials and most foodstuffs so that a quarter of imports were unaffected. Chamberlain, like his father, failed to achieve the dream of Empire Free Trade for the only return given by the Dominions was the undertaking not to impose on Britain any additional tariffs imposed on foreigners. (The Commonwealth countries had actually adopted tariffs to exclude British goods, beginning with Canada in 1868!) The results were predictable. Foreign manufacturers who found their goods excluded from the British market competed more fiercely against British exports in other markets and took less of them in their home market. The outcome was that British exports were reduced more than imports and the long-term trend whereby British overseas trade constituted a diminishing proportion of its trade as a whole was exacerbated. The only change was that trade within the Empire assumed a significantly higher proportion of Britain's diminishing overseas trade but this was a retrograde step because the foreign trade was the more dynamic. As always, tariffs would have had the effect of increasing prices of manufactured goods, for cheaper foreign goods would have been replaced by more expensive British goods, with the corresponding adverse effect on the rest of the economy. Thus even before the devastation of the war took its effect the British economy, in so far as it was being directed by the Government, was on the wrong track. Fortunately, however, there was that other dynamic part of the economy, the home market, which continued to expand outside the old industrial areas and especially in the South and South-East. The former became natural Labour territory and the latter Conservative – a division by 'class'. By so doing the former largely disqualified itself from enjoying the prosperity of the latter, a process which was exaggerated by the council house system by which after 1945 approximately one third of the population – the non-dynamic third – were virtually cordoned off from the rest of the population in areas that varied from the boring and 'humdrum' to the soul-destroying. There was no social or economic future for a country with such a 'system'. It was not until 1979 that this fact was recognized and acted upon.

The pre-war registered unemployment reached its height at just under three million in January 1933 (23–25 per cent) although the highest unofficial level was 3,750,000 in September 1932 (around 30 per cent)[1]

---

[1]In 1993, unemployment fell for five consecutive months, from February to June, from 2,992,000 to 2,922,100, and after a hiccup in July and August, the seasonally-adjusted total fell in September to December to 2,766,200 representing around 9.8 per cent of the workforce which has increased from around 12 million in 1933 to just above 28 million, mainly due to the significant increase in the number of women employed. In January 1994 there was an unexpected rise of 15,500 to a total of 2,787,600, around 9.9 per cent of the workforce. After then, the seasonally-adjusted figure for unemployment had fallen each month and in February 1996 it was at a low of 2,206,800 – 763,200 down on the peak of 2.97 million in December, 1992 – and 7.9 per cent of the workforce, the lowest since April 1991. In February the underlying trend of around 10,000 fall a month was reversed by an increase in the seasonally adjusted figure by 6,800. However, in March the falling trend continued and the jobless total fell by a seasonally adjusted 26,000 to 2,186,000 – 7.8% of the work force. This has continued in subsequent months and the seasonally adjusted total figure in December was 1,884,700, a decline of 45,100, to make the unemployment rate 6.7%, the lowest since January 1991 and continuing the historic break through the two million mark. A structural shift in employment is taking place whereby the decline in full-time manufacturing work is being more than offset by the creation of part-time service sector work following investment in new technology and capital-intensive equipment, designed to replace the machine-room floor with its high labour content, and by the self-employed and small firms.

but in 1933 there was a fortuitous recovery in world trade with UK unemployment falling half a million during the year and production recovering to exceed levels of 1929. The balance of payments problem was solved, although this was mainly the result of the continuation of the existing trend whereby the terms of trade were moving sharply in Britain's favour and a given quantity of exports was buying more and more imports. For those in work 'real' wages continued to rise as prices fell. Whereas the Government, the employers and the trade unions in the Depressed or Special Areas (Scotland, South Wales, West Cumberland and Tyneside) were concerned to help the producers in the old industries a boom in new industries was taking place to satisfy the demand of the now confident breed of consumer, namely in the electricity supply and electrical goods industries and in the automobile industry but, above all, in the housing industry whereby nearly 3 million houses were built in the 1930s without government aid,

> nearly twice as many as had been built with government aid during the preceding decade ... When recovery came, activity in the building boom accounted for 30 per cent of the increase in employment between 1932 and 1935. The indirect effects went wider. Men with new houses bought radio sets, electrical equipment, and new furniture. They raised their general standard of living, many of the houses had their own garages, and this went along with the sales of motor cars. Most of the unsubsidized houses were built in new districts. When men broke away from their old houses, they usually broke away from their old occupations and their old regions. The South of England, like the new houses and the new industries, was more high class. Hence there was a demand for new roads, new shops, new schools, new public buildings and cinemas; and these had to be of a higher standard. This was the new England which saved itself by its own exertions, or rather by preferring new amenities to exertions of the older type.[1]

And yet still the Government and what we would now call the Establishment directed all their attention and energies towards the fruitless task of engineering a recovery in the old industries while they were oblivious of the dynamism of the new industries which was evident all around them. Why not harness and encourage these dynamic forces by the use of incentives in the form of supply-side economics as opposed to the 'dead-end' of intervention? This did not happen until 1979.

---

[1] *English History, 1914–45*, by A.J.P. Taylor, p. 344.

As previously mentioned, economic and financial recovery was under way by 1934 when Chamberlain was able to cut the standard rate of income tax to 4s 6d and to restore the reduction in unemployment benefit and half that in government and local government salaries, which were fully restored in 1935. But there remained the problem of mass unemployment in the old industrial areas and although the restoration of the cut in unemployment benefit was a step in the right direction the glaring differences in the standards of living between the old and new areas led to 'class conflict' in and out of Parliament which at the time was polarized by the deep resentment of the 'means test'. As with his Housing Act of 1923 and his reform of local government in 1929 Neville Chamberlain, with his Unemployment Act of 1934, justified the judgment that 'he did more to improve it (i.e. local government) than any other single man in the twentieth century.'[1] Also, he is the archetype of that long line of Conservative ministers who have given that party the well-earned reputation as the party which is pre-eminent in the conduct of the nation's business. The main tenor of Chamberlain's local government reforms was to transfer the responsibilities of ad hoc bodies such as the boards of guardians administering the poor law to local government itself. However, with the Unemployment Act he took unemployment 'out of politics' by creating a statutory committee, the Unemployment Assistance Board, with its own offices and full-time staff to administer unemployment assistance, the new name for 'benefit'. This was not the end of the matter for there was continued dissatisfaction with the rates of assistance but the administrative change was successful. This was a step in the right direction for the 1929 reform of local government and previous development placed too many activities and too much authority in the hands of local government, for although it can be said that it has become merely the instrument of national policy, it has had enough power, in conjunction with other like-minded forces of total ignorance, to ruin aspects of our national life such as, for example, education and the social services. It was not until 1979 that anything was done (apart from the public wringing of hands by the Callaghan Government regarding the scandal of education) to deal with and curb the outrageous financial and social irresponsibility and decadence of the Labour-controlled local councils in the inner-city conurbations.

In these years Ramsay MacDonald mainly occupied himself by

---

[1] *English History, 1914–45*, by A.J.P. Taylor, p. 258.

'papering over the cracks' of his unnatural Coalition Government which was split from beginning to end over Protection and disarmament and in presiding over nebulous conferences and interesting himself in foreign policy generally. A typical MacDonald effort was the World Economic Conference which was held with much pomp and circumstance in London in June 1933. Like many of its successors, the conference was mainly concerned to eliminate tariffs, exchange controls and unstable currencies but it was adjourned for ever in July when President Roosevelt flatly refused to co-operate, by stabilizing the dollar following its recent severe devaluation. Ireland continued to be a problem because, as predicted when de Valera became Prime Minister of the Free State in 1932, he took advantage of its virtual independence to chip away at the remaining links with Britain as enunciated in the treaty of 1921. The Government of India Act of 1935, taking India further along the road to Dominion status, was mainly Baldwin's work in the course of which he was able to humiliate the bill's main opponent, Winston Churchill.

MacDonald's main preoccupation, as also was Henderson's, was the World Disarmament Conference which began in February 1932 and in which the two idealistic men placed such inordinate hopes. As has been said, the Labour and Liberal Oppositions continued to the bitter end to espouse disarmament and the Conservatives continued to give lip-service to the ideal. Nevertheless, unlike the twenties, in the thirties, however reluctantly, an element of realism gradually entered the minds and calculations of those people responsible for taking decisions and running the country. For example, ever since the war British governments and the chiefs of staff had agreed to the 'ten-year rule' that no great war need be expected for the next ten years. In March 1932 this rule was cancelled although it was typical of the times that in the next month's budget, as we have seen, Chamberlain's arms estimates were the lowest between the wars. However, the Disarmament Conference was a resounding failure for it broke down on the inability of France and Germany to agree, and Hitler, who had become German Chancellor in January 1933, withdrew from the conference in October 1933 and a week later left the League of Nations. At this stage, the leaders of all the British parties, and the public, regarded Communism as a greater danger than Hitler. Notwithstanding, the blame for the failure of the conference was laid at the door of the British Government by the Opposition parties and by the public for it was claimed that they should have 'pulled out all the stops' to gain agreement between the nervous French and the aggressive Germans. Less than two weeks after the German withdrawal, the Labour candidate in the East Fulham by-election reversed an adverse majority of 14,000 into a majority of 5,000 and Baldwin and his cabinet colleagues were panicked into the belief that this reflected the 'pacifist' mood of the electorate who were punishing them for the failure of the Disarmament Conference. More realistically, Chamberlain thought it was a protest against the means test for the public was much more interested in housing and unemployment, and the like, than in foreign affairs. But the Government was unable to escape from the consequences of Hitler and German rearmament. Whereas in 1932 the chiefs of staff had advised that Japan posed the greater military threat, by 1934 they were warning that the German threat was greater and pressed for rearmament although very little was done about it. More significantly, by 1935 the leading civil servants were openly deprecating 'collective security' and advocating rearmament to counter German rearmament and also the preparation for total war-rationing, mass evacuations, conscription of labour, and the like. The resulting White Paper announced:

> that the British government had ceased to rely on collective security and were now going to rely on the older security of armed force. The White Paper was initialled by MacDonald – almost his last act as Prime Minister. This seemed a bitter irony: the man who had earlier been accused of pacifism, however wrongly, now gave the signal for a renewed race to war.[1]

The new-found resolution of the Government was soon put to the test by Mussolini's invasion of Abyssinia but its nerve had previously been disturbed, if not shattered, by the preceding 'Peace Ballot' organized on a national basis by the League of Nations Union which once again emphasized the fact that the public still hankered after 'collective security', in the League of Nations sense, although by this time much play was being made of the addition of the (false) teeth of economic sanctions which, as we know, were applied unsuccessfully against Italy. With the forthcoming November election in mind, Baldwin had no intention of upsetting the important Liberal vote by taking a firm line over Mussolini's adventure. Although he asked for a mandate for rearmament 'to remedy the deficiencies which have occurred in our defences', typically, he added: 'I give you my word that there will be no great armament.' This was vintage Baldwin. As

---

[1] *English History, 1914–45*, by A.J.P. Taylor, p. 376.

it happened, the election campaign was dominated by the old home issues of housing, unemployment and the special areas.

> The turn-out on election day was lower than at any election since December 1923. The Conservatives held almost exactly their vote of 1931; Labour recovered those who had not then voted. This brought a hundred odd gains to Labour, less than they deserved on the figures (Conservatives 11.5 million; Labour 8.3 million), giving 154 Labour members and 432 supporters of the National Government. The Liberals slipped down further, from 33 to 20, and 4 of these were Lloyd George's family connection. National Labour also suffered. Ramsay MacDonald and his son Malcolm both lost their seats, though both crept back at by-elections.[1]

It has been said that a nation gets the leaders it deserves. This was never truer than of the British people in November 1935 under the leadership of Baldwin's so-called National Government but which was a Conservative Government to all intents and purposes. In his earlier days of the leadership of the Conservative Party the pipe-smoking Baldwin had been depicted on election posters as the advocate of 'Safety First', an image and a reality with which the British people felt comfortable for Baldwin was never one to rock the boat by espousing unpopular but possibly necessary causes while he also developed to a fine art the skill of keeping exactly in line with public opinion, even when subsequent events showed that the situation merited a measure of leadership. Unfortunately, although in the long-run the English people have proved their political maturity, in the short-run, unlike, say, the Germans and Japanese, they tend to be lazy (anything for a quiet life), which were exactly the sentiments of Stanley Baldwin – thus their compatibility and their incompatibility with the pre-war Winston Churchill. It is for this reason that the English/British people need to be confronted from time to time with a politician or statesman of genius to save them from themselves and to stir them out of their apathy and lethargy. Churchill, of course, did this for them during the war but they had to wait from the days of Disraeli and Gladstone until 1979 for it to happen in peacetime.

The Government of Baldwin from 1935 to 1937 is the story of how Britain prepared herself for war in spite of appeasement and in spite of Baldwin who from the early days of the Government seemed to lose his grip both in the country and the House of Commons. The

---

[1] *English History, 1914–45*, by A.J.P. Taylor, p. 383–4.

Abyssinian crisis was followed by the Spanish Civil War and Hitler's reoccupation of the Rhineland and, as in the former case, in the latter two cases great efforts were made to avoid any kind of practical or moral involvement in defence of a righteous cause or in opposition to a wrong or unworthy cause. For example, the reoccupation of the Rhineland was in violation of both Versailles and Locarno – and this was a precedent which was re-enacted on the occasions of each of Hitler's aggressions until the outbreak of war between Britain and Germany on 3 September 1939. But it will be remembered that the Government was elected on a qualified rearmament pledge and, due to the pressures that had already been built up in the top ranks of the civil service and by the chiefs of staff, from 1936 on this was done steadily and effectively in spite of a myth to the contrary. This was partly due to the fact that the contemporary figures for the extent of Germany's undoubtedly heavy rearmament were wildly exaggerated, thus goading our military leaders on to demand more arms and aeroplanes than they would otherwise have done. This did not apply to the navy which had always received the greater share of defence expenditure and which was superior to the German and Italian navies combined. However, the Washington Naval Conference, in 1921–22, was mainly concerned with naval rivalry between Britain and the United States who agreed to parity in battleships (five each) against three for Japan. '...this was the only effective international agreement on limitation of armaments ever concluded.'[1] The greatest efforts and expenditure were concentrated on air power, in the form of heavy bombers, which in pre-war days was regarded in somewhat the same way as nuclear bombs are now; that is to say, something that you had to have to win wars and against which there was allegedly no defence. However, fortunately, British scientists rose to the challenge and produced the all-important radar and at the last minute, as it were, the air lobby was persuaded to concentrate on building fighter planes in preference to the more expensive bombers, and the providential development of the Hurricane and Spitfire just in time for the Battle of Britain in 1940 is the stuff of legend. A point worth making is that the pre-war muddle and last minute effort in regard to rearmament did eventually react very much to our advantage for if it had all been done clinically, efficiently and well ahead of the time of need, the odds are that the resulting equipment would have been relatively out of date.

Another reason why rearmament was successfully pursued was that

---

[1] *English History, 1914–45*, by A.J.P. Taylor, p. 150–1.

the Chancellor of the Exchequer, Neville Chamberlain, was a consistent supporter of the programme even though he resented the money being spent on it. No two men could have been more different than Baldwin and Chamberlain. Whereas Baldwin was at the best, shrewd, at the worst, lazy and indecisive, he did come over nationally as an avuncular and human person. On the other hand, although Chamberlain had an outstanding record as a legislator and administrator in home affairs where he was motivated by a social conscience emanating from his non-conformist background, as much as from his God of efficiency, it must be said that he had a dry-as-dust, unsympathetic manner and that he was totally without charm or humour. In this respect, he was to compare so unfavourably with Winston Churchill who replaced him in such humiliating circumstances. However, after the retirements of both Baldwin and MacDonald following the Abdication crisis, which was made for a prime minister with Baldwin's particular qualities, and the Coronation of George VI, an era was ended and Chamberlain formed his National (Conservative) Government. In his subsequent ill-fated negotiations with Hitler, Chamberlain has been presented as the arch ditherer and appeaser but in my view both these descriptions do him a gross injustice. Unlike Baldwin, Chamberlain, as I have previously implied, was above all, a man of business who, again, unlike Baldwin, when presented with a problem would not wait for the resulting crisis to develop but would take positive action to forestall the crisis or meet it head on. This he did in his negotiations with Hitler over Czechoslovakia but here he made the mistake of assuming that Hitler was as rational and as honourable as himself. In this respect, some of Baldwin's shrewdness would have helped him. The capitulation at Munich in September 1938 which was presented by Chamberlain as a victory was undoubtedly the last and greatest of the failures of the pre-war policy of 'collective security' but it cannot be said that Chamberlain was the greatest appeaser of them all or that what he did was not supported by popular or informed opinion. It was his tragedy that he was at the helm of state when this particular 'consensus' finally broke down in such a dramatic way and that the qualities that would have made him an excellent peacetime prime minister were completely inadequate in the years between 1937 and 1940. The brilliant manner in which Winston Churchill 'picked up the pieces' is one of the high points, if not the highest point, of our history. So, too, is the way in which Margaret Thatcher reacted to and managed the Falklands crisis in 1982. With Pitt the Younger, she stands supreme as one of the two Tory leaders who have excelled in both peace and war.

As with the decline of the Liberal Party and the rise of the Labour Party, I have dealt in detail with the history of the Conservative Party in the pre-war years, partly because it is a necessary background to understanding the post-war era, especially as many, if not most, people are not as familiar with pre-war as with post-war facts, but also, so as to indicate what was the nature of the pre-war Conservative Party. Going further back the Tory party was, above all, the party of authority which believed that 'the King's Government must carry on.' In fact, Tories and Whigs first appeared after the Restoration of Charles II in 1660, in the Exclusion Crisis of 1679–81, the former being the descendants of the Cavaliers of the Civil War, the squires and gentry of the countryside for whom the Church of England must be supreme and the King their natural leader. 'Church and King' was the refrain of the squire and parson and although the 'Divine Right of Kings' no longer held sway, dissenters (Nonconformists) were proscribed and the doctrine of 'passive obedience' was applied against those who 'resisted the Lord's Anointed' or, in other words, the Tory leaders who had the ear of the King until the fall of the Cavalier Parliament which sat from 1661 to 1679. On the other hand, the Whigs, as in later years, were led by the greatest nobles in the land who, partly because they felt more confident and independent in relation to the monarchy and partly because they were more cosmopolitan, were cynical about the religious beliefs of the High Churchmen and High Tories; and became the natural leaders of the people who supported Cromwell in the Civil War, the Nonconformists and Low Church yeoman, or smallholder in the countryside, the new families who had bought estates in the Civil War and who had joined the Church of England in 1660, thus becoming eligible for membership of Parliament, together with the plebeian Nonconformists in the towns – thus their strength in the boroughs. Whereas the Tories stood for authority and the persecution of Nonconformists, the Whigs supported religious toleration for the dissenters and therefore, in the last resort, resistance to the authority of the King, especially if he should prove to be a Roman Catholic.

Although the Tory Party was from this early date one of the two great parties, one is inclined to assume that that was the end of the matter and that a continuation of this state of affairs was inevitable. But this was not so, for the weakness of the Tories was that in the case of Charles II the 'Lord's Anointed' was a Roman Catholic when he came to the throne, and took Mass on his deathbed in 1685, although he had the good sense to be a Protestant in-between-times, and James II was an active Roman Catholic. In spite of Charles II's moderation the scurrilous Titus Oates was able to embarrass the Tories by associating them with the Popish Plot in 1678, largely fabricated by himself, to such an extent that Charles II had to dissolve the Tory-dominated Cavalier Parliament. The subsequent Whig Parliament and leaders (and in those days, they were always in the House of Lords) attempted to exclude Charles II's brother, the Roman Catholic Duke of York, from the throne, intrigued with Charles II's illegitimate son, the Duke of Monmouth and, in the so-called Rye House Plot in 1683, conspired to murder the two royal brothers. When this failed Charles II deprived scores of Whig boroughs of their charters and created new boroughs, so returning new Tory Members of Parliament, which, when it was recalled on the accession of James II in 1685, was loyal to the new King. However, when James's army defeated the West Country rebellion fomented by Monmouth and his Whig allies at Sedgemoor in 1685, he moved quickly to appoint Catholics to army commissions, civil posts, university fellowships and even to benefices in the Church of England. The Declarations of Indulgence of 1687 and 1688 suspended entirely the penal laws against Non-conformists and Catholics (although, in point of fact, this had previously been the case after Charles II's Declaration of Indulgence in 1672) but, nevertheless, both Tories and Whigs saw these as a device to reimpose Catholicism on England, and all that went with it – royal absolutism, foreign Catholic influence and putting the clock back to the pre-Civil War era of 1641. The birth of a son to James's second wife clinched the matter for he would have precedence over his Protestant daughter, Mary, wife of the scourge of his neighbouring Catholics, William of Orange, Stadtholder (ruler) of the Dutch Netherlands (Holland). The leading Tories and Whigs combined to invite William of Orange to invade England in order to safeguard the Protestant Succession. With the desertion of the King's army and his escape to France the Tories were saved from the embarrassment of violating their doctrine of non-resistance by claiming that he had abdicated and they joined with the Whigs in making William III King, by Act of Parliament, with equal powers to Mary, Queen by inheritance. These changes, and the detailed safeguards ensuring the supremacy (sovereignty) of Parliament were embodied in the Bill of Rights of 1689, already mentioned in Chapter I (p. 23). However, the relevance here is that the Tory association with the Bill of Rights meant that the Party strengthened its position as the party of authority, in the Parliamentary sense, without the taint of the Divine Right of Kings or of Roman Catholicism. Even accepting the nineteenth-century interpretation of history that 1689 was a Whig triumph, in view of events and fact before and after that date, it could not be maintained that the Whigs were the inherent party of authority, in spite of Walpole's powerful position after 1720. The stage was therefore set for the domination of England by two political parties, one authoritarian and traditionalist, and the other, independent and radical.

But before this could really be said to be true, there was to be one great crisis which, if resolved in any way different from the actual outcome, would have altered the history of England and, for that matter, of the Tory and Whig parties. In 1701 a Tory Parliament passed the Act of Settlement which decreed that William III should be succeeded by his wife's sister, Anne, and that in the event of her death without children the Crown should pass to Electress Sophia of Hanover, an aged granddaughter of James I. It also removed the judges from the control of the executive by enacting that they should in future hold office 'during good behaviour' instead of during the good pleasure of the King and it also made them irremovable except on a joint address of both Houses of Parliament. In 1702 William died, the feeble Anne succeeded and with a new Whig ministry the war against Louis XIV, the war of the Spanish Succession, reopened. Since becoming Stadtholder in 1672 William of Orange had been fighting Louis XIV and between 1690 (after the Battle of the Boyne, securing Ireland) and 1697 (The Treaty of Ryswick) he had initiated what came to be the traditional English-Dutch policy of fighting any Continental aggressor (in this case Louis XIV) who threatened 'the safety of the Low Countries' (the Netherlands) by fighting them on land and sea. Owing to the decline of the once mighty Spanish Empire Louis XIV had his eyes on the Spanish Netherlands (Belgium) and for that matter the Crown of Spain for his grandson. Fortunately for England, and Holland, a military genius and statesman of outstanding ability, John Churchill (later Duke of Marlborough) was Commander-in-Chief of Anne's army and he continued William's work of organizing and leading the coalition against Louis XIV in nine years of bitter fighting, including the monumental battles of Blenheim, Ramillies and Malplaquet. Marlborough was the victor, and the Netherlands were saved from France, but the cost in blood and money was terrible. As has so often happened, opinion in England turned against this costly Continental involvement and on this issue the Tories won the general election of 1710, recalled Marlborough and opened peace negotiations.

In the meantime, all Anne's children had died young and she was delicate so that there was much apprehension regarding the

66

possibility of Jacobite attempts to upset the projected Hanoverian succession. Owing to the fact that the Act of Settlement did not apply in Scotland (for although the two countries had shared the same monarch since 1603 their parliaments were still independent) in 1707 the Whigs arranged the Act of Union between England and Scotland to obviate the danger of Scotland having a Stuart King and England a Hanoverian. Then, as now, the Union gave tremendous economic advantage to Scotland which had previously been kept poor by being excluded from trade with the English colonies by the Navigation Acts which confined this trade to English ships. However, in spite of these precautions the succession was disputed owing to the fact that the Tory party experienced its last serious flirtation with Jacobitism. The majority, led by the Queen's senior minister, Robert Harley, Earl of Oxford (the Baldwin of his day) were prepared to accept the Protestant, Elector George of Hanover, his mother having died, but a minority, led by Henry St John, Viscount Bolingbroke, favoured the Jacobite Pretender, a Catholic. Bolingbroke was not an out-and-out Jacobite but rather an ambitious and brilliant, but unrestrained, young politician who was playing for high stakes – the leadership of the Tory party. In 1714, he persuaded the dying Anne to dismiss Oxford but unfortunately for him and fortunately for England and Scotland, the Queen died in less than a week and he had calculated that he required six weeks to effect a Jacobite restoration. The Tory Party was split and the royal powers were still strong enough for the Whig lords to ensure that the Privy Council applied the provisions of the Act of Settlement by proclaiming the Elector, George I.

The Protestant Succession was ensured, as also were the provisions and philosophy of the Bill of Rights of 1689, namely that the King might not be a Roman Catholic, he was not to be absolute and therefore could not suspend or dispense with laws; subjects who might present petitions, elections and debates in Parliament should be free from royal interference (although that is not to say that the electoral influence of the Crown did not remain significant until at least the end of the eighteenth century); a standing army without Parliament's permission was illegal; taxes might be levied only by Parliamentary grant; and Parliament should be held frequently. The Church of England was to be the state religion (except in Scotland) and although Nonconformists and Catholics were to be disqualified from office, the former had been granted liberty of worship by the Toleration Act, and although it did not apply to the latter they were not prevented from worshipping in practice. The philosophy was that of the contemporary and most English of philosophers, Thomas

Locke, that government should be based on a contract to respect fundamental laws. These facts, and this philosophy, is not dry-as-dust history and I am recalling them now as they are in the psyche of English people who still bear them very much in mind when electing governments. It is why the early Labour party was accepted and why the present Labour Party had become unacceptable and unelectable owing to the fear that its programme and the attitudes of its members, in and out of Parliament, constituted a threat to our fundamental laws and way of life. As already mentioned, the desperate and strenuous attempts of the Labour Party under Neil Kinnock to change its programme radically and to muzzle its more wayward members, were a recognition of this fact, as have been the subsequent efforts by the late John Smith and Tony Blair. The Tory Party learnt this lesson in 1714 and has never been tempted in the slightest to offend it since.

In Chapter 1, I had much to say about English political maturity, culminating especially in the years and events leading to 1689. It was after the decisive defeat of the absolute monarch, Louis XIV, ('L'Etat c'est moi') that thinkers outside England began to appreciate the merits and strengths of the English system of government whereby the powers of the monarch were defined and limited by an elected parliament. Although the idea of the separation of powers can be traced back to English Republican theorists, like James Harrington and Neville, in the seventeenth century, it was paradoxical that it was in France especially, that this philosophy was developed by such thinkers as Montesquieu, Voltaire and Rousseau and that the French had to resort to a bitter and tragic revolution exactly one hundred years after the Bill of Rights to attempt to achieve for herself the rights and freedoms which the English had so successfully acquired by a comparatively peaceful and gradual process. I am positive that any impartial celestial observer would be much more impressed by the typically English and gradualist approach to the integration of Europe of Margaret Thatcher, than by the doctrinaire, impractical and hurried French strategy of M. Delors.[1]

---

[1]Written in August 1990. At the later date of October 1996, John Major is still pursuing the gradualist approach compared to the Bismarkian one of Chancellor Kohl. It will be remembered that Bismark said that the problems of Europe would be solved with 'iron and blood'.

5

The Years of Consensus, 1945–1964
The Background

One of the two purposes of the remainder of this book is to begin to answer the question (in view of the fact that it ends in 1964) as to why the pre-war British working class, who were paragons and the envy of the world, have degenerated to such an extent that they (meaning those who are of an age to be the products of this dismal period and who draw attention as a highly visible minority) are characterized as illiterate louts who can only be referred to as sub-human, and who are despised and feared throughout the world. It is certainly nothing to do with money as the church leaders and left-wing protesters would have you believe as they 'rabbit-on' about deprivation and poverty, for over the period and up until the present day the standard of living ('real' wealth per head) has increased continuously and so much so that, on the basis of income and occupation, whereas the pre-war working class comprised about 75 per cent of the population (p. 28), it now consists of only about 25 per cent. The obverse, of course, is that with post-war affluence many of the pre-war working-class families have moved into the middle-class bracket which on a narrow definition, counts for around 40–50 per cent of the population (and more on a wider definition) which is all to the good and in accord with Disraeli's dictum that the main object of the Tory Party is 'to improve the condition of the people'. However, in regard to the deterioration in such matters as education, law and order, general manners and morals, all of which, much more than material well-being, dictates the actual qualify of life of a nation, the enlarged middle class has been adversely affected. The second object is to enquire into the nature of the post-war consensus and to point out its inadequacy.

Although Churchill wanted the Coalition Government to continue until the end of the Pacific War the Labour Party was keen to have an election at the earliest time possible, after the Allied invasion of Europe in May 1945. After all, there had been no general election since 1935 and in spite of the enormous Conservative majority in 1940 when Churchill formed the National Government he had generously and wisely given Labour almost equal representation in his War Cabinet, and a disproportionate share of the junior government appointments. Thus, the leading men in the Labour Party, who were mainly concerned with running the home front, such as Attlee as Lord President and Deputy Prime Minister, Bevin as Minister of Labour, Morrison as Home Secretary, Dalton as President of the Board of Trade and Johnston as Scottish Secretary, were not only entirely confident of their ability to run a government but had become household names to the public who, in turn, would see nothing amiss in their so doing.

In the event, Churchill chose a date, 5 July, much earlier than Labour expected for he wanted to go to the country as a national leader, but the election had already begun in early April when Ernest Bevin attacked Churchill by declaring that 'this has not been a one-man government'. The Labour manifesto promised a programme of nationalization, a comprehensive social security system and a national health service, while the Tories made virtually the same offer in the way of social benefits for they were completely aware of the mood of the voting public. However, that same public had already come to the conclusion that the Labour Party, with its well-known leaders, were more likely to 'deliver the goods' than the Tories who were associated with the pre-war depression, unemployment and want, and the 'means test'. This was, of course, the main line of criticism of the Tories by Labour which was as wide of the mark as was Churchill's attempt to scare the public into believing that the Marxist Professor Harold Laski, the Chairman of the Labour party, was a potential head of the British Gestapo. He said that there was the need to

> guard the people of this country against those who, under the guise of war necessity, would like to impose upon Britain for their own purposes a permanent system of bureaucratic control, reeking of totalitarianism.

The warning against the heavy hand of bureaucracy was fair comment by Churchill and other Tories but it did not deter many older Conservatives from either abstaining or even voting Labour, as also with the majority of younger and first-time voters since 1935.

In spite of the fact that as early as 1943 there had been the accumulation of much evidence in the way of by-elections and the earlier polls that Labour would win the election, and the Tory Party Chairman had warned Churchill of the possibility of defeat, it was generally assumed by 'informed opinion' and the like that the Conservative Party would win. Some of the Labour Party leaders were not happy about breaking with the National Government and there was some apprehension among party activists. The outcome was one of the most memorable electoral victories in our long history.

Its absolute majority – Labour's first in British history – stood at no less than 146, and if this did not represent an absolute majority of the popular vote and was less than some previous government majorities, the swing recorded – about 12 per cent – was on the scale of 1832 and 1906; only after these elections had the Conservatives' position been worse. In the course of victory Labour had taken 210 seats from the Tory camp and recorded seventy-nine wins in seats which never before had returned a Labour member. The Labour vote compared with 1935 had increased from 8,325,000 to just 12 million, while the Conservative vote had fallen from 11,792,000 to 10 million. The Liberals had gained 2,248,226 votes but as a result of the first-past-the-post electoral system secured only twelve parliamentary seats. The electoral system as well as the outdated mal-distribution of seats had favoured Labour. It took 30,000 votes to elect a Labour member, 47,000 to elect a Conservative and no less than 187,000 to elect a Liberal. The results in tabular form, were as follows:

PARTY	Votes gained	% of vote	Average vote per MP	Number of MPs
Conservative	9,988,306	39.8%	46,892	213
Labour	11,995,152	47.8%	30,522	393
Liberal	2,248,226	9.0%	187,352	12
Communist	102,780	0.4%	51,390	2
Common Wealth	110,634	0.4%	110,634	1
Others	640,880	2.0%		19
TOTALS	25,085,978	100.00%		640

Source: Derived from D. Butler and A. Slogan, *British Political Facts, 1900–75.*

No less remarkable than the extent of Labour's victory was the geography of Labour's success. In 1935, there had been no Labour candidate in Northern Ireland. In 1945 there were six, and an Independent Labour candidate even managed to get elected. In

Scotland Labour consolidated its strength by winning another fifteen seats; in Wales it gained six seats, among them the three in Cardiff. It was, however, in England that the great landslide had taken place. The English boroughs, excluding London, returned 173 Labour MP's compared with only fifty-three beforehand. In London itself, Labour representation increased from twenty-seven to forty-nine MP's. Yet the chief sensation was the results from the English counties. These had traditionally been the strongholds of Conservatism, but they now returned 110 Labour members as opposed to 112 Tories. Moreover, in terms of the popular vote, Labour had actually come out on top in these areas with 4,606,000 votes compared with 4,412,000 for the Conservatives. The latter had to be content with wresting the West Country and parts of Wales – including Lloyd George's old seat of Carnarvon Borough – from the Liberals, who had suffered a great defeat and were reduced to a rump of twelve MP's.[1]

It is only by studying the details of the general election results that one can appreciate the exquisite way in which they reflect the wishes of the people in spite of the problem of the maldistribution of seats which was dealt with later by the activities of the independent Boundary Commission. However, under our system, it was inevitable that on this occasion it would work against the Conservatives in regard to the disproportion of votes required to elect a member while, in spite of later false starts, the system has brutally relegated the Liberal Party. The result was later summed up by Churchill who wrote that 'the verdict of the electorate had been overwhelmingly expressed'. Thus not only did the Labour Party come to power with an overwhelming authority which it never before possessed but which very few, if any, governments have possessed before or since. The Government embarked with confidence and enthusiasm on implementing its massive programme, twice the size of that of the pre-war era, as embodied in the King's Speech in August, namely the nationalization of the Bank of England and the basic industries, the implementation of a national health service and the expansion of social security provisions, the repeal of the Trade Disputes Act of 1927, the building of more houses and the production of more food, together with the financial legislation required to pay for this extremely ambitious programme. As already noted, the members of the Government were well-known to the public and very well qualified by dint of their wartime responsibilities. Although the

---

[1] *Post-War Britain*, by Alan Sked and Chris Cook, pp. 14–16.

Labour party remained an overwhelmingly working-class party, as with previous Labour Governments, it included men of middle and upper-class backgrounds.

> Labour had now much more the appearance of being a national party. Less than half the Labour MPs were classified as 'workers' (against no Conservatives), and forty-six had been to Oxford or Cambridge (against 101 Conservative), formerly the universities of the privileged.[1]

Clement Attlee, the new Prime Minister, had fought gallantly in the First World War, and returned a major despite his pacifist inclinations. Having been educated at Haileybury and Oxford, he gave up his earlier ambitions of becoming a barrister in order to do social work in the East End of London as well as to lecture at the London School of Economics. It will be remembered that he was active in the ILP and in the local politics of Stepney so that he naturally graduated to become MP for Limehouse in 1922. In 1935 he succeeded Lansbury as leader of the Labour party. What Clement Attlee lacked in charisma, he made up in sheer shrewdness and common sense and proved to be an ideal and effective leader or chairman of his brilliant Cabinet. Against expectations, Bevin became Foreign Secretary where he established himself as a statesman of world class and as the most powerful and influential figure in the Government. Hugh Dalton, the Chancellor of the Exchequer, was educated at Eton and Cambridge and was a member of the academic and intellectual establishment. Herbert Morrison, like Ernest Bevin, of a working-class background, was immensely experienced in local government and home affairs, and was promoted to Lord President and Leader of the Commons. Aneurin Bevan, the fiery, working-class Welshman, whose earlier left-wing and socialist background we have already noted, had played a prominent part in the Labour victory due to his oratorical skills and energy, was rewarded with the Ministry of Health. Stafford Cripps, the ascetic Wykehamist, like Bevan, temporarily expelled from the Party before the war for his extreme left-wing views, had his undoubted ability rewarded by being made President of the Board of Trade.

These were the men who, in accordance with public opinion, nay more, the public desire, gave a new direction and impetus to Britain and who established a political consensus which was to last until

---

[1] *English History, 1914–45*, by A.J.P. Taylor, p. 597.

1979 although it began to weaken from the late 1960s if not before. Winston Churchill, in his first speech as Leader of the Opposition, virtually accepted the consensus when he said:

> ...it is evident that not only are we two parties in the House agreed on the main essentials of foreign policy and in our moral outlook on world affairs but we also have an immense programme prepared by our joint exertions during the Coalition which requires to be brought in to law and made an inherent part of the life of the people. Here and there, there may be differences of emphasis and view but, in the main, no Parliament has ever assembled with such a mass of agreed legislation as lies before us this afternoon.

I have so far been critical of the concept of consensus in our political system but it is, of course, one of the political manifestations of the English capacity for pragmatism although fortunately the English are sometimes saved from themselves by their other capacity for radical or even revolutionary action which is necessary when the consensus had outlived its purpose. The British political system, culminating over the years in an electoral technique which inevitably leads to the rise of two powerful parties, has been criticized because of its adversarial quality. On the other hand, the two factors of government by debate together with the ability of the Opposition to form a government, agreed on its policy, at any time, is not only a major safeguard against the despotism of single party government but, although inconvenient, has a remarkably therapeutic effect on the party in power. Also, as with Hegel's concept of thesis and anti-thesis leading to synthesis, so too do the opposing views of British political parties lead to the consensus.

An excellent historic example is the acceptance of the Whig First Reform Bill of 1832 by the Tories after having opposed it for so many years under Liverpool (1812–27) and the Duke of Wellington (1828–30) with the result that they were out of power until 1841[1] with the election of Robert Peel, literally the founder of the modern Conservative Party (p. 326), but by his adoption of Free Trade by the passing of the Abolition of the Corn Laws in 1846 he broke the Party and he and his followers (including Gladstone) were absorbed by the Whigs and eventually became Liberals, although Peel himself died in 1850. When the Tories finally produced a political genius in the person of Benjamin Disraeli, who played a major part in bringing

---

[1] At the behest of William IV, Peel formed a minority government in November 1834 but in view of the hostile majority it fell in April 1835.

down Peel, he went one better than the Whigs by passing the Reform Bill of 1867 which gave the vote to urban artisans. The Tories did not win in the 1868 election so that Gladstone was Prime Minister from 1868–74 but it was due to Disraeli (1874–80) that the Tories won working-class support without which they might well have ceased to be one of the two great parties, if the Liberals had not failed in the way that I have described.

I have already described the famous pre-war consensus of appeasement, which was a good example of another aspect of the consensus which is the unspoken agreement of an elite or 'establishment', including and transcending the political and intellectual leaders of the two parties as well as senior civil servants and other leaders of the community such as businessmen, academics and communicators. In the last case, we have seen that the Editor of *The Times* played a prominent part but in our own day such elitism has been displaced by the concept of 'the media'. An important factor is the semi-permanence of important civil servants such as Robert Hall (later Lord Roberthall) who was chief economic adviser to all Chancellors of the Exchequer between 1947 and 1961 and who said that he gave virtually similar advice to them all.[1] Other examples of the post-war consensus are immigration, education and nationalization. Although Labour strongly opposed the Conservatives' early applications of immigration controls in 1955 and 1962 they never reversed the legislation and strengthened it in 1965 and 1968. In education, the Butler Education Act of the National Government in 1944 was accepted by all parties until Labour introduced the comprehensive system in 1965, but in spite of the Conservatives' hostility to this disastrous change they did nothing effectively to reverse it. The post-war Conservative Party was, of course, against nationalization, as we have seen from their election pronouncements in 1945 but apart from iron and steel and road haulage the nationalized industries were left alone. As Kavanagh and Morris says: 'No Labour Government seriously entertained ideas of widespread public ownership and no Conservative one until 1979 had tried to dismantle the nationalized sector.'[2]

Another variation on the same theme is the obsession of political parties, Left and Right, with attempting to control the 'middle

---

[1]*Consensus Politics from Attlee to Thatcher*, by Dennis Kavanagh & Peter Morris, p. 39.
[2]Ibid, p. 13.

ground'. This is beneficial in that the English electorate will never support an extremist party which threatens to subvert 'our fundamental laws and way of life'. For example, in the 1960s and 1970s the 'middle ground' moved well to the Left as the Conservative Party and governments attempted to come to terms with their interpretation of the prevailing consensus. Margaret Thatcher's successful rejection of this consensus shows how very wrong the Conservatives were and that it needs a politician of extraordinary strength of conviction, intellect and will to challenge the consensus. It will be remembered that Heath's Conservative Party, in January 1970, geared itself up to move to the Right at the Selsdon Park Conference but, faced by the problems of inflation, the balance of payments and a sterling crisis, in the course of 1972 it performed its massive 'U-Turn', to return to the policies adopted by the Wilson Government from which it had attempted to escape. It should never be forgotten that in spite of their long-term good sense and political maturity, the English are politically very lazy, want the minimum of involvement in day-to-day politics and are certainly averse to extremes of political or controversial hassle which is why an outmoded consensus can last so long. This is the reverse of the Scottish, Welsh and Irish who are prepared to spend inordinate amounts of time and energy pursuing lost political causes but seem blind to long-term issues and solutions. Finally, in regard to the 'middle ground', we have recently lived through a period in which Labour, under Neil Kinnock, correctly came to the conclusion that their extremist party had become unelectable so that with their unashamed adoption of Thatcherite policies the 'middle ground' has moved sharply to the Right. The late John Smith moved even further Right while the new Party Leader, Tony Blair, is indistinguishable from a Tory 'Wet'.[1]

To revert to the post-war consensus, this was implanted during the years of the first majority Labour governments, 1945–51. It has been analyzed and described as comprising:

---

[1]His creation of the New Labour Party is an attempt to emulate the Socialist parties in Europe which have turned their backs on old-fashioned socialism/communism (thus his rejection of Clause IV) and have become Social Democratic parties, appealing to a wider electorate, including the middle classes. If he wins the next general election it is to be hoped that he will continue to be successful in burying Old Labour. We can then look forward to constructive two-party government – one party Conservative and radical and the other Labour and liberal, with Tory 'wets' joining the latter party.

The mixed economy.
Full employment.
The role of the trade unions.
The welfare state.
Foreign and defence policy (the retreat from Empire, Britain's role as a nuclear power and membership of the Atlantic Alliance).[1]

In addition to dealing with each of these factors, I shall comment separately on other important consensus matters, namely Education, Housing, Local Government and the Law. I shall conclude with the following assessments: Social and Political.

---

[1] *Consensus Politics from Attlee to Thatcher*, by Dennis Kavanagh & Peter Morris, pp. 4–6.

6

The Mixed Economy, 1945–1964

The 1945 Labour manifesto advocated the public ownership of basic utilities and an active role for government in managing the economy in pursuit of certain social and economic objectives. A number of industries and services were taken over by the state and much of the rest of the economy operated within guidelines laid down by the government. The more active role for the state grew out of the wartime experience. A mix of public and private ownership was largely accepted by government until the late seventies.[1]

Before 1914 the capitalist system was, of course, unquestionably accepted by the Conservative and Liberal Parties and even the earlier members of the Labour Party and trade unionists took it for granted and were mainly concerned to ensure that a larger proportion of its impressive capacity for wealth creation should fall into the hands of the workers. As we have seen, by the end of the last century the idea of socialism was becoming a much stronger force and by 1918 it was a positive influence on what had become a much more independent and confident Labour Party which in Clause IV of its 1918 programme pledged itself to 'common ownership of the means of production, distribution and exchange and the best obtainable system of popular administration and control of each industry or service'. After 1918, unlike post-1945, the wartime government got back to normal as soon as possible so that deviations from peacetime practices, such as economic planning, were quickly eliminated. Nevertheless, early examples of corporatism can be seen under the 1924–29 Conservative Government which formed public corporations to run the electricity supply industry, the Central Electricity Board in 1926, and the BBC in 1927, while we have already noted the

---

[1]*Consensus Politics from Attlee to Thatcher*, by Dennis Kavanagh & Peter Morris, pp. 4–5. Further facts and figures in this chapter are attributable to Chapter 2 in this authority.

interventionist implications of the Conservative-dominated National Governments of the 1930s by their attempts to prop up the declining staple industries by the introduction of protective tariffs and quotas. This government also set up BOAC in 1939 in the form of a public corporation. Although the two Labour minority governments were in no position to introduce socialist-inspired measures we have seen that these governments were essentially moderate and conventional but that there was a distinct change in attitude in the Labour Party after 1931. This, together with the involvement of Labour ministers and the trade unions in the running of the economy during the war led to the enthusiastic belief that the nationalization of the 'commanding heights' of the economy (in Aneurin Bevan's words) would enable a socialist government to plan the use of the nation's resources within a mixed economy. As the 1945 Labour manifesto stated, Labour 'was a socialist party and proud of it'.

And yet, when it came to implementing the nationalization programme it was found that the Labour Party had in this respect been generating much more heat than light for there had been no thought or 'planning' for such a contingency. Herbert Morrison was put in charge of the operation and he fell back on the idea of the public corporation which had also been adopted by local government in the form of the Port of London Authority and the Metropolitan Water Board with which he was familiar. He said: 'We are seeking a combination of public ownership, public accountability and business management for public ends', the ideal which was never fulfilled. However, national boards were appointed by the appropriate Secretary of State who, in turn, was responsible to Parliament which nevertheless could not interfere with the day-to-day management of the industries as it could government departments. In subsequent years however, there was to be considerable governmental interference, direct and indirect, in the management of the nationalized industries while the attempt to compromise between providing a public service and profitability was impossible of fulfilment. A nationalized industry is subject to criticism if it makes a profit, on the one hand, and a loss, on the other, while experience has shown both here and abroad that they are subject to bureaucratic ossification. Finally, nationalized industries cannot go bankrupt which leads to all kinds of financial and economic distortions, especially the starving of new and more dynamic enterprises of capital and labour, thus reducing the growth of the national economy. However, back to the beginning of the story: the Bank of England and civil aviation were nationalized in 1946, coal, cables and wireless in 1947, transport and electricity in 1948, gas in 1949 while iron and steel had to wait until 1951, after the 1950 election, owing to the need for the Government to amend the Parliament Act so as to reduce the delaying powers of the House of Lords from two years to one year. In the end, the nationalization saga was an anti-climax. Its socialist critics complained that the previous owners were too generously compensated, the former management remained in place and nothing was done about introducing in whole, or in part, worker-control or profit-sharing. Far from capturing the 'commanding heights' of the economy, all that happened had been a change of ownership. Furthermore, the 20 per cent of the economy that had been nationalized was largely the unprofitable part while the remaining profitable part remained in private hands. Although the Conservatives remained hostile to the concept of nationalization, unlike their acceptance of full employment and the welfare state, it was perhaps the above facts that influenced them to accept the situation, apart from the Churchill Government's denationalization of iron and steel in 1953 and road haulage in 1954. Iron and steel was destined to become the nationalization and denationalization football, it being nationalized and denationalized twice. In the 1970s nationalization became one of the two great issues which seriously divided the Labour Party, the other being unilateral disarmament.

The other aspect of Clause IV was 'control' or, in other words, planning the whole economy which was a concomitant of the wartime writings of Beveridge and the pre-war writing of Keynes whom we shall discuss in detail in the next chapter. However, the attempt was made to plan the economy which, of course, included that part which was not nationalized and initially these efforts were not very effective. Keynes had recommended that the wartime Ministry of Production should effectively be retained in a peacetime form, under a new name, but this was not done and the Lord President, Herbert Morrison, supervised a number of cabinet committees while a number of advisory councils were set up by the Treasury, such as the National Investment Council, the National Joint Advisory Council and the National Production Advisory Council on Industry. All the evidence leads to the conclusion that the cabinet committees were useless, that the advisory councils were mere talking shops and that the Treasury merely reverted to its historic mission of doing its own thing in its own way. There was a pronounced change for the better when Stafford Cripps, the incorruptible, succeeded Dalton as Chancellor at the end of 1947 following the latter's unfortunate and famous budget leak. He had earlier succeeded Morrison on the latter's illness and later headed a new ministry as Minister of Economic Affairs with a new Central Planning Staff and a new Government Chief Planner, the respected Sir Edwin Plowden – all in place of the now abolished Lord President's Committee. Cripps's appointment as Chancellor of the Exchequer prevented the inevitable and destructive split between planning and finance and under his effective, puritanical leadership much was achieved.

> The system of interdepartmental co-operation was tightened up; general supervision was assigned to the Economic Policy Committee under the chairmanship of the Prime Minister; Cripps presided over a sub-committee on production; and a network of committees and sub-committees connected these to the Central Economic Staff, the Import Programme, the Investment Programme and all the other bodies – Regional Boards and Development Councils, etc., which co-operated both in drawing and attempting to achieve the 'targets' set out annually in the 'Economic Survey.'[1]

As we shall see later, this more effective planning coincided with an upturn in the economy but this could have taken place in any case for the really effective control of the economy was probably being exercised more directly by such methods as the old Conservative import controls which were still in place.

However, the last word on Labour planning must be mention of the infamous groundnuts scheme which proved to be the economic plan to end all economic plans. Devised in 1946, it was an attempt to combine planning for the home economy, in this case to reduce the UK deficit of oils and fats, with the new Government's attempts to make up for centuries of 'exploitation' of the Empire by investing idealistically in the colonial economies. It was described by John Strachey, the Minister of Food, as 'one of the most courageous, imaginative and well-judged acts of this Government for the sake of the world that had been taken in the life of this parliament'. The result was tragi-farce.

> By 1949 the scheme had come to nought, at a cost to the taxpayer of £36,500,000 having provided neither groundnuts nor margarine for Britain nor employment for the Africans. The groundnuts could have been used to increase the margarine ration in Britain; but even had they materialized no provision had been made for the transportation needed to bring them here.[2]

---

[1] *Post-War Britain*, by Alan Sked and Chris Cook, p. 34. Further facts and figures in this chapter are attributable to this authority.
[2] Ibid, p. 82.

At the time, the whole monstrous episode led to a noticeable collective pause for thought and great doubts about the desirability and efficacy of such grandiose economic plans and of such concepts as bulk-purchasing which had been naively propounded as a means of saving money by eliminating the middleman. How much better and more effective it would have been if such a desired end had been left to the devices of numerous entrepreneurs, both from the point of view of production and distribution, for if the project was practicable the individual entrepreneurs would have had the financial incentive to carry it through to a successful conclusion, while if it was impracticable it would have been the entrepreneurs and not the taxpayer who bore the loss.

Unfortunately, the groundnuts farce and other evidence of the inadequacy and undesirability of government planning led to no more than a pause for thought in the senior ranks of the Conservative Party. We find that Harold Macmillan had introduced indicative planning of the economy with the creation of the National Economic Development Council in 1962 as well as a National Incomes Commission. Indicative Planning, as practised by the French, did not mean central direction of the economy so that the object of the NEDC was to measure the growth of various sectors of the economy and to provide a means of the government, the unions and the employers co-operating so as to maximize economic growth. It was the forerunner of the ill-fated corporatist era between 1964 and 1979. Macmillan's interest in planning arose from the fact that he was very much a child of his time and, like Attlee in London, was much affected by the extremes of poverty in his northern constituency of Stockton-on-Tees. In the years before the 1929 election Lloyd George was taking note of and accumulating the 'dangerous' ideas that were being gradually worked out by academic economists of the times, including Keynes, and which were being promulgated by the ILP, to the annoyance of the leaders of the Labour Party and the trade unions who suspected the elimination of unemployment by government-sponsored public works, and the like, to be financed by deliberately contrived budget deficits with the possible prospect of the direction of labour. In 1929, as part of his election campaign, he published a pamphlet, entitled 'We Can Conquer Unemployment', on the above lines. As we know, it did not do him any good in the election and he failed to popularize his advanced ideas. Furthermore, we have also seen that when Sir Osbert Mosley, as a junior minister, tried to introduce them he was sacrificed on the altar of orthodox finance, following which he formed his own party, the New Party, and was expelled from the Labour Party in 1931. Herein lies the connection with Macmillan, for Mosley's economic adviser and a candidate of the New Party in 1931, one Allan Young, then became economic adviser to Harold Macmillan. While he had broken away from the pre-war economic consensus of balanced budgets, and the like, Macmillan, for worthy reasons, became a slave to the muddled post-war economic consensus.

There is no better example of this than his disastrous decision to split the new hot-strip steel mill between two locations, Llanwern, near Newport in South Wales and Ravenscraig, near Glasgow. This was a classic case of a political (and sentimental) decision taken in the face of economic reality, for ever since 1945 it had been appreciated that British steelmakers needed to concentrate output on fewer sites. As the leading historian of the industry commented in 1962, it was:

> a classic instance of bad planning. The decision led to the building of two major new plants when there was no near prospect of a market to use fully the capacity of one. The strip mill decisions rejected a strategy of development which ignored Britain's basic economic difficulties.

Fragmentation continued to weaken the industry until it was privatized in 1989 and a loss of millions of pounds a day was eliminated by long-overdue rationalization. Between 1975 and 1985, British Steel received £7.8 billion in public subsidies (more than £15 billion at current prices) while it lost £1.7 billion in 1979–80 despite receiving £715 million in subsidies. After 1986, it received no subsidies at all but the privatized company made £733 million profit in 1989–90. In May 1990 the necessary decision to close Ravenscraig was finally taken to the accompaniment of the predictable political lamentations from Scottish Labour – and Conservative – politicians. Even now, as from the beginning, it would have been far better both for Scotland and the national economy to have encouraged the development of other industries in which the area has greater natural advantages. There is absolutely no future in a locality clinging on to one major industry, and employer, which is not economically viable and which can only survive by virtue of subsidies. Not long before his much lamented death Lord Stockton showed by his jibe about privatization as 'selling the family silver' that he had not changed his spots and, in spite of his great intelligence, had learned nothing. He also showed and, this is to his discredit, that he was one of those ineffable patricians, and patrician 'hangers-on', who have pleasure in taking Margaret Thatcher 'down a peg or two'.

There is no doubt about one aspect of the post-war mixed economy and that is the vast increase in the role of the state resulting from nationalization, planning of the economy and the whole panoply of the Welfare State providing services for all in fields such as health, education and housing. With the consequent significant increase in the numbers employed in the civil service and local government, the government became, directly and indirectly, a major employer with the need for a significant increase in public expenditure and therefore of borrowing and taxation. The latter fell increasingly on the pre-war middle class so that there was a beginning of the tremendous redistribution of wealth that was such a feature of post-war Britain. This had actually begun during the war for in spite of a marked reduction in the average standard of living owing to wartime inflation ('guns' instead of 'butter' with a vengeance) the Coalition's policy of 'fair shares for all' resulted in large numbers of the population having a better standard of living than they had enjoyed before the war.

The inevitable propensity for the Labour Part to become the party of high taxation was increased while it was in Opposition in the 1950s but, on the other hand, the party leadership began to have serious doubts about nationalization. Although the 1950 election manifesto included a number of industries marked out for nationalization, the narrow margin of Labour's victory resulted in a sharp toning down of the nationalization issue in the 1951 election so that after the loss of this election there was a three-way split in the Party. As always, after an electoral defeat, the left wing moved further left and demanded more and more nationalization, the right wing and the leadership did not reject nationalization in principle but were disillusioned with it in practice while there emerged a third group, called the revisionists, who regarded it as irrelevant in achieving their ideal of socialism, which was equality. These ideas had been foreshadowed in 1952 in the 'New Fabian Essays', edited by Richard Crossman, which were a major attempt to revise Labour Party thinking away from its traditional socialist policies. The revisionists included men like Crosland, Healey and Jenkins and their ideas were formulated and popularized in Crosland's important book, *The Future of Socialism*, published in 1956, in which he advocated greater public expenditure and a further major re-distribution of wealth and income such as had already been achieved by the provisions of the Welfare State, but not by nationalization and economic planning. Like the earlier Labour men and trade unionists, the revisionists were impressed by capitalism's ability to create wealth but were mainly concerned to wrest this wealth from the capitalists, an attitude which was unforgettably enunciated by Denis Healey as Shadow Chancellor of the Exchequer, at the 1973 Party Conference, when he said Labour would impose taxes that would bring about 'howls of anguish' from the rich. However, herein lies the paradoxical failure of socialism for in whatever form it emerges it is obsessed with the redistribution, as opposed to the creation, of wealth so that eventually the power to create wealth is emasculated and finally destroyed. There have been many examples of the phenomenon but the greatest and most impressive is the collapse of the economies of Communist and Socialist Eastern Europe in our own day.

7

Full Employment, 1945–1964

The commitment to run the economy at a level to provide full employment was accepted in the White Paper on Employment in 1944. In line with the Keynesian ideas, governments accepted the duty of managing demand as a means of producing full employment. The policy succeeded. Compared to the double digit unemployment figure of the 1930s, the level did not exceed an average of 3 per cent in any full year between 1948 and 1970.[1]

In any field of study original thought is a very rare commodity which is why the names of such universal geniuses as Archimedes, Aristotle, Gallileo, Descartes, Newton and Einstein will never be forgotten. I would not claim that John Maynard Keynes falls into this class but certainly his book, *The General Theory of Employment, Interest and Money*, published in 1934, revolutionized the existing theories of economics and formed the intellectual basis for what can only be called the Keynesian revolution in the post-war management of their economies by governments throughout the world. We have already seen that as early as 1936 Keynes, and other economists, had identified lack of demand as the main cause of pre-war unemployment and that to ensure full employment governments had the responsibility of injecting demand by themselves investing heavily in the economy, even if this meant moving away from the pre-war ideal of balancing the budget to a budget deficit as a result of heavy borrowing. It was pointed out that pre-war monetary policies of stimulating investment by reducing interest rates did not work because the potential investors preferred to save any additional money in depressed times owing to lack of confidence in the economic future. This problem could only be resolved by government itself undertaking the act of investment which would in turn stimulate

---

[1]*Consensus Politics from Attlee to Thatcher*, by Dennis Kavanagh and Peter Morris, p. 5. Further facts and figures in this chapter are attributable to Chapter 3 in this authority.

spending and increase employment. The 'General Theory' was not only a brilliant intellectual explanation and justification of these concepts but its originality lay in the fact that it turned existing theory, based on common sense, upside down. The previous giant of economic theory, Professor Alfred Marshall, had said: 'common-sense is not enough'. Keynes successfully attacked the existing belief that there was a link between savings, investment and consumption and that whereas it was previously believed that investment depended on the prior act of saving he showed the opposite could be true. His sophisticated analysis of the relationship between demand and output, and their relationship, in turn, with inflation, employment, growth and the balance of payments was the bible of treasuries throughout the world, while in post-war Britain both Labour and Conservative parties claimed to be Keynesian and dedicated to the achievement of full employment by implementing widespread controls over the private sector. What was overlooked at the time was that in his report of 1942, Beveridge had assumed that unemployment would be normally about 8½ per cent while Keynes also expected it to be much greater than proved to be the case in post-war years.[1]

The fact that in post-war Britain, and Europe for that matter, unpredictably, unemployment ceased to be a problem, the new problem being overfull employment and that the imposition of Keynes's theories in this environment led to severe inflation, does not detract one jot from the importance of Keynes's contribution to the study of economics. In fact, his earlier economic milestone, *Treatise on Money*, published in 1930, before the Great Depression, was a brilliant analysis of monetary theory which is highly regarded by today's monetarists. In any case, as Marx once said, that whatever he was he was not a 'Marxist'; I am sure that Keynes would say the same. Classical economics are still of value in spite of the fact that the theory of supply and demand was misused when it was said that if there was unemployment it was because wages were too high, because the theory was only true in conditions of 'perfect competition' and the monopoly power of nineteenth-century employers made competition 'imperfect' as also does the monopoly power of twentieth-century trade unions, especially in conditions of full employment. Also, Keynes and his disciples assumed that public

---

[1]*Consensus Politics from Attlee to Thatcher*, by Dennis Kavanagh and Peter Morris, p. 74. Note however, the significance of the increase in the size of the workforce: (this book, p. 56). In order to make this adjustment the figure is usually quoted at around 2½–3 per cent.

spending would help Britain's declining staple industries but, of course, this did not happen because it mainly served to stimulate, if not over-stimulate, those industries which, as we have seen, were already prospering before the war.

It remains to record the main features of the British economy in the period under review. All was excitement when the new Parliament and Government met on 1 August 1945. As Hugh Dalton wrote: 'After the long storm of war ... we saw the sunrise. There was exhilaration among us. We felt exalted, dedicated ... we were 'walking with destiny'.[1] The sunrise, however, came in the form of a stern warning from the Treasury, actually written by Keynes, that the country was threatened with 'a financial Dunkirk'. After the exhilaration of victory the fateful prophecy of Churchill's first speech to the House of Commons as Prime Minister, on 13 May 1940 – the 'victory at all costs' speech – had become a reality. Britain had entered on her post-war economic agony of straitened circumstances.

> During the war Britain had lost approximately one quarter of her national wealth – some £7,000 million.[2] As a deliberate act of policy she had sacrificed approximately two thirds of her export trade; her economy had been distorted from top to bottom to produce the maximum war effort; and even in 1945 the number of people serving in the armed forces, civil defence and war industries amounted to 9 million – four and a half times the pre-war figure. Her total merchant shipping had been reduced by 28 per cent, and with the end of the war the terms of trade had turned against her. Clearly, therefore, it would take some years to re-establish her international trading position and to reconvert her industries to peacetime production. Meanwhile her internal economy also gave cause for concern. Wartime inflation – the cost of Britain's war effort for four years had exceeded her national income by 50 per cent – meant that as note circulation increased the value of the pound declined. In fact its purchasing power over the whole range of consumer goods and services, taking 1914 as 100, declined from

---

[1] *The Fateful Years*, by Hugh Dalton, p. 453.
[2] The sale or repatriation of overseas investments accounted for over £1,000 million alone. The rest of the figure is made up as follows:

Increase in loans and sterling balances	£3,000 million
Depletion of dollar and gold reserves	£152 million
Destruction and damage to property	£1,500 million
Shipping losses	£700 million
Depreciation and obsolescence of stock	£900 million

65 in 1937–8 to 43 in 1944–5. The national debt meanwhile had tripled, while the country's standard of living had fallen heavily.[1]

In his Treasury paper Keynes had also stated that without substantial American aid, the country would be 'virtually bankrupt and the economic basis for the hopes of the public non-existent'. The Government had no reason to think that American aid, in the form of Lend-Lease (the wartime system of aid to Europe) would not be continued, to strengthen the country's international trading position, in view of the enormous economic and other sacrifices that Britain had made during the war. But that was to reckon without the appalling ignorance and naivety of the Americans who under President Roosevelt regarded British imperial ambitions as the greatest threat to post-war world security and who under President Truman thought that the unrivalled economic gains that the United States had made during the war would be threatened by the revival of 'imperialist' Britain. VJ-Day was celebrated on 2 September and in the same month Lend-Lease was ended. The ubiquitous Keynes was immediately sent to Washington to negotiate a loan but the eventual loan agreed, signed with great reluctance in December at Bretton Woods, was much harsher than Britain had originally requested. Although the amount of the loan was very much less, owing to the fact that the terms of the loan agreement involved the cancellation of the greater part of the Lend-Lease account, with interest at 2 per cent, but they included an undertaking: to make the pound convertible in terms of current trading, within a year; that imperial preference should end; and that Britain should repay her sterling creditors by 1951, for during the war sterling debits had accumulated following imports of food and raw materials, and the like. All this, in spite of the facts of Britain's enormous wartime economic sacrifices and of America's refusal even to consider reducing her own excessive tariffs and of her formidable trade surplus which had led to the famous post-war 'dollar gap', an acute shortage of dollars in the international trading world, which the Americans seemed determined to exacerbate. An additional Canadian loan was negotiated in order to help with Britain's large dollar gap. The gravity of the outlook for international monetary and trading problems had already been foreseen in an earlier Bretton Woods conference in 1944 when the admirable Keynes was one of the main movers in establishing the International Monetary Fund and the Bank for Reconstruction. In

---

[1] *Post-War Britain*, by Alan Sked and Chris Cook, p. 26. Further facts and figures in this chapter are attributable to this authority.

spite of the differences between the Americans and the British in this negotiation and in the later one on the occasion of the American Loan Agreement of 1946, resulting from the latter's double standards in the matter of international trade, the important General Agreement on Tariffs and Trade (GATT) was signed in 1947.

Whereas economic recovery had been expected by 1951, by July 1947 the US loan was almost run down and the restoration of convertibility led to a run on the pound – the 'convertibility crisis' – and to the suspension of convertibility. The year 1947 was a nightmare year for the Labour Government. Income from invisibles deteriorated and, even worse, the terms of trade moved sharply against Britain, especially in terms of American dollar imports. Finally, following the hard winter of 1946–47 – the worst for 65 years – there was a major fuel crisis as the coal industry failed to meet the additional demand for power, a situation which was worsened by an outbreak of unofficial strikes in the mines. In February, Emmanuel Shinwell, the Minister of Fuel and Power, announced a complete cessation of the domestic supply of electricity to industry and the requisitioning of coal under the regulations of the Defence of the Realm Act, following which 1.8 million workers were laid off. It has been estimated that around £200 million of exports were lost as a consequence. By September there was both a financial and a political crisis for the balance of payments deficit had reached the then formidable figure of £435 million and Cripps and Dalton attempted to instal Bevin as Prime Minister in place of Attlee who proved to have barnacle-like, as well as other unglamorous but useful, qualities as a politician. I have already discussed how Cripps was promoted to be Minister of Economic Affairs in September and to succeed Dalton as Chancellor in October. The latter's main contribution to the economic crisis was to initiate a 'cheap money policy' by reducing the interest rates by ½ per cent on Treasury Bills and Deposit Receipts in his first budget in October 1945, while in May 1946 he announced a cut in interest on Defence Bonds from 3 per cent to 2½ per cent. Again, in his second budget in October 1946 the maturing 3 per cent local loans stock was effectively replaced by a 2½ per cent Treasury stock redeemable only at the Treasury's option in or after 1975 (i.e. undated) – the famous 'Daltons'. The object was to encourage capital investment but the policy was criticized by the bankers as being inflationary, and not deflationary, as claimed, on the grounds that the level of capital investment was not being controlled as effectively as the Government claimed. In spite of a measure of inflation, Dalton's Chancellorship was notable for the maintenance of the full employment of wartime while his budget of November 1947, which he never implemented because of his subsequent resignation, was disinflationary to the extent of around £200 million.

I have already commented on Britain's economic recovery in 1948 and the contribution made by Stafford Cripps. It was probably not so much the impetus that he gave to the planning machinery but the general effect of the sheer strength of his ascetic character which was just what was required at this stage in our history. After years of sacrifice during the war he asked the people to continue to make sacrifices in order to ensure national recovery. He outlined his policy in the following manner: 'First are exports...; Second is capital investment in industry; and last are the needs, comforts and amenities of the family.' People were asked to 'submerge all thought of personal gain and personal ambition'. The end-products of this policy and attitude were the capital levy on investment income and increases in indirect taxes in his first budget of April 1948 and his application of wage restraint. Cripps had already accepted the FBI proposals in March for voluntary price control and limitations of dividends, while in October he reduced capital expenditure by £200 million, thus temporarily ending the construction of new houses and factories. Significantly, Churchill supported the measures while also denouncing the policy of state planning. The obverse of the Coalition White Paper of 1944 on (Full) Employment was the acceptance of wage restraint which was of course agreed to by the Labour Party and the trade unions so that with the post-war phenomenon of 'too much money chasing too few goods', wage restraint was inevitable. A White Paper on Incomes, Costs and Prices of February 1948 denounced the wage-price spiral and called for voluntary collective agreements to regulate incomes in the following terms:

> It is essential that there should be no further general increase in the level of personal incomes without at least a corresponding increase in the volume of production.

The fact that the White Paper was approved by the TUC General Council was partly a reflection of Cripps's example and authority but mainly evidence of the responsible attitude of the early post-war trade unions. The result was certainly impressive.

> From 1948 'till August 1950 wage rates rose by only 5 per cent while retail prices rose by 8 per cent. Indeed between 1945 and 1951 average weekly wage rates rose in real terms by only 6 per cent, in other words, 'under six years of socialism the workers had

to work a great deal of overtime to improve their standard of living by a tiny 1 per cent a year.'[1]

Again, the pension of a married couple, 42s a week in October 1946, had by January 1950 fallen in purchasing power to 35s 8d. It is not surprising that by 1950 the trade unions began to oppose wage restraint. In September the TUC Annual Congress rejected it by a small majority and called for statutory control of profits. It was the latter demand which foreshadowed the later neanderthal proclivities of the trade unions.

There is one major reason for the 1948 economic recovery which has not yet been mentioned, namely Marshall Aid. In June 1947, before Cripp's appointment as Minister of Economic Affairs and later, Chancellor of the Exchequer, and before the July convertibility crisis, the United States Secretary of State, General George Marshall, called for a European Recovery Programme to aid the ailing European economies with the proviso that the Europeans would accept the responsibility for organizing it. With a trade deficit with the United States of £655 million by the end of 1947, Britain willingly took the lead, in company with France, the second largest beneficiary, in accepting Marshall Aid which came into force in 1948. In the wider historical perspective, Marshall's statesmanship was a pronounced improvement on the purblind ignorance that led Truman and his 'economic royalists' to cancel Lend-Lease so precipitously. Whereas in the nineteenth century Britain's international economic dominance did not lead to a disequilibrium of world trade (at least until the last quarter of the century), because of her immense capacity for importing commodities and raw materials, the protectionist traditions of the United States, together with the fact that this enormous continental country was virtually self-sufficient, seriously threatened such a disequilibrium. The chronic economic affliction of the 'dollar gap' was visible evidence of this and George Marshall and his advisers did an enormous service to the world, as well as to the United States itself, in recycling some of its vast trading surplus, $11 billion being granted to Western Europe between 1948 and 1951.

In Britain, unemployment and depression were held at bay by virtue of her own efforts as well as Marshall Aid and the 'Economic survey' for 1949 described 1948 as 'a year of great and steady progress' with a significant increase in production, an even greater

---

[1] *Post-War Britain*, by Alan Sked and Chris Cook, p. 36.

rise in exports and the balance of payments coming into surplus. Unfortunately, however, in spite of Cripp's gargantuan efforts, and because economic planning was incapable of making good the economic ravages of Britain's wartime economy, Marshall Aid being merely a palliative, in the course of 1949 Britain drifted into one of her many post-war 'sterling crises'. In his April budget Cripps warned of the growing dollar deficit and said that government spending on defence and social services necessitated an effective reduction in food subsidies and increases in direct taxes, while the effect of his initial allowances for new plant and machinery was extremely limited. The position, as reflected in the further fall in the gold and dollar reserves, continued to deteriorate during the summer although Cripps resisted devaluation before falling ill and going to Switzerland to recuperate, during which time his successor as President of the Board of Trade, Hugh Gaitskell, temporarily took his place. On his return in August, Cripps agreed to a devaluation which was announced in September after he and Bevin had visited Washington to arrange an increase in United States investment in Europe and the liberalization of trade in Europe. The extent of the devaluation, from $4.03 to $2.80, (over 30 per cent), has been criticized as excessive, for at first the Cabinet contemplated a level of $3.00, as also has been the fact that deflationary medicine was applied after rather than before devaluation, namely economies of £250 million in the 'capital expenditure of the fuel and power industries, the expanding education programme, new housing and the larger field of miscellaneous investment', as announced by Attlee in October. There was also the introduction of a charge of one shilling for National Health Service prescriptions, an innovation that was to have important consequences.

The situation at the end of 1949 has been succinctly summed up:

> Still, Labour's confidence was not broken. Austerity had, after all, become a way of life, and it might even be argued that the underlying trends in the economy gave room for optimism. Inflation was under control, full employment was being maintained, and exports were rising slowly but surely despite some recent setbacks. Moreover, if there was still a plethora of controls and if wage increases hardly kept up with the rise in prices, the standard of living had definitely improved since 1945. Labour's social reforms had seen to that.[1]

---

[1] *Post-War Britain*, by Alan Sked and Chris Cook, p. 37.

But perhaps the 'underlying trends in the economy that gave room for optimism' were that the pre-war dynamic economy, mainly in the South, South-East and the Midlands, had been stimulated during the war, together with the new industries that had been created during the war. There has been too uncritical an acceptance of the disappointing economic record of the Attlee governments which squandered the outstanding opportunity to increase national wealth that was provided by the release of large numbers of low-paid military servicemen into productive industry. We have already noted the meagre increase in the living standard in the period (pp. 91–2), admittedly partly due to the admirable restraint of the trade unions. Enormous resources were channelled into the burdensome nationalization programme while many foods, tea, petrol and newspapers remained rationed although items such as potatoes, bread, jam, footwear, clothes and other textiles ceased to be rationed in 1948 and 1949 (p. 377). The Government came to power with the belief in a planned economy which we discussed in Chapter 6, 'The Mixed Economy', (pp. 80–2), but this led to the economically debilitating direction of labour and to a myriad of regulations. For example, the manufacture and supply of such products as vacuum cleaners, washing machines, water heaters and refrigerators were all controlled by the Whitehall planners or otherwise these examples of the pre-war dynamic economy would have overtaken, even more, the old staple industries which should have been allowed to continue their decline without interruption.

Thus, this dynamic economy was still waiting to be really released so as to exhibit its full potential. The fact that it had to wait until 1979 is the reason why in the 1950s Britain was one of the ten richest nations in the world, with income per head 25 per cent higher than West Germany and 500 per cent greater than Japan, compared with the fact that by 1986 the former's income per head was 200 per cent greater than ours and Japan's 50 per cent greater, a trend which has continued. UK living standards, in terms of income per head, measured in real terms, show us well behind the USA, Sweden, Japan and the Federal Republic of Germany – with ninth place in the European Union at present (June 1994). However, as our place in the world's league of national wealth continues to slip, it is worth noting that these comparisons are largely based on industrial and manufacturing criteria, whereas our strength is based on our expertise in the commercial, financial, trading and service aspects of the economy, as indeed it has been since the eighteenth century, if not before. It is mainly for this reason that when it comes to comparisons based on the actual standard of living (such as the ownership of

94

homes and consumer durables) the British challenge the world's richest nations – the United States, Japan and Germany. And even in terms of traditional GDP comparisons it is important to keep a sense of proportion.

> According to the latest statistics (which cover 1991) Britain's gross domestic product was 2–3 times larger than China's, and that was produced by just 57 million Britons, or one-twentieth the 1.15 billion Chinese. If you combined the GDP's of China, Taiwan, Hong Kong, Thailand, Malaysia, Indonesia and Singapore, they would still not match Britain's GDP.[1]

Indeed, in view of the vast military machine and productive capacity which we had built up by 1945, the question has been asked whether our post-war decline was inevitable – if we had not flung ourselves headlong into the creation of the Welfare State.

However, that was not to be and the economy, and much else, during the second Labour Government of February 1950 to October 1951 was dominated by the outbreak of the Korean War in June 1950 and the Government's decision in July to send British troops to Korea in support of the United States forces and the other nations supporting the United Nations condemnation of the invasion of South Korea by the Communist forces of North Korea. In April Cripps had introduced a cautious budget with the reduction in taxes for the less well-off balanced by increased taxes on petrol and commercial vehicles and the limiting of food subsidies to £140 million. The Government was so well satisfied with the economy, as exports had attained the extraordinary level of £2,254 million compared with £920 million in 1946, that it did not utilize a further year's quota of Marshall Aid, as well as cancelling additional import restrictions. The Korean War soon ended this desirable state of affairs. Britain was already involved in fighting the Chinese Communists in Malaya at an annual cost of £50 million and a commitment of 100,000 men. In September, the month of the landing of United Nations troops in South Korea, the Government announced its gigantic rearmament programme which was to cost £3,400 million for a period of three years and which was increased to £4,700 million in January 1951. The new Chancellor of the Exchequer, Gaitskell, who had succeeded Cripps on his resignation due to illness in October, provided the additional money required in

---

[1]Quoted from Anatole Kaletsky's article in the *Sunday Telegraph* (21/11/93), 'The Chinese tiger turns out to be a minnow'.

his controversial 'Tory-like' budget in April. There was an increase of 6d in the pound on income tax, the doubling of purchase tax on motor cars, radios and domestic appliances, the tax on distributed profits was increased from 30 to 50 per cent, in spite of the abolition of initial allowances while, most controversial of all, half the cost of National Health Service spectacles and dentures was to be borne by adults. The balance of payments crisis in the summer of 1951 was due to the pronounced rise in world commodity prices following the Korean War, which was exacerbated by the 1949 devaluation, leading to a 50 per cent increase in the price of imports and a 12 per cent deterioration in terms of trade, as well as a physical increase in imports due to rearmament and the expansion of the domestic economy. During 1951 imports rose from £2,390 million to £3,501 million. The outbreak of hostilities in Korea coincided with the rejection of wage control by the TUC Annual Congress, as we have already noted, which, in turn, was followed by dockers' strikes in early 1951 and a series of wage increases. In September 1951, the TUC Annual Congress continued its demand for all-round wage increases together with that for equal pay for equal work while also supporting the Government's rearmament policy. In July, Gaitskell had already tried to appease the unions by announcing the imposition of anti-inflationary price and dividend controls in the autumn. However, in view of the political ruptions following his introduction of the NHS charges, the pound continued to come under international pressure, especially as there was the running down of their sterling balances by the sterling area members, whose increased wealth as raw material exporters led them to purchase from outside the sterling area. A surplus on current account of £300 million in 1950 had deteriorated to a deficit of £400 million by 1951. In the absence of any decisive change in policy, such as imposing import quotas, organizing standby credits, or even reducing the rearmament programme, the Government unsuccessfully went to the country in October.

Consequently, the Churchill Government (1951–55) inherited a vast balance of payments deficit of almost £700 million. In November, the new Chancellor of the Exchequer, R.A. Butler, the quintessential consensus-man, warned that the nation was in danger of being 'bankrupt, idle and hungry' and announced economies of £350 million per year which included reductions in imports, credit restrictions, reductions in food subsidies, travel allowances and, more important, in strategic stockpiling. In the defence debate in December Churchill said that the Government was unable to carry out the full programme of rearmament expenditure, and admitted that Bevan 'by accident, perhaps not from the best of motives, happened to be right'. Bevan, in his resignation speech over the NHS charges in April had said that the rearmament programme was not 'physically practicable' in view of the resources available, while Wilson, in his resignation speech two days later, for the same reason, said additionally that the economy could not bear the level of rearmament which the Government had undertaken. In his first budget in March, Butler reduced food subsidies as well as income tax and raised allowances to benefit about 2 million wage earners and raised Bank Rate to 4 per cent, which he had previously increased from 2 per cent to 2½ per cent, the first such increase since 1932. The reason for this attempt to restrain demand was the dramatic recovery by the economy due to the profound improvement in Britain's terms of trade in 1952 – by 6 per cent in 1952 and with a similar increase in the next year – which resulted in the balance of payments deficit turning into a staggering surplus of £300 million in that year, which continued for every year until 1957, except for 1955, when there was a deficit of £69 million,

This was the first Tory application of the 'Stop-Go' cycles of economic management that became so well-known in the 1950s and 1960s, under both parties, and which led to *The Economist* magazine using the famous word, 'Butskellism', in February 1954 for in his budget of 1951 Gaitskell had perhaps applied the most famous 'stop' of them all. However, in the management of the economy a big change was taking place, for although lip-service was still given to the ideal of full employment, increasingly in the 1950s and 1960s the main object was the protection of sterling from weakness caused by balance of payments deficits which was occasioned by the system of having a fixed exchange rate pegged against the dollar, together with the fact that sterling was an international currency. Every attempt to expand the economy led to a balance of payments deficit as imports expanded too rapidly, which was corrected by deflationary measures, and vice versa. Every government attempted to arrive at a stable relationship between the rate of inflation and unemployment, thus avoiding the extremes of too much expansion (demand) leading to inflation and overfull employment and too little leading to recessionary threats and a rise in unemployment.

Each party claimed it could deliver higher employment, lower prices, and faster economic growth than the other. There was relatively little conflict over the objectives themselves ... (the trade-offs were clearly understood) ... But in their electoral campaigns both parties preferred to claim that all the major objectives of stabilisation policy could be realized simultaneously.[1]

But 'Stop-Go', or 'fine-tuning', as it was called later, was an economic 'will o' the wisp' which was inherently unsound and impossible of fulfilment for it was really a form of central economic planning which foundered on such inconvenient facts as that it is impossible here and now to ascertain what the underlying forces in the economy are doing, for in an apparently recessionary situation the forces of recovery can be beginning to gather strength, and vice versa. Also, especially in the case of monetary measures such as changes in the interest rates, it takes between eighteen months and two years for them to become effective. There is only one thing worse in economic management and that is direct and interventionist controls so beloved of Labour Governments (and Tory 'Wets') which specialise in demand management by spending and borrowing until the economy is seriously out of control and which can only be slowed down by the imposition of the faster-working but hopelessly distortionary physical controls. Being the true man of the consensus, Butler used both monetary and direct controls but, to his credit, he was more a monetarist than an interventionist which led him in 1952 unsuccessfully to try to persuade the Cabinet to float the pound.

In October 1952, at the Conservative Party Conference, Butler attacked those Conservatives who were calling for more cuts in government spending as advocating 'radically unsound, cruel or unnecessary policies'. This statement emphasizes his 'middle of the road' approach to politics and life but, on this occasion, he was also right, for the underlying forces in the economy were beginning to slacken. Thus in his April 1953 budget 'Go' followed 'Stop' and income and purchase taxes were reduced, the levy on excess profits was abolished, initial allowances reintroduced and building license restrictions raised considerably. The budget also featured a minor historical landmark, for Butler and Gaitskell took part in the first television broadcast on the budget. With the continuation of the improvement in the terms of trade due to falling world commodity prices as well as to the benefits from the 1949 devaluation, now that the Korean War had ended, the British economy thrived between 1952 and 1955. Food was derationed during 1953 and 1954 while iron and steel and road haulage were denationalized in 1953. In 1954 the Ministry of Materials and the Raw Cotton Commission were

---

[1]*The British Party System and Economic Policy*, by Gamble and Walkland, p. 44.

abolished, the international commodity markets were restored, hire purchase trading encouraged, and wartime building restrictions reduced considerably. Finally, between 1952 and 1955 there was a boom on the Stock Exchange with the doubling of the ordinary share index, while prices, the cost of living, wages and output all rose moderately, until 1955 at least. With the balance of payments under control it was possible to reduce Bank Rate in 1952, 1953 and 1954 and to have a neutral budget in 1954, apart from the introduction of investment allowances which, although less of a distortion than the earlier initial allowances, were a dangerous and insidious form of applied socialism. Investment was subsidized for its own sake whereas unprofitable investment should have been actively discouraged for it deprived the more successful part of the economy of resources and thus reduced the economy's capacity for growth and wealth creation.[1] It is a similar kind of distortion to the subsidizing of export-orientated industries so necessary under a system of fixed exchange rates by which the economy, as such, is weakened by the squeezing of industries with more natural advantages but which might not necessarily be export-orientated. That is to say, it is better to import products that we cannot produce competitively than to subsidize uncompetitive home producers.

However, by 1955 the economy was beginning to overheat, with registered vacancies exceeding those unemployed so that in January, Bank Rate was increased from 3 per cent to 3½ per cent and in February to 4½ per cent. With the resignation of Winston Churchill, following his illness, in April, his successor, Anthony Eden, called for an election in May. Butler presented a frankly electioneering budget to emphasize the prosperity that Conservative rule had brought, in spite of the fact that he had already begun to curb the economy by his Bank Rate moves. Income tax was reduced by 6d, higher personal allowances were granted and purchase tax was halved on cotton, rayon and linen. Inevitably, the overheating of the economy

---

[1] An article in *The Accountant* (17/4/54, p. 409) stated: 'Initial allowances have been called, somewhat contemptuously, "interest-free loans", as though these were not worth having. They are at any rate better than no help at all. Now they are to be a gift.' The article then proceeded to demonstrate that a farmer paying tax at 19s in the £ (those were the days!) could make a profit by buying a tractor 'merely to scare the birds' through the accounting machinations of the investment allowance. As was later reported in the issue of 7 August (p. 159) the above article did lead to amendments of the original Finance Bill so as to reduce the possibility of abuse of the new investment allowances. The Inland Revenue was opposed to their introduction in the first place.

continued and Butler was forced to introduce a deflationary autumn budget in October (a regular feature in these years) increasing hire-purchase deposits and purchase tax and reducing both bank loans and the capital requirements of the nationalized industries – a fistful of the dreaded direct controls. In his reply in the budget debate, Gaitskell accused Butler of creating inflation as a result of his blatantly electioneering budget, as well he might. In a Cabinet reshuffle in December, Butler was appointed Lord Privy Seal and was succeeded as Chancellor of the Exchequer by Macmillan, fresh from his house-building exploits. In February 1956, Macmillan increased Bank Rate to 5½ per cent, the highest-ever rate since 1931, and his April budget, described by him as a 'savings budget' due to his typically gimmicky introduction of Premium Bonds, further attempted to deflate the economy by highlighting credit controls, reducing public investment and withdrawing investment allowances. This last excellent decision was offset by another move that was pure Macmillan: the increase in the tax on distributed profits to 27½ per cent and that on undistributed profits to 3 per cent, in that its aim was to bribe the trade unions to curb wage demands, on the one hand, and the application of wrong-headed socialist economics, on the other hand. The ploy of bribing and 'genuflecting' to trade unions was well-nigh played out, while the socialist policy of heavily penalizing the distribution of profits as opposed to their retention was, and is, the opposite of what should be done in the interests of the economy and the people; the former provides financial resources for up-and-coming commercial and industrial activities and the latter protects declining industries and companies from competition for these resources from more dynamic companies. We can already see Macmillan moving towards the 'dead-end' of corporatism and 'pink' Toryism which was to provide one of the most unfortunate, if not the most unfortunate, examples of the post-war consensus. While the Suez problem was developing, Macmillan's main preoccupation was the unions' continued wage demands in spite of his budget's concessions to them. In August he issued an appeal for wage restraint following the Government White Paper, 'Economic Implications of Full Employment', in March, which reiterated the problem that had been stated in the 1944 White Paper and which had become the model that later governments were to use to justify incomes policies, namely that the unions' excessive wage demands would have adverse effects on inflation and unemployment. *The Economist* magazine never tired of stating the aphorism that 'one man's wage increase is another man's job'. The height of the Suez Crisis and Eden's temporary retirement to Jamaica at the end of November, due to illness and exhaustion, leaving Butler as acting Prime Minister, was accompanied by the selling of sterling so that on 4 December, Macmillan announced large falls in the gold and dollar reserves and applied to the IMF to draw on the British quota to meet the shortfall (£201 million), the first such application in British history, while a stand-by credit of £246 million was announced in December.

On his unexpected appointment as Prime Minister in January 1957, Macmillan appointed Peter Thorneycroft as his Chancellor of the Exchequer who promptly announced cuts in social services and the raising of charges for school meals and milk. The euphoria of 1952–55 gave way to a period of Conservative stagnation for two years with the annual increase in the GNP falling to under 1 per cent. Although his budget in April provided major tax reliefs in the form of a reduction in purchase tax and higher earned income relief as well as the abolition of entertainment tax, Thorneycroft, like Macmillan before him, was concerned with the inflationary implications of excessive wage increases about which he warned publicly in July as well as establishing a purely advisory council on Prices, Productivity and Incomes, in August, in spite of trade union opposition. The hand of Harold Macmillan can be detected in this early manifestation of corporatism as also can his sharp intellect in detecting a trend, such as his 'wind of change' speech in Africa, or identifying and defining a development such as his remark, 'most of our people have never had it so good', in the same month of July in a speech at Bedford. This was criticized by his opponents as being excessively complacent and prized by his supporters as being a sharp reminder of the truth, but the words which followed were prescient:

> What is beginning to worry some of us is 'Is it too good to be true?', or perhaps I should say 'Is it too good to last?'. For amidst all this prosperity, there is one problem that has troubled us in one way or another – ever since the war. It's the problem of rising prices. Our constant concern today is – can prices be steadied while at the same time we maintain full employment in an expanding economy? Can we control inflation? This is the problem of our time.

By the summer, the gold reserves had been depleted by £186 million and Thorneycroft saw the continued wage increases as evidence of the need to deflate the economy further, so that in September he adopted the extreme policy of raising Bank Rate from 5 per cent to 7 per cent, and restricted public investment and intensified the credit squeeze in an attempt to curb inflation and hold the value of the pound, even if it meant higher unemployment. In September 1957, at 265,000, unemployment was 1.2 per cent of the working population and could still be described as full employment. However, the consensus of full employment at any price was now being questioned; it did not come under attack until 1979. Significantly, when the new Council on Prices, Productivity and Incomes approved the Chancellor's measures in its first report, the trade unions immediately withdrew what little support that they had given.

Nevertheless, Macmillan was not prepared to support Thorneycroft when he proposed further reductions in spending so that he dismissed him in January 1958, following which Thorneycroft's two Financial Secretaries, Nigel Birch and Enoch Powell, resigned in protest. Although Macmillan was adept at defining the problem posed by inflationary expenditure, he was too much of a child of his time to turn his back decisively on the bad old habit, but although he was wrong in the substance he was also wrong 'in style', describing the resignations as 'little local difficulties' as he took off for a Commonwealth tour. The three Treasury men were exceptionally able, as is now realized, and they were the first ministers to see through the bad advice that the Treasury mandarins had been giving, and were to continue to give, to both Conservative and Labour Cabinets, although it is understood that Thorneycroft believed that Sir Leslie Rowan, of the Treasury, supported him. In his first budget in April, Heathcoat-Amory, the new Chancellor, rectified the harm done by the previous policy of penalizing distributed profits, by imposing the single rate of 10 per cent on both categories while he also simplified purchase tax. Although he was not a 'high-flyer' Derick Heathcoat-Amory had a fund of common sense and good judgment which are the main qualities required to be a successful Chancellor of the Exchequer. A trained economist or financier might be more at home when presenting his budget at the dispatch box or on television, but a Sir Alec Douglas-Home,with his matchsticks, who makes the right decision, is preferable to the 'bravura' of a Nigel Lawson when he eased monetary policy in 1986, at the very time when he should have been strengthening it, (another example of the fatuity of fine tuning). This wrong decision was massively reinforced by significant interest rate reductions after he effectively took Britain into the ERM from February/March 1987 when he pegged Sterling at 3 Deutschmarks, a mistake which was compounded in the reaction to the collapse in world share prices in October 1987. In any event, and back to 1958, Heathcoat-Amory continued the restrictions but by July they had had sufficient effect for him to be able to relax the credit squeeze by introducing the option of a 'special deposit' system whereby the Treasury could compel banks to deposit required amounts in the Bank of England. Peter Thorneycroft and his two ex-colleagues, and those who were beginning to think like them, would have argued that such direct and physical controls would be unnecessary if the money supply were kept in control. It is interesting to note in passing that, unlike his present-day successors, that is, Cabinet ministers who have resigned or have been sacked, Thorneycroft, in a speech in the month of his resignation refused to organize a rebellious protest against the Party leadership. However, in November Heathcoat-Amory was able to reduce Bank Rate and abolish hire-purchase restrictions. For all his common sense, and on the failure of Macmillan to grasp the restorative nettle offered by Thorneycroft, Heathcoat-Amory was back on the 'Stop-Go' syndrome and his budget in April 1959 brought tax relief of £360 million, including reductions in income tax, purchase tax and the price of beer, while post-war credits were released and investment allowances were restored. Labour inevitably criticized the budget for its 'electioneering' provisions and equally inevitably Macmillan called an election for October which he won overwhelmingly on a tide of Tory prosperity.

Heathcote-Amory's sensible budget aims in April 1960 were 'to consolidate and fortify our present prosperity' but in addition to minor tax concessions he increased the tax on tobacco and on profits tax to 12½ per cent. This was really the beginning of another 'Stop' for in June, Bank Rate, which had already been increased to 5 per cent in January, was further increased to 6 per cent together with the imposition of a severe credit squeeze by the doubling of special deposits. In July Heathcoat-Amory retired to the Lords. It was said of him by a Cabinet colleague that 'it was evident that he had lost his grasp over economic matters', but what was evident to some, at the time, and what has become abundantly evident in retrospect, is that he was trying to work an unworkable system. Predictably, Selwyn Lloyd, his successor, did no better. After applying some counter-inflationary policies, including the new system of 'regulators', giving the authorities the right to raise specified taxes without reference, he announced a partial relaxation of hire-purchase restrictions in January and, probably on bad Treasury advice regarding the state of the economy, in his 1961 budget in April, increased the starting point of surtax from £2,000 to £5,000. In itself, this was no bad measure being one of the earliest examples of the application of 'supply-side' economics by a British government as opposed to the old-Keynesian consensus of 'demand management' and the new, ineffectual corporatist system, so beloved by Macmillan.

Unfortunately, by July another sterling crisis had erupted in the form of a £258 million deficit on the balance of payments and Selwyn Lloyd had to reverse gears sharply by raising Bank Rate from 5 per cent to 7 per cent and by arranging large loans from the IMF and central banks. He also announced a 'pay pause' for government employees. Only days before, the Plowden Report had emphasized the technical difficulties of controlling government expenditure and called for general surveys on spending over a period of years, together with a constructive parliamentary control. The immediate object of the projected 'pay pause' was to stop 35 wage claims which, it was estimated, would increase the nation's wage bill by £500 million and lead to wages rising by about 50 per cent greater than output. This drastic policy succeeded in that the pound stabilized by the autumn but it had inevitably incurred great hostility among government employees, especially the nurses, teachers and hospital workers who received considerable public sympathy and support. Like any policy of wage restraint, it foundered on the fact that the Government only controlled a secondary part of the economy while the employers and trade unions in the private sector were left comparatively free to make their own arrangements. Macmillan's answer to this dilemma was indicative planning.

In January 1962 the TUC General Council agreed to be represented on the new National Economic Development Council (NEDC) after overcoming the stiff opposition led by the left-wing secretary of the large Transport and General Workers Union, Frank Cousins, although paradoxically, the TUC Economic Committee had made the condition that the TUC should not be asked to support restraint! In February, the NEDC was established as a tripartite body and planning instrument; that is to say, the Government, the employers and the trade unions were to guide the economy on the French model, a development which had been foreshadowed by the so-called Planning Board of Treasury officials, businessmen and trade unionists. In hindsight, it is thought that the responsibility of indicative planning for the success of the French economy at this time was more apparent than real; that it was in a recovery phase for fundamental reasons, in any case. In Britain, it was certainly a total failure which is understandable now that we know that the British economy, especially that part of it that is dynamic, could not really thrive until the Government and the trade unions 'got off its back' – which did not happen until 1979 – in the sense of eliminating constraints on the capacity of the dynamic parts of the economy to develop.

The attempt, in March, to appease the unions by ending the 'pay pause' which had suffered its first major defeat by the electricity pay settlement in November and substituting a 2½ per cent 'guiding light' for pay rises and Selwyn Lloyd's imposition of a short-term capital gains tax on stock exchange profits on holdings held for less than six months, did not work, as neither would dividend restraint if the Government had been foolish enough to apply it. In January, the postal workers had already begun to work to rule and later in the year, there were strikes by the railwaymen and the nurses. In May, the dock employers breached the 'guiding light' principle by granting a 9 per cent rise to prevent a dock strike, after which the Minister of Labour announced that 77 industries had already had wage rises in excess of 2½ per cent.

Selwyn Lloyd was one of Macmillan's victims in his famous Cabinet reshuffle in July, 'the night of the long knives', his successor being Reginald Maudling, one of Butler's post-war young researchers in Conservative Central Office, who was experienced and articulate in economic matters and who was determined not to be another 'Stop-Go' Chancellor and who, incidentally, had opposed the creation of NEDC. However, before he had his chance, there was one last instalment of Macmillan's indicative planning, by the establishment in July of a National Incomes Commission to draw attention to important wage claims and wage increases, in view of the increases that were taking place in private industry, and with which the unions refused to co-operate! In accordance with *The Economist's* longstanding prediction (p. 100), by February 1963, unemployment had reached 878,000 or 3.9 per cent, although this was partly due to the coldest winter wince 1947. In the North-East, where it was as high as 7 per cent, Lord Hailsham was given special responsibility for the area while later in the year Edward Heath was appointed as Minister for Industry, Trade and Regional Development, a by-product of which was his Resale Prices Act of July 1964, abolishing resale price maintenance by which manufacturers enforced prices on retailers. This was the best thing that 'Ted' Heath ever did, not so much in regard to the actual measure, although it was enlightened, but in that he carried it out persistently in the face of vested interests in his own party without any hint of a U-Turn. It was the logical successor to the earlier Restrictive Practices Act of 1956 which was one of the earliest, if not the earliest, example of 'supply-side' economics being applied by a Conservative Government.

This was the background to Maudling's famous and futile 'dash for growth'. In October 1962 he announced the injection of £42 million spending power into the economy by releasing post-war credits, as well as promising an increase of £70 million in public investments and loans to local authorities. In November, he introduced new tax allowances for industrial investment and a reduction of purchase tax on motor cars. The culmination was his budget of April 1963 in which he reduced taxes by £250 million, mostly as income reliefs and provided tax concessions to firms setting up in areas of high unemployment, an unfortunate and early example of Conservative interventionism. Maudling claimed that his budget was based on a policy of 'expansion without inflation' and when his critics pointed out that it would exacerbate an already serious balance-of-payments deficit, his reply was:

> In so far as there is a stocking-up movement related to expansion, it is perfectly reasonable and sensible to finance such a movement out of our reserves or out of our borrowing facilities in the IMF and elsewhere.

In other words, he was gambling on an increase in productivity to balance the books – the stock answer of Labour manifestos and governments from that day to this and one of the reasons why the Macmillan Government can be correctly described as 'pink'. In spite of the fact that Maudling had the satisfaction of seeing unemployment fall to 480,00 or 2.1 per cent by June, in February 1964 Britain's trade deficit of £120 million was the largest monthly deficit ever recorded, following which he took £100 million out of the economy in increased indirect taxes in his budget of April 1964. In the meantime, Macmillan had resigned through ill-health in October 1963, to be succeeded by Lord Home, after he had become Sir Alec Douglas-Home and found himself a constituency. When Harold Wilson won the ensuing election in October 1964 by the narrowest of majorities, he had been able to destroy Maudling's and the Conservatives' credibility by his no doubt exaggerated forecast of an £800 million balance of payments deficit which turned out to be around £700 million – large enough indeed. Sir Alec Douglas-Home, with his matchsticks, could not have done any worse, while as Prime Minister for the last year of Maudling's Chancellorship, I am sure that he left the economy in the 'expert' hands of the Treasury mandarins and his Chancellor. Maudling's failure was not the result of inability or any kind of technical incompetence but simply of the fact that he was a prisoner of the 'Stop-Go' system of running the economy, that he inherited. He tried to break out of the straitjacket by spending his way out, but this was bound to end in failure. It was not until 1979 that the straitjacket was discarded.

The following depressing figures sum up the economic failure of the period:

The 1956 Report of the Ministry of Labour and National Service contained an ominous sentence: 'The post-war expansion in industrial production as a whole and output per man was halted in 1956, the rates remaining approximately at the 1955 level'. The middle years of the Fifties did indeed seem to mark a point of change for, in this respect, the worse. From 1948 to 1955 the average annual increase in the gross domestic product at constant prices was 3.5 per cent, between 1955 and 1961 it was up only 2.2 per cent. In 1954 Britain provided 20 per cent of the world's manufactured exports; by the early Sixties she was providing only 15 per cent. Meantime Germany's share had gone up from 15 per cent to over 19 per cent, and Japan's from 5 per cent to nearly 7.5 per cent; France was increasing her exports three times as fast, Germany and Italy six times as fast, as Britain. Taking 1950 as 100, British productivity per man in 1960 stood at 125; the German and French figures for 1960 were 159 and 177 respectively. The halt in industrial expansion meant a decline in unfilled vacancies and an increase in unemployment to, in 1957, an average level over the year of 313,000: at the end of the year unemployment in the hardest-hit communities, Wales and Scotland, were 3 per cent and 2.9 per cent respectively, still very low figures by pre-war standards. In 1958 and early 1959 there was a definite recession and unemployment rose to 621,000, the highest figure since the fuel crisis of 1947: Wales, Scotland and the older industrial areas of England stood out as centres of high concentration of unemployment. Productivity was lost not only through unemployment, but also through strikes.[1]

But as Marwick also points out (p. 461), in spite of the characteristic inability to exploit the fact, the inventiveness and success of British technology in the 1950s and 1960s were outstanding.

The first turbo-jets to go into civilian operation in the later Forties were British; the first pure jet to go into scheduled civilian air services was the de Havilland Comet (May 1952) ... An outstanding international success in the mid-Sixties was the BAC One-Eleven, the world's first economical short-haul jet. Hovercraft was a British intervention... The world's first nuclear power station was that opened at Calder Hall in October 1956.

Working in conjunction with Aviation Sud in France, British Aircraft Corporation developed the Concorde in the late 1960s. Owing to its

---

[1]*Britain in the Century of Total War*, by Arthur Marwick, p. 421. Chapter 8, 'The Role of the Trade Unions', pp. 216–17 – for figures on strikes.

phenomenal development costs, Concorde has been a financial failure but it has been a very acceptable 'loss-leader' and one of the more agreeable products and manifestations of the 1960s.

8

The Role of the Trade Unions, 1945–1964

The victory of the Labour Party in 1945 was also a victory for the trade unions. The Party had grown out of the trade union movement (out of its bowels according to Ernest Bevin); the Party leadership owed its position largely to the support of the trade unions: the unions contributed massively (and would soon do even more so) to the party's financial and organizational resources. Before the war the unions had not been regarded as an estate of the realm. In 1921 and 1926 they had actually flirted with direct action. High unemployment, hostile legislation and, after 1931, an unsympathetic government had weakened their position. All this changed in 1940.[1]

In the later Middle Ages the three great estates of the realm were the Baronage, the Church and the Commons. The Church had long since ceased to be an estate of the realm, in the medieval sense of importance, so that to recognize the fact that the trade unions had taken the place of, and were as important as, the medieval church gives some idea as to their post-war transformation. In the narrower sense, we can say that the Baronage was replaced by the employers but, in the very nature of things, these could not become an effective collective body: thus the failure of the Confederation of British Industry and the Institute of Directors to assume an importance in any way comparable to the trade unions – and one of the many reasons why corporatism was a failure. In the wider sense, the place of the Baronage was taken by the vaguer, but much more important body, the Establishment, which, in the elitist sense, was such an important part of the post-war consensus – for good and for bad.

---

[1] *Consensus Politics from Attlee to Thatcher*, by Dennis Kavanagh and Peter Morris, Chapter 4, p. 41. Further facts and figures in this chapter are attributable to the above chapter on the Role of the Trade Unions.

I have already mentioned that

> the involvement of Labour ministers and the trade unions in the running of the economy during the war led to the enthusiastic belief that the nationalization of the 'commanding heights' of the economy (in Aneurin Bevan's words) would enable a socialist government to plan the use of the nation's resources within a mixed economy (p. 79)

and that Ernest Bevin, the leading pre-war trade unionist, became a key figure in the wartime government, organized labour, as Minister of Labour, and that, as Foreign Secretary, he was the most powerful member of the Attlee Government. Significantly, he was succeeded as Minister of Labour by George Isaacs, the Chairman of the TUC. During the war, the TUC was represented on national bodies such as the National Joint Advisory Council to the Ministry of Labour, the Central Production Advisory Council and numerous regional and local supervisory bodies for industry. The number of government committees on which trade unionists served increased from 12 in 1939 to 60 in 1948–49. In July 1944 the TUC's 'Interim Report on the Post-War Reconstruction' not only accepted the wage restraint advocated by the Coalition White Paper of 1944 on Employment but called for nationalization and the need for the unions to have 'a decisive share in the actual control of the economic life of the nation'. In the event, the unions were consulted on both the terms and the running of the various nationalization issues, especially in the case of the nationalization of the mines, by the Minister of Fuel, Emmanuel Shinwell. This was also a natural concomitant of the facts that union-sponsored MPs were appointed to 29 out of 81 positions in the new Government and that the former comprised 120 out of the 393 MPs elected.

It also follows that the early repeal of the 1927 Trade Disputes Act reversed each of that Act's restrictions on the unions, namely the abolition of secondary strikes, the restrictions on picketing, the need to contract-in to pay the political levy as opposed to contracting-out and the forbidding of civil service unions from affiliating to the Trade Union Congress, not to mention the Labour Party. With the possible exception of the last provision, the repeal of the 1927 Act was a retrograde step, for each of the so-called rights restored to the unions has been a major cause of trouble and weakness in our political, economic and social life (p. 42). I can well remember canvassing as a local government candidate in the late 1950s and the 1960s when, without exception, civil servants and local government officials, and the like, would courteously explain their position and that they could not divulge their party preference and, in many cases, they would be genuinely neutral and would not exercise their right to vote. How much superior that situation was to the present one whereby local government officials are not only elected members of other local authorities than that in which they are employed, but are actually paid for it, a state of affairs that has been horrendously abused, with disastrous political and economic consequences, by members of the Labour Party and the Labour Party itself.[1] The same criticism can be made of the 1946 decasualization instigated by the Dock Labour Act which led to a progressive and systematic abuse of the powers granted to the unions, on the one hand, and the emasculation of the employers, on the other, until the Act was repealed as late as 1990, but not until it had virtually destroyed the old-established docks that came under its aegis and which were such an important sector of our economy. The only relief is that the post-war docks which did not come under its dreaded provisions, have mushroomed successfully.

There were, however, reasons why these pro-union Acts should have been passed and why the Attlee governments should have taken the unions so much into their confidence. The first was the important and responsible part played by the unions during the war, the second was the post-war continuation of the unions' responsible attitude, especially in regard to wage restraint. I have already noted the importance of the TUC's acceptance, in an emergency conference, of Cripps's wage freeze in 1948 and the restraint exercised in this respect until 1950. Since 1945, the unions had also agreed to a continuation of the considerable wartime restriction of their right to strike (Order 1305) and to the acceptance of compulsory arbitration. They also fully supported the measures, including the use of troops, employed to defeat the outbreak of unofficial strikes in the docks in 1948 and 1949. This followed from the unions continuing with their strong pre-war hostility to Communism which was embodied in the TGWU's 1949 banning of Communists from holding office in the union. Nor was there any of the latter-day opposition to foreign and defence policy in which the Government was given full support by the unions, including its culmination in the American Alliance. Thirdly, there were the implications of the fact of the unions becoming a part of the post-war consensus, namely that the political (Conservative as well as Labour) and administrative elites, or establishment, recognized the advisability

---

[1]The provisions of the 1972 Local Government Act prevented local government officials sitting on councils employing them ('twin-tracking') while those of the 1989 Local Government and Housing Act further confined the practice by restricting the possibility of an officer in a 'politically restrictive post' becoming a councillor in another council.

111

of working with, and not against, the trade unions. This conclusion was also reinforced by the impressive post-war growth of trade union membership. The number of trade unionists contributing to the political levy increased by about 2 million to 7,540,000 between 1945 and 1947 and union contributions to Labour's funds (membership – 5,040,000) rose from 80 per cent in 1945 to 96 per cent in 1955, a financial support which was reinforced massively in the political field by the use of the block vote to support the Labour Party leadership against the left-wing, a situation which many subsequent leaders of the party must have looked back on with the utmost envy.

For all these reasons, especially the third, the post-war Conservative Party accepted the trade unions' new and powerful position, as an estate of the realm. This is in spite of the fact that there were some reservations which, in retrospect, must be regarded as notably prescient. For example, in 1947, the Party's 'Industrial Charter' (p. 376) advocated the restoration of contracting-in and the prohibition of any connection between trade unions and political parties, on both of which factors I have already commented. A Conservative Party resolution in the 1947 Party Conference criticized the 'subservience of the present Socialist Government to the TUC'. In 1951, Churchill opposed the closed-shop principle after it had been enforced by Durham County Council. Nevertheless, in the end, Churchill's Conservative Party went out of its way to conciliate and work with the unions, a policy which would have been reinforced by both the Leader and the Party Chairman, Lord Woolton, determining to overcome the pre-war reputation in regard to relations with the unions. It was for this reason that the Shadow Minister for Labour Affairs, before the 1951 election victory, David Maxwell-Fyfe, was not appointed Minister of Labour. Maxwell-Fyfe, very sensibly, was not happy about the concessions made to the unions in the repeal of the 1927 Trade Disputes Act, and when he merely hinted at the possibility of some revision of the Act, he was immediately discarded in place of Walter Monckton, an emollient lawyer and well-known fixer, who was brought into the Cabinet from outside political life specifically to work with Churchill in keeping the unions happy – or, 'sucking up' to them, to use an unlovely but meaningful expression, by widely consulting them and, of course, by never again mentioning the possibility of revising trade union legislation. The invitation of union leaders to 10 Downing Street receptions was unexceptional but the stories of Churchill and Monckton giving in to the unions' excessive wage demands and strike threats and of their dispensing whisky at 'Number 10' have passed into our historical folklore as some kind of 'sick joke'. It will be remembered that it was at the TUC Annual Congress in

1950 that the Labour Government's excellent record on the wages front received its first rebuff when by a narrow majority the Congress rejected wage restraint. Far from opposing this development, Churchill and Monckton rolled over like the proverbial spaniels. In 1952, the TUC extracted from Churchill a promise that the Government would not interfere with pay awards in future after the latter had questioned some wage council awards. In 1953, last-minute major concessions by the Government averted a major railway strike.

On the other hand, there was the more acceptable face of the post-war Conservative Party's acceptance of the trade unions. The reassessment of the Party's thinking, under Butler, was based on the Disraelian concept of 'One Nation', for as Disraeli said, and acted upon when he passed the 1867 Electoral Reform Act, 'Unless the Tory Party is a national party it is nothing.' It will also be remembered that, with Gladstone, Disraeli was responsible for enlightened legislation strengthening the unions' legal rights. It was in this spirit that the party in 1947 set up its Central Trade Union Advisory Committee. Although always something of a 'Cinderella', the Committee, from the outset, portrayed itself as the voice of enlightened and independent trade unionism. For example, nationalization was opposed during the 1951 election campaign on the grounds that it involved a conflict between the unions' duty to its members and a nationalizing government. Taking the argument further, trade unions should be independent of political parties, a point which Margaret Thatcher was making years later when she stated that she was 'restoring the unions to their members'. The Advisory Committee also came more into its own when, under the Thatcher revolution, large numbers of the more skilled and highly paid workers and unionists, the 'blue-collar' workers, voted Tory. But back in the days of the Churchill Government the situation was very different. Whereas the Conservative Party reached a record membership of 2,805,832 in 1953, in 1952 the Labour Party membership was 6,108,000 and that of the TUC was 8,020,000.[1] In the

---

[1] In 1993 membership of the Conservative and Labour parties was around 1 million and 200,000 respectively while the TUC remained at around 8 million after having been as high as around 11 million. Since then the Tory membership has settled at around 750,000 while Labour has attracted new members, bringing their total to around 350,000. The difference between the Conservative Central Office unofficial figure and the more pessimistic one of 300,000, which has been quoted, probably arises from the fact that the local Tory branches are still counting as members those who have not paid their subscriptions for a year or so, which in my view, is acceptable, provided that those members have not yet sent in their resignations.

face of such overwhelming numerical superiority (even taking into account the nominal natures of the figures and the ramifications of the contracting-out principle) one has a sneaking sympathy for the 'old war-horse' dispensing whisky to the trade union leaders. It is also another reason why the Conservative Government not only continued to appoint trade unionists to consultative committee and executive positions at both national and local levels but outdid the previous Labour Government. In 1953–54 and 1957–58 trade unionists were appointed to 81 and 65 Government committees, respectively, while it has been estimated that by 1958 the trade union representation on around 850 Government committees, including the National Production Advisory Council and all the economic planning boards, was equal to that of the employers. Well might Anthony Crosland have commented in 1956:

> One cannot imagine today a deliberate offensive alliance between Government and employers against the unions ... Instead the atmosphere in Whitehall is almost deferential, the desire not to give offence positively ostentatious.[1]

However, from the mid-1950s a change in the relationship between the unions and the government, and the two main parties, can be detected. Partly in spite of and partly because of, the appeasement of the Churchill years, the unions were becoming more militant. For example, in 1955 the first national strike for twenty years took place in the form of an extended railway strike by ASLEF while in 1957 the number of days lost through strikes (8.5 million) was the highest since 1926.

> In 1959 days lost totalled the still high figure of 5¼ millions, 3½ millions of them due to a national printing strike. Many strikes seemed to be over somewhat trivial matters, demarcation disputes between different trades, the timing of a tea-break; the popular Press introduced the pejorative American phrase 'wild-cat strikes'.[2]

There was also a pronounced change in the philosophy and attitudes of a new breed of trade union leaders, compared with Bevin, and Deakin who had died suddenly in 1955, and who was succeeded as leader of the important TGWU by the explicitly left-wing figure,

---

[1] Quoted in *Consensus Politics from Attlee to Thatcher*, by Dennis Kavanagh and Peter Morris, p. 57.
[2] *Britain in the Century of Total War*, by Arthur Marwick, p. 421.

Frank Cousins, after an eleven-month interregnum by the moderate 'Jock' Tiffin. Cousins initiated the retrograde step of transferring the main responsibility for wage bargaining from the national union leaders to the negotiators on the shop floor, the militant shop stewards, who became even more militant when Cousins reversed the ban on Communists occupying union offices. From this time on, there was no question of the unions co-operating with government appeals for wage restraint with the result that they came increasingly to be seen as, and to be, a problem for the Government, which was no less true in view of the fact that the unions continued to retain their position as a major national institution. The ability to handle the unions came to be one of the staple claims and counter-claims in the confrontations between the main two parties, in and out of office. In effect, the two parties' attempts when in government to deal with the union problem led to what was virtually a new consensus, namely government intervention in the economy in the form of wage and other controls and indicative planning (corporatism) all of which was to prove to be extremely unsuccessful. Finally, and very important, it was also from this time that the unions became increasingly unpopular with the public in view of the inconveniences they suffered through strikes and through disapproval of their 'bloody-minded' attitude. The situation was brutally summed-up by Arthur Koestler in an article in the *Observer* in February 1963:

> In no other country has the national output been crippled on such frivolous and irresponsible grounds. In this oldest of all democracies class relations have become more bitter, trade union policies more undemocratic than in De Gaulle's France and Adenauer's Germany. The motivation behind it is neither communism, socialism, nor enlightened self-interest, but a mood of disenchantment and cussedness.

This was to prove to be a great disadvantage to the Labour party in view of their close association with the unions, in spite of the fact that it made the opposite claim that this would enable a Labour Government to deal more effectively with them. In June 1964, Ray Gunter, the Labour MP, in his 'Socialist Commentary', warned the unions that the state would intervene in their affairs unless they reform themselves. The article was received with great hostility by the union leaders who were greatly concerned, at the time, by the judicial decision in the previous January in the Rookes v Barnard case which threatened the right of the trade unions to strike, by returning to the pre-1906 period when, as we have seen (p. 36), unions were liable to damages for strike action. The TUC Annual Congress in September demanded legislation to give unions the protection of the 1906 Trade Disputes Act once again.

9

The Welfare State, 1945–1964

By 1914 the Welfare State was already on the British political agenda. The State provided benefits for some citizens in old age, ill health and unemployment. Whereas pensions were non-contributory and means tested, the national insurance benefits were contributory but not means tested. Provision in Britain, however, ran behind that of the authoritarian German State, a reminder that social welfare and political democracy do not necessarily go hand-in-hand. In Germany, welfare provision was introduced in the late nineteenth century as a trade-off against social democracy. The government hoped that by introducing measures to alleviate social and economic distress it would dampen working-class demands for political control. The example of the United States where levels of provision have lagged behind those of Europe, is further evidence of the non-convergence of universal suffrage and collective social welfare provision.[1]

I would agree with the authors as to the actual situation in Germany regarding social welfare but not so much with their trade-off theory for the newly created 'German State' in 1870, following the defeat of the historically more important Austria by Prussia in 1866 and of France in 1870, which enabled Prussia to unite with Saxony and Bavaria and the many other smaller German states which survived from the medieval Holy Roman Empire, of which it was said that it was neither Holy, Roman nor an Empire. However, unlike England (Britain) there was absolutely no democractic tradition for as late as the eighteenth century the rulers of all these states, large and small, were Absolute Monarchs, of whom some were enlightened and others were not. Thus by 1870 democracy had very tender and tentative roots in Germany but, on the other hand, Prussian efficiency was making very strong roots indeed and the

---

[1]*Consensus Politics from Attlee to Thatcher*, by Dennis Kavanagh and Peter Morris, Chapter 5, p. 71. Further facts and figures in this chapter are attributable to the above-named chapter on The Welfare State.

superior German welfare provisions, educational system, and much else, were simply a reflection of this fact – as also was the unquestioning obedience of the efficient German people in supporting their two power-crazed leaders, neither of whom was subjected to any democratic or constitutional restraint, in the pursuance of two extremely bloody and fruitless world wars. The fact that Bismarck passed anti-Socialist legislation, aimed against the Social Democratic Party, is not proof of the 'trade-off theory' but confirmation of the political ethos in pre-1870 Prussia and post-1870 Germany. In regard to the United States and welfare, I would say that although there is virtue in the adequate provision of welfare there is absolutely none in what has come to be termed as 'welfare-dependence'.

However, to revert to the 'creation' of the British Welfare State (which we must acknowledge by using capital letters!), I have made the point earlier in the chapters dealing with pre-war political history, especially concerning the reforming Liberal Governments, that its foundations were well and truly laid then, as the following summary illustrates:

Statutory Reforms	Benefit	Applicable to
Old Age Pension Act 1908	One to five shillings per week	The over seventies with annual income of less than £31.00
Unemployed Workmans Act 1905	Small supplements: assisted emigration	Groups of unskilled casual workers
1910 Introduction of Labour Exchanges	Nationwide organization of labour market	All workers
National Insurance Act 1911	Seven shillings per week during unemployment. Ten shillings per week Sickness benefit.	Restricted to small groups of low wage trades only. Applied to all paying the fourpence weekly employees' contribution.[1]

Although by 1920 widows' and orphans' pensions had been introduced and unemployment insurance was extended to cover most workers, the limitation of unemployment benefit to a fifteen-week period proved to be completely inadequate in view of the large rise in unemployment in the 1920s and 1930s so that it became necessary to

---

[1]*British Politics*, by Philip Gabriel and Andrew Maslen, p. 168.

extend the benefits by payment of 'the dole'. It was the introduction of the 'means test' in 1929, as the depression intensified, that led to the dissatisfaction that I have already described and the determination that something better would take its place after the war, in spite of the fact that total government expenditure (central and local) on social services had increased from a quarter of all public expenditure in 1913 to a third in 1935. However, by 1939 only half the population, the wage-earning half, were covered by national health insurance and although this figure does not take account of the membership of 'friendly' societies (p. 125), by this time it had been agreed that the poverty arising from unemployment among large working-class families, and the like, should be a charge on the state. The authority on the subject asserts that the state would have to 'guarantee a national minimum' to its citizens and that among leading politicians this was 'a private political consensus by the end of the 1930s'.[1] Accordingly, the wartime National Government established supplementary pensions, supplied milk to mothers and babies together with milk and meals to all schoolchildren, culminating in the Education Act of 1944, providing universal free schooling to the age of 15 while in 1945, Family Allowances were provided out of general taxation.

If the Liberal Party was the precursor of the Welfare State, it was the Labour Party which claimed it for its own. Before the publication of the Beveridge Report in December 1942 it had staked its claim in a motion at the Labour Party Conference of that year which committed itself to: (a) a comprehensive system of social security, (b) adequate cash payments to provide security whatever the contingency, (c) the provision of cash payments from national funds for all children through a scheme of family allowance, and (d) the right to all forms of medical attention and treatment through the National Health Service. Nevertheless, it was the Beveridge Report which really put the Welfare State 'on the map'. Sir William Beveridge had been asked to study the existing schemes of social insurance and services and to make recommendations regarding their integration. However, what was expected to be a rather technical report became instead:

a new declaration of human rights brought up-to-date for an industrial society and dealing in plain and vigorous language with some of the most controversial issues in British politics.

---

[1]*British Social Policy*, 1914–1939, by B. Gilbert, p. vii.

To the consternation and annoyance of Winston Churchill who resented distractions from his all-embracing mission of defeating Hitler, the Report, published soon after the victory of El Alamein, became a national best-seller and mightily reinforced the private 'political consensus' regarding social welfare, mentioned above, and turned it into a national consensus. Churchill, and the other Conservative leaders in the Government, correctly thought that Beveridge's recommendations were far too extensive and financially questionable so that when it was debated in the House of Commons in the following February, the Government confined itself merely to accepting the Report in principle, hoping that that would be the end of the matter, but instead it found itself faced with the greatest challenge by Parliament to its authority during the war, and although it won the vote easily (338 to 121) the combined challenge of the mass of Labour, Liberal, and some Tory back-benchers, forced it to think again. Following the appointment of Lord Woolton, as Minister of Reconstruction, the result was the acceptance of the Beveridge Report in the 1944 White Paper on Employment but the Labour Party still criticized this as being inadequate, thus reinforcing the view of the British public that it was more likely to 'deliver the goods' after the war. Not that it did it much good at the time, but the Conservative Party was right not to accept the Report unquestioningly for as A.J.P. Taylor shrewdly observed, it:

> came some forty years too late and provided, as might be expected, against past evils: abject poverty and mass unemployment, one, the great social evil before 1914 and the other, between the wars. Neither was to present a problem after 1945.[1]

However, there was to be no stopping the 'band-wagon' of the Welfare State as envisaged by Beveridge whom, I have already said, called for 'full employment, universal social security and a National

---

[1] *English History, 1914–1945*, by A.J.P. Taylor, p. 567. I had the pleasure and privilege of having the great man as my Modern History tutor at Magdalen, Oxford, immediately after the war and it was typical of his irreverent attitude that he refused to tutor myself and a handful of war veterans for our chosen European subject of 'Eighteenth Century Europe' on the grounds that anything before 1789 was irrelevant in European history. We were thus sent to C.T. Atkinson, an old Magdalen man, who had written an excellent book on the subject and he turned out to be an absolute character. Although he was about 75 years of age he still referred to Magdalen as 'the College' even though he had been a tutor at Exeter, apart from the First War, since he had graduated. A bachelor, he must also have

Health Service'. In his words, he wanted to overcome the 'five giant evils of Want, Disease, Ignorance, Squalor and Idleness' and there were a number of assumptions or stipulations that he made in his recommendations. First, there should be a 'national minimum' standard of living below which people should not fall, the pre-war 'private political consensus' of which we have already spoken. Second, the scheme should be financed mainly through a universal national insurance scheme consolidating the existing schemes for pensions, unemployment, illness, maternity, widowhood and funeral expenses, as well as family allowances. There were to be contributions from employees and employers and only partial finance by government. Beveridge's explicit idea was that people should not get something for nothing and that they should have the incentive to do more for themselves and their families. He warned: 'The State in organising security should not stifle incentive, opportunity, responsibility', while his original idea of unemployment benefit was that it should 'normally be subject to a condition of attendance at a work or training centre after a certain period'. Thus, like Marx and Keynes, Beveridge could say that whatever he was he was not an exponent of the Welfare State degenerating into Welfare Dependence. Nevertheless, he did provide a safety net in the form of means-tested national assistance benefits for those who were not properly covered by insurance – as a temporary measure only, for he envisaged this would need to wither away (like Marx's 'state') in the near future. Little did he realize that this was to become a main and increasing charge on the Welfare State as the post-war standard of living rose ever higher and higher with a corresponding increase in the level of the 'poverty-line', not to mention the ravages of inflation. (By end-1993 the cost of Social Security had become by far the Government's greatest financial burden, consuming a third of public expenditure – £80 billion a year, three times what we spend on defence, six times what we spend on law and order and much more than we raise by

---

been the last of the Oxford misogynists (another Oxford lost cause) for he had never accepted the entry of women to Oxford. When lecturing, he would make this point obvious at the beginning of term (including the use of doubtful language) and when the last of the women undergraduates had given up the class he would rub his hands together and say 'Now gentlemen, we can relax and enjoy ourselves.' Goodness knows what he would think of the present unnecessary and trendy situation whereby men are in women's colleges and women are in men's colleges and men run women's colleges while the distinguished Ancient Historian, Professor Averil Cameron, became the first woman Warden of Keble College, in October 1994.

income tax).[1] Thirdly, and mainly, Beveridge was concerned that benefits should be provided uniformly and equally and that, apart from the above 'temporary' exception, there should be no means test. The corollary of the universality, as opposed to the selectivity, of benefits and the absence of the means test was that there should be a flat-rate insurance payment by all: it was to be equality from beginning to end. In other words, Beveridge decided to adopt the uniform poll tax used by Lloyd George in his original 1911 National Insurance Act. In the hue and cry following the use of the uniform local rate for the 1989 Community Charge it was not appreciated by those who denigrated this as a 'Poll Tax' that this is by now a well-established British form of taxation, in spite of the efforts of John Ball and Wat Tyler and the other leaders of the Peasants' Revolt (against the poll tax) in 1381.

In the application of Beveridge's three main requirements in order to overcome the Five Giant Evils, I have already dealt with the post-war efforts to fulfil the full employment requirement. The remainder were embodied in the following Welfare Statutes, of which the first two were passed by Churchill's Coalition Government:

1944 Education Act:	Free secondary education for everyone and leaving age raised from 14 to 15.
1945 Family Allowance Act:	Made available out of general taxation
1946 National Insurance Act:	Benefits for the unemployed, sick, retired and widows: implemented in 1948.
1946 National Health Service Act:	Established to provide free medical service: implemented in 1948.
1948 National Assistance Act:	To provide benefits for those who did not have a complete record of contributions.

In regard to the two most important of these acts, the National Insurance Act and the National Health Service Act, the very foundations of the Welfare State, the Attlee Government adopted the Beveridge recommendation of universality with its implication that all

---

[1] In 1995–96 it is around £90 billion.

122

would have equal rights to social welfare, a policy which was both left-wing and collectivist. The opponents of the scheme, in and out of Parliament, argued correctly that it was based more on left-wing ideology than the needs of the poor and that these could be provided with more and better benefits if the principle of selectivity were applied. However, in view of the left-wing predilections of the Government and the Labour Party and the strength of the Welfare State consensus at the time, not to mention hostility to anything smacking of a means test, there was little point in doing anything more than expressing this sensible point of view. On the other hand, the whole of life is a means test. People with some degree of wealth spend their money in entirely different ways. One man might live very modestly so that he can enjoy owning a Rolls Royce while another might prefer to run a middle-range family saloon so that he can spend more money on holidays. What must be avoided at all costs, both politically and morally, is the 'politics of envy'. Besides, with the onset of post-war affluence, the objection to a means test is a good example of the socialist tendency to fight battles that have been won long ago. But back to 1946: the Conservative Opposition wisely declined to oppose both the second and third reading of the National Insurance Bill.

The preamble of the Act stated that it was designed 'to establish an extended system of national insurance providing pecuniary benefits by way of unemployment benefit, retirement pensions, widows' benefit, guardians' allowances and death grant'. It was compulsory for everyone of working age except for pensioners, married women and the self-employed earning less than £104.00 per annum. However, the Act applied the true Beveridge principle in that benefits, including sickness benefit, could only be drawn if the recipient had paid their share of national insurance contributions while benefits could only be claimed for a limited period. The more left-wing Labour back-benchers attempted unsuccessfully to establish the principle that the unemployed had an absolute right to maintenance. On the other hand, the Conservative Opposition succeeded in ensuring that benefits should be paid immediately to the unemployed self-employed compared with a time-lag of thirteen weeks suggested by Beveridge and of twenty-four days in the original Bill. In all, there were three categories of person entitled to become insured under the Act, and the rates paid varied with each category: employed persons who were eligible for all benefits, the self-employed who were eligible for all benefits except unemployment benefit and the non-employed who were ineligible for sickness and unemployment benefits. Finally, and most important, benefits were not open-ended, in the sense of their being tied to a cost of living index so that the assumption was that they could be supplemented by the individual arranging for additional private cover. This meant that the Act did nothing to establish a 'national minimum' in accordance with Beveridge's intentions and it was one of two important ways in which it deviated from Beveridge. The other was the continuation of the 'means test', as embodied in the 1948 National Assistance Act, and although, as had already been said, this was intended to be a temporary measure, it did in fact, become permanent. On a point of detail, Beveridge had recommended the establishment of a Ministry of Social Security for the administration of such benefits but the 1948 Act established a National Assistance Board, with regional area officers administering the means test. Nevertheless, although there were to be a number of ways in which the Welfare State was to depart from Beveridge's 'blue print', it cannot be denied that his hand is indelibly imprinted on it. It remains to deal with the establishment of the National Health Service.

By the eighteenth century the educated and richer townsmen objected to dirty drinking water, uncollected refuse, filthy ditches, muddy streets and footwalks, and the lack of street lighting so that although rates had been levied well before the eighteenth century, Parliament passed Acts empowering the formation of local councils with the right to collect local taxes or rates to spend on these improvements. The rates met with a great deal of resistance, for bad sanitation and the like were regarded only as a discomfort and not as an agent of disease, a view which altered radically as a result of the first massive outbreak of cholera in England in 1831, leading to numerous deaths. The struggle for town sanitation was led by Edwin Chadwick and John Simon, and it led to the various Town 'clauses' Act of 1847 and the Public Health Act of 1848, following the Report of the Royal Commission on the Health of Towns in 1845, a major social document. Thus, by the middle of the century, the local councils in most of the large towns provided hospitals in order to separate people suffering from infectious diseases from other patients, and prevented the building of houses which were damp or otherwise unhealthy. In 1872 these services were made compulsory nationally, culminating in the Public Health Act of 1875 dealing with sewage disposal, water supplies and the isolation of persons suffering from infectious diseases. The main object of this legislation was to provide healthy surroundings for people to live in, for it was assumed that this was the extent of the responsibility of the authorities, national and local, and it was not until after the First World War that the general public expected and the local health services accepted that they should serve persons, as opposed to districts, in the fight against disease and ill-health. After 1918, the local councils organized welfare services which gave medical treatment and advice to mothers and their young children, free of charge, together with the provision of doctors and midwives for childbirth, all of which led to a radical improvement in the rate of infant mortality. The health of pre-World War II children was also protected by the school medical services whereby the children of all local authority schools (the majority) were inspected medically and treated, free of charge of course, where necessary. For the adults, especially the half who did not contribute to the old National Insurance Scheme, the local authorities built many hospitals to which people were admitted free of charge. Our original hospitals were charitable foundations, the earliest being founded by the monasteries, as a part of their concern and care for the poor, such as St Bartholomew's in the twelfth century and St Thomas's in the thirteenth century, in London, the citizens of which made heroic efforts to save them after the dissolution of the monasteries. For example, St Bartholomew's passed into the hands of the Rich family, great Essex landowners. Indeed, by the first half of the seventeenth century London could boast a comprehensive, charitable and health provision – a veritable 'welfare state'. It was in this beneficent spirit that private charities and philanthropists continued to found hospitals, especially from the beginning of the eighteenth century when, between 1720 and 1745, Guy's, Westminster, St George's, London and Middlesex Hospitals were founded, as well as lying-in hospitals in the main towns, and those in the counties. Thus, by 1936 there were nearly a thousand voluntary hospitals, including small cottage hospitals and the great teaching hospitals in London and Edinburgh. Including the local authority hospitals, the pre-war total was in the region of 1,500.

Before moving on to the creation of the National Health Service, which became a national shibboleth, beyond criticism, it is worth making the point that the pre-war health set-up, private and public, had within itself the seeds of a system, when post-war affluence is taken into account, which would almost certainly have developed into one as effective as the National Health Service, but based more on selectivity, with a health insurance content, and therefore posing less of a financial drain and administrative strain on the state, than the post-war system, besides being able to concentrate more resources and effort on the needy. As early as 1909 more than 75 per cent of the working class belonged to 'friendly' societies to which they paid voluntarily something in the region of 3d a week for which they received all the health service benefits that the NHS provided after

1948. By 1948 it was only a small number of the more irresponsible poor who did not make provision although they were treated free in the voluntary hospitals, many of which were thus fulfilling their original function. It is true that the pre-war system lacked the economic resources to cope with the increasing demand for medical services and that there was variation in both the quality and quantity of treatment in various parts of the country, but it is not legitimate to compare it unfavourably with its post-war successor for, left to itself, it would have developed significantly in response to the demands and challenges of the post-war scene, as it has done in the rest of Europe.

However, it has been argued that by 1939 there was already a consensus for a national scheme.[1] Reports in the pre-war years such as the Dawson Report (1920) and a Royal Commission on National Insurance (1926) favoured this solution while the Socialist Medical Association had been active since the 1920s, advocating that there should be a full-time salaried medical service responsible to local authorities and working through local health centres. It was, of course, a part of Beveridge's plan, and the Coalition Government's White Paper of 1944 envisaged a national health service while the Conservative manifesto of 1945 proposed a 'comprehensive health service' as well as a social security system based on Beveridge. As we have noted already, the Welfare State consensus was a dominant factor with the electorate which therefore entrusted the Labour Party to impose it so that the National Health Service, the first in the Western world to provide free medical care for the entire population, was inevitably created in a consciously collectivist and egalitarian state of mind – and all evidence proves that such creations are bound to fail in practice. As a schoolmaster in the 1950s, I remember telling my sixth form pupils, at a time when it was uncritically accepted and even admired, that it would develop into 'a financial and administrative colossus that would eventually devour us all'.

Talking of colossi, there is no doubt that the outstanding personality, ability and beliefs of Aneurin Bevan, the Minister of Health responsible for the enormous task of setting up this collectivist monster, had an influence on the outcome, both at the time and since, out of all proportion to that usually associated with such ministerial responsibility. Apart from the gigantic scale of the operation, he had to contend with the implacable opposition of the major vested interest of the collective body of the general

---

[1] *The Politics of the National Health Service*, by R. Klein, p.3.

practitioners, the British Medical Association. The specialists, represented by the Royal College of Surgeons and the Royal College of Physicians, caused no great opposition for, being numerical, but extremely important, minorities it was comparatively easy to reconcile their interests with the new service. Also, unlike the National Insurance Bill, the Conservative opposition to the National Health Bill was much more vigorous. In spite of the fact that the Conservatives had accepted the principle of the comprehensive health services, 100 per cent acceptance was probably confined to the Tory Reform Group, led by the ever-flexible Butler, for there was strong criticism on grounds of costs, universality as opposed to selectivity, the threat to the individual's right to his family doctor and to the nationalization of the hospitals, with all that this implied in regard to local ownership, charitable foundations and the local authorities.

The nationalization of the hospitals was the first of the two major decisions that Bevan took in forming the National Health Service, the first being good, initially at least, and the second bad – and it will be dealt with later. As has already been mentioned, one of the problems was the great variation in the quantity and quality of health service in the country with, for example, the South-East having a disproportionate number of doctors and up-to-date equipment. It had been assumed by everyone, including Beveridge, the wartime government, the post-war Conservative Party and, above all, the Labour Party, with its historic strength in local government in highly populated areas, that this would play a key part in the new health service, following on from its importance in the health field before the war. However, Bevan, correctly, had no faith in the ability of the local authorities to achieve uniform standards in a decentralized health service so that to the amazement and consternation of Labour people such as Herbert Morrison, who had been nurtured on local government, he imposed the extremely radical solution of nationalizing the nation's hospitals in order to create a National Health Service on a rational basis. It is significant that at a time when the Labour Government was embarking on a spate of doctrinaire nationalization which was destined to impose an enormous economic drain on the state, there was little or no appreciation of the fact that a national service, whether health or otherwise (such as education), could never satisfactorily be run by local authorities if it was to be uniform and economic. Whereas I commend the 1990 reform of the Health Service by the Thatcher Government to give the hospitals a significant measure of independence and financial responsibility, I still support Bevan's nationalization of the hospitals in 1948 on the grounds that they had to be prized away from the local authorities in order to give them their independence at a later date. On the other hand, it can be argued that by nationalizing the hospitals the Labour Party itself began the process of reducing 'democratic accountability' when it created the NHS – but, in the last resort, Labour governments always plump for the collectivist, as opposed to the individualist, approach: thus the continuous propaganda about 'uncaring' Thatcherism both by Labour spokesmen and the egregious 'chattering classes'.

An inevitable result of the collectivist-style nationalization of the hospitals was the creation of a new administrative structure which only has to be described to indicate how it became a bureaucratic nightmare, the main feature of which has been the non-stop growth of its bureaucrats:

> Fourteen regional hospital boards, each centred on the medical faculty of a university and appointed by the Minister of Health were to be set up. These, in turn, were to appoint the management committees of 388 hospitals within the system, although in the case of thirty-six teaching hospitals the boards of governors were to be appointed by the Minister himself. In Scotland the situation was slightly different. The National Health Service (Scotland) Bill proposed five regional boards (four based on the ancient universities, the fifth based on Inverness) and eighty-four hospital boards of management. In Scotland teaching hospitals were not to be separately administered except insofar as medical education committees, appointed partly by the Secretary of State for Scotland, partly by the regional boards and partly by the universities, were to be set up to advise the regional boards on matters concerning teaching and research.[1]

The way in which Bevan succeeded in overcoming the extreme hostility of the general practitioners is a tribute to the great strength of his personality, as well as to his unexpected facility for compromise, and has been well described by our authority:

> In Britain as a whole a new administrative structure was to be established respecting the general practitioner, primarily, it may be said, as a result of pressure from within the medical profession itself. Thus the supervision of general practice was to be assigned to 138 executive councils in England and Wales (twenty-five in Scotland) on which local professional interests were strongly

---

[1] *Post-War Britain* by Alan Sked and Chris Cook, p. 43.

represented (twelve members out of twenty-five). These councils were to employ general practitioners, Bevan having rejected the idea that doctors should be in direct contact with the Ministry of Health or with local authorities. In similar fashion, Bevan had also rejected the idea of a full-time salaried service. He could not see how under such a system the doctor's right to refuse a patient or the patient's right to choose a doctor could be adequately upheld. Moreover this had been the issue over which the doctors had been complaining most. He therefore proposed as a method of payment the combination of a small basic salary plus capitation fees according to the numbers on the doctor's lists. Private practice, therefore, could continue as before and the medical profession was requested in return to co-operate in correcting the maldistribution of general practitioners by accepting a twofold system of controls. A Medical Practices Committee was to be established to prevent doctors setting up practices in areas in which they were not really needed, while the buying and selling of practices was to be stopped within the service. Bevan believed that as a result of these proposals he could create a health service which would not only be national in character but which would protect the professional interests of doctors.[1]

Whereas in February 1948 a BMA plebiscite indicated that about 90 per cent of its members opposed the plan, this had fallen to 64 per cent by April and on 5 July 1948, the date of the inauguration of the service, about 90 per cent (over 20,000) joined the service. By September, 93 per cent of the population had joined the scheme which covered general hospital and specialist services, research, bacteriological services, blood transfusions etc., domestic help, mental health services, general medical services, pharmaceutical services, general dental services and supplementary ophthalmic services. However, a number of 'local health services' were left in the hands of the large local authorities, the county and county borough councils, namely health centres, maternity and child welfare, domiciliary midwifery, health visiting, home nursing, vaccination and immunization, prevention of illness (care and after-care) and ambulance services. These services can all be regarded as either genuinely 'local' or capable of being run 'locally', with one exception, the ambulance service. No doubt, Bevan and his civil servants were pressurized to retain the pre-war, 'fuddy-duddy', local authority organization of this service but a splendid opportunity was missed to turn it into a national service with a much improved

---

[1] *Post-War Britain* by Alan Sked and Chris Cook, pp. 43–4.

129

career structure, economy in the purchase and maintenance of the fleet of ambulances, and geographical and administrative organization on a rational instead of an arbitrary local authority basis, thus eliminating duplication of the services, and the like. Finally, as before 1945, the medical inspection of schoolchildren, the provision of milk and, where necessary, of meals was left to the local authorities.

It was because of this measure of local authority involvement and the sharing of the cost with the central government, that one twentieth of the cost of the National Health Service was to come directly from the national insurance contributions.[1] But this was the full extent of the use of the national insurance contributions for the NHS owing to the second, and unfortunate, major decision by Bevan in setting up the service, namely his rejection of the insurance principle of funding the service which instead was to be unfunded and a charge on the state; that is to say, the taxpayer. This decision also left the NHS vulnerable, and without any effective answer, to the development of what has amounted to the situation in which the demand for its services has become, increasingly, unlimited. In doing this he went against the majority practice in the Western World and, as we have seen, directly against the recommendation and beliefs of Beveridge who wanted to encourage individual responsibility in the matter and who was interested in administrative efficiency and convenience and not in collectivism and egalitarianism, unlike the left-wing Bevan and the Labour intelligentsia, such as Tawney and Titmus, whose deceptively 'harmless' views permeated the grass roots. The result, not realized at the time by those 'woolly-minded' idealists, was to 'politicize' the Health Service owing to the fact that the Minister of Health had to compete for funds with the Treasury and with the ministers responsible for other services such as education and defence. Even worse, the elevation of the NHS into a national shibboleth, beyond criticism, following years of propaganda and brain-washing has had disastrous effects. How can it be believed for a minute that one of the largest organizations in the world, financially and numerically, should not be subject to continuous scrutiny with a view to improving performance by reorganizing and restructuring, and the like. And yet when even the slightest move was made in this direction, such as closing down a cottage hospital, the hue and cry was deafening. The result was that until 1990 the monster had remained unreformed for all these years, and even the radical

---

[1] *Post-War Britain* by Alan Sked and Chris Cook, p. 44.

130

Margaret Thatcher had perforce to give 'lip-service' to her determination to 'uphold' the National Health Service. Finally, in the period with which we are dealing at the moment (1945–1964), the Labour Party was for ever boasting of its post-war welfare reforms and that these would be jeopardized by the Conservatives. For example, the Labour 1955 election manifesto stated:

> Through the National Health Service and National Insurance the Labour Government began to abolish the fear of old age, sickness and disablement which haunted working class life before the war.

In the event, although the emphasis was different (equality of opportunity as opposed to social justice and the like), the Conservatives, in their own way, adopted the Welfare State as their own and in 'the thirteen wasted years' (1951–1964) there was a significant increase in spending on the NHS and welfare – and so it has continued from that day to this.[1]

However, as far back as the late 1950s the emergence of the 'age of affluence' alongside the intensification of the problems posed by budget deficits and adverse balances of payments, led to the re-emergence of the doubts expressed by Churchill and his Conservative colleagues when the Beveridge Report was first published, although at this stage it was confined to radical Conservative such as the Bow Group and radical Liberals, usually academics. Then, as now, the principle of universal, as opposed to selective, benefits was queried in regard to their financial viability, organizational practicability and, most important, as to whether the needs of the poor were being sacrificed on the altar of equality.[2] The belief was also expressed that, in an 'affluent society', the Welfare State should eventually become redundant[3] and that the object should be 'to restore the freedom of each individual to spend his income as he thinks best or to save it in order to provide for some future emergency'.[4] It was a short step from this view to recommending that people should be able to

---

[1] The Conservative Government had embarked after 1979 and well before 1990 on a programme of closing old hospitals and developing new, purpose-built, modern ones. The 1987 Campaign Guide suggested that, by then, the largest hospital-building programme in NHS history had been under way for eight years.
[2] *Choice in Welfare*, 1963, by A. Seldon; *Future of the Welfare State*, 1964, by P. Goldman.
[3] *Reform of the Social Services, Bow Group Principles into Practice*, 1961, by G. Howe, p. 59.
[4] *Ibid.*, p. 60.

contract-out of the National Health Service.[1] On all these grounds, the universal payment of family allowances, which did not apply to the first child, was attacked for being insufficient to help the poor and unnecessary for the rich, or even the moderately rich. Consequently, even though the allowances were liable to income tax, the Conservative Government introduced the principle of graduation in 1956 – 3s per week for the second child, 10s for the third and subsequent children. From that day to this there has been a strong minority group of Conservative MPs who have adopted the maintenance of universal family benefits as a principle which should not be violated under any circumstances. It is an outlook which I find entirely incomprehensible – in the context of Conservative MPs.

---

[1]*Ibid.*, p. 70.

10

Foreign and Defence Policy, 1945–1964

(The retreat from Empire, Britain's role as a nuclear power and membership of the Atlantic Alliance)

At the end of the war Britain was the only imperial and West European state with the status of a world power. Between 1945 and 1951 the Labour Government began a process of disengagement from empire, starting with the grant of independence to India and Pakistan in 1947, and promoted the idea of the Commonwealth, an association of equal states. It also helped to create the American-led Atlantic Alliance and started to develop an independent nuclear deterrent. Membership of European economic and political institutions was not at this time on the political agenda but became so in the 1960's. Questions of defence posture (particularly on the retention of nuclear weapons) and possible membership of the new European Community caused significant divisions in the Labour Party and, to a lesser degree, within the Conservatives. Yet these questions did not, apart from the period of Hugh Gaitskell's leadership of the Labour Party, cause difficulties for the leadership of either party.[1]

In summary, the post-war foreign policy and defence consensus, inaugurated by the post-war Labour Government was the creation of the Atlantic Alliance, the development of an independent nuclear deterrent, the process of imperial disengagement and reluctant Europeanism. Britain's post-war international situation was described by the prescient Churchill, immediately after the war, as consisting of three interlocking circles – in Europe, in the Empire and in the Atlantic 'special relationship'. This consensus has been described as 'damagingly overextended, both economically and

---

[1] *Consensus Politics from Attlee to Thatcher*, by Dennis Kavanagh and Peter Morris, pp. 5–6. Further facts and figures in this chapter are attributable to Chapter 6 on Foreign and Defence Policy, pp. 90–108, in this authority.

politically'[1] but such criticism of the consensus is no more than an interesting academic exercise – a classic case of reading history backwards in the sense of being wise after the event, or merely rationalizing. It is legitimate to write history in the vein of saying what should have been done or not done, provided that this idealistic point of view and objective is made clear at the outset, but any realistic and worthwhile history of a period should describe situations as they really were and should identify changes in attitude and policy as they came about in real life and not in the imagination of the historian in his ivory tower, many years later. For example, after the granting of independence to India in 1947 the Foreign Secretary, Bevin, stated in the House of Commons:

> So far as foreign policy is concerned we have not altered our commitments in the slightest ... His Majesty's Government do not accept the view ... that we have ceased to be a great power, or the contention that we have ceased to play that role. We regard ourselves as one of the powers most vital to the peace of the world, and we still have our historic part to play.

In spite of the fact that it was immediately accepted that Britain did not have the economic or military strength of the two Great Powers, Bevin's statement was quite literally true, in view of Britain's unique and outstanding performance in the war, of the weakness of the other West European countries (both victors and vanquished) and of the extent of the British Empire, which was greater in 1945 than ever before. Also, in accordance with our historic tradition this consensus, put forward by a Labour Government, many of whose leaders were virtually pacifists before the war, was marked by pragmatism and an absence of ideology, qualities which can only exist when there is a high degree of political agreement about ultimate political purposes and national identity.[2] This remains true in spite of significant differences over the years over issues such as the Boer War, the Spanish Civil War, appeasement in the 1930s and the Suez Crisis of 1956. It compared more than favourably with the political, military and moral disintegration of France during the war itself and in coping with the post-war crises in Indo-China, the American denouement in Vietnam, and Algeria – until in the last case she was rescued by yet another autocratic leader, Charles de Gaulle.

---

[1]*The Changing British Political System: into the 1990's*, by Ian Budge and David McKay, p. 199.
[2]*British Foreign Policy*, by J. Frankel, p. 32.

As with Stafford Cripps and Aneurin Bevan, Ernest Bevin, the man responsible for our post-war foreign and defence policy, was a man of outstanding character and intellect who implanted his giant personality on events and their solutions. Above all, he was a traditionalist and a pragmatist – in keeping with the traditions mentioned above. At a time when Labour left-wingers, such as Michael Foot and Richard Crossman, were venting their anti-Americanism by propagating grandiose ideas about Britain and the Commonwealth forming a 'third force' to contend with the USA and the USSR, the pragmatic Bevin recognized Britain's post-war weakness in comparison with the other two powers, and the futility of playing one off against the other, and rejected impractical notions such as the above by unerringly allying with the United States with a view to that country taking Britain's traditional place of maintaining a worldwide balance of power and furthering the cause of democracy and freedom. This is where Bevin's ability and powerful personality were of the utmost importance for such an eventuality was by no means inevitable. The United States had expected to withdraw all its troops from Europe at the end of the war, while we have already noted its hostility towards Britain's economic policy, by the precipitate ending of Lend-Lease, and the like, and its attitude to the 'threat' of British and European imperialism to which it gave voice by criticism in its popular press and elsewhere, between 1944 and 1947 of British policy in Palestine and by the support of the Indonesian nationalists against the Dutch colonialists. However, Bevin was not to be deflected in his main objective which was to make the ties of the United States and its troops to Europe, irrevocable. This he did as a result of the Truman Doctrine, the Marshall Plan (both in 1947) and finally, and the most important, of the North Atlantic Treaty of 1949 and the Atlantic Alliance.

As early as 1941, Roosevelt had included in the Atlantic Charter, negotiated by him and Churchill, 'the right of all people to choose the form of government under which they will live' and until his death in April 1945 he had complete faith that Stalin would help him to bring about 'a world of democracy and peace' through the self-determination of peoples since, in his belief, the Russians had 'no crazy ideas of conquest' whereas he distrusted Churchill's obsession with 'power politics'. On the other hand, from the earliest days of the war Stalin's objectives were those of Russian imperialism throughout the centuries, to gain control of, or to dominate Central and Eastern Europe and as much of Central Asia as possible. Stalin used the wartime conferences at Teheran, Yalta and Potsdam, and his

135

subsequent negotiations with the Allied leaders, to further these aims so that before the war had ended he had delineated the boundaries of the German occupation zones and the spheres of influence of the Allied powers. With his profound understanding of history and his appreciation of Stalin's character, Churchill was, of course, acutely aware of these inherent dangers which could have been largely obviated by his plan to invade Vienna, Prague or Berlin (the 'soft-underbelly' of Europe) before the arrival of the Russians. Far from doing this, the Americans, in the persons of Eisenhower and Truman made no attempt to exploit the fact that they found themselves, at the time of the German surrender, more than 100 miles beyond the boundary agreed upon with the Russians and unnecessarily surrendered a vast area of around 30,000 square miles to them as well as handing over millions of refugees who were being virtually consigned to a certain death or slavery in Russia. Also, let alone encouraging the creation of democratic governments in Russia's client states, in 1947 and 1948 Stalin imposed dependent communist governments on Poland, Hungary, Bulgaria, Romania and Czechoslovakia.

Yet even before these ominous developments, the purblind leaders of the United States had perforce to recognize the mounting threat of Stalin's ambitions, notably in Greece, Turkey and Iran – all areas outside the main European theatre. Both Russian and British troops entered Iran in 1941 when that country threatened to go over to Hitler but whereas the latter were withdrawn in 1946 the former remained with the obvious intention of exercizing a permanent influence. At the same time, the Russians attempted to impose a treaty on Turkey which would, in effect, have made it a Russian satellite. As a consequence, Britain and the United States made their hostility known to the Soviet Union in no uncertain terms regarding its policy in Iran and Turkey, and in August 1946 a naval contingent was despatched to the Mediterranean by the United States. The action was successful, for Russia withdrew her troops from Iran and Turkey made no concessions to Russia. However, the first post-war example of physically resisting communist pressure was taken by Britain in Greece where a civil war had been taking place even before the defeat of the German occupiers and which would have been won by the Communists had it not been for the landing and active intervention of a comparatively small British force, leading to the signing of a truce in January 1945. In spite of a general election in March 1946, won by the right wing, Greece's position remained precarious for the economy was exhausted by the war and she was surrounded by communist neighbours, namely Albania and

Yugoslavia where the communist partisans had established governments, and Bulgaria which had been occupied by the Russian Army. Greece was saved by Britain financing, equipping and training her army.

By the spring of 1946, Churchill had sufficient confidence to make his famous speech at Fulton, Missouri (already mentioned in regard to his ambitions for Europe) in which he said that 'an iron curtain had descended across Europe from Stettin to Trieste' and that 'our difficulties and dangers will not be removed by mere waiting to see what happens; nor will they be relieved by a policy of appeasement.' Unbelievably, the Americans had opposed Britain's successful action in Athens in 1945 and the great man's 'Iron Curtain' speech did not particularly impress them. However, it was events in Greece that were to decide the issue, although the mounting evidence of Russian recalcitrance during 1946 was gradually affecting the attitude of those ensconced in the White House. In the autumn of 1946, the Greek Communists who were being armed by their communist neighbours, embarked on a guerilla war which by spring 1947 was threatening to be successful, with the prospect of Turkey and Iran falling to the Communists, as well as Greece. Also threatened were Italy, with her strong and aggressive communist party and to a lesser extent, but for the same reason, France. The Eastern Mediterranean suddenly appeared to be extremely vulnerable and with exquisite timing Bevan let it be known in February 1947 that Britain was in no financial position to aid Greece and Turkey in their struggle against communist domination and that if this were to be done it would need to be by the United States, alone. Truman, ever a man of decision and action, in three weeks accepted that challenge when he said to a joint session of Congress in March: 'I believe it must be the policy of the United States to support free peoples who are resisting attempted subjugation by armed minorities or by outside pressure.' In other words, the United States would support any 'free people' struggling against Communism. In this case, financial, civilian and military aid were given to Greece and Turkey but, more important, President Truman had virtually announced an historic turning-point in the history and foreign policy of the United States – the rejection of isolationism and the assumption of the role that had been played by Britain for so many years, the maintenance of the balance of power in the western world and for that matter, the world. Bevin had thus taken the first step in achieving his primary objective, and the answer to the critics of his policy, and that of his successors in shaping our foreign policy, is that he envisaged Britain as paying a secondary but, nevertheless, a supporting role. It is also the answer to Dean

Acheson's unconstructive criticism in 1959 that Great Britain had lost an Empire but had not yet found a role, a point which seems all the more apposite as this is being written during the Gulf War.

Turkey, the 'sick man of Europe' throughout the nineteenth century, finally collapsed during the First World War when she joined Germany. After her defeat in Asiatic Turkey by the British, with the help of the Arabs and T.E. Lawrence (of Arabia), Syria, Palestine, Iraq and Arabia and their Arab inhabitants were freed from the hated Turk after six centuries of ruthless occupation. Hussein, the Grand Sheriff or Governor of Mecca, which position the Moslem Turks could not deny to this hereditary Arab family, and who had been the man with whom and through whom the British organized the Arab Revolt against their Turkish masters, became the independent overlord of Arabia proper, and his second son Abdulla, gained Transjordan. (Abdulla's grandson is King Hussein of Jordan.) Although Britain had conquered Mesopotamia (Iraq), including the oil-rich Mosul, Palestine (by General Allenby in December 1917) and Syria, the field of much of Colonel Lawrence's legendary exploits, with the invaluable help of Feisal, Hussein's third and most able son, she had to take account of France and, to a lesser extent, Russia, in the subsequent settlement. Whereas Britain had a 'protectorate' in Egypt and Sudan since 1882, and had recently acquired an 'influence' in Persia (Iran), France had more formal protectorates in Tunis and Morocco, and ever since the Crusades, had an absorbing interest in the Levant (Syria). In January 1916 Syria, including Damascus, Aleppo and Beirut, was allotted to France, and Iraq and Palestine to Britain, while Russian agreement was obtained by ceding Turkish Armenia, the present Moldavia, to her. The Kurds formed a separate nation in their own right but nothing was done about them so that they formed minorities in all these countries split-off from the old Ottoman Empire, including those still remaining in Turkey itself. In view of the continued problems in the Middle East, it is worth pursuing the outcome of these arrangements which were hideously complicated owing to the fact that simultaneously Hussein, who had asked for a British guarantee of independence for all Arab lands as a reward for the revolt against Turkey, was granted his wish, although there were vague British reservations that she could not disregard French interests (in Syria) and that Basra and Baghdad (Iraq) would be subject to British control. However, in spite of the first reservation and in response to Lawrence's pleadings with the British authorities not to let the Arabs down, Feisal was allowed to set up an Arab Kingdom in Syria, but by 1920 France had expelled him. What with this and similar problems in Palestine, the sensitive Lawrence

138

returned to Oxford to write *The Seven Pillars of Wisdom* and spent the rest of his life in purdah. The last was not to be heard of Feisal for the British transferred his kingdom to Iraq and it was one of his successors who was replaced by the Ba'athist revolutionaries, one of whom, Saddam Hussein, has ruled the country since 1968. In the meantime, the British were expelled from Iran in 1921 following a nationalist uprising led by an ambitious and able soldier, Reza Khan, who deposed the feeble ruler and himself became Shah in 1925. It was his descendant who was deposed by the dreaded Shiite fundamentalist, Ayatollah Khomeini. Unfortunately, the main Arab kingdom set up by Hussein in Saudi Arabia did not last. Although he was an honest man, Hussein had considerable defects of character which were embodied in his excessive jealousy of his able son, Feisal, and his extreme tactlessness such as when he proclaimed himself, 'King of the Arab Nation' in October 1916 and, again, 'Commander of the Faithful', once ensconced in Mecca in 1918. One of the many people whom he upset on both occasions was a warlike inland Arabian chief, Ibn Saud, who ruled over the fanatical Wahabis and who, single-handed, subjugated the undisciplined tribes of the interior. When he had completed this task in 1924, much to the satisfaction of the British, he entered Mecca and replaced Hussein, who fled, again to the satisfaction of the British. For the first time for centuries, Arabia was under the control of one man. It is his descendants who are the present rulers of Saudi Arabia and although, unlike Hussein, they cannot claim descent from the Prophet, they positively exude an aura of dignity and gravitas.

It remains to deal with Palestine which is one of the early examples of the post-war consensus of 'disengaging from Empire' as well as a reminder of the present intractable problem of Palestine. In spite of the promise to Hussein in 1916 regarding Arab lands, the British were submitted to Zionist and international pressure to declare the mandated territory 'a national home' for the Jews, at the same time undertaking not to 'prejudice the civil and religious rights of existing non-Jewish communities' there – all of which was embodied in the famous, or infamous, Balfour Declaration of 1917. The fact that the Arab inhabitants were a significant majority (about 650,000 compared with the Jewish 84,000) explains the twists and turns of British policy in subsequent years. With the sharp increase in the number of refugees to Palestine in the 1930s, following the rise of Hitler, the Arabs revolted and were suppressed by the British between 1936 and 1939 but at the same time a limitation of 75,000 was placed on the number of Jews who could enter Palestine by end-March 1944, together with restrictions on Jewish rights to buy land and the

139

promise of eventual Palestinian independence under Arab majority rule. This pro-Arab stance was due not only to the predilections of Bevin and the Foreign Office but also to the need to ensure the security of the Middle East. However, as the war progressed and as the truth of the horrific Nazi-Jewish atrocities gradually dawned, especially after 1945 when public knowledge became much more specific, the pressure on the British Government to relax its restrictions on Jewish entry to Palestine knew no bounds, especially in the United States where pressure groups openly advocated the setting up of a Jewish state in Palestine 'as soon as possible', together with sustained immigration so as to establish a Jewish majority. Both American political parties gave lip-service to these proposals and the Labour Party passed such a resolution in its Conference in December 1944. Typically, Bevin refused to be panicked or bullied into the adoption of a blatantly pro-Zionist policy but he had no success in his negotiations with Arab and Jewish leaders while the Americans, in general, and Truman, in particular, were long on words but short on practical help. A reference to the United nations in February 1947 was of no avail. It was a hopeless cause. What should have been done was to enforce a solution by partition, the solution preferred by the wartime Coalition Government, with 'enforce' to be taken literally, if necessary. In the event, British public opinion was deeply affected by the outbreak of outrageous Jewish terrorism and atrocities while the enormous cost of the operation made no sense in view of the economic crisis of 1947. In September 1947 it was announced that the Palestine Mandate would end at midnight 14–15 May 1948. As in the case of Greece and Turkey, Bevin had served notice on the United States that the problem was theirs. In other words, if the people of the United States were so desperate to create a Jewish state in Palestine, in spite of its indigenous Arab population, it was up to them to do it. They are still grappling with the horrendous problem.

In the meantime, Truman's historic declaration in March 1947 was followed by the Marshall Plan which was the economic counterpart to the former and which has already been mentioned when dealing with the economy. Dean Acheson, the American Under-Secretary of State, said that the United States was prepared to facilitate long-term help 'to aid free peoples to preserve their independence and their freedom from Communism, both internal and external'. In June, in his famous speech at Harvard University, the Secretary of State, George Marshall, went much further by proposing that it was only 'logical' for the United States 'to assist in the return of normal economic health in the world without which there can be no political stability or assured peace'. It will be remembered that Marshall made the proviso that 'the Europeans would accept the responsibility for organizing it' (i.e. the Aid) which, under Bevin's leadership, was the beginning of Britain's post-war involvement with Europe and, indirectly, that also of the United States, the outcome of which was the Atlantic Alliance. Initially, the American project had included Russia, and excluded the 'fascist' Spain, but the former, following a meeting in Paris, in June 1947, between Molotov, Bevin and Bidault, did not accept the invitation in which Britain and France, following Bevin's immediate initiative, invited 14 other European nations to meet in Paris in April 1948 in order to deliver to Marshall a four-year programme and organizational mechanism for European economic reconstruction – the Organization for European Economic Co-operation. From this evolved the European Payments Unions which replaced bilateral trading arrangements between the members while trading restrictions, in the form of import quotas, were lowered. In general, however, the OEEC was an outstanding success.

> Even by 1950 the success of the Marshall Plan was plain: Europe was already exceeding its pre-war production level by 25 percent; and by then the dollar gap had been reduced from $12 billion to $2 billion. British exports were doing well, West German production had reached Germany's 1936 level, and French inflation was being brought under control. America had also benefited from the plan, since at a cost of only a tiny fraction of her national income she had achieved a brilliant diplomatic success and engineered a domestic economic boom.[1]

The success of the OEEC also gave a boost to the ideal of Europe becoming something more than a geographical expression, first enunciated by Jean Monnet in pre-war France, but the war induced the leaders of France, Germany, Italy and the Benelux countries to think in terms of a 'supra-national culture' so as to counter the warlike threat of nationalism as well as the economic and political benefits of European integration. The 'reluctant Europeanism' of which I have spoken, certainly applied at this time to the Labour leaders and, especially, the Foreign Secretary, Bevin. But this cannot be said of the leader of the Opposition, Winston Churchill, who enjoyed enormous international prestige and who virtually took the lead, both nationally and internationally, in promoting the grand concept of the 'European idea'. This has been much misunderstood,

---

[1] *Post-War Britain*, by Alan Sked and Chris Cook, pp. 68–9. Further facts and figures in this chapter are attributable to this authority.

141

not least by Sir Geoffrey Howe (now Lord Howe) in his resignation speech in the House of Commons in 1990, in which he castigated Mrs Thatcher for not sharing Winston Churchill's faith in Europe, but the truth is that Mrs Thatcher is much closer to his concept than is Lord Howe and those who think like him, for Churchill, like Bevin and everyone else in Britain, from the Duke to the dustman, never contemplated for a moment that Britain should play a direct or integrated part in any European institutions. It all began with Churchill's speech in Zurich in September 1946, following that in Fulton, Missouri, earlier in the year, when he referred to the necessity to create 'a kind of United States of Europe', embodying a Franco-German reconciliation, and to set up a 'Council of Europe' in which Britain was to be not a member but a 'friend and sponsor'. In January 1947 Churchill became Chairman of the United Europe Committee, formed in London to promote the creation of a 'unified Europe', which he further encouraged in a speech in the Albert Hall in May, while in July British, French, Belgian and Dutch members formed an International Committee for a United Europe, the Chairman of which was Duncan Sandys, Churchill's son-in-law. This momentum led to the setting-up of a 'Congress of Europe' at the Hague in May 1948, at which Churchill was the main speaker and which as attended by leading and other Conservative MPs but by very few Labour MPs who had been discouraged from attending by the Government.

Churchill's emotionally stirring peroration called, among other things, for a Council of Europe, 'including Great Britain joined with her Empire and Commonwealth' as well as one in the Western Hemisphere with which Britain would be linked through Canada and 'other sacred ties' – all very vague and harmless. Not so vague, was the Congress's resolution to form a European economic and political union together with a European Assembly, consisting of Parliamentarians of the member states. Not so vague either, was the response of the Labour Government and its spokesmen which reflected the views of the British 'man in the street' that the Europeans consisted of countries that had either been enemies or had been defeated, and that Britain's natural friends were her wartime allies from the Commonwealth and the United States. Bevin stated:

> I feel that the intricacies of Western Europe are such that we had better proceed ... on the same principle of the association of nations that we have in the Commonwealth. The right way to approach this Western Union problem should be by adopting the principle of an unwritten constitution, and the process of constant

association, step-by-step, by treaty and agreement, and by taking
on certain things collectively instead of by ourselves.

From this early date Bevin had enunciated the British sensible and
pragmatic approach to European integration and in spite of the fact
that although the Conservative Party came to be regarded as the pro-
European party, when it came to the crunch the Conservative
approach was just as pragmatic as was that of Bevin, or Churchill, if
he had been in office at the time. Conservatives would have had no
difficulty in agreeing with the down-to-earth Clement Attlee, when he
wrote in 1948:

> The Labour Party is a characteristically British production differing
> widely from Continental Socialist Parties. It is a product of its
> environment and of the national habit of mind.

Thus, in 1948, Bevin repulsed a French proposal to establish a
European Customs Union and emasculated a French attempt to
strengthen the powers of the OEEC Secretariat. The Customs Union
proposal was early evidence of the backward-looking attitude of the
French in economic matters for customs unions, as they were known
in the nineteenth century, were essentially protectionist devices.
Again, in 1949 Bevin dismissed a French initiative to set up a five-
year plan for Anglo-French economic co-operation, as follows: 'We
don't do things like that in our country: we don't have plans: we
work things out practically.' If only Labour Governments had carried
out that excellent philosophy in running the British economy!

On the other hand, Bevin was all in favour of European co-
operation, especially with France, when it came to the all-important
question of defence for he knew that he would be more likely to
achieve his ambition of committing the United States to the defence
of Europe when that power saw that the Europeans, especially
Britain and France, were giving a lead. Thus, in 1946 he was
enthusiastic about the French proposal for an Anglo-French military
alliance which led to the signing of an Anglo-French Treaty at
Dunkirk in 1947. Coming so soon after the war, this treaty was
aimed at Germany but a year later, March 1948, the relations
between the Allied powers and Russia had deteriorated so much in
Germany, that the alliance was widened by the inclusion of the
Benelux countries – Belgium, Holland and Luxembourg – in the
defensive Brussels Treaty, to be known as the Western Union. The
fact that the Berlin blockade began two weeks later was largely
coincidental but it nevertheless strengthened Bevin's determination to

143

establish the Western Union with an effective military organization so that in September 1948 the members' Defence Ministers met in Paris to set up a permanent organization with headquarters at Fontainebleau with a Chiefs of Staff Committee under Field Marshall Montgomery and with French and British senior officers sharing the higher commands, although the latter were loath to treat the French as military equals! There were further differences between the French and the British when the former, in conjunction with the other European members (plus a further five new signatories), attempted to give the Western Union a political, as well as a military, significance. Instead of the French proposal for a European Assembly, the British agreed to a much less ambitious Council of Europe, consisting of the Ministerial Council and a 'Consultative Assembly' of parliamentarians with deliberately vague aims and with the right of veto exercisable by ministers in 'important matters'.

It was to be the momentous events in Germany that were to lead to the culmination of Bevin's diplomatic efforts. The Western powers had had no intention, initially, of dividing Germany but as a result of the hostile Russian policy of treating its Eastern zone as a fief of Russia, exploiting its grain supplies for the use of her home market, and denying them to the Western zones, as well as expropriating the industrial plant in its own zone, by 1948, the Western powers had no alternative but to develop their zones as a separate entity. The Soviet blocking of the Western access by land to Berlin in 1948 has already been mentioned, nine days after which she left the four-power military control in Berlin. The threat of serious shortages of food and other necessities was alleviated by the historic Berlin Air Lift, organized by the United States, with significant British help, which, after 324 days of non-stop flights led to the ending of the blockade and the Russian admission of defeat. The political consequences of the division of Germany were soon manifest in that the Western Powers drew up a West German constitution for approval by the West German political parties, and after the elections in August 1949 Konrad Adenauer was elected by the Bundestag as the first West German Federal Chancellor. Meanwhile, the four-power military control of Berlin functioned intermittently right down to the 1990s.

The Berlin Air Lift was thus the first and most important watershed in post-war world history. On the one hand, a world war would have threatened if the West had endeavoured to break the blockade by land or if the Russians had opposed the air lift. As it happened, it was the first important example of the policy of peace through strength, applied by the United States, with important British support, in opposing post-war Russian aggression, a policy

144

which was to be crowned with success, after backsliding in the Carter years, following the brilliant years of Reagan and Thatcher. On the other hand, it was the event that finally persuaded the Americans to involve themselves actively in defending the security of Europe, in addition to the Truman Doctrine and the Marshall Plan. It has already been noted that events in the Eastern Mediterranean soon alerted the American leaders to the relevance of Churchill's 'iron curtain' speech in Missouri in 1946 as also did the setting-up of client states in Poland, Hungary, Bulgaria and Romania, culminating in the Communist takeover of Czechoslovakia in February 1948. As early as June 1948 a resolution was passed overwhelmingly by the United States Senate, paving the way for a series of talks and negotiations with the Western Union countries and Canada, which culminated in the Atlantic pact of April 1949, a defensive and military alliance, embracing the North Atlantic powers of the United States and Canada, and the original Western Union powers, as well as Norway, Portugal, Italy and Iceland, while Greece and Turkey were soon to be included. Thus, in accordance with Bevin's original wish, the whole of the Mediterranean was protected. As Truman stated:

> If (this document) had existed in 1914 and 1939, supported by the nations who are represented today, I believe it would have prevented the acts of aggression which led to two world wars.

Ernest Bevin therefore occupies a place of the utmost importance in post-war world history for it was he, more than any other man, who was responsible for binding the United States to Western Europe by a formal military alliance in peacetime, against all that country's traditions. Indeed, Bevin's achievement was an act of political vision which must rank among the greatest in history. Furthermore, although the Atlantic Alliance has been described as 'American-led', which indeed it is, it is extremely important to recognize that it was not imposed on Europe by the United States but that the initiative and pressure came from Europe, under British leadership. In Britain the consensus was virtually complete. Whatever the views and the prejudices on the fringes of the two parties, whenever they have been in power, each has clung tenaciously to the Atlantic Alliance, both in terms of the defence of Europe and the maintenance of the world balance of power as well as in those of the 'special relationship' between the United States and Britain.

It has already been explained that the first steps taken by Bevin and Britain to involve the United States in a much wider post-war world involvement than the latter had ever envisaged was the

145

former's withdrawal from Greece in 1947 and from Palestine in 1948. This was due to the fact that the Labour Government acknowledged at the outset that Britain's economic weakness precluded her from playing the world and imperial role that she had done before 1939. Nevertheless, she still, rightly, regarded herself as a world power, as we have seen from Bevin's statement in Parliament in 1947. It was a combination of these two factors – financial constraint and the continuation of world-power status – that led the Labour Government to decide in 1946 to develop its own independent nuclear deterrent, the theory (not borne out in practice) being that a nuclear bomb would be cheaper than the maintenance of formidable conventional arms. This decision was taken even before the passing of the United States' McMahon Act in 1946 which ended Anglo-American nuclear co-operation and which reflected the American fear at that time of the resurgence of British imperialism. The Conservatives' hydrogen bomb was successfully tested in 1952 but in view of the strong vein of pacifism in the Labour Party, in his development of the earlier atomic or A-bomb Attlee employed the greatest secrecy throughout, without most of the Cabinet, not to mention the Parliamentary Party and Parliament itself, being informed, to which strategem the Conservative party did not object. Sir Anthony Eden wrote of his agreement on the matter with Bevin: 'I would probably have agreed with him more, if I had not been anxious to embarrass him less.'[1] However, in spite of Britain's attempt to limit the financial and geographical extent of her worldwide obligations, the fact was that she was a world power and, with no German Army and a questionable French one, she was the only nation in Europe which could help the United States to defend Western Europe, as we have seen in the Berlin Crisis of 1948. This led to the introduction of conscription by a call-up period of eighteen months under the terms of the National Service Bill of March 1947 which came into effect in January 1949 – another brave effort by the Labour Government, considering the unpopularity of conscription in the party. Montgomery said at the time: 'When all is said and done one must pay tribute to the courage of the Labour Government.'

With the defeat of the Nationalists in China by the Communists in 1949, Stalin turned his attention to the Far East where he assumed that the United States would not take an active interest as it had done in the Mediterranean and Western Europe, but the invasion of South Korea by communist North Korea in 1950 led to the

---

[1] *Full Circle*, by Sir Anthony Eden, p. 5.

successful repulse of the invasion by United Nations forces on the initiative and under the leadership of the United States. In spite of the fact that British forces took part, there were some strains in the 'special relationship' owing to Britain's recognition of communist China, and to British worries that the United States would use the atom bomb and cause a world war. The Americans suspected the British of being 'soft' on Communism (those were the days of McCarthyism and of the ambitious 'prima donna', General Douglas MacArthur) but this charge could not be sustained in view of the fact that Britain was spending £50 million per annum and utilizing over 100,000 troops opposing the Chinese Communists in the 12-year campaign in Malaya – thus the need for conscription – while the Americans were assuaged by the ever-pragmatic British also recognizing Chiang Kai-Shek's Chinese regime in Taiwan. The Korean war dragged on until 1953 when Korea was divided along the 38th parallel and South Korea signed a defence treaty with the USA. The war had decisive consequences in Western Europe where it was feared, quite incorrectly, that Stalin was due to attack the West. West Germany felt especially threatened owing to the fact that American and British troops there were massively outnumbered by the Soviet Forces in the East. As a result, German rearmament was initiated under the auspices of NATO with the consequent strengthening of the Western Alliance, as also was the United States's acceptance of its role as leader of the Western World. But the cracks were beginning to show in her partner, Great Britain. We have already seen how the attempt to finance the war by the Chancellor of the Exchequer, Gaitskell, led to a crisis in the Labour Government and contributed to its loss of will to survive. The problem was not easily solved. In 1952, Britain's defence expenditure was higher per capita than that of the United States. For a convalescent economy, the commitments were enormous and unsustainable. The British Army of the Rhine was in place in West Germany, the RAF was preparing to be able to deliver an independent nuclear deterrent, a large contingent was fighting in Korea as part of the United Nations forces, troops were fighting against guerillas in Kenya and Malaya, the British garrisons in Suez, Aden and Cyprus were increasingly resented by the indigenous populations, nationalist aspirations were mounting in the African colonies and the Royal Navy still operated a 'Pax Brittanica' in the Persian Gulf and Indian Ocean.[1]

---

[1] *The Changing British Political System: into the 1990's*, by Ian Budge and David McKay, p. 203.

There were thus pressing economic reasons for the process of disengagement from Empire as well as the indigenous pressures for independence which were well described by the nineteenth-century colonials by the expression: 'Self government is more important than good government'. When the process of disengagement took place the British received no thanks or praise for it was regarded merely as bowing to the inevitable but, in fact, it was, on the whole, an act of enlightened and deliberate decolonization – probably unique in world history. Although European decolonization took place elsewhere at the time, such as in the Belgian Congo and French Africa, it is notable that it was accompanied by less domestic upheaval in Britain than elsewhere. The Labour Party, of course, inherited the 'Little Englander' mentality of the nineteenth-century Liberals and was anti-imperialist and concerned with racial equality and making links with future nationalist leaders such as Menon, Nkrumah, Nyerere and Banda. Labour wanted to make up for past colonial exploitation by providing resources for the economic regeneration of the colonies, under the terms of the Colonial Development and Welfare Act of 1940. Whereas this had originally provided for around £10 million for the colonies, it was increased by £120 million for the years 1945–55 and to £140 million in 1950. Two public corporations were established in 1948 to improve living standards in the colonies while there was a significant expansion in colonial education. It is needless to say that the staff of the Colonial Office trebled between 1938 and 1950. Finally, they believed in the colonies achieving self-government by a gradual process culminating in their ideal of a multiracial Commonwealth. On the other hand, the Conservatives were identified indubitably with the British Empire, where they had strong personal and economic links with the settlers while they were, of course, of the same class as the colonial civil servants and the service officers, whose raison d'etre was largely due to the existence of the Empire. In all, as embodied in the attitude of Churchill, which was typical of Conservative Members of Parliament as well as the rank and file of the Party, the Empire had a mystical element and a right to exist in its own right. And yet, paradoxically, in spite of these enormous differences in the imperial outlook between the two parties, it is probably the field in which post-war bipartisanism was most successful. This was true from the very beginning for in spite of Churchill's protestations for many years over the plans to grant India self-government, and the unhappiness of Conservatives over Indian independence, when this came about they made only token resistance to what they knew was the inevitable. Again, Churchill, speaking for his fellow Conservatives, grumbled over the policy of 'scuttle' from

Greece and Palestine, and the like, as he also did in his much quoted remark about the Empire on becoming Prime Minister in 1951. But both in his ministry and in those of subsequent Conservative governments the policy of retreat was carried on almost as if there had been no change of government. The consensus worked, as usual, not only by virtue of the Establishment acceptance, but also because of the part played by important key individuals in the Conservative Party in accepting the consensus, notably Oliver Stanley, the post-war Shadow Colonial Secretary, Harold Macmillan and Iain MacLeod.

In 1942, Bevin had written that 'empires as we have known them must become a thing of the past'. We have already seen that Attlee was an enthusiastic supporter of Indian self-government, while in 1942 Cripps had planned a 'Social and Economic Policy for India' but by the end of the war this would have been far too costly to implement so that the Government decided to proceed with the plans to give India her independence, with the Indians hopefully solving their problems themselves. Britain attempted to mediate between the Hindu Indian Congress Party under Nehru and the Muslim League under Jinnah but after prolonged and unsuccessful negotiations between 1946 and 1947, Britain withdrew from India in August 1947, leaving it partitioned between two sovereign states, India and Pakistan. The ensuing slaughter of minorities by majorities, both of and by Indians and Pakistanis, mainly in the Punjab, leading to about 200,000 deaths, drew strong Conservative criticism of the Government, although it had the undoubted support of the British people who regarded it as the far-sighted and courageous act that it undoubtedly was. In 1948, Burma and Ceylon also gained their independence and all three countries, except Burma, decided to remain in the Commonwealth. Burma, following its war-time occupation by the Japanese, who recognized its independence in 1943, went into a Communist 'limbo', notable only for the excesses of its repressive regime and the courageous resistance of Aung Sang. The 'new' Commonwealth, the proud creation of the Labour Government was initiated at the Commonwealth Premier's Conference of 1949 whereby the King, previously 'the King' in each Commonwealth country became 'the symbol of the free association of its independent member nations and as such the Head of the Commonwealth'. Thus, the three new Republics were also, at the same time, able to become members of the British Commonwealth. Whereas to Conservatives this was a soul-destroying diminution or 'watering-down' of the concept of Empire and Commonwealth, to the Labour (and Liberal) Parties it was the foundation of a multiracial Commonwealth – a worldwide free association of independent states.

149

As we have seen from the above defence commitments which, in retrospect, were impossibly excessive, the withdrawal from the Indian sub-continent was not accompanied by a re-appraisal of Britain's commitments East of Suez. This cannot be accounted for by stupidity or by 'delusions of grandeur' for it was mainly due to Britain's sense of responsibility – the 'White man's burden' concept at its best. Thus, the fastidious Auchinleck thought that Britain was 'still morally bound to aid India and Pakistan against an aggressor' in deference to which view Ceylon agreed to provide British naval and air bases on the island. It was also assumed that an attack on Australia or New Zealand would be treated like an attack on Great Britain herself, which was perfectly understandable in view of the way in which these two countries had recently supported their 'Mother Country'. However, they both sensibly came to the conclusion that they were now essentially Pacific countries so that in 1951 they signed the ANZUS defence agreement with the United States from which Britain, again rightly, was excluded, although co-operation with Britain in intelligence matters was envisaged. The communist violence in Malaya began in 1948 and who is to say that the defeat of the Communists after a 12-year struggle was not an entirely commendable and beneficial action on the part of the British and is certainly not something that can be decided by drawing up a balance sheet. Also, Britain was responsible constitutionally for the defence of her remaining colonies in Africa and Asia and had signed defence treaties with the sheikhdoms and emirates of Arabia and the Persian Gulf. A what stage were those responsibilities to be abrogated? In 1945 Attlee had queried our Middle Eastern strategy but in view of the above commitments, as well as the problems in Palestine and Egypt, where Britain's military presence had been confined to a base on the Canal Zone and where the annexation of the Sudan was being demanded by the nationalists, it was decided that 'the route to India' would have to continue to be protected.

The weak Labour Government of 1950–1951, with its majority of only five, cut a poor figure in the field of foreign affairs, partly because Ernest Bevin, who had retired as Foreign Secretary in March 1951, due to ill-health, and was to die in April, was succeeded as Foreign Secretary by Herbert Morrison who failed to bridge the gap between a lifetime spent in local government and home affairs, and the international scene. We have already seen how it was seriously weakened by the financial ramifications of the Korean War. The Middle East also presented it with intractable problems – and forebodings for the future. The Prime Minister of Iran, Dr Mussadeq, had the not-unnatural ambition of obtaining a greater share of the proceeds from the Iranian oilfields for his own country. He was in the position to put pressure successfully, to this purpose, on the Anglo-Iranian Oil Company, which controlled the oilfields. Instead, he expropriated the oil company which was a pointless act as Iran had neither the tankers nor the marketing expertise to sell and deliver the oil. Morrison could think of no constructive way of solving the problem, apart from threatening 'sharp and forceful action' which, fortunately, did not take place as the United States disapproved of stirring up trouble in the Middle East. The crisis therefore subsided ingloriously and Dr Mussadeq was left to his own devices, whereby Iran's economy began a period of serious decline. In the event, Britain and the United States, working behind the scenes, engineered the coup, in August 1953, which led to the fall of Dr Mussadeq and the restoration of the Shah, together with the reorganization of the Persian oil industry in 1954 by an international oil consortium, with Britain holding 40 per cent of the shares after having sold the rest of her stake to the Americans and others. In Egypt, where the forces of nationalism were already stirring strongly, Britain's earlier embarrassment and weakness in Iran were noted, for Britain regarded her control of the Suez Canal as of major importance, although she was prepared to compromise in view of the high cost of maintaining her bases there, the 1936 treaty for the occupation of which was due to be renewed in 1956. Apart from the growing Egyptian nationalism, the situation was complicated by Britain's refusal to recognize Egypt's claim to the Suzerainty of Sudan so that the negotiations, which had been proceeding fitfully since 1946 were brutally terminated in October 1951 when Egypt abrogated the 1936 treaty and proclaimed her monarch, Faruq, King of Sudan. To make matters worse, this action was accompanied by a spate of anti-British feeling which was vented specifically on British troops and civilian personnel in the Canal Zone, a situation which was much resented by the British public who felt that the Foreign Office, in general, and Morrison, in particular, were inept in the matter. In retrospect, it can be seen that this was a part of the drama of imperial disengagement, and that in regard to Egypt it was soon to reach a disastrous climax. In May 1951 the defection of the Foreign Office spies, Burgess and Maclean, to Moscow had already seriously damaged the credibility of that department while, although the signing of the ANZUS pact in September was regarded as a blow to British prestige at the time, it was merely the response to post-war reality in the Pacific.

In the same way as Churchill's peacetime Government (1951–55) was characterized by 'Buskellism' in economic and social affairs so, too, in foreign affairs the consensus was continued as it had been ordered by Bevin. Churchill had said in 1952 that on social services, foreign affairs and defence, nine-tenths of the people agreed on what had been done and what would be done.[1] The exception to this benign state of affairs was the consequence of the loss of the election by the Labour Party whereby the left wing advocated the desirability of more socialist policies, including a more socialist foreign policy, such as opposition to German rearmament, and a return to the left's pathological anti-Americanism. In spite of the difference in the approach of Labour and Conservatives to Imperial and Commonwealth matters, in the matter of decolonization there was a consensus that self-government should be attained gradually. However, in Opposition, Labour rejected gradualism in favour of outright independence and, moralistically, attacked colonial economic exploitation, and the brutality of the British forces in British Guyana, Malaya, Kenya and Cyprus. Although officially a non-party organization, these views were expounded by the Labour-dominated Movement for Colonial Freedom (MCF) founded in 1954 and of which the indefatigable Anthony Wedgwood Benn was treasurer.

There was, however, one way in which foreign policy under Churchill differed dramatically from that in the previous short-lived Labour Government, under the unfortunate Morrison, and that was the outstanding part played by the Foreign Secretary, Anthony Eden, both in regard to style and achievement. For the last time in British history, apart from the renaissance under Margaret Thatcher, Britain confidently and successfully played the part of a world power (in this case the third world power) and it was due to this inspired period of office that Eden, also helped by his aristocratic background and bearing, created the 'Anthony Eden legend'. Much has been made of his pre-war role as an anti-appeaser but this was a low profile and indeterminate effort while his Prime Ministership was disastrous. However, the first of his achievements was to settle the twin questions of German rearmament and European defence. I have already mentioned that the outbreak of the Korean War in 1950 had led to the German Chancellor, Adenauer, demanding greater protection for West Germany from the Russian military threat, including the formation of a 'West German Federal Police Force' of 150,000 men. The European nations, mainly Britain and France, could not agree on the practicalities of German rearmament

---

[1]*Churchill's Indian Summer*, by A. Seldon, p. 35.

while the Americans were not prepared to commit more troops to Western Europe without West German participation. In the end, Bevin was able to effect a compromise whereby NATO was strengthened by the provision of an integrated army with a central command structure under an American supreme commander, General Eisenhower, thus enabling the United States to commit more troops to Western Europe. As we shall see later, there were stirrings of a specifically European defence commitment and organization at this time and it is significant that Bevin took the route of strengthening the Atlantic Alliance. (It was also necessary, in view of the way in which the European nations have adopted such supremely narrow and nationalistic attitudes, both prior to, during and since the Gulf War.)

Nevertheless, this was no more than a compromise and the German question did not go away. The Soviet Union was obviously hostile to West German rearmament and put forward abortive proposals for a 'four power conference' on Germany in 1952, while in January 1954 such a conference took place in Berlin but, once again, it was abortive. The reason, in both cases, was the failure to agree on the holding of free elections, for whereas East Germany's population was only one third of that of West Germany and its government was not independent and representative (a fact emphasized by the 1953 uprising there), Russia wanted equal representation for the two Germanys. Russia, for its part, disagreed with the Western Allies' proposal that a re-unified Germany should be able to join any alliance – that is to say, NATO. In 1952, Russia had actually proposed the withdrawal of foreign troops and the reunification and rearming of a neutral Germany which therefore could not be a part of NATO. In retrospect, this might appear to represent an important lost opportunity but, in reality, owing to Russia's stranglehold over East Germany, the Allies and West Germany were correct in regarding this as a tactical and spoiling move.

More important and significant, as already hinted, was the parallel activity of the European Federalists, under the inspiration of the irrepressible Jean Monnet, culminating in the proposal to associate the rearming of West Germany with the creation of a European Defence Community. This was part of the resurgence of European federalism, which I will deal with later, but in this context it was the catalyst that brought the problems that we have been discussing to a head. Between 1950 and 1952 France, West Germany, Italy and the Benelux countries took part in negotiations which resulted in what has been called the Pleven Plan, after the French premier who led the negotiations. Under its terms:

There was to be a European Defence Community paid for by European taxes, controlled by a council of European ministers and run by a European commissariat. The analogies with the European Iron and Steel Community and the later European Economic Community are too obvious to need outlining.[1]

Although the European army was to be integrated, in the sense that national forces were to be inter-mixed, the West German and Italian armed forces (the latter were to be rearmed also) were the only nations whose armies were to be confined to the European army. The plan was also extremely complicated and therefore regarded as impractical, while it was not popular in West Germany and the Europeans still had doubts about German rearmament. Also, initially, the United States was not in favour for the Americans were mainly concerned with integrating any European army into NATO which would necessitate renegotiating the legal position of West Germany, among other things. Finally, true to form, the Labour Government was no more than sympathetic and confined itself to sending observers to the 1950–51 negotiations which by now had become the standard British response to manifestations of European federalism.

With the formation of Churchill's Government in October 1951 the architects of the European Defence Community thought that there would be a change in British policy in view of Churchill's pro-European pronouncements since 1945, the latest of which, in 1950, called for the creation of a European army but this proved to be purely quixotic as far as Britain was concerned for Churchill had never contemplated Britain joining a United Europe and thereby surrendering British sovereignty. Similarly, Eden, following Bevin and Churchill and in line with British public opinion and his own concept of Britain as a world power, stated categorically in November that Britain would not become a member of the EDC, in spite of the fact that the Government's spokesman in the Council of Europe at Strasbourg, Sir David Maxwell-Fyfe, had implied to the contrary. The fact of Britain's representatives at European institutions becoming 'Europeanized' has, of course, become a recurring syndrome. Nevertheless, like Bevin, but even more so, from November 1951 Eden took every possible step to ensure the success of the EDC, without actually joining it, pledging military aid and the like, by a series of treaties, and undertaking that a British minister

---

[1] *Post-War Britain*, by Alan Sked and Chris Cook, p. 111.

would attend the meetings of the EDC Council of Ministers and that a permanent British representative would liaise with the EDC Board of Commissioners. By 1954, all the signatories of the Pleven Plan had ratified the treaty, apart from France, and the failure of the French National Assembly to do so in August 1954 was the end of the European Defence Community. The immediate reasons were that the French were still not fully convinced of the advisability of German rearmament while, without Britain, France suspected that the EDC would be dominated by the United States and West Germany. The deeper reason was that France had still not regained her national confidence after her wartime humiliations and instinctively regarded Britain as her senior partner. With the resurgence of the French economy and the advent of Charles De Gaulle it was to be a very different story.

After Eisenhower's election as President of the United States in 1952, he and his Secretary of State, John Foster Dulles, became enthusiastic supporters of the EDC as it conformed with the American requirement that its major contribution for the defence of Western Europe should be matched by that of the Western European nations themselves. Thus, in December 1953, Dulles, a man of strong personality and great experience in the field of foreign affairs, uttered his famous warning that if France did not ratify the 1952 treaty there would be an 'agonizing re-appraisal' of the United States's commitment to European defence. The failure of France to do so was received very badly in Washington and, for the first time, it can be seen that the Americans regarded the 'special relationship', so cherished by Churchill and Bevin, as detrimental to their interests – a sentiment which has reappeared from time to time but which has yet to be proved true, in spite of the logic in its favour, from the American point of view. However, Eden had the confidence and ability to grasp the 'poisoned chalice' and he embarked on an orgy of diplomatic activity in which, on a worldwide basis, he negotiated and settled all the outstanding issues, culminating in a nine-power agreement signed at Lancaster House, in London, in October 1954 by representatives of the Six, Great Britain, USA, and Canada, and ratified by the French Parliament before the end of the year and coming into force, as the Paris Agreements, in May 1955. It was one of the great post-war diplomatic watersheds for after years of uncertainty it put Western defence on a permanent and stable basis, ending the occupation of Western Germany by the Allies, procuring German and Italian membership of NATO, confirming the presence of the US and Canadian troops in Europe and, above all, ensuring a significantly stronger British military presence in Europe than

155

heretofore, and with even stronger undertakings against withdrawal than had been given to the EDC. In all, it was Eden's greatest diplomatic achievement and the high point of his political life which soon went into sharp decline. The other side of the coin is that Russia's answer to the Paris Agreements was to set up the Warsaw Pact which cannot be said to have ushered in any change in the relationship of its members with Russia except that it formalized the latter's practice of retaining troops in them. Similarly, the Russian granting of independence to Austria, as a neutral country, by the Treaty of May 1955, did not disguise the fact that Austria regained her independence as a result of four power agreement, and her approaches to West Germany in June with a view to establishing diplomatic relations, were attempts to ensure that she would not become totally isolated from Western Europe.

It has already been noted (p. 147) that the Korean War ended by a moderate peace in 1953 in which Anthony Eden played an important diplomatic part and, on this occasion, it was the British who were increasingly unhappy about the 'special relationship' for they were very uncomfortable about the excesses of American anti-communism and, rightly or wrongly, suspected that they might mistakenly use the atomic bomb in North Korea. In the Middle East it also appeared that Eden had been successful. As we have seen, in 1953, Dr Mussadeq's government was overthrown in Iran and the Shah was restored to power, following which, in 1954, the British set up an international consortium to reorganize the Persian oil industry. The 'foreign exploitation' of Persian and other Middle Eastern oil resources was, obviously, something that could not go on forever but, at the time, the British and the Americans felt that as they had financed the projects it was only right that they should recoup the capital invested by receiving the income. Over the years, in one way and another, the transfer in ownership and control to the indigenous people has been made, but the whole process, from beginning to end, has been perfectly natural and, in practice, the only way it could have taken place. The moralists forget that literally both sides have benefited. Meanwhile, in Egypt, King Faruq and his Government were forcibly replaced in 1952 by the army, under Colonel Neguib, who thus initiated a clean break or revolution in Egyptian life – diplomatically, politically, economically and socially. In 1953 Neguib and the British agreed that Sudan should attain self-government in three years' time after the departure of British and Egyptian forces. There remained the problem of the Suez Canal Zone which was made easier by the fact that the British Army's headquarters in the Middle East were transferred from Suez to Cyprus and in October in 1954 a seven year agreement was made for the gradual withdrawal of British troops from the canal over a period of twenty months, with the joint maintenance of key installations by British and Egyptian civilians and the reactivation of the base on any armed attack on Egypt or her Middle Eastern allies. In return, Egypt undertook to guarantee freedom of navigation through the canal. However, this compromise was extremely unpopular with the extremists in both Britain and Egypt. In the former, the 'Suez Group' of Conservatives voted against the Government and in Egypt the moderate Neguib was replaced by the younger, more dynamic and radical Colonel Nasser who was to prove to be the Cromwell of Egypt.

The break-up of the French Indo-China empire after a period of round a hundred years led to the Vietnam problem. After 1945 France set up three independent states – Laos, Cambodia and Vietnam – as members of the French Union but Ho Chi Minh and his Viet-Minh nationalists proclaimed the 'Democratic Republic of Vietnam' and by 1954, with the aid of the Communist Chinese, had taken much of North Vietnam and were successfully conducting the siege of Dien Bien Phu against the French who, having been financed to around 80 per cent of their war effort by the United States, now called for American miliary participation if the war was not to be lost. Dulles, whose ambition was to 'roll back the Communist world empire' and to 'liberate the captive peoples' of Eastern Europe and who, along with other right-wing Republicans, had resented Eden's influencing Eisenhower in the matter of the moderate Korean peace settlement, was enthusiastic to help the French but, once again, at Eden's behest, moderation prevailed. At the Geneva Conference of May 1954, which Dulles attended for only a week, Eden negotiated the partition of Vietnam along the 17th parallel, with the later holding of free elections to decide the future relationship of north and south as well as separate treaties determining the neutrality and independence of Laos and Cambodia. This was another diplomatic triumph for Eden but Dulles was extremely critical for in his view, due to Eden, the Communists had once again gained a political, military and moral victory. The United States refused to sign the agreements and the relationship between the two diplomats deteriorated further. Eden's victory was to cost him, and Britain, dear as Winston Churchill intimated at the time.

This then, was a period when the 'special relationship' was at a low ebb and in view of this and the hostility of the Eastern Communist 'block', Churchill and Eden became convinced that the peace of the world depended on a strong British presence which could be best enhanced by the deterrent power of nuclear weapons. Thus, in March

1955 a Defence White Paper announced a decision to manufacture a British hydrogen bomb although, like Attlee before them, they had secretly made the decision earlier, in 1952. In the meantime, and, following the Geneva Conference, Eden took part in a frenzy of diplomatic activity with a view to strengthening world peace and security. First, he joined the South-East Asia Treaty Organization (SEATO) which Dulles had organized when he left Geneva in a huff, including Great Britain, France, Australia, New Zealand, Pakistan, the Philippines and Thailand with separate protocols to include Laos, Cambodia and Vietnam although these states could actually sign the treaty. SEATO was a much less significant military alliance than NATO for it did not involve an automatic response or the creation of a standing army or joint command. Nevertheless, Dulles was pleased with it but when he called a meeting of the non-Asian members of SEATO while Eden was still at Geneva, the latter objected forcibly for he felt that this would threaten his attempts at Geneva to preserve the peace in Asia. Following a hostile telegram sent by Eden to Dulles the meeting was postponed, which emphasises both the importance of the part played by Eden, acting on behalf of Britain, and the further deterioration in Anglo-American relations. Secondly, in April 1955 Eden joined the Central Treaty Organization (CENTO) which already linked Turkey and Iraq and which was joined later in the year by Pakistan and Iran. As Turkey and Great Britain were also members of NATO, and Pakistan and Great Britain were members of SEATO, Eden envisaged CENTO providing a link between NATO and SEATO so as to establish a worldwide defence strategy against Communism, but with the refusal of the United States, the strongest link, to join CENTO, Britain and Eden were rebuffed and Dulles had repaid an old score against Eden. The United States resented the British presence and influence in the Middle East and as Russia had not been particularly active there since 1946, and as Egypt and Syria (who were allies in those days and flirting with Russia) were against the idea, the United States did not feel inclined to further British interests there.

Anthony Eden's short Prime Ministership (April 1955 to January 1957), on the retirement of Winston Churchill, due to ill health, was dominated by the Suez crisis. At its very beginning his reputation as an international statesman was enhanced by his taking part in the summit conference with the Russians in Geneva where he arranged for the controversial visit of the two Russian leaders, Bulganin and Kruschev, to Britain. However, very soon his Government appeared to be in total disarray, not only on larger issues such as the overheating of the economy, which we have already discussed, but on

158

more straightforward matters such as the free vote on the abolition of capital punishment in July 1956, following the execution of Ruth Ellis a year earlier, which was passed in the House of Commons, to the Government's surprise, but in line with a shift in public opinion over the Ruth Ellis case, and defeated in the House of Lords – an unsatisfactory conclusion. Even in his own field, the dismissal of General Glubb (the Commander of the Arab Legion in Jordan) and the disappearance of the frogman, Commander Crabb, at the time of the Russian leaders' visit, were ineptly handled while his failure to appoint an ambassador to the United States in the month before the Suez expedition and his replacement of the Minister of Defence and the First Lord of the Admiralty, shortly before it, were inexplicable lapses. The cabinet reshuffle in December, already mentioned, (p. 100) replacing Butler, as Chancellor of the Exchequer, by Macmillan, and Macmillan as Foreign Secretary, by Selwyn Lloyd, were probably partly motivated by his uneasiness in having such a strong personality as Macmillan as Foreign Secretary – at the very time when he needed a strong figure in this post. In January 1956 there were rumours of his pending resignation, which had to be denied, the *Daily Telegraph* called for the 'smack of firm government' and the polls and by-elections went badly for him and the Government. All this in spite of the fact that his Cabinet colleagues received repeated and frenzied telephone calls from the Prime Minister who seemed to be unable to give an effective lead to the running of the Government. Many reasons were advanced as to how such a transformation in a man's reputation could take place so suddenly, including ill health. However, in my view there were two factors. First, there is a type of politician who is much more at home by temperament and knowledge, in running the Foreign Office, than in the unpredictable jungle of, say, the Home Office. In this respect, the names of Sir Alec Douglas-Home and Douglas Hurd spring to mind – but the quintessential example is that of Sir Anthony Eden. Secondly, the first requisite of a successful Prime Minister is the possession of supreme physical and mental toughness, exhibited to a degree by Sir Winston Churchill and Margaret Thatcher. Anthony Eden notably lacked these qualities, increasingly so and disastrously as the Suez crisis escalated.

Whatever the rights and wrongs of the Suez imbroglio there can be no doubt that it began with the seizure of power in Egypt by Gamal Nasser who set out to emulate Mehemet Ali, the Albanian adventurer and Napoleon's protégé and founder of Egyptian independence and the royal house, which had fallen in 1952, by expelling the Turks, beating the British and slaughtering the Mamelukes. Nasser was the first of the post-war Middle Eastern secular, non-hereditary leaders to attempt to lead the Arab world to which end he set himself up as the spokesman for the neutralist and non-aligned countries, made a treaty of friendship with India, visited Moscow in August 1955 and made an arms deal with Czechoslovakia so as to reduce his dependence on the West. At the same time, he persuaded the Western powers to support his project to build a high dam at Aswan on the River Nile although he had also made the same request to Russia. In the event, the US, Britain and the World Bank promised financial contributions ($56m, $14m, and $200m respectively) provided that Egypt contributed $900m, but this was ruled out by Egypt mortgaging her cotton crop in order to pay for Czech arms. Nasser said that he had expectations of a Russian loan, and this is how the dam was eventually built, but Dulles and the American politicians in Washington were suspicious of Nasser's ambitions and withdrew their offer of a loan in July 1956, to be followed by Britain and the World Bank. Nasser's riposte was to nationalize the Suez Canal Company in order that its revenue could be used to finance the building of the Aswan dam.

The reaction in Britain was like the exploding of a bomb and violently different sides were taken among friends, families and politicians who usually found themselves in agreement. The country was divided as it had not been in living memory. However, the majority, including the Labour-voting working man, took the same view as the Government, that Nasser should not be allowed to break the bounds of international law, agreed to by his predecessor Neguib, with impunity. Against the popular view were those who felt that the canal was Egyptian, in any case – the 'bleedingheart' and left-wing brigade, the former including three members of the Government, Anthony Nutting, Sir Edward Boyle and Walter Monckton, who all resigned, as well as around 30 Conservative MPs who were against the action but who nevertheless did not attack the Government. Although the parallel should not be carried too far, this was a pre-play of the Gulf Crisis of 1992, the difference being that the former was the 'mere' violation of a treaty while the latter was, in addition, the violation of another, smaller country. Another difference was that in the case of Suez there was never any question of the United Nations sanctioning the use of force. True to form, the Labour Party, and its leader, Gaitskell, were belligerent both in and out of Parliament but would only agree to the use of force if this was under the auspices of the United Nations, but these were the days of the Russian veto and the domination of the UN by the Third World and non-aligned countries that Nasser had been so busy cultivating. As it was, there were a number of compromises suggested by, among others, Dulles, effectively proposing the internationalization of the canal with all kinds of guarantees for Egypt, such as the recognition of her sovereignty, agreement on tolls and the arbitration of disputes, but they were all rejected by Nasser. When, in desperation, Britain and France approached the UN with a similar proposal it was vetoed by Russia. Bearing in mind the mounting evidence of Eden's indecisiveness a most important factor was the crescendo of conflicting advice that he received from all sides. On the one hand, there was the aggressive stance of the Conservative 'Suez Group', which had popular support, and, on the other hand, there was the minority who made a moral issue of the matter with, in the middle, those who fell between the two extremes. From the beginning to the end the Americans, and especially Dulles, took all three positions. Initially, Eisenhower and Dulles advised caution for, as we have seen, they were not happy about supporting British interests in the Middle East while the former was due for re-election in November and was standing as a peace candidate. Dulles played a key role in the negotiations which attempted to find a peaceful solution. In his words: 'A way has to be found to make Nasser disgorge what he has attempted to swallow,' but on another occasion he went further and hinted that the use of military force might be called for. Having decided to use force, Eden's greatest mistake was to trust the Americans, in general, and Dulles, in particular, in view of the extent of the deterioration in Anglo-American relations and the personal antipathy between Dulles and himself, especially as he acted a week before the holding of the Presidential election. However, it must be said that Eden did not take the Americans into his confidence over his military plans. Also, and although I cannot prove it, I am sure that Eden was swayed by the publishing, at the time of the crucial parliamentary debate, of a very strongly worded leading article in *The Times* which implied that there was a time in the life of all nations when they had to defend their vital interests, by force, if necessary, and that this time had now arrived for Britain. It will be remembered that Eden had had personal experience of the failure of appeasement to deter Mussolini and Hitler.

Finally, there was the most important pro-war influence of all – that of France. The Suez Canal was also the route for the transit of French oil and, even more important, France was fighting Algerian rebels whose main ally was Nasser. The fatal 'link' was the intense cultivation of the new Israeli state by France who throughout 1955 and 1956 was busy arming Israel so that she could withstand the expected Arab attack in return for the humiliating defeat following their attack in 1948. The Egyptian army was making preparatory incursions into Israeli territory at the time. (It is interesting to note that prior to the Gulf Crisis the French had been prominent in selling arms to the Arabs, notably Iraq.) This fateful combination led to the French concocting a plan whereby Israel, on the pretext of Egyptian provocation, would attack Egypt in Sinai and British and French intervention would take place in order to preserve the security of the Suez Canal. During six weeks in October and November the French worked on Eden and persuaded him to agree, which agreement was embodied in the Treaty of Sevres, signed on 26 October. Eden's dilemma was that, rightly, he was not prepared to 'appease' Nasser but unfortunately he did not have the 'stomach' and nerve to do the only thing that could have been successful – to have attacked Nasser alone, on the moral and legal grounds of enforcing the treaty of 1954 regarding the Canal. Instead, Israel attacked on 29 October, and an Anglo-French ultimatum was issued which expired on 31 October. Following the bombing of Egyptian airfields, Anglo-French paratroopers landed at Port Said on 5 November and captured it within 24 hours. However, at midnight the next day there was a ceasefire following the precipitate action of Eisenhower who, acting through the United Nations a week before his election, condemned the war and ordered the combatants to withdraw. Also, there was the veiled threat of nuclear war by the Soviet Union. We have already noted the severe run on the pound, following the withdrawal of American support, which led to misgivings by Macmillan, Chancellor of the Exchequer, and previously, probably Eden's main supporter in the Cabinet. Finally, there was the humiliating recourse to a loan from the IMF, as well as Eden's exhaustion and his need to withdraw to Jamaica to recuperate at the end of November. He had paid a very heavy price for his alienation of John Foster Dulles.

The recriminations were immediate and violent and the repercussions were profound. Some of the newspapers which had supported Eden turned against him and there were frenzied scenes in the House of Commons between 6 and 8 November, following Gaitskell's call to the Conservatives on 3 November to replace him. Churchill, profoundly, said, 'I am not sure I should have dared to start, but I am sure I should not have dared to stop'. The unkindest cut of all was Dulles's informal comment: 'Why on earth didn't you go through with it?'. But Eden was never tempted to do this because his respect for international law and order (the reason for his initial action), in the form of the UN order to withdraw, was absolutely sincere and more important to him than the protection of Britain's interests in the Middle East which had already been covered by his

162

1954 undertaking to withdraw from the canal and by the move to Cyprus. As in the lives of individuals, so in the lives of nations, decisions leading to major changes in direction and lifestyle are not made intellectually, in a vacuum, but more usually, as the result of some action or event, usually unpremeditated. Eden summed it up when he wrote, retrospectively: 'Our intervention at least closed the chapter of complacency about the situation in the Middle East.' More immediately, the crisis further weakened Anglo-American relations, (the 'special relationship'), it soured the incipient accord between Britain and France which was to have profound consequences, it gave the Soviet Union the opportunity to crush the Hungarian revolt which coincided with the Port Said landing and it permitted Nasser to reinforce his position in the Middle East, although his wings had been undoubtedly clipped. Finally, the action provided a watershed of the utmost importance in post-war British history. I have already noted (p. 147): 'In 1952, Britain's defence expenditure was higher per capita than that of the United States. For a convalescent economy, the commitments were enormous and unsustainable.' It was for this reason that Britain undertook to evacuate the Canal Zone in 1954 and from that year to reduce defence expenditure from its peak level at the time of the Korean War. But whereas Churchill and Eden thought in terms of Britain playing a major and comparatively independent part in maintaining world peace, Suez cruelly exposed both Britain's dependence on the United States and her economic status as no more than a second-class power. Too much has been made of this by the ever-present anti-British, British contingent for it was on this assumption that Bevin constructed his initial consensus of persuading the United States to play the leading part, but it is notable that after 1956 there was never again any serious attempt by a British government to play the part of a Great Power. In this respect, Eden's aberration was not Suez but that period between 1951 and 1955 when he was so scintillatingly successful as Churchill's Foreign Secretary. The failure at Suez was not necessary and was mainly the result of Eden's inadequacy as a decisive leader in times of crisis. Margaret Thatcher, on the other hand, would have carried it off brilliantly, in spite of the odds being stacked against her.

There are three interlocking strands in the foreign and defence policies of the Macmillan governments (1957–1964), all a part of the post-war consensus – imperial disengagement, the development of the nuclear deterrent (the fact that it was no longer independent being a tribute to the rebuilding of the 'special relationship') and reluctant Europeanism giving way to the earliest attempts to come to terms

163

with the strong tides of Europeanism flowing on the Continent. We shall deal with imperial disengagement first remembering that the effect of the Suez crisis was to strengthen the disillusionment of the British people with the Empire and its responsibilities, and to prepare them for the period of imperial disengagement which was to follow. Churchill was true to his word in that, apart from the withdrawal from the Canal Zone, the only 'retreat from Empire' in his peacetime government, was the granting of independence to Sudan, which was intricately involved with Anglo-Egyptian relations and one of the causes of Egyptian hostility when it was not ceded to Egypt. On the other hand, Churchill's Government played its part in the difficult business of transforming the British Empire into the British Commonwealth. There were three types of colony. First, there were those such as the West African colonies where there were few whites and where it was believed that it would be irresponsible to grant self-government prematurely, so that a lengthy period of preparation was envisaged by means of education and a gradual introduction to the processes of government by the membership of legislative councils, and the like. Secondly, there were those such as the East African colonies with large numbers of white settlers of British descent (the 'Kith and Kin' colonies) who had important and valuable interests to defend. The Churchill Government set the pattern for these colonies when in 1953 it established the Central African Federation consisting of Southern Rhodesia, Northern Rhodesia and Nyasaland, with settler-dominated constitutions. The federation device was later established in the West Indies Federation, Malaysia, the South Arabian Federation, Nigeria and Uganda. Thirdly, there were the fortress colonies which were regarded as vital for strategic reasons (Malta, Gibraltar, Aden, Suez, Hong Kong and Singapore); we have already seen that there was the withdrawal from one of these, Suez, in 1954. The problems were the persistent agitation of the indigenous peoples for self-government, sooner rather than later. For example, limited representative government had been introduced in West Africa as early as the 1920s – in Nigeria in 1922, in Sierra Leone in 1924 and in the Gold Coast in 1925. There was also the perpetual problem of tribal rivalries in Africa, as well as the opposition of the native populations to the constitutions of the East African Federation and the stresses and strains between black and white in the other major 'Kith and Kin' colony, Kenya. There, the Kikuyu tribe had been active since the early 1920s, with Jomo Kenyatta its leader since 1928, culminating in the Mau Mau rebellion between 1952 and 1956. At the same time, there was violent opposition to the British in Cyprus where EOKA under Colonal Grivas, and Archbishop

164

Makarios, were endeavouring to attain a union with Greece.

The conventional view is that Macmillan's Government was overwhelmed by its problems soon after the election of 1959 but this was certainly not true in regard to its handling of imperial disengagement for it was in this period that attempts to restrain the ambitions of the indigenous peoples were finally abandoned, even though it was realized that with the departure of the British there would be severe problems, at the best and, at the worst, political and economic chaos. It was summed up in Macmillan's famous 'Wind of Change' speech in South Africa in 1960, which was doubly important for it struck a cord with British popular opinion, which as a result of Mau Mau atrocities, EOKA violence and the Suez debacle was becoming disillusioned with the 'burdens' of Empire. The process had already begun before 1959 with the granting of independence to the Gold Coast, as Ghana, in 1957, under the charismatic Kwame Nkrumah, and to Malaysia, as a federation, in 1957, and to the West Indies Federation in 1958. However, it was the advent of Iain Macleod as Colonial Secretary in October 1959, immediately after the election, which gave decolonization an impetus which was unstoppable. It was a classic instance of consensus, for although he clashed with the Foreign Secretary (who said, memorably, that Macleod was 'too clever by half'), over the speed at which he was progressing, he was in line with the elite around which the new consensus was forming, as also was Macmillan. Therefore, owing to the tight discipline of British party politics, especially under the Conservatives, Macleod arranged a number of Party conferences over Kenya, Nyasaland and Northern Rhodesia which broke the hopes of the white settlers who had been so strongly supported by the Conservatives. In February 1961 James Callaghan, the shadow Foreign Secretary, said in the House of Commons: 'I have not been conscious of any gulf [between himself and Macleod] over the last eighteen months.' Thus, although Macleod was only Colonial Secretary until 1961 it is fair to link his name with the granting of independence during the rest of the Macmillan Government. In West Africa, Nigeria (1960) and Sierra Leone (1961) followed Ghana. In Nigeria, like Cyprus (1960) and Uganda (1962) it was realized that future troubles were on the horizon. Also, in Africa, there was Tanganyika (1961), Kenya (1963–4) and Zanzibar (1963–4). The first of the fortress colonies to achieve independence was Malta (1963–4) following unexpected anti-British developments and a change of government, the process, which was begun under Macmillan, being completed under Wilson. Finally, the compromise of creating federations of colonies broke down in the face of the opposition of the indigenous peoples and secessionist forces which were not disregarded by Macmillan and Macleod. The West Indies Federation ended in 1962 and in the same year Jamaica and Trinidad became independent. The first and most controversial of the federations, the Central African Federation, broke up in 1963 and Northern Rhodesia (Zambia) and Nyasaland (Malawi) attained independence under both the Macmillan and Wilson Governments. The remaining federations, Malaysia and South Arabia became independent under the Wilson Government. All these countries joined the new, multiracial Commonwealth, with only three doing so as republics, so that in spite of the later trauma posed by Rhodesia it can be said that by 1964, 'Britain succeeded in divesting herself of her empire with remarkable dignity and skill,'[1] not to mention rapidity.

However, the successful creation of the multiracial Commonwealth did create problems the first of which led indirectly to the departure of South Africa from the Commonwealth. Following the election of the Afrikaans National party in 1948, the racist policy of apartheid which it had developed was, naturally, unacceptable to the new, emerging African states in the 1960s as well as to the other members of the 'new' Commonwealth, especially Canada. Macmillan's 1960 'Wind of Change' speech was delivered to the South African Parliament in Cape Town, and although it could be used to justify political freedom for all Africans it was, in fact, specifically aimed against apartheid which he had told the South African Government that Britain could not support. Although Macmillan, correctly, refused to adopt the calls of the Labour and Liberal Parties to impose a boycott of South African goods, on the grounds that there were many offensive governments which went free, the Sharpeville Massacre of 1960, when Africans were shot by the police, put further pressure on the British Government which was induced to state the unacceptable nature of the laws of apartheid at the 1960 Commonwealth Conference, in spite of the fact that there was an understanding that British governments would not interfere in the domestic concerns of Commonwealth members. The South African response was to declare itself a republic in 1961, following a national referendum and, much to the disappointment of Macmillan and the members of his Government, Dr Verwoerd, the South African leader, who was himself not in favour, found that a majority of his colleagues were unwilling to apply for Commonwealth membership. Although noises were made about continued co-operation between

---

[1] *Post-War Britain*, by Alan Sked and Chris Cook, p. 144.

the two countries, such as the maintenance of South Africa–Commonwealth trade preferences, it was the end of one era and the beginning of another very unhappy one.

The second problem, immigration, arose from the fact that the nineteenth-century fiction that all British subjects had the same rights, regardless of where they were born in the Empire, ceased to be fiction. It will be remembered that in the events leading up to the Crimean War (1854–6), Lord Palmerton blockaded Greece, at Piraeus, in 1850, on the grounds that the Greeks had transgressed against a British subject, Don Pacifico, whose rights were to be regarded and protected in the same way as those of a Roman citizen of old – '*civis Britannicus sum*', in Palmerston's idealistic words. But the reduction of pre-war constraints, the improvement in travel facilities, the affluence of Britain and the security of its Welfare State, together with its political freedom and liberalism, made it a magnet for the members of the Commonwealth – 'a quarter' of the world's population! Furthermore, because of the low level of unemployment in Britain immigration was encouraged by people such as Enoch Powell's Ministry of Health, in order to overcome the shortage of nurses and other staff, as well as those responsible for running the transport and postal services who were desperately short of labour at this less-skilled end of the market. By the 1950s, there was a significant increase in Indians, Pakistani and West Indian immigrants, the last-named arising largely from United States legislation in 1952 banning them from that country. Whereas there were around 20,000 immigrants annually by 1959, the number had risen to 115,150 in 1961. By this time the Government had been alerted to the attendant problems such as the tendency to congregate in certain areas, especially in London and the Midlands, leading to racial violence in Nottingham and Notting Hill Gate, in London, in 1958, as well as the consequent strain on social services such as housing, health and education. In fact, the Cabinet papers of the 1950s show that a ban on inward immigration was considered. In passing its Commonwealth Immigration Act of 1962 the Government took the only responsible view and action. The Act was to be for a trial period of five years and did not apply to those Commonwealth citizens who could support themselves from private means, which the Act's opponents criticized on the grounds that it discriminated between black and white Commonwealth citizens. For the remainder, they needed to have a job to go to, or the requisite skills or qualifications or, lastly, they could enter as part of a quota of immigrants which was to be decided by the Government. Although the Bill was popular with working-class opinion, which was eventually to be led by Enoch

Powell, the Labour and Liberal Parties both roundly condemned it as racist and thoroughly unenlightened, in spite of its popularity with the former's traditional supporters. It is not therefore surprising that when Labour came to power in 1964, the Immigration Act was neither repealed nor amended. I have already written that it has become a part of the consensus in spite of periodic alarums and excursions.

In dealing with the second strand in the foreign and defence policies of the Macmillan Government, the development of the nuclear deterrent, we shall also take note of the rebuilding of the 'special relationship' with which it was intimately connected – the consensus of Atlanticism, in a word. Macmillan's first objective when he 'emerged' as Prime Minister on 10 January 1957 was to restore good relations with the United States, although he made a point of not apologizing about Suez, saying in his first broadcast as Prime Minister:

> True partnership is based upon respect. We don't intend to part from the Americans and we don't intend to be satellites. I am sure that they don't want us to be so.'

However, after his re-election Eisenhower showed his appreciation of the continued problems and dangers in the Middle East by enunciating the 'Eisenhower Doctrine' on 5 January to the effect that any Middle East nations threatened 'by alien forces hostile to freedom' could call on American military aid and assistance to withstand 'armed attack from any country controlled by international Communism'. As early as April, King Hussein of Jordan had to call on the United States when faced with a Nasser-inspired revolt and a year later (1958) it was necessary for American marines to land in Beirut to secure the safety of the Lebanese Government. Further evidence of mounting tension in the Middle East was the formation of the United Arab Republic by Syria and Egypt, as also was the pro-Nasser Ba'athist coup in Iraq in 1958 – in which Saddam Hussein was involved from the beginning and of which he gained control in 1968. The wheel had turned full circle when, with American approval, British paratroopers were landed in Amman to support the still threatened King Hussein. The stage was therefore set for a symbolic gesture giving evidence as to the restoration of the Anglo-American Alliance, the occasion for which was the meeting of Eisenhower and Dulles with Macmillan and his Foreign Secretary, Selwyn Lloyd, on British soil at Bermuda in 1957. Seven months later the Queen and Prince Philip visited the USA following the tour of Canada. At Bermuda, Eisenhower and Macmillan (who took complete charge of his foreign policy) had reaffirmed the resolution of the Security Council of October 1956 regarding the freedom of the Suez Canal, in case Nasser needed reminding of this fact, and, following the Queen's visit they signed a Declaration of Common Purpose.

After Macmillan's cabinet reshuffle in March 1957 he retained only four of Churchill's old cabinet and appointed younger men who had been elected after 1950. However, he appointed Duncan Sandys as Minister of Defence, with increased powers over the other service ministers, to help him with his next task which was to restructure British defence policy. This was embodied in the White Paper on Defence, in April 1957, which announced the end of National Service by 1960, a drastic reduction in the number of servicemen from 700,000 to 400,000 and the establishment of the nuclear deterrent as the corner-stone of Britain's defence policy. It cannot be claimed, however, that this was a new departure for it was only another instalment, albeit a fairly decisive one, of Britain's perpetual post-war dilemma of reconciling her worldwide defence commitments with her economic constraints. Britain was spending 8 per cent of her GNP on defence, compared with 3 per cent between the wars, and this compared with 6 per cent by France and 4 per cent by Germany, both of whose economies were now growing faster than Britain's. As before, it was hoped that Britain's hydrogen bomb – successfully tested in 1957 – would permit defence economies following reductions in conventional forces and arms. Furthermore, the possession of an independent nuclear deterrent would assert Britain's literal independence, with no more dependence on the United States. I disagree with the charge that Britain was still hankering after superpower status for in view of the Russian nuclear threat it was legitimate to seek the security that could best be guaranteed by an independent nuclear deterrent.

In 1958 the delivery of the British hydrogen bomb to the Vulcan bomber force began and in the same year Macmillan succeeded in obtaining amendments, in favour of Britain, to the American McMahon Act of 1946 whereby foreigners were prohibited access to American nuclear secrets. One result of this was that the British learned that their nuclear technology was inadequate now that they began to develop Blue Streak, a ground-based missile, but by 1960 this had also been abandoned so that arrangements were made with Eisenhower to replace it by the American Skybolt missile while the Americans were enabled to lease a nuclear submarine base near Glasgow. As Skybolt was an air-to-ground missile it could be delivered by Vulcan bombers so to that extent it could still be regarded as British, but unfortunately this satisfactory arrangement came to an untimely end when the Americans cancelled Skybolt in 1962. In the meantime, they had developed the submarine-based Polaris missile which Macmillan was granted the right to purchase by the new US President, John Kennedy, by the Nassau Agreement, when they met there in December 1962. Several factors arise from these developments. First, and most important, whereas the Eisenhower administration had returned to accepting the 'special relationship' as the natural order of things, in 1961, Kennedy, under the influence of his Under-Secretary of State for Western Europe, George Ball, sought to encourage the Western European countries to strengthen their conventional arms and to leave the nuclear response to the United States, with her 'tremendous (nuclear) arsenal'. Furthermore, it was the express intention to downgrade the importance of the 'special relationship' by treating Britain, and encouraging Britain to regard herself, as an ordinary Western European power. This was not to be, however, partly because Macmillan (whose mother was American) exercised his considerable old-world charm on the younger man, and partly because of the extremely close personal relationship between the British Ambassador, David Ormsby-Gore, and the Kennedys, but also because, when it came to the point, the Americans were not really prepared to ditch the 'special relationship' which was to pay them dividends in the years to come as it had already done in the form of British support during the Cuban Missile Crisis in October 1962. Secondly, Britain's nuclear deterrent could not now be called truly independent in spite of the fact that it was to be fitted with British nuclear warheads into British nuclear submarines. On the other hand, Macmillan negotiated better terms with Kennedy than Attlee did with Truman in 1950, for although Polaris was to be used mainly for Western defence there was a clause adding, 'except where the British Government may decide their supreme national interests are at stake'. At the time, the Nassau Agreement was regarded as a British diplomatic triumph and, in spite of the contrary view of the British, anti-British, school of thought there is no necessity to differ from that conclusion or to agree with the latter's view that it was all the more disastrous in view of the fact that it was probably this that decided General de Gaulle to reject Britain's attempt to enter the European Economic Community in 1963. Thirdly, the policy embarked upon in 1957 of reducing Britain's defence expenditure was not fulfilled. In the first place, the expenditure on the nuclear programme had escalated, as was inevitable, and secondly, there was no diminution of Britain's conventional involvement in the world's trouble spots. In

1958 there were more than 100,000 British troops in the Middle and Far East but even these were insufficient in view of the crises in Kuwait and Berlin in 1961, and the confrontation between Malaysia and Indonesia in 1963.[1] In all, in 1963 the defence estimates were around £150 million more than those for 1962 which was bad news for the Chancellor of the Exchequer, Reginald Maudling. Nevertheless, by this time, and in spite of Britain's worldwide commitments and excessive defence expenditure, the Cuban Missile Crisis emphasized once again that there were only two world powers and that Britain was not one of them. Significantly, it was in the previous month that the former American Secretary of State, Dean Acheson, made his memorable remark that 'Great Britain has lost an empire and has not yet found a role'. In point of fact, his views were identical to those of George Ball.

Whereas Atlanticism and the development of the nuclear deterrent had the undivided support of the Conservative Party, it was not so easy for the Labour Party which, as we have already noted, shifted to the left after its defeat in 1951 so that, together with its further defeats in 1955 and 1959, the Labour leadership and its left wing were split during the period over Atlanticism, defence and nuclear policy. For example, Aneurin Bevan, the leader of the left-wing 'Bevanites', was persistently critical of NATO, CENTO and SEATO (which last he criticized as being an embodiment of anti-colonialism in Asia) while he attacked not only Churchill and Eden, but also Attlee, when he heard about the construction of the H-bomb. Yet, after he had lost the Labour leadership to Gaitskell, on the retirement of Attlee, as shadow Foreign Secretary, he opposed the left-wing campaign for nuclear disarmament on the grounds that it would not be right to send a Labour Foreign Secretary 'naked into the conference chamber'. However, after 1959 the left wing, now afforced by the dreaded Frank Cousins, the leader of the Transport and General Workers Union, both of which supported the campaign for Nuclear Disarmament (CND), founded in 1958, challenged the leadership over defence policy, culminating in the Labour Party Conference of 1960 when they won a resolution calling for nuclear

---

[1] In view of the Gulf War in 1990 it is interesting to recall that following the termination by the British of the Protectorate of Kuwait in 1961, the new-found independence of Kuwait was rudely interrupted by the new Ba'athist regime in Iraq which reasserted the Iraqi claim to Kuwait. The intervention of British troops removed the Iraqi threat after which the Arab League (Egypt and Syria) assumed a peacekeeping role.

disarmament. Fortunately for the Labour Party, Hugh Gaitskell had a clear head and strength of character. He had already shown his mettle when he had threatened to resign from Attlee's Government in 1951 if it did not support a UN resolution which declared Communist China to be the aggressor in the Korean war. He now threatened to resign from the leadership of the Party if the 1960 resolution was not rejected, denouncing the 'pacifists, unilateralists and fellow-travellers' who had supported it and promising that he would 'fight, fight and fight again to bring back sanity and honesty' and 'to save the Party we love'. In the 1961 Party Conference the offending resolution was reversed although the left wing were still fulminating about such things as training German soldiers on British soil and the establishment of American Polaris bases in Britain – and so it continued in the Labour Party.

The opening quotation in this chapter on Foreign and Defence Policy includes the statement: 'Membership of the European economic and political institutions was not at this time on the political agenda but became so in the 1960s.' The chapter shall be completed with the discussion of this topic. In dealing with the 'reluctant Europeanism' of the post-war Labour Government, I have already emphasized the pragmatic and positively insular approach of Attlee and Bevin to any vestige of a supra-national Europe compared with Churchill who propagated the idea sedulously, on a world stage, but I have also emphasized that the difference was more apparent than real, for Churchill and his Conservative colleagues did not ever contemplate direct British involvement in any form of European economic or political union. Anthony Eden summarized the post-war consensus in regard to the British attitude to European federation when he said: 'We know in our bones that this is something we cannot do.' Thus, the formation of the OEEC and the Churchill-inspired 'Congress of Europe' conference at the Hague, took place contemporaneously in April and May 1948, respectively. The former was the successful and practical institution resulting from the equally successful and practical Marshall Plan but Bevin made sure that it stayed that way by eliminating the bureaucratic and supranational threats embodied in a French attempt to strengthen the powers of the OEEC Secretariat and to set up a European Customs Union. The latter was an embarrassing political 'hothouse' as far as Bevin was concerned who rebutted 'the Congress's resolution to form a European economic and political union together with a European Assembly', in the manner already quoted on page 142 which spelt out the British way of proceeding from the particular to the general as opposed to the Continental way of proceeding from the general to

172

the particular. In other words, European economic and political union should only come about as the result of many years of practical co-operation and not as the result of a collective glint in the eye of a conference in the Hague in 1948 or a body of bureaucrats in Brussels 40 years later. On the other hand, as has already been noted (p. 143), 'Bevin was all in favour of European co-operation, especially with France, when it came to the all-important question of defence' which resulted in the Anglo-French Treaty at Dunkirk in 1947, culminating in the wider-ranging Brussels Treaty in 1948 – the Western Union. However, as we have seen, the culmination of Bevin's work as Foreign Secretary was the linking of the Western Union with North America by the Atlantic Alliance of 1949. Thus, as I have described on page 147, as a result of the Korean War (1950–53) 'German rearmament was initiated under the auspices of NATO with the consequent strengthening of the Atlantic Alliance as was the United States's acceptance of its role as leader of the Western World' – all of which was a fitting memorial to the work of Ernest Bevin as well as being a rebuff to the concept of European federalism.

The European federalists, however, were to be rebuffed no longer and during the 1950s there were a number of important moves that made the ideal of Europeanism a reality. The first, the proposed formation of the European Coal and Steel Community, had already been announced in May 1950 as the 'Schuman Plan', and it established a common market and supranational control of iron and steel production for France, Germany, Belgium, Italy, the Netherlands and Luxembourg. Predictably, the indestructible Jean Monnet was the author of the idea which was espoused by Robert Schuman, the French Foreign Minister, the initial object being to limit any future German rearmament, but there was also the allied aim of curbing German nationalism by absorbing it in a supranational structure as well as the benefits of economic integration. The treaty creating the Coal and Steel Community was signed in April 1951 – without the adherence of Great Britain. This was inevitable in view of the fact that the Labour Government had not been consulted before the original announcement in 1950, the supranational concept conflicted with the recent nationalization of the British iron and steel industry and, finally, Britain could not accept the condition that the fact of supranationality should be accepted in advance. This last condition rings 'a bell' of recognition 40 years later and the pragmatic words of Attlee and Bevin are as true today as they were in 1950, and should have been weighed much more by subsequent commentators who have blithely lamented our failure to join the Community there and then. The Conservatives were not

173

unsympathetic to the Schuman Plan, in view of Churchill's romantic Europeanism, but, as we have seen, when it came to the point they were no more likely than Labour to encourage British participation in European institutions. It was due to them, and Churchill and Eden in particular, that the second important move to advance European federalism, the European Defence Community, failed in 1954. Originating in the dying days of the Labour Government in 1950, its gestation period, in the form of the Pleven Plan, lasted until 1952 and paralleled the successful Schuman Plan. I have described the birth and death of this particular saga on pages 153–5.

The third, and most successful and significant move of the European federalists was the creation in 1957 of the European Economic Community, together with Euratom, the common atomic programme. The initiative on this occasion came from Belgium, whose Foreign Minister, Paul-Henri Spaak, called a meeting of the Six in June 1955, to discuss the proposal by the Benelux governments to form a European Common Market. Britain had been invited but did not attend, in spite of the fact that there was no insistence on a prior supranationalist commitment as in the Schuman Plan, and Harold Macmillan, the Foreign Secretary at the time, sent only an under-secretary from the Board of Trade to represent Britain on the Spaak committee, which was formed to prepare a detailed report on the proposals. Events moved much faster than the British Government expected and the treaties establishing the European Economic Community and Euratom were signed in Rome in March 1957, subsequently ratified by the Six and became effective on 1 January 1958. As with the Schuman Plan, the anti-British, retrospective myth has arisen that the British failure to sign the Treaty of Rome was inexcusable, both absolutely and relatively. The first charge is wrong and the second, that if we had joined we would have been in the position to remedy the plan's defects, is highly questionable. From the British point of view, the favourable factors were the absence of the prior supranationalist commitment and the fact that it was an economic concept, a Common Market, for as we shall be discussing in the next few pages, there were good reasons why the British were interested in this. On the other hand, there were the negative and reactionary aspects, especially in the cases of France and Germany, with which Britain, correctly, was unable to comply. The Common Market was to include agricultural as well as industrial products and from the beginning there was a trade-off between France and Germany whereby the former opened her market to the latter's industrial products in return for Germany supporting virtual protection for France's backward agricultural industry. Whereas

174

England, from the later middle ages, saw a movement, culminating in the late fifteenth century, whereby the inefficient medieval agricultural system was replaced by a modern system which is recognisable today, following enclosures, and, in the eighteenth century, the Agrarian Revolution led to the application of modern methods such as the rotation of crops and the sowing of seed by Jethro Tull's drill, European agriculture was little changed, especially in France. England also had the advantage of primogeniture, which meant that family estates and farms were not split up on death while in Europe there was continuous subdivision into smaller and more uneconomic units. Apart from Denmark, English agriculture was by far the most efficient in Europe, as it remains today. The terrible device to be used to protect both the industry and the agriculture of the Six was the external tariff, to be applied against the rest of the world. Apart from the facts that this was incompatible with Britain's system of Commonwealth Protection and that it was supranational, the main objection was that it was an inward-looking, exclusive and old-fashioned protectionist device whereas Britain looked to the more inclusive OEEC to undertake European tariff negotiations which, together with the early post-war GATT, was a free-trade-orientated organization. While European agriculture was hundreds of years behind the times, European industry had grown in the second half of the nineteenth century behind rigid protective barriers. It is inconceivable that Britain should have joined such an outfit and equally inconceivable that, having joined, she would have had any success in altering for the better the well-laid plans of France and Germany.

Nevertheless, then, as now (written in March 1991), Britain looked favourably on a non-protectionist, inclusive European economic market so that as a riposte to the Common Market Spaak talks she produced the idea at the beginning of 1956 of a European free trade area to include the Six, Great Britain and the other OEEC countries. Unlike the Common Market, it was not supranational so that its members would negotiate through their respective governments, there would be no common external tariff and it would not apply to agricultural products and foodstuffs. After consultation with the OEEC, Eden produced the British proposals for European free trade in October 1956, and although they were looked upon favourably by Erhardt in Germany and Mendes in France – both liberal-minded men – there was no real chance that they would be accepted by their respective countries. Germany was tempted by the prospect of an enlarged market for its industrial products but the French were not prepared even to contemplate a system without a common external

175

tariff behind which her inefficient agriculture could hide, and which would keep cheap Commonwealth foodstuffs out of Britain without which, as a result of her cheap food policy, she would be a much less formidable industrial competitor to France and Germany. As we have seen, the Treaties of Rome were signed without her but Macmillan, who was now Prime Minister, was determined to establish a European free-trade area, including the Six EEC countries, a task which was made all the more difficult by the return of General de Gaulle to power in France in 1958. De Gaulle's pathological aversion to the 'Anglo-Saxon' hegemony of the United States and Great Britain was reinforced in 1958 when he received two major rebuffs from the former, in the first place when he proposed that France should join the US and Britain in controlling the Western Alliance and, secondly, when, unlike Britain, France was excluded from sharing American nuclear secrets under the terms of the McMahon Act. Similarly, Macmillan's influence with Adenauer was constrained after he visited Moscow following the 'Berlin crisis' fomented by Kruschev's demand in November 1958 that the Allies should leave Berlin, for Adenauer was suspicious of secret agreements leading to a recognition of the East German Government or the inclusion of West Berlin with East Germany. Thus the negotiations which were taking place between Britain's Reginald Maudling and the Six were promptly ended in November 1958 on the grounds that it was 'not possible' to create a free trade area without a common external tariff. Thus the brilliant and exciting concept of the Six being included in a genuine free trade area was sacrificed on the altar of French agriculture, as has been so much else since then. Consequently, Britain formed the European Free Trade Association (EFTA) in Stockholm in January 1960 which included the Scandinavian countries, Switzerland, Austria and Portugal. (Soon after going to the City of London as an economist my first ambitious undertaking was to write a review of 'The Investment Implications of the European Free Trade Area'.) Owing to the economic division of Europe, the OEEC could no longer perform its original function so that it became the Organization for Economic Co-operation and Development (OECD), including the United States and Japan, in which guise it has achieved much respect as a body concerned with the attainment of international economic and financial stability.

This brings us to the end of the period which we have called 'reluctant Europeanism'. We now have to deal with the change in emphasis in the 1960s when membership of European institutions appears on the 'political agenda' and in doing so we have to remind ourselves of Churchill's 'three circles' – Europe, the Commonwealth and the Atlantic 'special relationship'. Politically, it was only natural that with the 'process of imperial disengagement' Britain began to look with more interest at the European circle as a means of increasing her world influence. Diplomatically and strategically the older Commonwealth countries were drifting away from the British influence, Canada aligning herself with the United States, while we have already noted the ANZUS pact between Australia, New Zealand and the United States as well as South Africa's withdrawal from the Commonwealth in 1961. In spite of the idealism of the Labour Party in regard to the 'new' Commonwealth it was destined to be a political chimera in view of the extensive 'watering-down' of the Royal or Imperial connotation and of the fact that its members eventually lined up with the hostile Third World countries when it came to the point. Following Suez, India's Nehru and Ghana's Nkrumah were involved in diplomatic manoeuvres which led to the creation of the Non-Aligned Movement in 1963. The first Commonwealth Immigration Act of 1962 emphasized the problems posed by the 'new' Commonwealth, many of whose countries were in receipt of British aid as well as adding to the burden of the defence budget. A second influence inclining Britain towards Europe was the fact that from the immediate post-war period and throughout the subsequent years the United States encouraged Britain to involve herself in anything that would improve Europe's hegemony. Initially, this was incompatible with Britain's heavy political and emotional imperial commitment, and eventually with the 'special relationship', in view of the supranational and protective connotations of the European idea. Indeed, it was de Gaulle's preference for a European Community of sovereign states in place of a supranational Europe that was the key to Macmillan's decision that this was a Europe which Britain could contemplate joining. However, throughout the period British governments sedulously fostered co-operation in matters of defence and, as we have seen in the events leading to the formation of EFTA, they were interested in increasing trade by eliminating political and economic barriers. In fact, the third and most important reason for Britain turning towards Europe was economic.

The 'never had it so good' euphoria at the time of Macmillan's successful election in 1959 was replaced by 1962 by a sense of failure and pessimism, especially in the economic field. We have seen that balance of payments problems led Heathcoat-Amory to initiate a credit squeeze in 1960 which was intensified in 1961 by his successor, Selwyn Lloyd, as the sterling crisis escalated. At the same time, Britain's faltering economic performance was compared unfavourably

177

with that of the Six member countries of the EEC whose economies were growing dynamically, as the following table illustrates:

Industrial Production Figures[1]

Year	UK	The Six
1950	94	80
1958	114	144
1963	119	142

Note. 1953 = 100.

What was worse, from the point of view of Britain's morale, was that French industrial production had overtaken Britain's for the first time since the nineteenth century. But the figures that clinched the argument were that the sterling area's share of total British exports diminished from 48 per cent in 1950 to 30 per cent in 1960 while, on the other hand, total trade with the Six, both imports and exports, was on a significantly rising trend. In other words, the dynamics of post-war trade were favourable in Europe and unfavourable in the Commonwealth, but this argument can be used to deny that the industrial and economic expansion of the Six was due to the Common Market or that it was necessary for Britain to join the Common Market in order to participate. The figures show that this was happening in any case before the formation of the EEC, and the fact that it was greater in the Six than in the UK was the result of the need to rebuild a greater degree of wartime devastation in Europe, especially in Western Germany, than in the UK. Academic studies have also concluded that the economic expansion of Europe and the existence of the EEC were a mere coincidence and that the former did not necessarily follow from the latter. The above table also indicates that there was no growth in this respect in the Six between 1958 (a year after the foundation of the EEC) and 1963, and marginal growth in the UK. Similarly, the decline in the traditional British trade of importing food and raw materials from the Commonwealth, in return for the exporting of manufactured goods, was offset after the war by the dynamic growth of trade with Europe, in the form of both export and import, of finished and semi-finished

---

[1]*Diplomacy and Persuasion: How Britain Joined the Common Market*, by Y. Kitzinger, p. 29.

manufactured goods. There are many examples of this kind of situation throughout economic history. The state-regulated and protectionist method of running the English economy during the sixteenth and seventeenth centuries, coincided with a great increase in English trade and wealth but it is now felt that this satisfactory outcome took place in spite of the system and not because of it. Again, in the years following the achievement of independence by both the American colonies and the Indian continent, trade with Britain increased dramatically, a result which no one would have predicted. Nevertheless, in July 1961 the Macmillan Government decided to seek the possibility of entering the EEC and the negotiations were led by Edward Heath who had been appointed Lord Privy Seal with special responsibility for European affairs.

Heath had early established his credentials for the task for, as a backbencher in 1950, he was the strongest defender of the Schuman Plan and was supported by a minority of pro-Europeans whom Macmillan had also appointed to office, such as Duncan Sandys and Christopher Soames. There was an equally determined and vociferous minority of Tories who were totally against joining the EEC, all led, after 1961, by the barrister MP, Sir Derek Walker-Smith. At this time, I was an enthusiastic 'European', in spite of my New Zealand origins, for, like Ted Heath, I was intellectually convinced of the truth of the argument that the nineteenth-century European nation state (Britain, France and Germany) was irrelevant, politically and economically, in the post-war world and that it was only by acting in a 'European' guise that they could exercise political and economic power – a belief that was reinforced by the facts of economic life that have already been stated. In spite of the obscenity of the Common Agricultural Policy, I continued to support this view but then, as now, I assumed that anything in the nature of a supranational and federal United States of Europe would only come about as a result of years of successful co-operation (and by years I mean 50 to 100 years) and not as a result of a bureaucratic 'diktat'. Thus I now agree with Margaret Thatcher and the Bruges Group.[1] On the Labour side, there was a small number of Euro-enthusiasts, such as George Brown and Ray Gunter, but the left was very much against the EEC (in accordance with its insular predilections) and the Party leader, Gaitskell, initially confined himself to warning the Government not to disregard Commonwealth ties and interests, while the shadow Foreign Secretary, Harold Wilson, characteristically non-committal,

---

[1]Written in March 1991.

took his lead from the majority of hostile sentiment in the Labour Party. In fact, in the course of 1961–62 Labour became increasingly hostile towards the European idea under the leadership of the conviction politician, Hugh Gaitskell, who declared at the 1962 party conference that entry into the Common Market would mean 'the end of a thousand years of British History'. In all, it can be said that there was no question of a national consensus for entry into Europe, either in terms of the two main parties or in that of popular sentiment which was mainly neutral at first but which tended to turn against the idea as the negotiations became more and more difficult, especially in regard to our trading links with the Commonwealth and the prospect of dear food. In view of the above and of Commonwealth apprehensions it is little wonder that Macmillan proceeded initially with extreme caution both at home and in relation to the Commonwealth countries while he emphasized the economic, as opposed to the political, aspects and benefits of joining. However, Alan Sked and Chris Cook allege that the Macmillan Government's application to enter Europe had been taken 'dishonestly as far as Britain was concerned'.[1] Excellent as these historians are in so many ways, I would disagree with them entirely in this case for I consider that their view is judgmental and is not in accordance with the historical facts. Furthermore, the autobiographies of Denis Healey and Roy Jenkins take the view that the debate was more evenly balanced than I have stated.

It is well known that the application failed on two main counts, first, the ramifications of the EEC Common Agricultural Policy in regard both to British agriculture and to British agricultural imports from the Commonwealth and, secondly, the veto by de Gaulle. As in 1957, the Common Agricultural Policy applied an external tariff so as to protect the inefficient, but politically important European (and especially French) farmers. This took the form of a system of levies on agricultural imports, a system of price supports for European agriculture, financed through a Common Agricultural Fund, and a system of subsidies for European agricultural exports. Owing to the fact that world food prices were much below European prices, farmers in the EEC received, and consumers in the EEC paid, high food prices by virtue of the CAP's artificial mechanisms. On the contrary, the traditional British system was the much more sensible and efficient one of ensuring cheap food for the consumer by paying world prices and subsidizing the British farmer by way of deficiency

---

[1] *Post-War Britain*, by Alan Sked and Chris Cook, p. 168.

180

payments where necessary. For Britain the CAP meant that she would be the main contributor to the Common Agricultural Fund because of massive levies she would pay on Commonwealth food imports, while the British people would suffer from the retrograde step of departing from the cheap food policy adopted in 1846 by the abolition of the Corn Laws. For the food exporters of the Commonwealth it would mean a significant reduction in their exports to Britain. Negotiations on these matters proceeded from October 1961 until January 1962 when, for the first of many times there was an agreement in principle on a policy which had the intention of helping and modernizing European agriculture. Nevertheless, France insisted on protection for her agriculture in return for accepting industrial competition from Germany and Britain. Some progress was made in regard to the 'new' Commonwealth countries in the West Indies etc., by proposing that they should become 'associate members' of the EEC but by October 1962 negotiations had virtually broken down following the French refusal to grant Britain a long transition period to change over from her system to that of the CAP, which was to apply as soon as Britain entered the Market: so much for the myth that if Britain had entered Europe then she could have improved the system from the inside. Heath had negotiated transitional arrangements but they were for far too short a period and were therefore cosmetic both in regard to Britain and her Commonwealth suppliers. The CAP could not have been more retrograde – and the same still applies. A country such as New Zealand, with enormous natural advantages in the production of primary products, which could transport lamb and butter 12,000 miles, and even undercut the efficient British farmer, was threatened with the denial of her traditional market and the adverse effect of dumped EEC products elsewhere in the world. It was a system calculated to make Adam Smith 'turn in his grave'.

I have already mentioned on page 176 'de Gaulle's pathological aversion to the "Anglo-Saxon" hegemony of the United States and Great Britain' and the way in which this was reinforced in 1958, as well as Adenauer's distrust of Macmillan which did not help the latter in the subsequent negotiations with the EEC. Macmillan had shown great willingness to discuss the general European political situation with de Gaulle in 1962 in spite of the fact that the latter had moved away from his original concept of a *Europe des nations* to one which was supranational enough to imply a breach with NATO, but no discussion took place because de Gaulle irrationally thought that Macmillan's intention was to turn his European partners against him, whereas they were more 'European' than either

181

Macmillan or himself. In fact, it is possible that the greatest factor influencing de Gaulle in exercising his famous veto was his fear that Britain would upset the balance of power between the members of the EEC, for it must be appreciated that whereas Britain had been the leading power in Europe ever since the war, at this time France was the leading power in the EEC, and de Gaulle was intent that it should remain that way. However, when the negotiations about the reconciliation of the CAP had all but broken down in late 1962, de Gaulle's fear of the 'Anglo-Saxon' hegemony came to a head when, with the cancellation by the American Government of the Skybolt missile system that Britain had agreed to buy, Macmillan accepted Kennedy's offer of Polaris as a replacement, as we have already seen. De Gaulle was also offered Polaris but Macmillan failed to persuade Kennedy to amend the McMahon Act in regard to France so that de Gaulle was able to say: 'It would be truly useless for us to buy (Polaris missiles) when we have neither the submarines to launch them nor the thermonuclear warhead to arm them'. It has been said that

> de Gaulle apparently regarded the cancellation (of Skybolt) as a great opportunity to develop Anglo-French nuclear collaboration and for the UK to reduce its military dependence on the United States.[1]

In my view, this assessment is special pleading, reading history backwards, and the creation of yet another anti-British and anti-American myth. Unlike the authors of the above quotation, I think that de Gaulle did use Macmillan's acceptance of Polaris as a convenient excuse to veto the British application in January 1963 for, to tell the truth, his decision was probably made on much more mundane grounds such as French and German farmers' political importance and the near-impossibility of reconciling Britain' entry to the EEC with the CAP. As he said:

> You who eat the cheap wheat of Canada, the lamb of New Zealand, the beef and potatoes of Ireland, the butter, fruit and vegetables of Australia, the sugar of Jamaica – would you consent to feed on continental – especially French – agricultural produce, which would inevitably cost more?[2]

---

[1] *The Changing British Political System: into the 1990's*, by Ian Budge and David McKay, p. 207.
[2] Quoted in *Post-War Britain*, Alan Sked and Chris Cook, p. 173.

But even if one agrees that this was a great issue of principle I would not accept the naive proposition that the pro-European de Gaulle was 'the goody' and the pro-American Britain was 'the baddy' for although I accept that de Gaulle was quite entitled to be anti-American there was, and is, no reason whatsoever for Britain to be anything else than pro-American – not that this implies an anti-European stance. Consider that the Anglo-American alliance or relationship was based on the British hope and intention that the United States would take over the part played in the world since the sixteenth century by Britain in opposing attempts to dominate Europe and the world by Spain, France and Germany, respectively. These countries no longer pose a problem for the world but, as we have recently seen, other countries do – and all the evidence leads to the conclusion that it is only the Anglo-American alliance which has the political, military and moral stature to ensure the security of the world, even though it is modestly content to hide its 'light' behind the United Nations' 'bushel', an assertion proved by the events of the Gulf War. Although no European country any longer poses a threat to the world or their neighbours the British cannot have the same confidence in their motives or predilections as they can those of the United States. Hopefully, we shall never have to choose between one or the other, but let us not refrain from saying that if we do, we would choose the United States.[1]

---

[1]Since my having written the above conclusion, in June 1993, the Major Government is following the historic policy of the Foreign Office of acting against Britain's (and international) interests by not supporting President Clinton's (admittedly feeble) initiatives in Serbia and Bosnia in deference to the non-policy of the EEC. During 1996 the Conservative Government has been under tremendous pressure to join the European Monetary Union and to accept the single European currency, to give up the United Kingdom's veto and thus her Sovereignty. The hope and expectation is that the whole bureaucratic, centralized and undemocratic structure will be asphyxiated by its own entrails and be still-born – sooner or later.

11

Education

As with so many of our institutions, King Alfred can be regarded as the founder of English education. He found most of the ninth-century clergy to be illiterate and he called upon the Welsh and Franks to educate them. In the secular field, he founded a school for boys and he encouraged his adult friends and followers to follow his own example of regular study. Although half a century later Archbishop Dunstan had still to deal with clerical ignorance, (which remained a problem for centuries to come, in the dark corners of the land) and monastic worldliness, it can truly be said that in secular education Alfred markedly improved its level and that he created a tradition which has been maintained throughout the centuries.

In the following centuries educational progress was spasmodic and was, of course, usually associated with the monasteries. For example, Repton School, which realistically dates from 1557, can trace its origins back to a school for the local children in the Augustinian Priory establishment at Repton in 1172, but with its dissolution by Thomas Cromwell in 1538 one, Sir John Port, endowed the refounding of the school in 1557 in what remained of the old priory. Many cathedral schools could tell a similar story. For example, in 1896, a letter to *The Times* claimed that King's School, Canterbury, was older than St Peter's School, York, (founded by St Paulinus in 625) in that it was started by St Augustine when he established Canterbury Cathedral in 598. The claim was based on the Venerable Bede's 'Ecclesiastical History', written in 731, and although the case for 598 is circumstantial, or by analogy, there is good evidence that there was education going on at Canterbury from about 600 and that there was a well-established school at Canterbury immediately before the Norman Conquest.

When Christianity first came to Britain, it brought with it services, prayers and songs that were all in Latin. Whenever a cathedral, monastery or even a large church was built, therefore, they were almost invariably accompanied by schools. These were of two sorts

184

(often combined): a song school to teach choristers to sing, and schools to teach Latin for the services. For this reason the last were called grammar schools.[1]

Following the Conquest there were another 200 years of uncertainty about education at Canterbury but there is no doubt that by 1259 the Archbishop's school existed and that from this date and the appointment of John Everard in 1310, the continuous history of the school can be said to have begun. It was refounded by Henry VIII after the dissolution of the monasteries but it had the same headmaster, before and after – the learned John Twyne.

Not much happened educationally as late as the thirteenth century when the mass of people were servile and ignorant 'beasts of burden', while in the fourteenth century the emphasis was on the struggle of the latter to end their bondage and become free, in addition to the significant minority who had already become freemen and freeburgesses. The Black Death (1349–50) played an important part in ending servile status because the acute shortage of labour increased immeasurably the bargaining power of the labourers, both free and of villein status. However, in spite of the violence – military, political and social – of the fifteenth century, culminating in the Wars of the Roses, it was notable for the founding of schools, in the main associated with chantries or other religious institutions. My own Oxford college, Magdalen, was founded in 1458. Before one attaches too much importance to the glib generalization that England was in a state of chaos during the period of the Wars of the Roses (1455–1485), one should visit Magdalen College and feast one's eyes on the majesty and delicate beauty of its original buildings, as well as read the Paston Letters which give an insight into the everyday life of this East Anglian family which was prosaic and peaceable in the extreme. Besides, although they were fought with great ferocity and cruelty, many of the battles of the Wars of the Roses, whose names still resound in history, were mere skirmishes, in military terms. Also, many, if not most, of the political achievements, which have been accredited to the Tudors, can be dated back to that every effective Yorkist King, Edward IV.

Nevertheless, it would be unhistorical as well as uncharitable to deny to the Lancastrian Tudors the extent of their great political achievements and of their association with the amazing flowering of the genius of the English people in literature, art, architecture, music

---

[1] *The Public School Phenomenon*, by Jonathan Gathorne Hardy, p. 22.

and education. The religious educational foundations of the fifteenth and earlier centuries were suppressed, and their endowments confiscated, during the Reformation of the Church of England, initiated by Henry VIII in 1534 and continued by the Protestant extremists who reigned from 1547 in the name of the delicate, nine-year-old Edward VI until his death in 1553. However, in the latter's time many of the schools were refounded as secular establishments which is why Edward VI's name is associated with the founding of around 40 of England's grammar schools, including the school where I taught for seven years (1949–56), Shrewsbury School, in 1552.[1] Under Elizabeth I (1558–1603) the process continued with the foundation of more grammar schools and with further improvement in education. From those days until the establishment of the fatal comprehensive system the English grammar school has been its finest and most important educational institution, in spite of the fact that, superficially, it has been overshadowed by the prestigious public schools (originally grammar schools, themselves) and Oxford and Cambridge. From the time of Shakespeare to that of Harold Wilson, James Callaghan,[2] Edward Heath, Margaret Thatcher and John Major, the vast majority of England's leading citizens in every field, but especially the professions and business, have received what was (with the Scottish schools) undoubtedly the best education in the world, in English grammar schools. The classical education which they imparted initially was in one sense, narrow, but in another, rich and varied, but as the years went by the classics were afforced by history, literature, science and mathematics – all to the highest of standards whereby both minds and characters were trained.

It is remarkable that in spite of the fact that public schools only educate about 7 per cent of the school population they occupy such a vital and dominant place in the English educational system, both historically and currently. One of the main reasons is the ancient nature of the earliest public schools with Winchester College and New College, Oxford (1382 and 1379 respectively), being twin foundations by William of Wykeham,[3] Bishop of Winchester and Chancellor, and Eton College and King's College, Cambridge (1440)

---

[1] *A School at Shrewsbury*, by Colin Leach, p. 11 et seq.

[2] James Callaghan attended a 'central' school which was the equivalent of the new secondary schools created by the Education Act of 1902 and which later became grammar schools, in emulation of the historic grammar schools (pp. 202–3).

[3] He was born at Wickham and was therefore originally, William of Wickham, but he became popularly known as William of Wykeham – thus Wykehamist, not Wickhamist.

by King Henry VI. The symmetrical and wholly satisfying lines of King's College Chapel and the Founder's Quad at Eton are further tributes to the magnificence of fifteenth-century architecture, while William Wykeham's educational activities remind us that one should beware of generalizations regarding the fourteenth or, for that matter, any other century. Another factor is how quickly and successfully the later schools emulated the two original foundations. For example, although it was situated in a comparatively remote part of the country, Shrewsbury School, both in terms of size and reputation, became one of the largest and most important schools in the kingdom as early as 1570. Its most famous Old Salopian is Sir Philip Sidney (1554–86), the quintessential Elizabethan – soldier, statesman, diplomat and poet – a distinction he shares with the nineteenth-century Charles Darwin, the author of *The Origin of Species*. In view of the numerous schools whose headmasters are entitled to attend The Headmasters' Conference (the traditional definition of a public school) it is remarkable that as late as 1868 the Public Schools Act, which embodied the findings of the Clarendon Commission, which was formed to investigate and define these schools, limited their numbers to the following:[1]

> Eton
> Winchester
> Westminster
> Charterhouse
> Harrow
> Rugby
> Shrewsbury

Westminster was refounded and re-endowed by Henry VIII, following the dissolution of the monasteries, as one of the new schools which were to be associated with the cathedrals. Henry also founded Trinity College, Cambridge which was closely connected to Westminster as also was Christ Church, Oxford. Similarly, St Paul's was associated with St Paul's Cathedral but it was in the modern tradition, being founded by a merchant's son, John Colet, in 1510, who was an educational innovator of his day, while the school was to be administered by the Company of Mercers. Merchant Taylors was founded on the model of St Paul's in 1562 by the Worshipful

---

[1] St Paul's and Merchant Taylors were originally included but they were finally omitted for technical reasons.

Company of Merchant Taylors in the new sixteenth-century manner of schools being founded as charitable institutions and by successful businessmen, rather than as 'colleges' with Royal or ecclesiastical patronage. The school had a strong connection with St John's College, Oxford by virtue of scholarships founded by the Merchant Taylors. Harrow was founded in 1571 by John Lyon, a yeoman landowner, as a grammar school for the local poor. Rugby, founded in 1567 by a London grocer, Lawrence Sheriff, was also intended for the free education of the local children. Although its original buildings had a long history before they were used as a school, Charterhouse was founded in 1611 by Thomas Sutton, an immensely rich businessman and financier. At around the same time Dulwich College was founded by the successful actor and theatre-owner, Edward Alleyn. Christ's Hospital was founded in 1553, in the reign of Edward VI, to provide for 'fatherless children and other poor men's children'. In this, it has much in common with other public schools but it is probably unique in that it still literally confines its pupils to the sons and daughters of a parent or parents who could not otherwise afford a public school or comparable (independent) education although they pay, if at all, according to their means. In fact, on average, its 800 pupils have 75 per cent of their fees paid through the school's charitable income of about £8 million a year so that the school and its pupils would be a major sufferer from any abolition of the charitable status of independent schools, as has been threatened by the Labour party and to a lesser extent by the Liberal Party. The Roman Catholic public school, Stoneyhurst, was originally founded at St Omer's in 1592 in order to escape the penalties of English law while it was refounded in England in 1794. Ampleforth and Downside have similar histories.

It will be noted that the Clarendon Commission's list of 'the seven' public schools omitted many of the old-established schools which have become acknowledged public schools – and there are many of them. For example, there are the schools which had been recently founded in the mid-nineteenth century to educate the sons of the middle and upper-middle classes following the reformation of the public schools in the earlier years of that century. These include Cheltenham (1841), Marlborough (1843), Rossall (1844), Radley (1847), Wellington (1853), and Clifton, Malvern and Haileybury in 1862. This list is by no means exclusive while there are the many excellent schools which have been founded since 1868, not to mention the schools which at about that time were grammar schools but which made the transition to public school status, such as Repton, Sherborne and Uppingham. There are many other grammar schools which later became public schools. A good example is Chigwell School which was founded in 1629 by Samuel Harsnett, Archbishop of York, the son of a baker from Colchester, who had previously been vicar of Chigwell. The school's most famous Old Boy, William Penn, the founder of Pennsylvania, entered the school in 1655. In 1813 a prospectus described the school as one

> Where Young Gentlemen are Boarded and Classically Educated by Mr Edwards at Forty Five Guineas per annum. Writing & Arithmetic, Four guineas per annum. French or any other Modern Language usually taught, Four guineas each, & Geography with the Use of Globes, Two guineas. Young Gentlemen may also be instructed in mathematics if required. Dancing & Drawing on the usual terms. A seperatc (sic) Bed, if desired, Three guineas, & each Young Gentleman is requested to bring a Knife & Fork, Silver Table Spoon & six Napkins. N.B. Chigwell is Ten Miles from London & Stages pass every Day.

Like most schools, Chigwell had its ups and downs. In 1840 the Latin School comprised only one pupil. (Harsnett originally provided for a twin foundation including an 'English School' where boys should be 'taughte & to reade & write Cypher and cast Accounts and to learn their Accidence'.) In 1868 the new Headmaster inherited 47 boys and when he left in 1876 there were 142 but unfortunately he took all but 2 of the boarders with him to his new school. His successor, the Reverend R.D. Swallow, remained at Chigwell until 1912 when there were only 85 boys in the school of whom 40 were boarders. The present role is around 630, including about 70 boarders.

Shrewsbury School did well to be included for it had, according to the various reports, dwindled to between one and twenty pupils in 1798 but it was revived under the headmastership of the great Samuel Butler (1798–1836) and thrived for the rest of the century under two very able headmasters, Kennedy and Moss. Butler is a most important figure in public school history for it was his educational reforms at Shrewsbury, including the introduction of examinations, together with the moral standards introduced to Rugby by Dr Thomas Arnold (1828–42), chronicled for posterity in the book *Tom Brown's Schooldays*, that created the public school tradition that is so well known – the scholarly athlete and sincere Christian leading a disciplined life dedicated to the service of others, whether it be the Church, politics, the Services or the Empire. When one compares it with the barbarity and fruitlessness of what preceded it, this educational revolution was and is a most impressive example of

189

human achievement, and can be compared with that of the ancient Greeks, as enunciated by Pericles in his famous funeral speech of 431 BC to commemorate the Athenians who had fallen that year in the war against Sparta. His conclusion is a remarkable parallel to the ideals of the public school tradition, quoted above:

> What made Athens great was men of daring, who knew their duty, and were ashamed to fall short in action. They contributed their lives to Athens, and for themselves won praise that never grows old – not in the sepulchre where they lie, but in the glory that remains eternal in men's minds. For heroes have the whole world as their tomb. Take these as your model and reckoning that happiness depends on freedom, and freedom on bravery, never shirk the dangers of war.

The public schools, then, are essentially the nineteenth-century creation of the upper and middle classes, on an entirely 'laissez-faire' basis, to organize the education of their sons, with the emphasis on sons, for during the greater part of the century their daughters were educated by governesses, although the pioneers of women's secondary and university education were active from the middle of the century. Public schools exhibit the English genius for elitism at its best, although their enemies would say, at its worst, associated as they were with the primacy and exclusiveness of Oxford and Cambridge, and vulnerable to the criticism that their way of life had become a mere convention – an end in itself. (Throughout the centuries a goodly number of poor boys also went to Oxford and Cambridge but, in their own way, these boys were also an exclusive elite.) However, an elite based on high standards of social, moral, educational and physical behaviour can be no bad thing, and is a sure way of discouraging and eliminating elites of a much more dubious and dangerous kind which have fouled the pages of history.

Much of their success is due to their single-sex tradition for, especially during and after puberty, it really is preferable for young boys' and girls' sex-drive to be channelled in the direction of organized games and activities. As a schoolmaster, I found, especially in the sixth form, that one could achieve a rapport with the boys that would have been impossible in a mixed class and I feel sure that most public school mistresses would agree with me, from their own point of view. This is especially true in that in today's more 'liberated' world boys and girls in single-sex schools do not need to suffer from lack of contact with the opposite sex. In my view the only justification for not having single-sex state schools is economic

190

necessity and I need hardly say that the recent trend of introducing girls to the sixth form in public schools is unnecessary (apart from economic factors) and does much more harm than good, while the decision to make Rugby School co-educational is depressing. The only justification can be economic and, if this is true, I would say, 'poor Rugby'! In spite of their high academic standards, Continental schools are nothing more than glorified 'crammers', and due to the mixture of sexes and lack of organized other activities, the pupils do not benefit from the useful experience and discipline of communal living and group activity. People who have had to endure the experience of exchanging children with the French, especially Parisians, will take the point.

If there is any one quality that is the secret of the public schools' success and which they share with so many other English institutions, from the Monarchy down, it is their ability to change with the times while at the same time appearing to retain their traditional character. Eton is the best example, although it applies generally, with each school giving its own flavour to a fairly uniform 'system', which is another admirable factor. At Eton the 'fancy' uniforms (please may they never be abolished for 'politically correct' reasons) and general air of aristocratic indifference may tend to the completely erroneous belief that the place just muddles along and hopes for the best. On the contrary, it, and other public schools, are miracles of organization and one has the feeling that during a long period of time every eventuality has been encountered and provision made for dealing with it. Examinations are regular and meaningful, ominously called Trials at Eton, and boys are regularly promoted and demoted, and even expelled, on their results. End of term reports are lengthy and detailed and masters put a great deal of time and thought into writing them. Each boy has a form master who varies as he progresses up the school and he has, of course, the same housemaster throughout his school life but, unusually and importantly, he has a tutor who is usually unchanged. Together with a small group of boys he will spend an hour or so, at least once a week, with his tutor when they will read and discuss books, plays or poetry, listen to music and discuss anything under the sun, including sex. At a time when it was considered 'progressive' to present cultural subjects to scientists and scientific subjects to non-scientists, Eton, and other public schools, in their own way, had been doing it for years. There are many other examples in public schools of the English capacity for combining tradition with change and radicalism, one example of which is the introduction of girls, as initiated at Bedales! Another is the fact that Eton has its own pub, called 'Tap', which can be used by boys over 15 years of age.

This is an outstanding example of the way in which public schools place so much emphasis on making boys independent and able to accept responsibility. The best-known method of achieving this is the famous prefectorial system which has been emulated in schools throughout the world wherever the British have been, and not only in English-speaking countries. Once again, Eton is extremely 'progressive' for there the prefects are self-elected and glory in the name of The Eton Society, or 'Pop', for short, it originally being a debating society formed in 1816. It was once stated that a boy was never better fitted to be Viceroy of India than in his last year at a public school, but although this was a cynical remark it contains a great deal of truth and sums up the aims and achievements of a public school education.

My own experience is of interest and relevance. Although, as I have said, I am a third-generation New Zealander, I had decided that I wanted to go to Oxford (not Cambridge!) and teach at a public school, and the war merely interrupted these ambitions. A tremendous number of ex-servicemen read History with the intention of teaching so that for every public school vacancy for a History master there were as many as 80 applicants. Therefore, much to the surprise of the President of Magdalen, the charming Tom Boase,[1] and others, I refused the comparatively plumb post of Sixth Form History Master at Peterborough School, a perfectly respectable grammar school, on the dubious grounds that if I could not teach at a public school I would go into industry. Within weeks the 'magic circle' went into action and a place was eventually found for me at Shrewsbury to introduce and teach Economics. This was possible because the Headmaster of Shrewsbury, J.F. Wolfenden, had been a Don at Magdalen before being appointed Headmaster of Uppingham School at the early age of 27 from where he went to Shrewsbury at 38. Although my Oxford degree is in Modern History I was able to teach Economics because of my New Zealand degrees, Bachelor of Arts and Bachelor of Commerce, both of which included History and Economics to three stages as well as Accountancy and allied legal subjects in the latter case. I completed two degrees with only one year at university, 1941, at the end of which I spent around five years in the services, owing to the facts that I studied for these degrees as an external student for two years in the sixth form at school, for a year while in the army in New Zealand and in the last year of the war

---

[1]T.S.R. Boase, MC, FBA, Professor of History of Art, London University, and Director of Courtaulds Institute of Art 1937–47, President of Magdalen 1947–68, Vice-Chancellor 1958–60, Slade Professor 1963–64.

while in the navy, sitting my finals, History III and Economics III, in the Captain's cabin in Tokyo Bay – all of which is a tribute to the ingenuity of the New Zealand educational system and to my own determination!

J.F. Wolfenden was the retiring Headmaster of Shrewsbury and I was his last appointment, his successor being J.M. Peterson. No two men could be more different. Wolfenden was the precocious and enormously talented grammar school boy from Wakefield in Yorkshire who, after leaving Shrewsbury, went on to lead a distinguished life in public service, being knighted and then ennobled after the Wolfenden Report on homosexuality. He was a complete man of the world, not in the sense that he cultivated a worldly sophistication, but in the sense that he found his way about it easily and without hesitation or doubt. Two examples prove the point. The first is that, unknown to both of us, he had offered the same post to a friend and myself and, in a way, my friend was better qualified than I, for he had taken a First in Politics, Philosophy and Economics, and although not a Blue, had rowed with distinction at his Oxford college – and Shrewsbury was and is one of the great rowing schools. Neither of us heard from Wolfenden during the long months of the summer vacation and at almost the same time we both took independent action, my friend sending a telegram to JFW simply asking him whether he had the job – yes or no. I wrote to ask him if I could visit him. Wolfenden solved the problem in a thoroughly worldly way. He telegrammed my friend in the negative and greeted me in his study at Shrewsbury, with his feet literally on his desk, and gave me the job! Secondly, at the annual dinner of the New Zealand Society at The Savoy, Lord Wolfenden was the main guest speaker in what threatened to be a disastrous evening from an oratorical point of view. The President of the Society, wrongly, considered himself to be a talented speaker and had prepared a long and tedious diatribe, carefully written on pages of foolscap, which he proceeded to deliver and before too long losing his way and ending up in a literally muddled fashion. This nightmare was followed by a couple of indifferent speakers who went on far too long, by which time the audience was on the point of fainting with boredom and almost drowning the speakers' voices with the scraping of chairs and coughing. To such an unpropitious audience Lord Wolfenden rose to deliver the last speech, and one wondered if it could possibly survive the next 10 of 15 minutes. I shall never forget the way in which, in a matter of minutes, the bright and cerebral John Wolfenden had the audience enraptured and completely awake just as much as if he had waved some kind of magic wand. He completely saved the evening.

193

Jack Peterson, on the other hand, was the modern equivalent of Chaucer's 'parfit gentil knyght' and was the embodiment of the public school virtues, being an accomplished classical scholar, a sincere Christian touched with saintliness and a brilliant athlete having excelled at cricket, football and Eton Fives as a boy at Shrewsbury and winning Blues in the latter two with the reputation of being one of the two best Eton Fives players in the country in subsequent years. It is little wonder that the great Dr Alington made sure that this brilliant Salopian should follow him to Eton as a master, and subsequently housemaster, as he had as Headmaster of the two great schools. But whereas, in my view at least, Peterson was much more a man of the world in the upper-class, social sense than Wolfenden, he was eminently not a man of the world in the Wolfenden sense, and whereas, in one sense, unfortunately, public school headmasters were becoming increasingly imbued with Wolfenden-like, twentieth-century qualities, Peterson would have been much more at home in the nineteenth century. A good example is that whereas I was entitled to append after my name in the official school list, the degrees MA (Oxon), BA, B Comm (NZ), he was unhappy about the vocational connotation of the last degree, so that I ended up as R.G. Wood, MA (Oxon), BA (NZ) – in spite of all my hard work in attaining the Bachelor of Commerce degree and, in view of the fact that with my non-numerate mind, accountancy was the hardest of all.

However, Jack Peterson fully encouraged my brief to introduce Economics at the Sixth Form 'A' level which I taught, together with History, in a form subsequently to be called the History Lower Sixth, to boys who were not achieving their potential in the other sixth forms, or who were due to enter the sixth form and for whom this was an alternative course. The founder-member of my new form was one Michael Ray Dibdin Heseltine, who had mistakenly elected to go on the science side and who occupied a lowly position in the Science Sixth due to his lack of interest in the subject. After two years in my form Heseltine left for Oxford with two respectable 'A' levels in History and Economics, became President of the Oxford Union, a millionaire by the time he was 30 – and the rest is history, as they say. My best known other pupils were the late William Rushton, the versatile cartoonist, writer, publicist and comedian whom I always thought of as much more a man of the world than myself, in spite of the difference in age and experience, and the brilliant Christopher Booker, the writer and journalist, who was by far the cleverest boy whom I taught. There was also Christopher Gill whose quiet charm belied the fact that he would become the effective Eurosceptic Tory

194

MP which he undoubtedly is. Much as I enjoyed Shrewsbury I began to feel envious of the boys whom I was sending out into the world, which could mean that I did not have the necessary vocation for the job, but I believe that my interest in the outside world made me a better, not a worse, master. After a year's sabbatical in New Zealand where I divided my time between writing *From Plymouth to New Plymouth* and working as a financial journalist I left Shrewsbury to become an economist in the City of London, with the express intention of gaining a seat in Parliament. Little did I realize what a clean pair of heels my first pupil would show me! One of the greatest pleasures of my life has been the friendship of the boys whom I taught at Shrewsbury, especially those whom I knew in the City of London, but there were and are many others. Public school boys have a great regard for their old schoolmasters but they do tend to regard them as cardboard figures – caricatures. I have had the great satisfaction of enjoying their pure friendship.

I have already said that the creation of the public schools, flowering as it did in the mid-nineteenth century, was an act of 'laissez-faire' by the English upper and middle classes. This was necessary because, as in public health, there was no recognition of the responsibility of the government to provide a general system of education for the mass of people, as there already was in Europe and in Scotland where they have been educating peasants such as Robbie Burns (who knew Latin) for centuries although, admittedly, in this case it was done by the villagers communally hiring a headmaster to teach the local children. That is not to say that there was not a great deal of 'laissez-faire' activity in this direction, in accordance with the English tradition. There were the questionable private schools, both for boys and girls, for those who could pay, but these have been well described by Dickens.

> It was to distinguish themselves from the private schools that the term 'public' school evolved during the 18th century to describe the leading old grammar foundations. They were public in that they were not privately owned but incorporated under statute at law. The use of the term was never consistent during the 18th century and it was not really until the latter part of the 19th century that it became general. The new foundations and revived old grammar schools of this period called themselves 'public schools' in imitation of the old leading grammar schools in order to gain something of their cachet.[1]

---

[1] *The Public School Phenomenon*, by Jonathan Gathorne Hardy, p. 32.

There were also the mechanics' institutes where working men could study. As always, the man or woman with a voracious appetite for education and knowledge can never be denied. For example, David Livingstone, who later achieved fame as Dr Livingstone of Africa (1813–73), began life working in a cotton mill near Glasgow at the age of ten and managed to educate himself. There were men like the Reverend William Rogers (1819–96) who founded more non-state schools than any other Victorian, including schools for ragamuffins, when he was appointed curate at St Thomas's, Charterhouse, as well as various primary schools. After becoming rector of St Botolphs, Bishopsgate, in 1863, he turned his attention to secondary education and formed a number of middle-class schools, culminating in his taking a leading part, as a governor of Alleyn's charity, in the changes which transformed Dulwich College into one of our leading public schools.[1] However, the main instrument for educating the working classes before 1870 was that provided by the voluntary agencies, in other words, the churches. The pioneers were the Quaker, Joseph Lancaster, who was a 'non-sectarian' in regard to education, and Andrew Bell, an Anglican, who believed strongly in inculcating religious teachings in popular education. Lancaster's principles were embodied in the British and Foreign Society, founded in 1808, and Bell's in the National Society, in 1811.[2] Later, there were Joseph Chamberlain's National Education League and the church-supported National Education Union. The state had made grants in aid to popular education since 1833, the reformed parliament thus gently dipping its toe into what was to become such a large pool. In the meantime, the voluntary system became deeply rooted and from that time to the present day, in spite of numerous Education Acts, including that of 1944, public education policy has been concerned with the extent of the aid to be given, and the conditions on which it was given, to the two original voluntary societies and to those subsequently established by the other churches, such as the Roman Catholics, Methodists and Congregationalists.

It was significant that the Education Act of 1870, instituting for the first time the provision of primary education on a national basis, was passed in the early days of Gladstone's great reforming ministry of 1868–74, for one of the main criticisms of the Second Reform Bill of

---

[1]*England, 1870–1914*, by R.C.K. Ensor, p. 146. Further facts and figures in this chapter are attributable to this authority.
[2]The National Society for Promoting the Education of the Poor in the Principles of the Established Church.

1867 was that many of the new voters were illiterate. After it was passed, one of its critics said that 'we must educate our masters'. The Act was typically English in that it provided the new without dispensing with the old. A survey of the schools of England was ordered and, in districts where there were not enough charity schools, ratepayers were ordered to elect School Boards which were to have the duty of establishing schools and to pay for them by levying an education rate, the schools thus becoming known as board schools. In addition, the Government agreed to aid the poorer districts with funds deriving from national taxes. In all the state primary schools, old and new, it was accepted that the main task was to win the battle against illiteracy so that the 'three Rs' were taught in accordance with a standardized curriculum imposed by the central authority, which gives the lie to the criticism of our present national curriculum that it is a new and retrograde step, for it, in its turn, is attempting to overcome a new wave of illiteracy. In this respect, the 1870 Act succeeded comparatively in its endeavours for in the general election of 1886, out of 2,416,272 votes cast in England and Wales only 38,457 were those of illiterates. The 1870 Act did not make attendance at elementary schools compulsory, because initially there were not enough schools until they had been produced under the terms of the Act, but this provision was included in Disraeli's Education Act of 1876, by which time both parties had accepted the state's responsibility in educational matters and in which a great deal was subsequently done by the time of the First World War. For example, after 1870 Gladstone doubled the state grant to voluntary denominational schools which accepted inspection and proved satisfactory. In 1880, the lowest age at which pupils might leave school was fixed at 10 years old and it was raised to 11 in 1893 and 14 in 1900, which was doubly important in that it acted as an indirect Factory Act by preventing the full-time employment of people under that age.

As has already been intimated, there was an unhappy dichotomy between the well-established voluntary church schools and the new board schools. On the one hand, the simple religious instruction in the latter suited the non-conformists or dissenters, but not the representatives of the former on the school boards. On the other hand, the voluntary schools could not afford to build or maintain sufficient buildings for their schools, but they resisted pressure from the school boards to finance them through the rates because they would then lose their independence in the matter of religious instruction. Consequently, the first Salisbury Government (1886–92) sets up an important royal commission 'to enquire into the workings of the Elementary Education Acts, England and Wales' whose majority and minority reported in 1888. On the first question of the voluntary schools, the former took the view that they ought to be maintained (by grants from the Government) and even have a share of the local rates. The latter, mostly radicals and non-conformists, did not agree, on the grounds that any payment to the voluntary schools out of rates were 'certain, if it became law, to embitter educational politics and intensify sectarian rivalries'. Thus although Lord Salisbury's Act of 1891 abolishing school fees in all elementary schools (both voluntary and board) was an important landmark, it was significant that it was passed by a Conservative Government, for as Salisbury said:

> If their opponents should obtain a majority in a future Parliament, they would deal with it in such a manner that the voluntary schools would be swept away.

That is to say, if it was left to the Liberals they would abolish fees only in the board schools which would put the church schools at a distinct financial disadvantage although they would have more independence. However, it was 14 years before anything positive was done to settle the rivalries between these two factions. The second main question considered by the commission was, apart from religious instruction, the curriculum of the elementary schools. The Education Department stipulated in 1886–87 that:

> The course suited to an elementary school is practically determined by the limit of fourteen years of age, and may properly include whatever subject can be effectively taught within that limit.

The natural consequence was that many school boards developed 'higher-elementary' or 'higher-grade' schools which had their own laboratories, apparatus and drawing facilities, and entered their pupils for examinations so that they could earn grants from the Department of Science and Art at South Kensington; about which more anon. This was another example of the admirable system of 'payment by results' which had been employed from 1870 in regard to the teaching of the 'three Rs' and which, predictably, the minority, the early 'progressives', condemned wholeheartedly, and as a result of which the majority agreed for it to be 'modified and relaxed', which was done in 1890. By this time then, we see the development of the earliest secondary instruction by the school boards under the elementary school code. Outside religion, the curricula of those pupils who had passed their 'three Rs' examination, the Proficiency Test, was a matter of 'laissez-faire' which was implied in the above Education Department statement in 1886–87.

With the return of Gladstone's Liberal Government (1892–94) this typically English 'laissez-faire' development was taken in hand by the appointment of the very able A.H.D. Acland as Vice-President of the Council for Education, with a seat in the Cabinet. He inaugurated his important Code for Evening Schools in 1893, together with a national investigation of the suitability of school buildings which drew attention to the poor accommodation in the voluntary schools. In 1894 he formed a special inquiries branch in his department to investigate and report on education abroad and which was to play an extremely important part in the coming English educational reforms. However, probably Acland's main achievement was to persuade Gladstone at this time to appoint a Royal Commission on Secondary Education under the chairmanship of the great Scottish jurist and historian, James Bryce, later, Lord Bryce. By this time it was realized that in state education in general, and technical education in particular, England was lagging seriously behind her competitors – the United States, Germany, France, Belgium and Switzerland – which had been making progress for 25 to 40 years. From at least 1870 German industrial competition seriously affected England and this was attributed to their superior state educational system – *'plus ça change'*! German administrative efficiency had become a byword and by 1870 they had revolutionized the art of military warfare, logistics and the like, a direct result of which was the reform of the British Army by Gladstone's great Secretary of State for War, Edward (later Lord) Cardwell (1868–74), culminating in the abolition of the system of obtaining commissions and promotions in the army by purchase, in 1871. In the civil field, Gladstone declared by Order in Council in 1870 that all appointments to permanent positions in the civil service, except the foreign office, should be by open competitive examination.

By the time of the Bryce Commission the main educational objective in England was the attempt to create for the first time a national system of technical education which until this time had been mainly confined to the various efforts of private enterprise such as the formation of mechanics' institutes, the precursor of which was Dr Birkbeck's London Mechanics Institute in 1823. By 1850 there were 622 mechanics' institutes in England and Wales with over 600,000 members but, as we have already seen, although the more dedicated artizan working man took advantage of their faculties to learn to read and write, they never became popular centres of technical education as they were mainly attended by the literate middle class. However, they did lead to the development of national examination systems in the technical fields, at first by voluntary bodies – The College of Preceptors (1853) and the Society of Arts (1856–57) and from 1859 on by the state, namely the Department of Science and Art at South Kensington which, as we have already noted, paid government grants to schools whose pupils passed their examinations. It was characteristic of the times that the Department of Science and Art was quite distinct from the Department of Education, in spite of the fact that many of its grant-earners were pupils in the 'higher-grade' elementary schools. Finally, in 1879, a new body, the City and Guilds of London Institute, took over from the Society of Arts examinations in 'technological subjects' on which it issued certificates and paid grants to schools, from funds supplied by the City livery companies. Thus, the only element of central planning, whether state or private, in technical education was restricted to examinations and grants made on them but, as we have stated, it was not sufficient in view of the progress being made by contemporary nations. For example:

> At the Great Exhibition of 1851, out of a hundred different departments in which goods were displayed, Great Britain had won the palm of excellence in nearly all. But at the Paris Exhibition of 1867 she excelled her competitors in only 10 per cent. Lyon Playfair, who had been a juror at Paris, wrote a letter ascribing England's loss of ground to the fact that her competitors possessed 'good systems of industrial education for the masters and managers of factories and workshops', whereas England possessed none. A committee appointed to probe the matter confirmed his statement; but for fourteen years little came of it. In 1881 the problem was remitted to a Royal Commission under Mr (afterwards, Sir) Bernard Samuelson, which reported in 1882 and 1884. It was in belated conformity with these reports that the Technical Instruction Act 1889 was passed, twenty-two years after Playfair's letter'.[1]

The Technical Instruction Act was passed by Lord Salisbury's Government for, by now, both parties were dedicated to educational reform, with one party passing legislation resulting from the report of a commission set up by the other party while civil servants of great ability were appointed to the educational fields which kept the momentum going whatever government was in power. Under the

---

[1] *England, 1870–1914*, by R.C.K. Ensor, p. 319.

terms of the Technical Instruction Act the county and county borough councils were made responsible for technical education while the responsibility of the central authority, the Science and Art Department, was enlarged. Whereas it had previously only been permitted to give grants for examinations passed to non-taxpayers (members of the 'industrial classes'), this had excluded most of the future 'masters and managers' so that in reply to Playfair's, and others', strictures, this exclusion was discontinued. Furthermore, the Act empowered the councils to levy a penny rate for their new responsibility and their financial position was improved dramatically by a further Act in 1890 by the Chancellor of the Exchequer, Goschen, passing on to them for technical education his tax of an extra 6d a gallon on spirits, the so-called 'whisky money' (in order to curb the drunkenness of these prosperous years), when he was prevented from giving it to the licensees of redundant public houses which was his original intention. The councils also financed an ambitious building programme by raising large loans. For example, in London the Technical Instruction Committee of the LCC, under the chairmanship of Sidney Webb, was extremely active, while in Manchester the city council developed its famous School of Technology.

Thus, when the Bryce Commission came to survey secondary education it found, on the one hand, the Department of Education, through the school boards, providing limited secondary education in 'higher-grade' elementary schools and, on the other, the Science and Art Department's county and county borough councils providing technical secondary education, as a part of their general responsibility for technical education. Thirdly, there were the grammar schools and the numerous but small and poor ancient endowed foundations – and although these were independent their curricula were sometimes influenced by their desire to obtain the Science and Art Department's grants. Accordingly, the Commission recommended the formation of a central education authority to be:

> a Department of the Executive Government, presided over by a Minister responsible as the one to whom the charge of elementary education is entrusted.

This was done by the Education Act of 1899 under Lord Salisbury's second administration (1895–1902) which established the Board of Education which amalgamated the old Department of Education and the Science and Art Department. The Commission also recommended that the authorities for controlling education should be county

201

councils, and borough councils in populous places, whose education committees should contain co-opted members, and empowered them to create secondary and technical schools where none existed. The Schools Boards of 1870 were abolished and the term 'board school' passed from use. This was done by the Education Act of 1902 in Balfour's Government (1902–5) so that these two important Education Acts were passed by Conservative Governments, implementing the recommendations of the Bryce Commission which was appointed by the Liberal, Gladstone. This Royal Commission was probably the most important and effective of all such commissions on education and it is most unfortunate that Lord Bryce, who died in 1922, was not around in 1944 in order to remedy the great error of omission in implementation that so marred the Education Act of that year – technical education. Again, whereas in 1904 it was stated that children must learn English, science, mathematics, geography, history and a language, as well as participating in physical exercise, drawing, singing and manual training for boys and 'housewifery' for girls, the 1944 Education Act hardly referred to the curriculum which was, in effect, left to the teachers. Thus, on two counts, the 1944 Act badly failed the nation.

On the other hand, the Acts of 1902 and for London, of 1903, led to striking advances in education. The Act, opposed by the Non-Conformists, led by Lloyd George, finally placed the 'non-provided' (the old 'voluntary') schools under the authority of the local education authorities so that, as all elementary schools were now benefiting from the rates, there was a general improvement in physical and educational standards, for although the managers of these schools still controlled religious education, they were subject to the directions of the local education authority in the secular field. A system of scholarships was introduced which made it possible for clever children of poor parents to obtain a university education. Until this time scholarships were confined to those given for education in the endowed grammar schools by some of the school boards in the larger towns such as Manchester, Birmingham, Leeds and Bradford. Teachers' salaries, although still low, were improved and regular scales were set by the county councils, while there were strenuous efforts made to reduce the size of classes, although this proved difficult to achieve, especially in London. The 'higher-grade' schools which had been (illegally) created and run by the school boards mostly became secondary schools, but in London the LCC built new secondary schools and developed the old 'higher-grade' schools as 'central' or 'intermediate' schools of a higher-elementary type, a policy which was soon to be recommended by the Board of

Education. It will be remembered that, under the influence of Acland, Gladstone's· administration formed a special inquiries branch in its Council of Education in 1894, to which R.L. Morant was appointed. It was under Morant that the Board of Education made such great progress in extending and improving the facilities for secondary and technical education. Although the numbers of pupils in grant-aided secondary schools do not compare with the post-war figures the increase from 94,000 in 1905 to 156,000 in 1910, and to 200,000 in 1914, was very impressive and did much to remedy England's educational weakness which had become so apparent by 1870.

Post-war historians, influenced by the euphoric belief in socialist centralized planning, advocated by writers such as R.H. Tawney, were unimpressed by this achievement. For example, speaking of the 200,000 pupils in secondary schools, one says:

> The remainder (3 million or so in the relevant age group) sat out a miserable elementary education until the expiry of their allotted span, when, ignorant and uncaring, they were released upon the world.[1]

Yet the reality is (and I have known many of these 'ignorant and uncaring' victims) that owing to the inculcation of the 'three Rs', they were able to go from strength to strength in their chosen occupations and in their own intellectual development in comparison with the present-day victims of 'progressive' educational methods and ideas, a significant number of whom are illiterate and the rest most inadequately prepared for life at work and in general. Again, whereas most of the smaller historic grammar schools had been modernized as a result of the Technical Instruction Act, after 1902 they became fully subject to the local authorities as secondary schools, as also did some of the larger ones which had previously been members of the Headmasters' Conference and which could no longer afford to be independent. On the other hand, the remaining members of the Conference, the non-local public schools, retained their financial independence and entered on a period of unparalleled prosperity and expansion. In regard to the state educational system, the reforming Liberal Government, elected in 1906, carried on the good work initiated by both parties since 1870. In 1906 there was a great extension of the scholarship system whereby additional grants enabled secondary schools to give 25 per cent 'free places'. On the

---

[1]*Britain in the Century of Total War*, by Arthur Marwick, pp. 34–5.

broader front, there were a number of new measures such as the establishment of school medical services in elementary schools, together with the provision of free meals where necessary, which has already been noted in the section on the creation of the National Health Service. More imaginatively and controversially, the councils opened nursery schools for the very young and special schools for deaf, blind and crippled children.

Whereas after 1870 the development of elementary education became the responsibility of the State, that of higher education, the universities, was left to independent institutions which had very little financial help from governments. As has already been noted, the dominance of Oxford and Cambridge (dating from the twelfth and thirteenth centuries respectively) was complete and the inevitable consequence was that the number of university students in proportion to population in England was far less than in comparable foreign countries, and in Scotland. To make matters worse, the ancient universities were still dominated by the classics (although the 'transference' into other subjects worked brilliantly among the academic elite) and were still virtually closed to non-conformists and Roman Catholics by the imposition of religious tests which Gladstone abolished by his University Test Act of 1871. Together with his imposition of competitive entrance examinations for permanent positions in the Civil Service, Gladstone gave a formidable stimulus to universities, in general, and university teaching, in particular. Of course, another reason for the small proportion of university students in England was that the cost of residing at the Oxford and Cambridge colleges debarred them to all but the richest of the middle classes and, of course, the upper class. Therefore, before 1870, both for reasons of finance and religion, there was a serious need for institutions of higher education other than Oxford and Cambridge which led to the foundation of London and Durham universities in the 1830s, although Durham remained small while London was confined to two teaching colleges and the right to conduct examinations and grant degrees. This latter became important, however, for it applied nationwide and led to the foundation of higher education colleges such as Owens College at Manchester in 1850 and Mason College at Birmingham in 1875. A landmark was the foundation in 1884 of the first of the modern provincial universities, Victoria University, which had a federal constitution, comprising the existing colleges at Manchester, Liverpool and Leeds which had previously used the London University examination system but which now had its own authority to examine and grant degrees. Fortunately, unlike the secondary

204

universities in the United States, Victoria ensured that education in the provincial universities would be comparable to that in Oxford and Cambridge by instituting a high standard for its degrees, thus also maintaining that excellent English educational tradition of excluding those students who were not suitable for a university education before they reached university, and not after, as in America and, to a lesser extent, Europe. A further necessity was the modernization of Oxford and Cambridge which, following the Clarendon Commission and Public Schools Act of 1868, was undertaken by the Royal Commission of 1876 and the Universities of Oxford and Cambridge Act of 1877 whereby, continuing the mid-century reforms, the two universities were given a more distinct status and function, as opposed to their constituent colleges, utilizing the latters' endowments for more educational purposes, thus making it possible to widen and modernize their curricula, the need for which was urgent. Apart from Geology, throughout the nineteenth century there was no work of importance done in any natural science at either university until the appointment of a professorship of experimental physics at Cambridge in 1871. All such work had been confined to the Scottish universities – Glasgow, Edinburgh and Marischal College, Aberdeen – the Royal Institution in London, the School of Mines, the 'mechanics' institutes' and the local scientific societies, usually called 'philosophical' societies, in the industrial towns.

Following the formation of Victoria University, in 1893, the three Welsh colleges (Aberystwyth, Cardiff and Bangor) established the University of Wales in which women were accepted equally with men, as in Victoria, a departure which was also followed by Durham University when it gained its supplementary charter in 1895. In 1900, Mason College became Birmingham University, the first example of a large industrial city having a university of its own. In 1889, Parliament gave financial support for the first time to the university colleges by voting an annual sum for allocation among them which, by 1900, became £25,000 distributed between thirteen of these institutions, three in London and ten in the rest of England, the three Welsh colleges enjoying a separate grant. In 1898, by Act of Parliament, seven commissioners were appointed for the University of London who issued statutes in 1900, following both of which the university, for the first time, became comparable with Oxford and Cambridge, with a senate, an academic council, a university extension board and eight faculties. Included in it as 'Schools of the University', were the three university colleges receiving grants (University College, King's College and Bedford College) as well as ten medical schools, six theological colleges, Holloway College (founded in 1883 by the manufacturer of patent medicines and philanthropist, Thomas Holloway, as a separate residential women's university), the London School of Economics (founded in 1895), the South-Eastern Agricultural College and the Central Technical College of the City and Guilds Institution. Although London University had further to go in the achievement of centralization it became more of a teaching institution than heretofore. Nevertheless, apart from medicine, the university colleges were mainly staffed by men from the reformed Oxford and Cambridge, whose intake was largely from the reformed public schools, and although the standard in both cases was very high, this still narrowly based system could never have produced a sufficient output of educated persons, so that, in proportion, Scotland was still far ahead of England in this respect. By the end of the century it was recognized that a solution to this problem was urgently needed.

As the lower levels of education benefited greatly and expanded following the Education Acts of 1899 and 1902, so too did the new century see a great expansion in the universities. Both Oxford and Cambridge increased their range and facilities for teaching as well as their numbers of undergraduates, but the period was notable for an impressive increase in the number of new universities. Following the example of Birmingham in 1900 the three university colleges comprising Victoria University became universities in their own right, Manchester and Liverpool receiving charters in 1903 and Leeds in 1904 followed by Sheffield in 1905 and Bristol in 1909. Additionally, outside London, there were six university colleges established by 1914, namely Nottingham, Newcastle, Reading, Exeter, Southampton and the Manchester School of Technology. The three colleges incorporating the University of Wales continued their growth while London maintained its development as a centre of learning both in content and organization. In 1907 University College became a part of the university itself and a similar 'transfer' was made of King's College in 1910, with the exception of its theological faculty. On the other hand, together with many others, the institutions with the two largest numbers of students remained not wholly integrated as 'schools of the university', the first being the great medical schools associated with the main London hospitals, and the second the Imperial College of Science and Technology with which was merged the City and Guilds Engineering College and the School of Mines. The London School of Economics and Political Science also retained this same status and although it was to become a very much larger institution after the war, by 1914 it had attained a national and even

206

an international reputation in the subjects that the older universities had comparatively neglected. In all, it can be said that by 1914 there had been a substantial increase in the provision of university teaching in England.

Economics and industrial history were the subjects mainly studied by the earliest exponents of adult education who were drawn largely from the activists in the trade unions, co-operative and socialist movements. From its beginnings as a university extension movement in Cambridge from 1873 and in Oxford from 1887, adult education blossomed in the new century in the form of the Workers' Educational Association, the four earliest branches of which were founded between 1904 and 1905 in Reading, Derby, Rochdale and Ilford. The movement was essentially co-operative in nature, as opposed to the negative process of merely listening to lectures, and it received a great impetus by the formulation of the 'tutorial class' method at Rochdale in 1907. Whereas in 1905 the WEA had 8 branches and about 1,000 members, in 1914 it had increased to 179 branches and 11,430 members. At the university level, the Oxford and Cambridge university extension movement culminated in the foundation (by Americans) of Ruskin Hall (later Ruskin College) at Oxford in 1899 as a residential college for the training of future working-class leaders. Whereas these had previously been self-educated and any extremism often moderated by the responsibilities of leadership, the segregated contact with the lecturers at Ruskin led to a 'hothouse' atmosphere in which extremism flourished and which led to movements such as the Plebs League in 1908 to urge 'independent working-class education on Marxian Lines'. This militantism or syndicalism of the trade unions in the years leading up to 1914 has already been mentioned and in this the Plebs men played an important part, notably in the 1911–12 strikes.

I have already mentioned the pioneers in women's education, of whom there were two outstanding personalities, Frances Mary Buss (1827–94) and Dorothea Beale (1831–1906) both of whom were Victorian evangelicals imbued with a strong sense of personal discipline and service which had been the feature of the great Victorian public school headmasters' beliefs. Miss Buss founded the North London Collegiate School in 1850 and although she continued to direct it until 1893 she transferred the property to a body of trustees in 1870 thus forming the Girls' Public Day-Schools Company, or Trust, which proceeded to establish high-quality girls' day schools based on the example of the North London Collegiate School, such as the Manchester High School for Girls in 1874. The resulting nationwide coverage of these schools was of supreme importance in English women's education and can be compared with the boys' grammar schools, including the fact that they have received much less publicity than the girls' equivalent of public schools. The first proprietary boarding school for girls was Cheltenham Ladies College (1854) where Miss Beale became headmistress in 1858. Both of these great ladies were called upon to give evidence before the Endowed Schools Inquiry Commission in 1865, whose reports on the education of girls in 1869 were very important. However, it was some years before girls' boarding schools were developed on the splendid lines of Miss Beale's example, two of the most important being Roedean (1885) and Wycombe Abbey (1896).

The greatest problem for the pioneers of women's education was the shortage of women university graduates to do the teaching. University education for women was initially provided by the opening of Queen's College for women, Harley Street, London in 1848 where Miss Beale was among the first students. Also, it was supremely important that from the beginning London University had made its examinations and degrees available to women for, as we have already seen, all provincial university colleges which took London's examinations and degrees initially accepted women on the same terms as men. Typically, Oxford and Cambridge, tentatively accepted women. Girton College was opened in Hitchin in 1869 and moved to Cambridge in 1872, while Newnham was founded in Cambridge in 1871. Again, typically, Oxford dragged its heels but Lady Margaret Hall was established in 1878, Somerville in 1879 and St Hughes in 1886. In 1893 the indomitable Miss Beale founded St Hilda's as a teachers' training college and an extension of the college that she had run for many years at Cheltenham. Equally typically, the members of these six colleges were not admitted as members of their respective universities, but they were permitted to attend lectures and take the degree examinations. Inevitably, with women throughout the country taking the same university examinations as men there was no question of there being developed distinct curricula for women which, however, was no bad thing for it placed women on an equal footing with men. Our contemporary 'women's libbers' would have approved of the benefactor, Thomas Holloway, for not only was the actual building and fabric of Holloway College extremely ambitious, on the lines of an enormous French chateau, but also he envisaged it as an independent residential women's university; yet, as we know, he had to run it as an adjunct of London University so that its teaching had to conform to London's examination and degree requirements. On the question of women's rights in education in general, and in university education in particular, Miss Emily Davies, a

208

contemporary of the Misses Buss and Beale, played an even more important part than these two formidable ladies.[1]

In the years prior to 1914, an important educational influence was the rapid growth of free libraries which was initiated by the Scottish-born American millionaire, Andrew Carnegie, who presented a free library to his home-town of Dunfermline and who between 1886 and 1900 established others in Great Britain (and many others in the United States). J. Passmore Edwards, a retired London newspaper proprietor, also founded 24 free libraries throughout the country, many of which still survive. With this impetus, the original Public Libraries Act of 1850 was extended in 1892, and in 1894 Fowler's Local Government Act

> made it possible for even a rural parish to have a public library. As a result of all these things, such libraries in the nineties were rapidly multiplied.[2]

The years between the two World Wars was a period of useful consolidation in the educational field but, naturally, the wars themselves had adverse consequences.

> Government plans for large increases in its education grants were announced in the Speeches from the Throne of 10 March 1913 and 10 February 1914, but, as the Board of Education subsequently reported, they were 'arrested by the outbreak of war'. Within a year the Board was being subjected to heavy pressure from local authorities who argued that the national emergency required a suspension of the school attendance by-laws ... At the same time the school medical services were severely curtailed, with a 28 per cent cut after 1916 in the number of children medically examined.[3]

The man brought in by Lloyd George as President of the Board of Education to cope with these disruptions was the distinguished Oxford historian of Europe, H.A.L. Fisher, who was responsible for the 1918 Education Act. After the raising of the school-leaving age to 14 in 1900 there remained exceptions to the rule, but Fisher's Act succeeded in enforcing this requirement without exception, although:

---

[1]*The Public School Phenomenon*, by Jonathan Gathorne Hardy, pp. 236–238.
[2]*England, 1870–1914*, by R.C.K. Ensor, p. 322.
[3]*Britain in the Century of Total War*, by Arthur Marwick, p. 64. Further facts and figures in this chapter are attributable to this authority.

209

the classes remained grotesquely large. In 1922 a quarter of the classes had more than sixty pupils. The highest ambition of educational policy between the wars was to reduce the classes to under fifty. Even this was not achieved.[1]

Another effect of the war was a shortage of teachers which Fisher proposed to remedy by both a significant increase in teacher's salaries, to be decided by a joint committee under Lord Burnham, to be nationally uniform and to be subject to a national pension scheme. There was a further increase in the number of free places at secondary schools to 34 per cent by 1922 – all of which led to an expensive increase in expenditure on education. Whereas Fisher estimated in 1918 that the increase would be about £3 million a year it proved to be more than ten times that amount and, while the local education authorities administered education, half the cost was borne by the central government which was, of course, responsible for the policy – which made it vulnerable in times of economic contraction.[2]

In the event, education was the greatest casualty of the 'Geddes Axe', the swingeing reductions in public expenditure in 1922. Whereas teachers' salaries had previously been decided by local authorities, they were now reduced by Parliament as also was expenditure on school buildings and free places. Although these economies were soon restored, the question of educational expenditure was never the same again, for from that time on the government was to decide how much of the national income was to be spent on education – a far weightier and more important question than the old educational controversy about religious teaching in elementary schools. Besides, it was inevitable that the central government would become more and more involved for only it could finance the increasing educational needs and demands. On the other hand, unlike France and the other Continental countries, although the State increasingly bore the cost of education, the 1918 Education Act, unlike the previous Education Acts, did not determine what should be taught, except in the case of religious instruction. Thus England established a tradition of unplanned diversity in education which was left in the hands of examining boards, headmasters and teachers, a system which worked well until it was undermined in the last 30 years or so by the combination of a 'trendy' educational establishment and recalcitrant left-wing Labour councils.

---

[1] *English History, 1914–45*, by A.J.P. Taylor, p. 184. Further facts and figures in this chapter are attributable to this authority.
[2] Ibid, pp. 184–5.

The end of the First World War brought about the active involvement of the State in the university sphere, for the first time. Previously, the State had played a passive part by granting royal charters to the new universities and reforming Oxford and Cambridge by the appointment of commissions. We have already noted that there were the small beginnings of financial support in 1889, which was extended in 1911, but, apart from this, the universities' income was derived from fees and endowments. As the Board of Education traditionally acted through the local authorities there had to be a change in the system when it was decided to subsidize the universities more substantially, as they, in the manner of Oxford and Cambridge, were national institutions. Thus in 1919 the University Grants Committee was established by which this committee of academics distributed an annual grant made directly by the Treasury. This led to an increase in standards as a result of the levelling of salaries between Oxford and Cambridge and the newer universities, the creation of state scholarships, and the like. But the main point was that the Minister of Education was precluded from interfering in education at the highest level so that the universities retained, and even increased, their traditional independence, and English university teachers enjoyed what was probably an unparalleled freedom throughout the world. Although not spectacular, there was a steady increase in the foundation of new university colleges, preparing their students for London University degrees, namely Swansea, Leicester, Hull, Nottingham, Southampton and Exeter, while Reading became a university in its own right. Marwick makes the point regarding the 'red brick' universities that:

> There remained class distinction as between different universities: Oxford and Cambridge ranked above the newer foundations in much the same way that the old-established public schools ranked above all other institutions of secondary education.[1]

On the other hand, the truth was, and is, that in spite of the fact that the earliest civic universities were founded partly to provide higher education for dissenters, and partly to provide an alternative to the unattainable Oxford and Cambridge, they became national institutions and consciously strove to emulate the upper-class aura of the latter. Unlike university students in the rest of the old world who traditionally have had to accept a much lower standard of living at

---

[1] *Britain in the Century of Total War*, by Arthur Marwick, p. 182.

university than at home, in England's newer universities, as at Oxford and Cambridge, they have often enjoyed higher standards, especially the teachers. In other words, Marwick's undiluted view is biased and negative – especially, in view of the fact that in these days many young people prefer to go to the newer universities rather than to the two old ones.

However, it would be equally foolish to deny the 'class' structure of pre-war English education. It is well described by A.J.P. Taylor:

> The children of the masses went to free day schools until the age of 14; the children of the privileged went to expensive boarding schools until 13.[1] The dividing line was as hard as that between Hindu castes. No child ever crossed it. At the secondary level, the division was almost as complete. Nearly all the children of the privileged proceeded to expensive private schools – public schools as they were perversely called. A minority of children from the other classes went to modern day schools, maintained from public funds. The grammar schools straddled in between, mainly and appropriately for the middle class, and with a few poor boys as well. At the highest level, the modern universities in large towns were socially inferior to Oxford and Cambridge, which remained in spirit, and largely in numbers,[2] preserves of the privileged classes. The two systems of education catered for different classes and provided education, different in quality and content, for rulers and ruled.[3]

Marwick makes the same point:

> Educational opportunity in England in the 1920s was openly governed by social class, and as a natural consequence, served to reinforce it. However, this consideration was swamped ... by the more oppressive fact that the educational provision for the lower classes was appalling. In 1923 rather more than 1,600,000 children between the age of 11 and 14 (72.5 per cent of this age group) were being educated in elementary schools which did not even claim to provide 'advanced instruction'; in other words, they were simply receiving a repetition of the same rudimentary material until the

---

[1] Taylor is referring to the private preparatory schools to which boys went from the ages of eight or nine before going to public school.
[2] 'Though about a third of the students at Oxford and Cambridge now came from grammar schools, only one in a hundred came from a working-class family'. Quoted on p. 171 (see below).
[3] *English History, 1914–1945* by A.J.P. Taylor, p. 171.

blessed day of release, which was at the end of the term in which the pupil reached the age of 14.[1]

Thus although it is quite legitimate for the historian to point out the class structure of pre-war English education, we note once again that Marwick's bias and pessimism, in quoting what appeared to him to be 'blood-curdling' figures, serve to give a serious distortion of the pre-war situation. What he should have used the word 'appalling' for was the gross neglect of the education of the English masses before 1870, for it is quite incorrect to use it to describe the strenuous efforts made between 1870 and 1914 to redress the situation, which is why I have taken the trouble to describe them in some detail. Admittedly, these were carried out on a class basis, elementary school classes were far too large and there were many other imperfections, but the all-important fact was that the age of neglect was decisively terminated and honest endeavour had taken its place. Furthermore, it was extremely important that, before both World Wars, the education system, to a considerable degree, opened up the possibility of advancement, with the consequent social mobility, to children of poorer backgrounds. Also, and of the utmost importance, the basic and conservative education up to the age of 14 was infinitely superior as a preparation for life as an individual, on the one hand, and as a member of a community, on the other hand, than that suffered by today's 'little victims', in the words of the poet, Thomas Gray, in his 'Ode on a Distant Prospect of Eton College'. (I refer to the question that I pose in the first sentence of Chapter Five.) We have seen that H.A.L. Fisher continued this good work in 1918 and it remains to describe the situation leading up to the Education Act of 1944.

We have already seen that the minister in charge of education during the Labour minority Government of 1924 was C.P. Trevelyan and he was able to restore most of the cuts imposed by the Geddes Axe on public education, especially in secondary education, but we must remind ourselves that although he had as tender a social conscience as any Labour man, the Chancellor, Philip Snowden, believed even more in a balanced budget and unlike later members of his party, he had a healthy distrust of the efficacy of state expenditure. It is also worth noting that whereas the Geddes Committee originally envisaged a reduction in educational expenditure of £18 million the Lloyd George Government, in fact,

---

[1] *Britain in the Century of Total War*, by Arthur Marwick, p. 179.

'only' reduced it by £6½ million and did not adopt the retrograde suggestion to raise the school entry age to six. In his brief but important period in charge of education Trevelyan inherited a Labour policy statement, 'Secondary Education for All', adopted by the Party Conference, and drafted by R.H. Tawney who had become a significant moral and intellectual force in the Labour Party. Tawney's statement was doubly important for its views were those of a wide range of informed opinion and were mainly concerned with the fact that elementary education continued to the age of 14 or later and that although 5.5 per cent received 'advanced instruction' in 'all-age' schools or in separate 'central' schools (p. 202–3) only 7 per cent attended the grant-aided secondary schools which involved a working-class child passing the 'Free Place Examination', usually at the age of 11. The aim of 'Secondary Education for All' was:

> That all normal children, irrespective of income, class or occupation of their parents, may be transferred at the age of 11 + from the primary or preparatory school to one type or another of secondary school, and remain in the latter till sixteen.

Trevelyan appointed a consultative committee of the Board of Education under Sir Henry Hadow to deliberate on these matters and, even though the committee did not report until 1926, he deserved most of the credit for the fact that, as A.J.P. Taylor says: 'The Hadow report set the pattern for English publicly maintained education to the present day.'[1] Its main proposal, following 'Secondary Education for All', was the abolition of the old concept of elementary education which was to be replaced by primary education, after which there was to be a clean break at the age of 'eleven-plus', followed by secondary education. The existing secondary schools were to be called 'grammar schools' (a brilliant idea because they were to be upgraded in the mould of the historic grammar schools, an objective which was achieved in practice) and a new type of less academic secondary 'modern' school was to be created. Finally, it was recommended that after a period of five years the school-leaving age should be raised to 16. Unfortunately, owing to the economic crisis of 1931, the Hadow Report was not implemented but its proposals, including the leaving-age of 15, were embodied in the Education Act of 1944. In the second minority Labour Government of 1929–31 Trevelyan was again in charge of

---

[1] *English History, 1914–45*, by A.J.P. Taylor (published in 1965), p. 211.

214

education and it is ironic that his Bill to raise the leaving age to 15 was defeated by Roman Catholic Labour backbenchers, representing working-class constituents. However, in 1926 the Baldwin Conservative Government had made an important move, which in years to come was to result in centres of outstanding educational excellence, and that was to permit fee-paying grammar schools, which were not in the public system and were in the larger towns, such as Manchester and Bristol Grammar Schools, to qualify for 'direct grants' from the government without becoming subject to the local authorities. In view of the small-minded and misguided policies of many of the latter in future years this was indeed fortuitous. Marwick describes this successful development as 'a new refinement in the class structure of English education',[1] yet another example of his negative egalitarianism and class-conscious defeatism.

By 1939 then, although there was little increase in the numbers being educated over the compulsory age, in regard to the proportions of students at secondary school and proceeding from the latter to university, there were some achievements. It had been agreed that the compulsory leaving age of 15 would be enforced from 1 September 1939 but unfortunately this date coincided with the outbreak of war so that, once again, the matter was delayed. But there had been definite progress in relation to the size of classes in primary schools where those of over 60 had virtually disappeared, there being only 56 of such by the end of 1938, while two-thirds of children over 11 were in senior departments of one kind or another. The war, however, was to bring about a significant set-back to this quiet progress for air raids destroyed a fifth of all the country's schools. Nevertheless, it was to be in the field of education that there was the first manifestation of the wartime hopes for post-war England for as has been mentioned on several occasions, R.A. Butler's Education Act of 1944 was the only one of the great Acts of Parliament setting up 'The Welfare State' to be passed by the wartime Coalition Government, and which had been preceded by the Board of Education's 'Green Book' in 1941 and the White Paper of 1943. The Act was the natural corollary of all that had been done since 1870 and embodied the pre-war consensus which had been set out in the Hadow Report. That is to say, the school-leaving age was to be raised to 15 by 1947 (leaving time to build more schools) and there were to be three types of free secondary education – grammar, modern and technical – without means tests or similar restrictions. Although it was not specifically

---

[1]*Britain in the Century of Total War*, by Arthur Marwick, p. 181.

mentioned in the Act, it was implied that selection to a grammar school would be determined by success in the 'eleven-plus' examination. The similar Act of 1945 for Scotland emphasized Scotland's longer and superior tradition of secondary education, for there were a greater number of grammar school places in proportion to demand than in England, and their 'twelve-plus' exam, on the change from primary to secondary education, was retained. Finally, in regard to the 1944 Act for England, the requirement to begin each day with a non-denominational act of collective worship, for the first time in educational history, was socially significant. Previous Acts had assumed that there would automatically be religious worship and they were only concerned that this would be non-denominational. The religious clause admits that this assumption could no longer be made.[1] The change, subtle at the time, can be seen to set the stage for so many of the differences to be seen gradually in post-war England – notably an increase in materialism and the questioning of authority.

The post-war consensus has 'brain-washed' us into thinking of the 1944 Act as the beginning of a great educational adventure but, as I have implied, it was the end of an enlightened process dating from 1870. In so far as it was the beginning of something it was the beginning of our greatest educational missed opportunity and this was due to the Labour Party and to the attitude of 'egalitarian' socialists and, it must be said, to a supine Conservative Party, influenced initially by the most supine character of them all – 'Rab' Butler. Marwick aligns himself decisively with the former attitude, pouring scorn especially on the 'outmoded' ideal of 'diversity' which the Act embodied with its three types of secondary education which we now know was entirely beneficial. But according to Marwick,

> ...when a comparison is made between the utterly deplorable state of English education prior to 1939 and its condition after 1945, (the English Education Act of 1944) is a great Act but which, when thought is given to the continuing inadequacies of English education since 1945, (it) seems a bungled opportunity. ... both fee-paying direct grant schools and the exclusive public schools were left untouched. A left-wing Labour amendment on the committee stage of the Bill, seeking to abolish fees in all schools, would with one blow have provided for the rebuilding of the system on a fresh basis: the amendment was not successful...[2]

---

[1] *English History, 1914–1945*, by A.J.P. Taylor, p. 568.
[2] *Britain in the Century of Total War*, by Arthur Marwick, p. 319.

The naivety is staggering as also is the total failure to think in terms of emulating the good, as has happened with the universities and as was happening with the secondary modern schools before their unfortunate abolition. Instead, Marwick is implicitly critical of the 'eleven-plus' and to this day people with his cast of mind continue to fulminate against this eternal 'red-herring', for if the matter were to be decided by a show of hands instead of by examination the outcome would be virtually identical, for only a minority of people are of an academic inclination.

I have said on more than one occasion that there was one monumental omission in the application of the 1944 Act, and that was the failure to provide technical schools, apart from a very few. As we have seen, the English weakness in technical education has been recognized since the time of Playfair's letter of 1867 and the Technical Instruction Act of 1889, and in view of the continuation of that weakness to the present day, the perpetrators of this grotesque omission can never be forgiven. The reason was that the left-wing elements in the Labour Party, such as those MPs whose amendment attempted to abolish fees in all schools were so obsessed by their objective to attain educational 'equality' that they were completely against any form of 'diversity', as represented by the technical schools, especially as these, to their twisted minds, relegated working-class children to an inferior form of education. In other words, their class bias and hostility to elitism blinded them to the real needs of the working-class and non-academic (not necessarily the same) children of the day, which was, and is, diversity. From the opposite end of the spectrum they were exhibiting the same prejudice as was Jack Peterson and, sad to say, so was Arthur Marwick in his knowledgeable and brilliant but prejudiced account of the period. So obsessed was he about 'class' that he wrote

> ...if ever there was a good psychological moment for dealing with the snobbism built into the (educational) system, it was in the aftermath of the 1945 election victory.[1]

But he completely failed to appreciate the awful significance of the failure to establish technical schools after 1944. Literally, his only comment on the subject was: '...it had been the intention of the framers of the Act that there should also be "technical schools", but very few of these in fact materialized.'[2] Nevertheless, apart from this

---

[1] *Britain in the Century of Total War*, by Arthur Marwick, p. 358.
[2] *Ibid.*, p. 319.

serious defect, the Act succeeded in increasing the school population significantly. By January 1955 the number of pupils at school until 17 and over was twice the pre-war total, although as a percentage of the age group it was only 7.9 per cent in England and Wales and 9.1 per cent in Scotland. If the creation of technical schools had been pursued vigorously these percentages would have been much higher. Finally, education provided a good example of the post-war consensus, for under Labour the 'eleven-plus' examination was applied, in spite of its unpopularity with the left wing, and under the Conservatives, in the 1950s, the first three comprehensive schools were opened by the Labour London County Council, in spite of the fact that the Government believed in the grammar and secondary modern system of education. In the Labour party's 'Challenge to Britain', issued in June 1953, the abolition of grammar schools was demanded, but better sense prevailed at their annual conference in September which rejected the proposal in favour of a milder resolution expressing preference for comprehensive education. Unfortunately, the undertaking in the Labour Party's election manifesto in September 1964, to reorganize education in accordance with the comprehensive system, effectively condemned a whole generation of schoolchildren to illiteracy and semi-literacy, because of the 'progressive' ideas that accompanied it, as much as to the mixed ability system itself.

It is satisfactory to be able to report that there was the usual steady and sensible progress on the university front. In 1946 the powers of the University Grants Committee were considerably enhanced, as also were its grants from the Government from 1952–55 so that by 1956–57 the Treasury was providing around 70 per cent of the income of the universities. Following the granting of university status to Southampton (1952), Hull (1954), Exeter (1955) and Leicester (1957), there were 21 full universities and one university college (North Staffordshire). The university population was inflated after the war by the presence of ex-servicemen and reached 85,421 by 1948–49 but after declining to 80,602 in 1953–54 it expanded to 89,886 in 1956–57. It was under Macmillan in 1961 that the Robbins Committee on Higher Education and the Newsom Committee on Secondary Education were appointed, while Sir Alec Douglas-Home accepted the former's recommendation for the expansion of higher education as well as appointing the Franks Commission to deal with the special case of Oxford in this expansion. But even before the Robbins expansion, under the Conservatives new universities were founded at Sussex (Brighton), York, East Anglia (Norwich), Lancaster and Essex (Colchester), and plans made for those at Kent and Warwick. The man who, in practice, was mainly associated with this exciting period of university expansion was Keith Murray (later Sir Keith Murray and then Lord Murray of Newhaven), chairman of the University Grants Committee from 1953 to 1963. Murray had had an extremely successful career in administration at Oxford University, before and after the war, during which he was appointed Director of Food at the Middle East Supply Centre, GHQ Cairo, in 1942. On his appointment to the UGC there were sixteen universities, five university colleges and two institutes of science and technology but when he retired, there were thirty-two independent universities and one institute. We have already noted, above, the increase in student numbers during his time while annual recurrent grants had increased from £20 million to £56 million and capital grants had risen from £4.6 million a year to £29 million. It was under his leadership that the UGC established that university places should be available to all qualified for them, thus leading to the appointment of the Robbins Committee. He was instrumental in ensuring that as expansion mounted financial control was maintained, while perhaps his greatest contribution was his success in maintaining the independence of the universities from direct government interference, both before and after his time.

12

Housing

Britain's housing problem was and is unique. This arises from the two facts that she was the first country to experience the industrial revolution and that, unlike the United States and the continental countries of Europe (except Belgium), being a small island, space was very limited, so that the houses in the towns that sprang up around the new factories were confined and concentrated in the way that has become associated with the grim and forbidding environments of Britain's nineteenth-century industrial towns. For example, it has been said that the industrial Clyde area of Glasgow was the most densely populated area in the world. In continental countries such as Germany and France one can see that, although there are 'black spots' in Northern Europe, on the whole, industrial activity and the consequent urban development were and are comparatively widely spread. In neither country is there any 'great wen'[1] dominating the whole country, such as London, compared with which Paris and German towns were and are mere provincial cities. The catalyst that made these two factors so important was an explosive growth in population which, during the reign of George III (1760–1820), doubled itself in England and Wales from around 6½ million to around 13 million. Coming after centuries of slow population growth this unparalleled increase in numbers was a revolution in itself and put great pressures on the social framework, including housing. It has been seen that Edwin Chadwick, one of the Poor Law Commissioners, played an important part in the passing of the first Public Health Act of 1848 (p. 124). He wrote:

> The prisons were formerly distinguished for their filth and bad ventilation; but the descriptions given by Howard of the worst prisons he visited in England (which he states were among the worst that he had seen in Europe) were exceeded in every wynd in Edinburgh and Glasgow inspected by Dr Arnott and myself. More

---

[1]The name given to London by the essayist, William Cobbett (1762–1835).

220

filth, worse physical suffering and moral disorder than Howard describes are to be found amongst the cellar populations of the working people of Liverpool, Manchester or Leeds and in large portions of the Metropolis.[1]

In the usual fashion, I shall examine the problem in detail, but in spite of all that has been done to rectify the situation the fact remains that British housing is still bedevilled by its unique origins.

Apart from education (and in this case only from 1870), there was no development of social services as a result of a social conscience. We have already seen in the case of public health that nineteenth-century legislation was confined to providing a healthy environment and that:

> It was not until after the First World War that the general public expected and the local health services accepted that they should serve persons, as opposed to districts, in the fight against disease and ill health (p. 124–5).

The same was true of housing. It was significant that the first effective legislation in this field was during Disraeli's great reforming ministry of 1874–80. It will be remembered that although Disraeli put through the Second Reform Act of 1867 as a member of the Earl of Derby's administration of 1866–68, Gladstone won the election of 1868 at the time of Disraeli's first short-lived administration. In giving the vote to the town-dwelling artisan Disraeli was conscious of the fact that he was striking a blow at the middle-class era of 'laissez-faire' which was initiated by the First Reform Act of 1832 giving the vote to the middle classes. After 1867 governments were much more inclined to take action when nothing would have been done in a 'laissez-faire' situation, as we have seen in the case of education, but whereas Gladstone was mainly concerned with sweeping away disabilities, Disraeli consciously initiated legislation that would help the new working-class voters, thus returning to the Tory tradition of radical reform during the years 1822–29 in the ministries of Peel, Huskisson and Canning. To keep things in perspective, it is necessary to mention the two great humanitarian reforms initiated by evangelical Tory peers and passed by the reformed Whig Government in 1833, Wilberforce's abolition of slavery under the British flag and Lord Ashley's Factory Act by which children under nine were not to

---

[1] Quoted in *Illustrated English Social History*, (Volume 4), by G.M. Trevelyan, pp. 66–7.

be employed, those under twelve were not to work more than eight hours a day and those under eighteen not more than ten hours a day. Ashley (later the Earl of Shaftesbury), followed this up by the Coal Mines Act of 1842, prohibiting the employment of women and children underground and initiating safety measures for men, and by two more Factory Acts of 1844 and 1847 further limiting the employment of children and establishing ten hours as the normal working day for men. Significantly, these Acts were strenuously opposed by MPs such as John Bright who spoke for the Midlands manufacturers, the exponents of 'laissez-faire'.

The great year of Disraeli's social reforming legislation was 1875. The Trade Union and Public Health Acts have already been mentioned on pages 36 and 124 respectively, the Sale of Food and Drugs Act was the first, really effective measure on the subject, as also can be said about the Artisans Dwelling Act.

> Till then, there had only been Lord Shaftesbury's two acts of 1851, permitting local authorities to supervise common lodging-houses (and in some cases procure their erection), and the Torrens Act of 1866, enabling them to compel the owners of individual insanitary houses to put them in proper condition.[1]

The way had recently been shown by the radical mayoralty of Joseph Chamberlain (later Liberal and Conservative MP and minister, 1876–1906) in Birmingham (1873–76) where, in his own words, the town was 'parked, paved, assized, marketed, gas-and-watered, and improved – all as the result of three years' active work'.[2] In the early days of the new towns thrown up by the Industrial Revolution the prevailing 'laissez-faire' outlook led to anomalies such as three or four competing gas and water mains in the same streets. The recognition that these were 'natural monopolies' led to amalgamation and local monopoly, and finally to the local authorities, under Private Acts of Parliament, buying out the companies and running the services themselves. With the advent of electricity supply and street transport in the 1870s and 1880s, Parliament recognized that these were also 'natural monopolies' and provided in advance that they should be undertaken either as regulated private monopolies or as public monopolies undertaken by the local authorities.

However, back to 1875 when Cross's Housing Act (Cross having

---

[1] *England, 1870–1914*, by R.C.K. Ensor, p. 127. Further facts and figures in this chapter are attributable to this authority.
[2] *Life of Chamberlain*, by J.L. Garvin, p. 202.

been Disraeli's brilliant Home Secretary) was the first, following Chamberlain's work in Birmingham, to authorize national clearance schemes by empowering local authorities to condemn, demolish and rebuild whole areas. In spite of second Cross and Torrens Housing Acts in 1879 it was felt that much more needed to be done so that in 1881 there was a Select Committee of the House of Commons, in 1882 another Housing Act and in 1883 a pamphlet, 'The Bitter Cry of Outcast London', led to the important Royal Commission on Housing in 1884, chaired by Dilke and including such notables as the Prince of Wales, Cardinal Manning, Lord Salisbury, Goschen, Cross and Torrens. Their report in 1885 was followed by yet another Housing Act. In the meantime, the local authorities began clearing the worst slums, as in London when between 1876 and 1884 the Metropolitan Board of Works displaced 22,872 persons and rehoused 28,352; however here, as elsewhere, the local authority did not undertake the rehousing but offered the sites for sale on the condition that they should be used for this purpose only, so that this was confined to the activities of philanthropic bodies such as the Peabody Trust. Nevertheless, municipal enterprise in the great provincial cities preceded even Birmingham, notably Liverpool, Manchester, Bradford and Glasgow, with their confidently ambitious municipal buildings and undertakings such as the Liverpool docks, as well as slum clearance after the first Cross Housing Act. It was in these cities rather than London, that the regulation of the 'natural monopolies', referred to above, was developed and where 'municipalization' became increasingly important, although it was not until the end of the century, with the influence of the Fabian intellectuals, that the collectivist implications of municipalization were defined. Initially, the motives had been purely pragmatic.

However, although England's skilled workers (the trade unionists) were the most highly paid in Europe, the unskilled, casual and sweated labourers, were still bedevilled by poverty, and poor housing and environment, in spite of the fact that the very worst housing conditions, such as one room tenements containing nine or more people, had been severely curbed. England and Wales were better than Scotland or Dublin but even in the former the number of tenements was not increasing as fast as the increase in population. I have already referred to Charles Booth's *Life and Labour of the People of London*, 1889, in which he estimated that 30.7 per cent of the inhabitants of London lived 'in poverty', as well as to Rowntree's survey of York. But, apart from certain areas in London, the greatest overcrowding was in the North-East, in 1899 the counties of Durham and Northumberland having 34 and 38 per cent respectively of their

223

populations overcrowded, with Gateshead, Newcastle and Sunderland being the three most overcrowded towns. Other bad areas were Liverpool, near the docks, the South Wales coalfield and the Clyde – all of which, unsurprisingly, were 'hotbeds' of militant trade-unionism down to 1914. But as much as, or even more than, overcrowding, there was the devastating effect of the fact that:

> the typical homes of the artisans in the manufacturing towns – cottages in long rows lining mean streets, quite sanitary, but ugly, smoke-blackened, and monotonous – were apt to be starved of all such amenities as access to parks, or indeed to beauty of any sort.[1]

Nevertheless, the housing situation was affected favourably by the revolution in urban transport that took place in the 1890s, namely the advent of the first electric trams and the early motor cars which enabled the towns to widen their perimeters, thus leading to the building boom of 1900–1910. For example, in London when people from old houses in Poplar, Walworth and North Camberwell moved to new houses in East Ham, Wandsworth and Lewisham respectively, the old houses were occupied by poorer people from the more central and crowded areas. Thus, although the building boom was for the benefit of the better-off workers, the worse-off benefited indirectly. The main reason for the end of the boom was the projected Land Value duties in Lloyd George's controversial 1909 Budget which was also the prime cause of the opposition of the land-owning Conservative peers and which threatened to deprive the speculative builders of the main part of their profit – the increase in the value of the land. It is worth recording that owing to the refusal of the House of Lords to permit trams over the bridges of the Thames or the Embankment, the City and West End of London remained tramless, while electric trams, mostly in municipal ownership, became such an important feature of provincial cities. Prior to the advent of the first motor omnibuses in London in 1905 the capital was dependent on slow-moving horse omnibuses so that the 'atmosphere' of London was that of an earlier age compared to that of the provincial cities. However, 1905 also saw the opening of the Bakerloo and Piccadilly tubes and the partial electrification of the shallow underground railways which had previously been steam-driven, but all the metropolitan transport was more expensive than the economical trams in the provinces.

---

[1] *England, 1870–1914*, by R.C.K. Ensor, p. 302.

From the human point of view, and in spite of the fact that real wages and real living standards rose significantly during the nineteenth century for the lowest income groups, the combination of poverty and poor housing meant that the lowly-paid town labourers of Edwardian Britain, together with the 'sweated' workers and casual labourers, were living below minimum standards – 27.84 per cent of the whole population or 43.4 per cent of the wage-earning class, according to Rowntree. Contemporary statisticians stated: 'To raise the wages of the worst-paid workers is the most pressing social task with which the country is confronted today.'[1] All this was reflected in the alarmingly poor physical condition of the poorer inhabitants of the towns, enormous numbers of whom were rejected as being unfit for service in the South African War, in spite of the fact that the standard had been reduced to the lowest since Waterloo. This was the background to and the incentive for the unprecedented social reforms of the pre-war Liberal Government which bear repeating: free school meals and a free school medical service, non-contributory old-age pension, a Children's Act, the establishment of Labour Exchanges and of Trade Boards (to curb the abuses of 'sweated' labour), a Housing and Town Planning Act in 1909, the National Insurance Scheme of 1911 dealing with both sickness and unemployment followed by a Shops Act and an eight-hour day for miners. Whereas most of these reforms and Acts can be regarded as the forerunners of the much more ambitious social reforms of the post-1945 Labour Government, the Housing and Town Planning Act made no new contribution and was disappointing in its actual achievements. The former did not depart from the traditional 'laissez-faire' policy of merely enabling local authorities to build houses for the poor without any degree of compulsion or financial assistance from the Treasury. The Town Planning part was so hedged with conditions that it was virtually ineffective, which was extremely disappointing in view of the examples which had already been set by enlightened private enterprise at Port Sunlight, Bournville and Letchworth, not to mention Hampstead Garden suburb which, in turn, had been partly inspired by the pioneering work in Germany on town planning. Thus, instead of a surge in house-building and the development of an effective planning structure in the years before the First World War, we learn that 'the shortage of houses in 1913 was officially estimated as between 100,000 and 120,000.'[2] As we have learnt from our own

---

[1]*Livelihood and Poverty, 1915*, by A.L. Bowley and A.R. Burnett-Hurst, p. 5.

[2]*Britain in the Century of Total War*, by Arthur Marwick, p. 35. Further facts and figures in this chapter are attributable to this authority.

post-1945 history and from that of the old Soviet Union and its East European satellites, centralized planning of the national economy is economically disastrous and, if applied relentlessly, is incompatible with political and personal freedom, but if there is any field in which planning has a place it is in local government. The reason is that the inherent defects of planning soon come into play when the scale of activity is widened from the municipal to the national.

The pre-war shortage of 120,000 houses had escalated to 610,000 by 1919 which was due not only to the virtual cessation of building since 1910 but also to the pre-war increase in population, especially of married couples, and to the continued decline of older houses into slums.[1] Furthermore, the crowding of large numbers of people into the new munitions centres, hostels for war workers and for other war-time industrial expansion such as in the ship-building and steel industries, exacerbated the old problem of over-crowding. For example, conditions at Barrow were officially described as 'a crying scandal'. Indeed, so great was the perceived problem that the Salisbury Committee on Housing in England and Wales, which reported in October 1907, suggested that the State would need to be more active in the housing field, while the earlier Royal Commission on Housing in Scotland made the then revolutionary declaration that the problem could not be solved by private enterprise, and that it could only be done by government action and by the massive injection of public funds.[2] During the General Election of 1918 Lloyd George had promised to build 'Homes Fit for Heroes' and the Housing and Town Planning Act of 1919 was the instrument designed to achieve this aim but, more important, as in public health, it acknowledged for the first time the State's responsibility to society to provide decent housing, as opposed merely to the financing of sporadic private building initiatives.

Acting through the Ministry of Health (the ministry concerned) the Act required the local authorities to survey their local housing needs within three months, and periodically thereafter, and to submit plans. On approval by the Ministry, all losses in their execution were to be the responsibility of the Treasury which greatly exceeded the income from the penny local rate which the authorities were to levy for the purpose. Thus, in 1919 there was established the principle of the State accepting the direct financial responsibility for the provision of homes

---

[1]*English History, 1914–45*, by A.J.P. Taylor, p. 122. Further facts and figures in this chapter are attributable to this authority.
[2]Commission of Enquiry into Working Class Unrest, 1917–18, xiv, Cd.8663, p. 31.

for a large section of the working classes. The second important feature of the Act was that the controlled rents, based on the 1914 level, could be altered, above and below this level, in accordance with the amenities of the house and, more important, the tenants' ability to pay. It is sad to think that this original enlightened view that the Government was subsidizing the tenant, as such, and not the house, was eventually replaced by the latter concept, which resulted in the creation of needless financial and community problems in the matter of 'council housing'. The Minister of Health, responsible for putting the Act into effect, Dr Christopher Addison, had been extremely successful during the war in the Ministry of Munitions with Lloyd George, and he immediately applied the same enthusiasm to the building of houses by instructing the local authorities to build unlimited houses and to let them at controlled rents, which was, of course, another expense for the Government. Unfortunately, the building programme coincided with the post-war, explosive boom which collapsed just as suddenly in 1921 so that houses which cost the Ministry £910 in early 1921 could be built several years later for £385. As a result of this 'Housing Scandal' Addison left the Ministry of Health in early 1921, in July 1921 the grants for new houses were heavily reduced and in 1922, the era of the 'Geddes Axe', they were ended. The last houses under the programme were built in 1923 which was unfortunate for, by then, building costs had declined and house-building would have reduced unemployment. With the continued increase in the number of married couples, the shortage of houses had increased to an estimated 822,000 by 1923. Nevertheless, Addison cannot be said to have failed. He succeeded in building 213,000 houses, established the principle that housing was a social service and the practice that the local authorities should be the instruments of the Government's housing policy and, finally, by his Housing (Additional Powers) Act, he provided small monetary subsidies for private house-builders, provided that they maintained certain standards as to size. For Lloyd George, who by 1921 had become extremely unpopular with the working classes owing to the sharp fall in wages, with the collapse of the boom in 1921, and to his defeat of the striking miners, it could be said, however, that he had honoured his 1918 election pledge to build 'Homes Fit for Heroes'.

It was only natural that the Conservatives should have attributed the escalation of house-building costs in 1921–22 to Addison's unlimited subsidies so that Neville Chamberlain's Housing Act of 1923 was framed to enable private enterprise to show that it could solve the housing problem better than the local authorities. His limited subsidy of £6 a year for 20 years for houses of a maximum size of 950 square feet was available to both private and public builders, but in practice most of the 436,000 houses built before the subsidy was ended in 1929 were built by the former – and all of these were for sale. In spite of the fact that the houses were limited to the 'non-parlour type', and were therefore at the lower end of the social and financial scale, they did not benefit the manual workers but mainly the lower-middle-class office workers who were moving to the outskirts of the towns although, as always, the houses vacated by them provided housing for the former. Nevertheless, this was the main achievement of Bonar Law's 1922–23 Government and, as Minister of Health, it was the first of Chamberlain's great administrative achievements for the Conservative Party and the country. The Act, however, caused great hostility among working-class electors who took their revenge in the December 1923 election, and poor Chamberlain, with his cold and impersonal manner, was singled out as the oppressor of the poor.[1]

With the minority Labour Government of 1924, housing was again the Government's most impressive achievement, owing to the brilliance in conception and execution of the Minister responsible, John Wheatley, who was the first housing minister to recognize the long-term nature of the housing problem. He increased the subsidy to £9 a year for 40 years, with an additional £4.10.0 if, as in rural areas, the controlled rent was not enough to cover the cost, he restored the main responsibility to the local authorities and he insisted that the houses should be built to be let at controlled rents, and that the scheme would operate for 15 years. This last was a part of his historically important and unique innovation of negotiating with both sides of the building industry so that much higher levels of productivity were achieved from the expanded industry. The only thing he failed to do, although it was in accordance with official Labour policy, was to replace the annual subsidy by low-interest loans from the central government in order to obviate the necessity of local authorities having to borrow money to cover the capital cost, and thus to give up much of the government subsidy in the form of interest payments. However, in spite of the fact that Wheatley's programme was terminated in the course of 1932 and 1933, as a result of the economic crisis, it led to the construction of over half a million houses, and virtually ended the housing shortage, although it did nothing to eliminate the slums.[2] The 1931 Census showed that in England and

---

[1] *English History, 1914–1945*, by A.J.P. Taylor, p. 206.
[2] Ibid, p. 210.

Wales 35 per cent of the population lived more than 2 to a room, 15 per cent more than 3 to a room and 6 per cent more than 4 to a room, with the position even worse in Scotland. Once again, the new houses benefited the better-off members of the working and middle classes, and the only benefit to the slum-dwellers was that they could move into the houses that had been vacated. But now that the system of universal controlled rents had been adopted, and that the very poor could not afford these, the people in real need, and those for whom the State should have been making provision, were not helped. The better-off artisans and office workers should not have been subsidized or should have been offered houses to buy, while the subsidies should have been concentrated on the poor. That is to say, the subsidies should have been concentrated on people, not houses. In my years as a local councillor in the 1960s, I noticed two aspects in the housing field. First, the dear old Conservative councillors were always on about the fact that there was a housing queue, even though I continually explained to them that as long as the subsidized rents were below the market price, there would inevitably be a queue. Secondly, the Housing Committee vetted council house applicants rigorously with a view to eliminating any family whose financial position or record was not impeccable. There was not the slightest indication that the council's houses were for the benefit of the community's poorer members. This is a very different situation from that prevailing since Labour has gained control of the inner city authorities which have presided over millions of pounds of unpaid rent and hundreds of thousands of council houses being left derelict.

Once again, housing was a main feature of the legislation of the 1929–31 Labour Government. Arthur Greenwood, the Minister of Health, retained Wheatley's subsidies, which Chamberlain would have abolished, and in his Housing Act of 1930 envisaged an ambitious programme of slum clearance. However, with the advent of the National Government and the financial crisis of 1931, building under Wheatley's Act was ended in 1932, as were the remaining housing subsidies in 1933, while Greenwood's building programme was never started. But with the beginning of economic recovery his slum clearance scheme was instituted in 1934, and although it was only half the number planned by Greenwood, a quarter of a million houses were demolished by 1939, more than in the previous 50 years. In Opposition, the weakened Labour Party was also stressing the importance of slum clearance, rather than house-building, which made sense in view of Chamberlain's and Wheatley's achievements in house-building, in their different ways, and the continued existence of unacceptable slums.

Undoubtedly, the main feature of housing in the 1930s was the phenomenal private housing boom which, as already indicated (p. 57), was the most important vehicle of the consumer-led pre-war economic recovery which took place in spite of the Government which, as we have seen, spent its energies on endeavouring to prop up the declining old staple industries. The boom was dynamic because, owing to the cheap money policy, investors who were buying houses to rent found it much more profitable than investing in public funds and other fixed interest investments, while low interest rates were also beneficial to the builders. New houses therefore made up a quarter, or more, of the total national capital investment in the 1930s while activity in the building industry increased at about twice the general rate, and was responsible for 30 per cent of the increase in employment between 1932 and 1935. This went along with the dynamic growth of another new industry – the motor industry. In 1920 there were under 200,000 registered private cars but by 1930 there were more than a million and nearly two million by 1939. This was about one car for every five families (much less, however, than in the United States), and although motor cars were now being used for day-to-day transport as opposed to prestigious purposes, it was the advent and development of the motor bus which was the dynamic element. Few new railways were constructed after 1914 and after 1928 buses were superseding trams, whose tramlines were now being torn up, a development which was only delayed by the compromise of using trolleybuses. By 1932 buses were transporting more passengers than trams, and country buses were competing successfully against the railways and servicing regions where there was no railway. Whereas in the earlier part of the century towns were built around the railway stations and expanded as far as the tramlines could take them, in the 1930s houses were built wherever cars or buses could go so that instead of spreading from a central point they spread along the main roads with side roads forming little tributaries – the classic era and example of 'ribbon' development. It was not exactly a pretty sight but it was dynamic and extremely practical besides enabling a much larger proportion of people than heretofore to enjoy the benefits of fresh air, a garden of their own and a less crowded environment. Light industry, using electricity and transporting their products by road instead of rail, also sprang up in these areas as also did shopping areas to service the new houses.

I have mentioned in Chapter 1 that the middle and upper classes consisted of about 25 per cent of the population. Although during and since the Great War the incomes of the upper classes (comprising around 5 per cent) had been gradually reduced by taxation they still enjoyed enormous wealth. Of the remainder, the highest paid artisans topped the European league but as the 1931 Census confirmed, poverty was endemic while in spite of the building boom and slum clearance of the 1930s deplorable housing conditions persisted. On the definition of three adults to two rooms or five adults to three rooms, or worse, a government survey in 1936 came to the optimistic conclusion that the average was as low as 3.8 per cent in England and Wales but in the northern industrial areas such as Sunderland or Liverpool it could be as high as 20 per cent. These were also the areas where infant mortality was as high as 134 per thousand, compared with around 32 per thousand in the prosperous South-East, and where malnutrition was still to be found; and even when a poorer family moved into a council house it usually meant paying a higher rent which, with additional expenditure on tram or bus fares, left less money for food and clothing. It is not surprising therefore that, as I have already commented on page 60, the Labour triumph in the East Fulham by-election in 1931 was not to do with a popular cry for disarmament but was a protest against bad housing, unemployment and, above all, the hated 'means test'. Soon after its election the National Government, concerned at the high level of public expenditure for the relief of unemployment, applied a 10 per cent reduction in unemployment insurance payments and laid down by Orders in Council that additional 'benefits', for the long-term unemployed, should only be paid after the applicant had been subjected to a test proving that neither he, nor his family, had any other means of support, an assessment that was to be made by the public assistance committees of the local councils. The 'means test' became a matter of great social cleavage. Whereas the body of taxpayers complained that public money should not be used to pay 'benefits' to men who had resources of their own, the unemployed were very bitter that they should be penalized if they had been provident enough to accumulate savings or if other members of their families were in employment. Again, in the General Election of 1935, although the main issue was allegedly rearmament, once more the electors' main concerns were housing, unemployment and the special areas, as well as the 'means test'. We have already commented on the Unemployment Insurance Act of 1934 (page 58) inspired by Neville Chamberlain (Chancellor of the Exchequer from 1931–37), and passed soon after the 10 per cent cuts were restored. The new Government soon returned to the perennial problem of housing and its 1936 Housing Act consolidated all the post-war Acts – those of 1919, 1923, 1924, 1930 and 1935. As municipal subsidized housing was for the benefit of the working classes the 1936 Act broke new ground by attempting to define 'working class' as anyone 'whose income in any case does not exceed an average of £3 per week'. Unfortunately, as I have already indicated, these good intentions of confining this housing to the needy was not maintained by the post-war governments which, following the pre-war hostility to 'means tests', conferred universal benefits in every sphere. In housing, in a period of full employment and increasing affluence among the working classes, a limitation to those beneath a certain income would have been in order but, instead, subsidized council houses, very often containing a number of wage earners, passed from one generation to another, in the manner of feudal estates. Once again, we note that in this field the post-war consensus was singularly unfortunate.

In spite of the fact that in many ways the 'average' person was better off during the war, the main area where there was material hardship was in housing. Whereas before and at the outbreak of war, the extent of civilian casualties resulting from the expected German air raids was wildly exaggerated, the damage to housing and the like was very much underrated. In the event, 200,000 houses were completely destroyed and another 250,000 rendered uninhabitable. The building of private houses virtually came to an end with only 9,000 being completed in 1943 compared with 360,000 in 1938, while even the repair of houses damaged by air raids was not undertaken seriously until 1943. By the end of the war 200,000 houses had been built although the manpower in the building industry had been reduced from one million in 1939 to 337,000 in 1945. In all, as a result of the war, there were 700,000 fewer houses than in 1939. Thus, as in 1918, there was a determination to replace the bombed slums with something very much better. As the journal of the Federation of British Industries put it in 1940: 'Bombs have made builders of us all.' Unfortunately, due to the naivety and woolly-thinking of both the planners and the building industry, especially in the 1960s, this aspiration was not fulfilled. However, as on so many previous occasions, at the General Election of 1945 the electorate were not interested in Winston Churchill's wartime exploits or in his grasp of foreign affairs, but in housing, full employment and social security.

As I have implied, it was not for lack of planning that the great post-war adventure of rebuilding Britain was undertaken. In his report, Beveridge identified 'squalor', namely bad housing and environmental conditions, as one of his 'five giant evils'. The wartime Government considered that 750,000 new homes would be needed to fulfil its objective of a 'separate dwelling for every family which desires to have one' and a further 500,000 in order to complete the

232

pre-war slum clearance and overcrowding programmes. A two-year emergency programme was put into effect and a work force of 800,000 was provided by special releases from the forces, by training programmes and by the use of new methods of construction such as prefabrication. The Housing (Temporary Accommodation) Act of 1944 authorized the spending of £150 million on temporary houses, with a target of 300,000 by the end of the second year and in spite of disruptions as a result of the shortage of materials and the flying-bomb raids of the summer of 1944, after August of that year the programme got under way satisfactorily. For its longer-term housing programme the Churchill Government completed the payment of subsidies to both local authorities and private builders and, to avoid Addison's problems after 1918, it planned to control the prices of building materials and also building contracts. Significant wartime developments in this field were the Barlow, Scott and Uthwait reports of 1940, and 1942 respectively which set forward the merits of town and country planning and, in the case of the Scott Report, the 1930s concept of the 'Green Belt' was revived. Following the Barlow Report the Government set up the Ministry of Town and Country Planning in 1943 to which Sir Patrick Abercrombie, who was to produce his famous Greater London Plan in 1944, presented his plan, which included the recommendation to create 'New Towns' to deal with London's problem of population overspill. The Town and Country Planning (Interim Development) Act of 1943 extended interim development control to areas where there were no planning schemes in preparation whereas the previous law confined it to those where the local authority had decided to prepare a planning scheme. The Act significantly increased national control of town and country planning by giving the new Minister the power to revoke local authority decisions, and to make decisions on development in accordance with national policy. The Town and Country Planning act of 1944 increased his powers still more by extending them to areas which were already developed, provided either that they were areas of 'extensive war damage', or of 'bad layout and obsolete development', with government grants payable in the former but not the latter case.

It is sometimes said that Aneurin Bevan was a comparative failure as the post-war Housing Minister in comparison with his historic efforts in setting up the National Health Service. In this respect it is unfortunate that the Labour Government did not implement its election undertaking to create a separate Ministry for Housing, which was something that had to come in any case, for undoubtedly it would have been humanly impossible for Bevan to have spent the same amount of time, energy and sheer dynamism in two undertakings. Also, as on so much else and as has become its custom, the Labour Party's rhetoric proved to be facile in the extreme. 'Then Bevan had promised "five million houses in quick time" and Cripps, allegedly, had claimed that "housing (could) be dealt with in a fortnight"'.[1] Finally, there was the unpredictable nature of post-war British society. In the first three years after the war there were 11 per cent more marriages and 33 per cent more births than in the 3 years prior to the war, while full employment and a changing social outlook increased the demand for separate houses to an extent that was unprecedented. However, the fact that Bevan failed to meet this unpredictable increase in the demand for new housing should not be allowed to detract from the fact that on conventional assumptions his record was quite impressive, taking into account post-war dislocations and severe shortages of building materials. The figures for new house completions are 55,400 in 1946, 139,690 in 1947 and 227,616 in 1948 which total, including other forms of housing, was increased to 284,230, very close to Macmillan's much-heralded later figure – and Macmillan had none of Bevan's post-war disadvantages. Bevan also handicapped himself by his stress on quality over quantity (unlike Macmillan). He said,

> While we shall be judged for a year or two by the number of houses we build we shall be judged in ten years' time by the type of houses we build.

Local authorities were therefore instructed to build houses of an average 1,000 square feet, compared to the previous average of 800 square feet. Without this enlightened limitation (but whatever happened about housing the poor!) Bevan could well have achieved 300,000 houses in 1948 and after but, once again, the financial crisis of 1947 intervened, so that after 1948 the number of completions declined to 217,240, 210,253 and 204,117 in 1949, 1950 and 1951 respectively. Nevertheless, the Churchill Government's target of 750,000 new houses had been reached by 1948 and by 1951 around twice that number of new units of accommodation had been provided. This was largely due to the fact that in spite of his preference for quality Bevan wisely put into effect the 1944 plans to build 'temporary' prefabricated houses, 157,000 of which were completed between 1947 and 1950.

---

[1] *Post-War Britain*, by Alan Sked and Chris Cook, p. 46. Further facts and figures in this chapter are attributable to this authority.

A feature was the marked degree of consensus between the Government and the Opposition over housing. Bevan's Housing (Miscellaneous and Financial Provisions) Bill, passed in 1946, was simply an extension and amendment of the 1936 Housing Act with its preservation of the principle of direct state subsidies to the local authorities, county and non-county, which would provide the capital by borrowing, repayments being by a combination of an annual grant per house from the Government, payable for 60 years (as opposed to the previous 40 years), by a contribution from the local authorities' own rates and by the rent paid by the tenant. Conservative criticism was mainly confined to the absence of any provision for private builders, on the absence of subsidies for conversion, on the inadequate provision for housing in agricultural areas (the parties disagreeing over the 'tied house' principle) and over the Government's financial forecasts, for, as usual, Labour were over-optimistic on that question. There was a separate Scottish Act along the same lines as the English one. The housing conditions in Scotland continued to be worse than in England and Wales for relatively fewer houses were built there between the wars, with a relatively larger proportion being subsidized local authority houses; the stage was set for the unedifying spectacle of Scotland's municipal, Labour-controlled slums, especially in Glasgow.

Finally, whereas, as we have seen, the 1936 Housing Act defined the 'working class' to whom the benefits of subsidized local authority housing were to be confined, Bevan refused to have any such limitation so that not only were council houses to be of a higher quality but that the subsidized benefit of their occupation was to be open to all – universal. Bevan's idealistic aim was to avoid having depressing housing estates populated by the poor: what the country ended up with, in an increasingly affluent society, were council estates (still depressing) but occupied by the more virile of the working classes who jumped quickly on this particular 'bandwagon', while the poor were left to rot in the inadequate and soul-destroying inner-city tenements. The Housing Act of 1949 expressly eliminated the words 'working class' from housing legislation, and satisfied the Conservative Party by allowing subsidies for conversions and renovations. There were two further Acts, in 1946 and 1949, which secured the continuation of rent tribunals and rent control so as to protect the interests of the tenants of private landlords. Thus, in the years following 1918 this country had saddled itself with a housing system which, by definition, was incapable of achieving its objectives. In the first place, subsidized council housing meant that demand was artificially stimulated, thus causing an increasing financial burden and

235

ever more 'council estates', separate from the rest of the community but excluding its poorest members. Secondly, rent control meant a cessation of private building for rent so that the remaining privately-rented accommodation became slums, or near slums, and there was virtually no temporary accommodation for young married people or for families on the move following a change in employment, and the like – 'the road to Hell is paved with good intentions!' As I have said, the Conservative Opposition, led by the urbane Captain Cruickshank, made no objections on principle. This came from left-wing Labour MPs and the one Communist Member of Parliament, who, predictably, wanted the nationalization of house-building, which even the Labour Party now knows would have been catastrophic.

On the other hand, one can report much more favourably on Bevan's general environmental planning, although the main legislative responsibility for this was in the hands of Lewis Silkin, the Minister of Town and Country Planning, while it followed from the very valuable wartime reports, legislation and developments which have been already described. Thus the Town and Country Act of 1947 continued the process further by removing planning functions from the smaller local authorities, increasing the responsibilities of the larger ones, extending powers of compulsory purchase and undertaking aid to planning authorities from central government. Planning authorities were also authorized to control advertisements and to preserve historic buildings, while the Government introduced a development charge on any increase in land values arising from development or projected development. Following on Abercrombie's wartime vision, the New Towns Act of 1946 was the most important and successful of this environmental legislation. A number of development corporations were created which were responsible for the building of new towns in London, North of England, and Scotland and which was continued with great success under later Conservative governments. Less important, but significant in view of the neglect of two centuries was the National Park and Access to Countryside Act.

It will be remembered that in pre-war elections housing was perhaps the main issue with which the electorate was consistently concerned, and that the Labour Party made great play as to what it was going to do about it, in the 1945 election. As always, Britain's housing was still unsatisfactory and the Census of 1951 revealed that one third of the houses in England and Wales had no bath and over a million had no water closet. The Tory Conferences of 1950 and 1951 highlighted housing, and passed resolutions demanding the building of 300,000 houses per year for which task Churchill

236

appointed Macmillan, telling him that his success or otherwise would 'make or mar' his political career. Thus Harold Macmillan became Minister of Local Government and Planning, for the Labour Government had latterly transferred the housing responsibilities of the Ministry of Health to this new ministry, which the Conservatives renamed the Ministry of Housing and Local Government. It is well known that in this undertaking Macmillan succeeded magnificently and that he laid the foundations for his future elevation to the leadership of the Conservative Party and to the Prime Ministership on Eden's resignation, thus more than fulfilling Churchill's challenge. His achievement of building 327,000 houses in 1953 and 354,000 in 1954 was reminiscent of John Wheatley in 1924 in that not only was he single-minded in the matter but he used considerable organizational powers. In the first place, he selected a particularly able team, including Dame Evelyn Sharp and Ernest Marples, whose experience in the construction industry was invaluable, while he ingeniously co-ordinated the work of his own department with that of others by utilizing to the full the building committee of the Cabinet, and the like, and he made sure of the support of the Prime Minister and of important Cabinet ministers, thus overcoming the financial constraints that the Treasury would otherwise have imposed.

Harking back to Neville Chamberlain's efforts in 1923, Macmillan's radical change was to depart from the Labour policy of relying wholly on the public sector and to utilize to the maximum extent private building. The Housing Act of 1952 increased subsidies in England and Wales from £22 to £35, in recognition of rising building costs and interest rates, and it reduced Bevan's ambitious building standards, so that slightly smaller houses could be built, both of which helped the local authorities, as also did Macmillan's efforts to ensure the efficient allocation of supplies and the use of non-traditional building methods. However, it was the encouragement of private builders that was the hallmark of Macmillan's policy. From 1 January 1952 local authorities were enabled to issue licences to private contractors for as many houses as they were building themselves, whereas throughout 1950 and 1951 the ratio was one private house to four local authority houses. In 1953 all restrictions were removed on the building of smaller houses and licences for large ones could be issued on their merits. Under the Small Dwellings' Acquisition Acts and the 1949 Housing Act local authorities were empowered to issue mortgages to house purchasers and builders, a practice which was positively encouraged by Macmillan. As a result of this policy, in 1954 28.5 per cent of houses completed were built by private builders. Other measures ensured this outcome. Local councils were encouraged to obtain loans on the open market, rather than from the Treasury, through the Public Works Loan Board when the Government allowed Section 1 of the Local Authorities Loans Act of 1945 to lapse at the end of 1952. Thus in 1953–54 the proportion of new loans raised through the above institution fell from 79 per cent in the previous year to 54 per cent. The Town and Country Planning Acts of 1953 and 1954 abolished the development charge on land which could well have been better retained as a means of curbing the excesses of future building booms. Finally, in November 1954 the Minister of Works revoked the Defence Regulation 56A, enacted during the war, so as to release private enterprise house-building from licensing control. As already indicated, in these first five years of post-war Conservative government the 12 New Towns designated by the Labour Government were substantially developed although no new ones were begun. However, the Town Development Act of 1952 made a sensible amendment to the New Town ideal, as it was conceived, to enable the expansion of existing small towns prepared to accept overspill population. Due to his house-building achievements, Macmillan was the 'darling' of the 1954 Tory Party Conference and in view of the efforts made by all governments in housing, certainly since 1918, that recognition was deserved. In retrospect, it could be said that he was risking inflation or overheating in the housing market, and that the human and capital resources could have been better utilized in industrial development, but Macmillan could answer that morally, medically and industrially it was necessary for Britain to have better-housed workers and that, in any case, Britain's housing problem could not be solved by half-hearted measures.

A major deficiency in the situation, on which I have already commented, led to the passing of the Rent Act in 1957 which removed from control all houses of an annual rateable value of £40 in London and Scotland, and £30 elsewhere, and allowed 'creeping decontrol' for all other tenancies as they became vacant. The Act released 810,000 houses from rent control and allowed increases for 4.3 million still controlled. The Act generated more heat than light for, in the short term, rents did not rise significantly, as predicted by Labour, and few new houses for rent came on the market, as argued by the Conservatives. Nevertheless, the main object surely was to increase the number of and improve the quality of private rented accommodation, and in this respect the principle of the Act was correct. It was also gratifying for the Conservative Government that by 1959 30 per cent of the people owned, or were buying, their own homes while it was estimated that in 1960 37.7 per cent of people

238

purchasing their houses by mortgage were wage earners. But it was equally depressing that around one-third of the population lived in council-house 'estates', whereas ideally they would have been better spread further afield in privately-rented accommodation, even if subsidized, or if the number of owner-occupiers were to be significantly increased – but this was not to happen until after 1979! Macmillan's contention that housing was still inadequate was proved by the fact that in 1963, with a total of just over 16 million houses more than 5½ million were built in the nineteenth century (which, in itself, was not unremarkable), but that about 4 million had no baths, a proportion of which had no hot water systems or inside lavatory facilities – which brings us back to the opening sentences of this chapter.

13

Local Government

Although, as mentioned on page 14, the Norman Feudal system of justice utilized, but never supplanted, the Anglo-Saxon system of law and local government (the county courts under the sheriffs appointed by the King), in the Middle Ages (from about 1200 to 1500) village and agricultural affairs were settled by the Manor Court where the chief landowner met with his tenants. It was this court, where quarrels were settled and offenders punished, that elected the first part-time, unpaid 'constables' who had the task of keeping order by apprehending and arresting law-breakers for the year in which they held office. During this medieval period, and for years later, two factors dominated the development of local government – poor communications and the lack of trained officials. The roads in those days were no better than tracks for walking or riding horses, and it was not until the time of Queen Elizabeth (1558–1603) that they were good enough to enable wheeled carriages to travel from London to other parts of the country. Even as late as 1800 there were some parts of England to which it was impossible to travel in the winter except on horseback. Although we have seen (p. 17) that as early as the twelfth century the King was able to use the new profession of lawyers as officials, before the machine age in the nineteenth century the necessity for the vast majority of the population to be engaged in agricultural pursuits meant that there was not sufficient 'manpower', let alone the financial resources and organizational skills, to provide a body of full-time local officials. Indeed, as late as 1914 agricultural labourers, together with domestic servants, were, numerically, the two most important occupations.

Before the sixteenth century, life was very hard and expectations were low, a sufficiency of food and clothing and simple accommodation being the only requirements so that, apart from the management of the royal estates, the administration of justice and tax gathering, royal governments were mainly concerned with defence and the maintenance of national law and order. However, with the ending of the Wars of the Roses the authority of the central

240

government was strengthened under the Tudors, a development which was foreshadowed under the able Edward IV (1461–83), and expectations increased. For example, in 1555 Parliament passed a law requiring the local citizens to maintain the roads and in 1598, following the first 'Poor Law' passed by Henry VIII in 1536, it enjoined them to care for the poor by enacting that officials called 'overseers of the poor' were compulsory in every parish. With the enclosures of the late fifteenth century, and the breaking-up of the old farming system based on and around the village, although they survived well into the eighteenth century, the Manor Courts declined and their place was taken by parish meetings, the Church being the other main influence in the life of the people in the Middle Ages. There they met to discuss the repair of church buildings, burials, charity funds, festivals and the like. It was only natural therefore that the new obligations regarding roads and the relief of the poor, especially the latter, should become the responsibility of the Church meetings, and they have taken the name of the room in which the meetings were held – the vestry – so that parish meetings for local government business were called vestry meetings until as late as 1894, by which time there were more than 15,000 parishes in England and Wales.

There was never any Parliamentaiy legislation to define the proceedings of vestry meetings so that the annual meetings to appoint local officials in both villages and towns were informal. The part-time and unpaid officials were the farmers, shopkeepers and traders who used to meet informally after work or during the holidays. As there were very few people living in the villages, elections were not necessary and as the new duties of the Overseer of the Poor and the Surveyor of the Highways entailed more expense, it was felt that only those who paid the local rate or tax, mainly property holders, should vote on the dispensing of the money, so that the poorer labourers were mainly excluded from the village meetings. In some of the towns the richer citizens obtained Parliament's approval to undertake all local government affairs, although this was rare before 1660, and in a few towns a small group of wealthy people did the same thing, through 'close' meetings, without Parliament's permission. However, in most parishes, local government was carried on by a far greater number of people, but it was inevitable that there should have been tremendous variations in the standard of local services – the state of the roads, the welfare of the poor and the apprehending of criminals. It was the job of the local Justices of the Peace to supervise and control the local government activities of the many parishes in their districts, there being about 60 local groups of justices. It will be recalled (p. 22) that this late-thirteenth-century and fourteenth-century development in the field of local government was described as 'an extra-ordinary experiment in justice which was at once anti-feudal and a reversal of the hitherto universal trend towards centralization'. Nevertheless, they were agents of the King or central government and since 1388 they had been required by statute to hold their sessions four times a year to hear lawsuits in their areas, and by the sixteenth century they were dealing with complaints against Constables, Surveyors of Highways and Overseers of the Poor and, if necessary, punishing them with heavy fines for errors of omission or commission. In the same way as the parish vestry was an informal meeting of neighbours, the Justices of the Peace, who were also local men, used to hold their meetings in a comfortable room at the local inn. Thus, the administration of local services by local people and in accordance with the ideas of local people became an ingrained part of the English way of life. Finally, although they were administering national laws, owing to the difficulties of communication, there were often periods when the local leaders, despite their best efforts, were out of touch with the central government. It has therefore been necessary for the latter to assert itself from time to time, a requirement which, in our own day, was overdue by 1979. In spite of its defects ours is a better system than that on the continent of Europe where the governments were late in gaining central control but, having achieved that, proceeded to impose it with scant regard for local requirements or feelings. It is significant that the Prefect, the most important person in French local government, is appointed by the central government.

By the eighteenth century there was an increased demand for new and improved services, especially in the towns, where the better-educated inhabitants wanted pavements and street lamps, drains and water supply, and civic amenities such as gardens and assembly halls. As in the sixteenth century, groups of richer citizens requested Parliament's permission to form select councils, usually known as 'Boards of Improvement Commissioners', with the legal right to raise a limited local rate with which to add to the basic services provided by the parish vestries. In the course of the century the general public took an increasing interest in these developments and began to demand elected councils so that by the beginning of the nineteenth century Parliament consented to the election of Improvement Commissioners by the local ratepayers. As from that day to this, there were marked variations in the standards of local government, the best of the Boards making their towns the subject of civic pride, while the worst either neglected their responsibilities or, even worse, used the ratepayers' money to 'feather their own nests', or those of their friends and relatives.

It was, however, with the coming of the Industrial Revolution that the 'modern' history of local government began. We have already seen at the beginning of Chapter 12 on Housing (p. 220) that the reign of George III (1760–1820) coincided with the doubling in population as it also did with the creation of the Industrial Revolution which brought in the 'machine age' which, in turn, led to the growth of towns and the necessity for increased and improved services, together with the increased manpower to facilitate a class of officials, both central and local. There were a number of consequences in local government. First, there was the creation of the first 'modern' organs of local government elected by the middle-class voters who had just received the franchise by virtue of the First Reform Bill of 1832. Under the terms of the Municipal Corporation Act of 1835 reformed Municipal Borough Councils were established in the older and larger towns, the first and chief duty of which was to administer through Watch Committees the new police forces, the first of which, as described in Chapter 14 in the section on Law and Order and the Police (p. 313), had been established in the Metropolis in 1829 by the reforming Home Secretary, Sir Robert Peel. This was, partly a reflection of the second major development in local government at the time, a reaction against one council, the parish vestry, being responsible for too many duties, in favour of each major service being administered by its own elected council. Accordingly, the Elizabethan system of poor relief was removed from the jurisdiction of the vestry councils and the Poor Law Act of 1834 established special councils, elected by the ratepayers, the 'Boards of Guardians', whose sole duty was to administer poor relief. The Act abolished the notorious Speenhamland system which is discussed in Chapter 14 on The Law (p. 319). It was the first instalment of Benthamism. Bentham and his followers (p. 322) were highly critical of the old amateurish and inefficient system of local government in town and country, especially the latter. In their place they wanted a combination of locally-elected bodies carrying out the policies of centrally-appointed, bureaucratic functionaries. With its locally-elected Boards of Guardians and with its three Poor Law Commissioners, appointed by and responsible to the central government, the new Poor Law set the pattern for the reform of local government. This was in spite of the unpopularity of the harsh 'workhouse test', in place of outdoor relief, which was adopted for the 'utilitarian' reasons that the Benthamites always applied. In the preamble to the description of the setting-up of the National Health

Service we have already commented on the earliest attempts in the eighteenth century to combat insanitary conditions and on the salutary effects of the first serious outbreak of cholera in England in 1831, including the Public Health Act of 1848 (p. 124). This Act provided for the election by ratepayers in town and country of councils, 'Boards of Health', to regulate water supply, drainage and medical services. Similarly, when it was decided to improve the roads an Act of 1862 divided England into districts, each with a 'Highways Board', elected by the local ratepayers. In the chapter on Education, the creation of yet another group of elected special councils, the 'School Boards', by the Education Act of 1870, whereby England was divided into School Board Districts, has been described on page 197. However, as mentioned on pages 124–5 and 221, it was not until after 1918 that social services were developed as a result of social conscience – the serving of persons as opposed to districts. The fact that the one possible exception to this was Education proves the point, for it was as a result of this attitude that the creation of a national education system was delayed until as late as 1870.

By 1870, although the parish vestries still met, there was very little for them to do. Also, public opinion was going against the system of having a number of different councils in the same district (ad hoc authorities as they would be called today) and Parliament had already allowed some of the Boards to unite. By the end of the century there was a complete reorganization of local government, the Boards being entirely replaced by a series of councils based on traditional, non-specialist lines. On page 242 it was pointed out that local government in England had acquired, partly by cause and partly by effect, what might be called a strong tradition of local independence. The virtue of this worthy spirit does not need to be emphasized, but the obverse, an equally strong tradition of conservatism, has meant that any attempt at reform or to introduce new methods into local government or to impose a measure of central control, has been resisted wholeheartedly. The result has been that the history of English local government has been dominated by the conservative, and not the radical, aspect of the English character which has resulted in a series of unsatisfactory compromises. This is what happened in the Local Government Acts of 1888 and 1894 with the abolition of the system whereby each major service was administered by its own council, which could have developed into a single-tier form of local government, which reconciled both national and local requirements, in favour of a reversion to an entirely locally-based and largely two-tier system. But before dealing with these Acts it is necessary to point out that the third important local government development of the nineteenth century – municipalization – was radical in its concept and even more so in its later collectivist implications. This has been dealt with in the early pages of Chapter 12 on Housing (pp. 221–2) where the anti-'laissez-faire' implications of the Second Reform Act of 1867 were noted, together with the way in which Disraeli pragmatically put this into effect during his ministry of 1874–80. It was also mentioned that by this time the provision of services, such as gas and water by 'laissez-faire' means, had already broken down and that the recognition that these were 'natural monopolies' led to them being largely taken over by the local authorities, a trend which was strengthened with the advent of electricity supply and street transport in the 1870s and 1880s. This, in turn, was the dynamic force behind 'municipalization' and the flowering of municipal enterprise in the great provincial cities in the last quarter of the nineteenth century. In the same way as it has been said that 'a self-made man is a good example of unskilled labour' a criticism of 'municipalization' is that it was the product of comparatively uncultured self-made men who, with little interference from the centre, perpetuated the harsh ugliness and poor amenity of Victorian industrial towns.

The actual term, 'local government', was first used in 1858 by a Conservative, C.B. Adderley. But as we have seen above, the granting of the franchise in 1867 to the town-dwelling artisan was the stimulus that led to a marked increase in political activity and consciousness in the town constituencies, especially among the radicals of the Liberal Party, and which, in turn, resulted in the radical concept of 'municipalization'. Compared with this positive development, there was a muddle at the centre, mainly due to Gladstone's benign disinterest in local government in spite of the deep interest and involvement of Liberals in local government. On the other hand, we have seen that Disraeli responded wholeheartedly to the electoral reform of 1867. Nevertheless, something had to be done by the central government in view of the repercussions of 1867, and in 1871, the year of much of Gladstone's 'liberalizing' legislation, an Act was passed by which the Local Government Board (the forerunner to the Ministry of Health) was formed by the amalgamation of the old Poor Law Board, the local government branch of the Home Office, the medical department of the Privy Council and some other minor departments. Its first president and author of the Act was the able James Stansfield who was the last President of the Poor Law Board and who also piloted two bills in the House of Commons based on the proposals for the implementation of the sanitary laws by a Commission appointed by Disraeli in 1868, presided over by C.B.

245

Adderley and reporting in 1871, although in his Act of 1872 he failed in his attempt to extend the laws owing to lack of support. Similarly, Goschen, his predecessor at the Poor Law Board, and later Chancellor of the Exchequer, failed with an enlightened Bill to introduce representative government in parishes and counties, for it was opposed by the landowners who, as JPs, were still in control of the counties through the oligarchical quarter sessions – and was dropped, mainly due once more, to Gladstone's disinterest. Goschen was later to describe local government as 'a chaos of authorities, a chaos of jurisdictions, a chaos of rates, a chaos of franchises, a chaos worst of all of areas'. It is significant that Goschen was the son of a German merchant based in London so that he would have heard from his father how much better local affairs were arranged in Germany.

In the administrative field, the new Local Government Board got off to a bad start for Stansfield allowed its Poor Law component to wield the greater power so that local government became infected with the negative, restrictive and financially stringent traditions of the old Poor Law Board, a situation which, unfortunately, appertained until 1914. During the same period (1870–1914), German local government, through its Prussian influence and with positive leadership and financial support from the centre was positively thriving, producing, for example, its first national health insurance scheme in the 1880s. The late nineteenth century, unreformed English local government is well described by Ensor:

> The only nation-wide scheme of local authorities was that of the boards of guardians administering the 1834 Poor Law. For the rest, the counties were still ruled by the justices of the peace in quarter sessions; and in the urban areas responsibility for such primary services as paving, cleansing, lighting or drainage devolved sometimes on a municipal corporation, sometimes on an improvement commission, sometimes on a local board, sometimes on a London vestry; not infrequently being divided between two of these bodies . . . Hence though sanitary administration was at that time better understood in England than anywhere else, its practice remained very inadequate in the towns, while in rural districts it barely existed. It was not a party question; the opposition was that of 'interests'. Possibly the liberal party included more of the few enthusiasts among its rank and file. But, as between the party chiefs the balance was the other way round; Disraeli expressed a concern in sanitation quite exceptional among the politicians of his day; whereas Gladstone showed none at all. Indeed the blind eye, which he consistently turned towards the importance of local

246

government, explains some of the gravest gaps in his statesmanship, and in its effect on history may be counted a national misfortune.'[1]

The facts of the matter were that in 1883 there were 27,069 independent local authorities taxing the English ratepayer by 18 different kinds of rates. The authorities included 52 Counties, 239 Municipal Boroughs, 70 Improvement Act Districts, 1,006 Urban Sanitary Districts, 41 Port Sanitary Authorities, 577 Rural Sanitary Districts, 2,051 School Board Districts, 424 Highway Districts, 853 Burial Board Districts, 649 Unions, 194 Lighting and Watching Districts, 14,946 Poor Law Parishes, 5,064 Highway Parishes not included in urban highway districts and about 1,300 Ecclesiastical Parishes.

In the same way as the Reform Bill of 1832 led to the Municipal Corporation Act of 1835, and the Reform Bill of 1867 led to 'Municipalization', the Reform Bill of 1884 led to the Local Government Act of 1888 for whereas the Act extended the parliamentary franchise to householders in the counties and country parishes these latter could no longer be denied the right to elect their local rulers, which is emphasized by the fact that the Conservative Prime Minister at the time, Lord Salisbury, opposed the Reform Bill, as indeed he did that of 1867. The 1888 Act was popularly known as the County Councils Act for it provided for the creation of 62 'Administrative Counties', coterminous with the 52 historic shires, but with some of the larger ones being sub-divided. The second main provision of the Act created a new kind of borough called a County Borough whereby the larger boroughs, normally towns with over 50,000 population, were effectively 'taken out' of their counties and each was set up as a county in itself. The creation of these 'single-tier' authorities was unpopular with the 'gentlemen' of the counties but it was a beneficial import from the German system of local government, in the absence of the unthinkable but better alternative of reforming and systematizing the ad hoc authorities. Thirdly, the Act established the London County Council. Whereas the historic 'square mile' of the City of London had been organized as a shire by the time of the Norman Conquest, and had established the right of a small body of aldermen to elect a mayor by around 1193, London was not affected by the Act of 1835. London outside the 'City' boundaries was still an aggregate of parishes governed like the

---

[1] *England, 1870–1914*, by R.C.K. Ensor, p. 125. Further facts and figures in this chapter are attributable to this authority.

smallest country parishes by their vestries, but since 1855 subject, in particular matters, to the control of a central authority, the Metropolitan Board of Works. The 1888 Act abolished the Board of Works and converted this large area into an Administrative County with a council like the other County Boroughs. The London City Corporation retained a great deal of its autonomy but it was included in the County and was represented on the new Council by four members. Outside London, both the County Councils and the County Boroughs were to be represented by councils whose councillors were to be elected for a term of three years by the ratepayers and the number of co-opted aldermen were not to exceed one third of the elected councillors. The actual rates were based on property values, and not on income, while local government, which had already pioneered in 1882 in giving unmarried women, aged 30 and above and with a small property qualification, the right to vote but not to be elected, extended this right to the new councils. The administrative functions of the Quarter Sessions, as distinct from their judicial and licensing responsibilities, were transferred to the councils, the most important of which were the care of roads and bridges. Outside the City, the police of London continued under the Commissioner appointed by the Home Office, but in view of the combination of administrative and judicial functions, in the other counties their control was committed to a Standing Joint Committee of Justices of the Quarter Sessions and County Councillors. However, boroughs with populations of 10,000 or more at the time of the 1881 census were permitted to retain separate police forces, controlled by their own Watch Committees.

As might be expected, Goschen, as Chancellor of the Exchequer, was generous financially and both in London, where Lord Rosebery was the first chairman of the council, and throughout the country there was a significant increase in public activities resulting from the new authorities created by the 1888 Act which was generally regarded as a successful English compromise, especially as the county magistrates carried on their 600-year tradition of voluntary public work by throwing themselves wholeheartedly into the work of county councillors. In other words, this is a good example of a radical (but not radical enough) Act being administered conservatively – a change in form but not in substance. We have already seen that Parliament soon added to the powers of the new councils under the terms of the Technical Instruction Act of 1889 (pp. 200–1) and the Education Acts of 1899 and 1902 (pp. 201–2). The Education Act of 1902 introduced the admirable requirement that the Councils' Education Committees should include members co-opted from outside the council, including women, which led to the setting up of similar committees dealing with important matters such as childcare and unemployment. Unfortunately, this excellent tradition was abused by the Labour Governments of the 1960s and 1970s with their Quangos which degenerated into organizations which attracted the worst type of interfering 'busybodies', so many of whom had not made great successes of their own private affairs, not to mention 'jobs for the boys'.[1] However, the radical Liberals were not happy about the monopolization of the County Councils by the squirearchy and, in the Newcastle Programme, pressed successfully for elective District and Parish Councils where those other than the country gentlemen could exercise their influence. This was especially important to the many non-conformists in rural areas where, administratively, the parishes were controlled by the church wards and vestries of the Established Church of England, the church of what was later to be called the Establishment. Even Gladstone could not disregard this strong Liberal feeling in regard to local government so that in 1893 H.H. Fowler introduced what became the District and Parish Councils Act of 1894. Under the terms of the Act every County Council was divided into Districts, Urban and Rural, and every District into Parishes. In every District and in every Rural Parish, with more than 300 inhabitants, there was an elected council, and in the smallest parishes there was to be a primary meeting of all persons on the local government and parliamentary register. As well as the transfer of the civil functions of the vestries to the Parish Councils and meetings such as control of parish properties, charities and footpaths etc., wider powers were conferred, including the right to provide libraries, baths, lighting and recreation grounds etc. It is necessary to understand what an important and controversial Bill this was, which is borne out by the facts that the Commons spent 38 days on it, that there were 619 amendments and that the admirable Fowler spoke over 800 times, while it was necessary for it to go to and from the two Houses three times before the Lords agreed to pass it, subject to their many amendments, the most important of which was to ensure that the Parish Councils were to be starved of funds by restricting their ordinary spending to the equivalent of a threepenny rate. Thus, although this was later increased and, although 6,880

---

[1]Although the Conservative Governments which followed Labour undertook to reduce the number and power of Quangos, they have continued to multiply and unfortunately have often become vehicles for the pursuance of politically correct prejudices.

Parish Councils were established under the Act, most of their powers, especially the wider ones, were little used and, in retrospect, it can be seen that Fowler's Herculean efforts were in vain. Apart from their opposition to Home Rule, this was one of the many examples of the Lords' recalcitrance that led to the constitutional crisis of 1910–11.

On the other hand, in another respect the 1894 Act was successful and of significance to this day, for the Urban and Rural District Councils have played an important part in local government ever since, as well as initiating the questionable 'two-tier' system of local government. Initially, Fowler successfully transferred to them the responsibility for the application of the sanitation laws which since Stansfield's Act of 1872 (pp. 245–6) had been divided between the Municipal Boroughs, local boards in the more populous districts outside these and the Board of Guardians in the countryside, all of which appear in the summary on page 247. Highways were also added to the District Councils' responsibilities while Rural District Councillors also acted as Poor Law Guardians so that in Rural Districts there were no longer separate elections for Guardians. Urban Districts became virtually Municipalities without mayors and the larger of them applied for and obtained 'incorporation' as 'boroughs'. Finally, in the 1894 Act the Tories further extended women's voting rights in local government by allowing married women to vote, as well as those who were unmarried, and by permitting women who were qualified to vote to stand for election as well. With the electoral rights of women for local government so far ahead of those for the national government (p. 24), an intensification of the suffragette movement was inevitable. But it was also inevitable that in England, which was capable of being so radical, the suffragettes had to withstand such a strong vein of conservatism.

In 1910, the respected Oxford Constitutional historian, Sir John Marriott, wrote:

> The Acts of 1888 and 1894 have unquestionably done much to bring order out of the chaos which had existed in local government for the previous half-century, and more recent legislation has shown an increasing tendency to simplify areas and consolidate authorities. Notably the Education Act of 1902, which abolished the ad hoc education authorities known as School Boards, and transferred their duties to the several councils of counties, boroughs and districts. Should the proposals of the Poor Law Commissioners of 1909 become law, this tendency will be still more strikingly illustrated. Nor can it be doubted that it is in the main healthy and sound. The more varied and important the functions

250

committed to the local governing bodies, the more likely are they to enlist the services of men of position, character and independence. And, on their doing so the future of local government obviously depends. Should they fail to attract such men (and women), the multiplication of responsibilities and the concentration of powers can have only one result: the development of a local bureaucracy and the increased authority of a vast army of local officials. Signs of such a tendency are not lacking even now, and with the aggregation of population in urban areas it is probably inevitable; but it is one which must be carefully watched, for it is foreign to the genius and tradition which have made England pre-eminently the land of vigorous and independent local government.[1]

It is depressing to recognize the fact that as far back as 1910 Marriott was much more prophetic than the typical historian and social commentator of the 1960s whose naive complacency and optimism about post-war developments has been proved to be so wrong, so fast, so often. 'Poplarism', (p. 51), is one thing but local officers of inner city councils being elected as paid councillors of adjacent councils is entirely another (p. 110–11). The fact that these 'councillors' do not fulfil Marriott's requirements of their being 'men of position, character and independence' has been disastrous for local government and did more than anything else to disqualify Labour as an alternative national government, in recent years. Marriott's prediction of the growth of bureaucracy was fulfilled, both nationally and locally. The Board of Agriculture was formed in 1889 and the Board of Education in 1899, (p. 201), while the functions and activities of the Home Office, the Board of Trade and the Local Government Board were growing apace, the last especially after the increase in officials necessary to deal with the tremendous increase in local authorities following the Acts of 1888 and 1894. In spite of the fact that the newer Ministries were often busier and making more important national decisions than the older, historic ones, such as the Exchequer, the Admiralty and the War Office, their ministers were paid significantly less which, in retrospect, is regrettable but entirely in keeping with the hierarchical and 'stiff-necked' attitude of the times, the pros and cons of which were discussed in Chapter 1. It was not too many years after the Charge of the Light Brigade!

In the meantime, the new London County Council, with Lord Rosebery as its first chairman, had made an excellent beginning for

---

[1] *English Political Institutions*, by J.A.R. Marriott, pp. 263–4.

instead of its members being Conservatives and Liberals, special municipal parties, 'Moderates' and 'Progressives', were created, with the latter soon becoming the governing party until around 1906 when the system collapsed owing to the fact that many of the Progressives became Liberal Members of Parliament, with the Liberal 'landslide' of that year. It should be noted that the Progressives were widely based for besides socialists and Fabians they included a number of Conservatives, the upshot being that the LCC established an entity in its own right which transcended 'party'. There was, however, still one significant weakness and that was the continuation of the old 30 vestries and 12 district boards which had been traditionally responsible for London's paving, cleansing and public health. In 1884 an attempt had been made to reform the situation by the introduction of a Bill to create a unified London with a greatly enlarged City Corporation as its main authority with the power to delegate authority to District Councils, but the Bill failed owing to the Corporation's opposition. Institutional 'vested interests' have always been a formidable enemy to imaginative reform, none more so than in local government. Accordingly, the County Councils Act of 1888 avoided the issue, as also did Fowler in 1893–94 for, as we have seen, he encountered formidable opposition in passing his great Act as it was, without raising further controversial matters. Thus a Royal Commission on London Government was appointed and it reported in 1894 following which Lord Salisbury's Government passed the London Government Act in 1899 which made no alteration to the LCC and the City Corporation but which abolished the vestries and local boards, and created in their place 28 'Metropolitan Borough Councils' each with its own mayor, alderman and elected councillors. In the nature of things, these councils could never have enjoyed the full powers of ordinary borough councils, for this would have meant diminishing the powers of the increasingly prestigious and popular LCC, so that their financial independence was impaired not only by the Local Government Board but also by the LCC.

A further problem was that because of the poor East End and the rich West End the London Boroughs with the lowest rateable revenues were burdened with the highest needs – shades of 'Poplarism'! Attempt have been made to remedy the anomaly such as the Act of 1904 which levied a 6d rate from all the London Boroughs and the City Corporation on the basis of assessments and redistributed it on the basis of population, but to little avail. The problem was, and is, fundamental, although Tory Inner City London Councils, adjacent to their struggling Labour counterparts, have shown that it is soluble by good management and that 'Poplarism' was not necessary after all. The antics of the 'Loony Left' councils have made a serious problem desperate and, in their unreformed state, virtually insoluble. Nevertheless, the London Metropolitan Councils were a considerable improvement on the old vestries. In the words of Marriott:

> The brand-new bodies brought into being by the Acts of 1888 and 1899 have wrought a marvellous change in the metropolis, alike in outward visible form and in administrative symmetry. The County Council has been the object of much criticism; the local boroughs of some ridicule; but both are what Londoners make them and neither ridicule nor criticism has done harm.[1]

Although during the war years, 1914–18, the war effort, such as the manufacture of munitions, entailed considerable changes in the machinery of government, none of these was retained after the war, the exception being the absorption of the Local Government Board by the Ministry of Health in 1919. For the rest, there was no logical disposition of authorities. For example, in what might be broadly called welfare, the old Local Government Board was responsible for the Poor Law, the Home Office for the Factory Acts, the Board of Trade for the Labour Exchange created in 1911 and autonomous Commissions for National Insurance. However, the point has been made several times, in particular when dealing with earlier health and sanitation legislation and with housing that it was not until after 1918 that 'social services were developed as a result of a social conscience' and that 'the general public expected and the local health services accepted that they should serve persons, as opposed to districts, in the fight against disease and ill-health', pages 244 and 124–5 respectively. In housing, page 226 explains that the Housing and Town Planning Act of 1919 was the legislation by which Lloyd George, through his Minister of Health, Dr Christopher Addison, called upon the local authorities to build unlimited houses – 'Homes fit for Heroes'. Thus in 1919 there was established the principle of the state accepting the direct financial responsibility for the provision of homes for a large section of the working classes' (pp. 226–7), and that Addison 'established the principle that housing was a social service and the practice that the local authorities should be the instruments of the government's housing policy' (p. 227).

Post-1919 was thus also significant for local government in that

---

[1] *English Political Institutions*, by J.A.R. Marriott, pp. 273.

they (the local authorities 'acquired new functions in social services, just when their share of financial contributions to these services was decreasing'.[1] A corollary of this development was that the local authorities were acting much more as agents of the central government than heretofore. Another example is that Fisher's 1918 Education Act was administered by committees of the local councils (the Local Education Committees) while half the cost was provided by the government – and all the policy. One of the earliest examples of the central government grant was the payment to councils of half the cost of the policeman's pay and uniforms which, after World War II, had escalated to half the cost of all police expenses. The traditional way in which the sovereign democratic state has set limits on the powers of local government has been by its Parliamentary Acts, by judicial control of these Acts, by the administrative control of the central civil service and by the limited nature of its revenue, notably rates and other forms of income such as that from corporate property, trading revenues and charges for additional services. However, it is by reason of grants and subsidies by the State that, in practice, the greatest control has been exercised. To take the case of the cost of policing, the earlier authorities were very keen to save their ratepayers money by satisfying the Home Office inspectors as to the efficiency of their local forces. This is also an example of administrative control while government departments also provide technical information and expertise. A notable feature of the relationship between English governments and their local authorities[2] has been that in spite of increasing financial support of the former for the latter, these have retained their freedom of action in day to day administration and have not been subjected to detailed restraints such as in France, where a Minister of Education once boasted that he could tell precisely at any day or time precisely what lesson was being taught in any school in France. This remains true today in spite of the virtual breakdown of traditional relationships and assumptions that Sir John Marriott would have regarded as essential, between central government and some areas of local government, necessitating much greater financial and legislative control – and also in spite of the National Curriculum!

After housing, the second way in which Lloyd George made the

---

[1] *English History, 1914–1945*, by A.J.P. Taylor, p. 148. Further facts and figures in this chapter are attributable to this authority.

[2] The Local Authority Acts only applied to England and Wales as Scotland had its own distinctive system of local government.

transition from the pre- and post-war attitudes to social reform was his massive extension of insurance against unemployment to virtually the whole of the working class. As we have seen (p. 118) the original Insurance Act of 1911 had been strictly limited to three vulnerable trades (building, engineering and ship-building) which included about 3 million workers and which was increased to about 4 million when it was extended to munition workers during the war. The big change occurred because of the necessity to give ex-servicemen, and their families, temporary and non-contributory security against unemployment until they established themselves in peacetime. Thus, whatever its importance, it was not planned and by 1920 extended to about 12 million workers earning less than £5 a week (a comparatively large sum in those days), except domestic servants, agricultural labourers and civil servants, to be financed by contributions from employers and employees, although the inevitable deficit was effectively paid from the Exchequer. It was not foreseen that the boom of 1920 would come to an end and that the expectation of a 4 per cent unemployment rate would soon become irrelevant for years ahead. A.J.P. Taylor summed up the situation as follows:

> A strange new system thus grew up haphazard. Unemployment insurance, administered through the labour exchanges,[1] cut across the Poor Law, which was in local hands. The foundations of 'laissez-faire' were shaken. 'Insurance', though largely fictitious was not felt to be humiliating as reliance on the Poor Law had been. Men were no longer driven to work at lower wages, and harsher conditions, by the lash of hunger. If they could not find employment at their usual jobs, they drew prolonged benefit at the expense of the taxpayer and the employed.[2] Unemployment insurance retarded the shift of workers from declining to rising industries. On the other hand, it took the edge off discontent. Even when the unemployed rioted, this was to get higher rates of 'benefit', not to bring down a system which had made them unemployed. Once Labour had demanded 'the Right to Work'. Now it demanded 'Work or Maintenance', and the emphasis was on maintenance. Thanks to Lloyd George, barricades were not set up in English streets. At the time he did not appreciate what he had done. He wanted to get rid of unemployment, not to make it bearable.[3]

---

[1] These were, of course, local offices of central government.
[2] In 1926 it was found that 48 per cent of insured workers had not drawn any benefits for the preceding five years.
[3] *England, 1914–1945*, by A.J.P. Taylor, p. 149.

However, once again, haphazard reforms and developments had put a strain on the facilities of local government which, as we know, was last reformed in 1888 and 1894. We have already seen (p. 58) that the great reformer of local government between the wars was Neville Chamberlain who, typically, when he became a government minister in 1922, planned 25 Parliamentary Bills of which 21 became Acts. After his Housing Act of 1923 he next addressed himself to curbing 'Poplarism', for his tidy administrator's mind was offended by the defiance of parliamentary authority when Labour Councils and Boards of Guardians paid higher wages and rates of relief than those stipulated by the Ministry of Health, which was given the power to supersede offending Councillors and Guardians by an Act of 1926. One of the three Boards to be superseded was West Ham: it is interesting that when I was on leave in London during the war, a relative by marriage who was Assistant Director of Education at that worthy Borough told me that it was commonplace for appointments to headmasterships, and the like, to be made on political grounds – 'plus ça change'! Opprobrium was heaped on Chamberlain by Labour as an 'enemy of the poor', but the administration of unemployment insurance and poor relief was very much simplified by the abolition of the last of the ad hoc authorities, the Board of Guardians, by his Local Government Act of 1929 which, as we have seen, placed it in the hands of the newly-created Public Assistance Committees of the Counties and County Boroughs, in the manner of Education in 1902. The necessity for Chamberlain's Unemployment Act of 1934 arose by virtue of the imposition of the 'means test' as one of the economies of 1931, for whereas the temporary unemployed were paid from the Insurance Fund, which was not open-ended and which therefore took little account of actual need, the long-term unemployed were paid with funds that came directly from the Exchequer as they were no longer entitled to money from the Insurance Fund. As this was taxpayers' money the view was taken that the recipients' resources, or lack of resources, should be identified but, on the other hand, the latter felt equally strongly that they should not be penalized if they had been thrifty or if other members of their family were employed. 'Poplarism' reared its head again and Labour Public Assistance Committees either refused to carry out the 'means test' or did so ineffectively. As we have seen, Chamberlain took unemployment 'out of politics' or, more correctly, out of local politics, by recreating an ad hoc body by statute, the Unemployment Assistance Board. In the event, the ideal of an independent statutory authority was not realized for the Government had to intervene, in the face of strenuous public protests, when the Board reduced the rates of relief.

This did not happen again and the Board became responsible for yet more varieties of the unemployed so that the local councils' Public Assistance Committees had only tramps and the aged to look after. In 1940 the Board became the Assistance Board and it could be said that thanks to Neville Chamberlain the hated Poor Law was no more.

It is notable that in dealing with Chamberlain's Acts of 1920 and 1934, Arthur Marwick does not even mention that he was their author, so intent is he in his mission to vilify pre-war Britain and to ensure that any suggestion that the social reforms of the pre-World War I Liberal Government were a precursor to the Welfare State are killed at birth. References to obscure survivals of the old Poor Law, and the like, are highlighted to this end. In spite of the brilliance of his research, Marwick's tendency to write history backwards means that he is oblivious to the slow but solid progress made in this field and to other significant developments. Rightly or wrongly, after the 1929 Local Government Act, British local government was notable in Europe for the extent of its responsibilities and for the fact that, apart from pensions paid by the post office and the Ministry of Labour's Employment Exchanges, all services emanated from the Town Hall which, together with local authority councillors, enjoyed great prestige as the agent of government policy. The point has already been made that with around two-thirds of their income deriving from government grants they had much less independence than their nineteenth-century predecessors in spite of their manifest responsibilities and apparent powers – although the tradition of independence died hard. The Local Government Act of 1929 also introduced some important modifications to the financial relationship between central and local government which were something of a watershed. Chamberlain's reforms added about £3 million to the Exchequer's costs while the Chancellor of the Exchequer, Winston Churchill, against the former's wishes, embarked on an ambitious scheme to 'derate' about three-quarters of certain classes of manufacturing industry and the railways, as well as to remove entirely the remaining 25 per cent due by agriculture. This was one of the many attempts to prop up the staple industries by subsidizing both the efficient and inefficient at the taxpayer's expense with the result that the Exchequer's deficit from the rate revenue was increased to around £24 million. Prior to 1929 general state grants to the local authorities had been on a percentage basis (usually 50 per cent) but this had come under criticism, in the interests of economy, as leaving the Government with an open-ended commitment. Thus the 1929 Act introduced the concept of the Block Grant, called 'The General

Exchequer Contribution' which was fixed for a period of five years with provision for the subsequent periodical adjustments by Parliament. In order to deal with the old problem of maintaining uniform standards of service in areas of varying financial resources, which had been a criticism of the percentage grants, the new system of distribution was based on population figures, 'weighted' in a number of respects. Although the Block Grant was a highly controversial innovation, as with almost everything that Chamberlain turned his hand to, it was an administrative improvement, especially in regard to the problem of dealing with various levels of local financial resources. The Local Government Act of 1948 renamed the Block Grant 'the Exchequer Equalization Grant', as it attempted the perennial problem of distributing it with the object of eliminating the large differences in the rateable values of the various Local Authorities.

An extremely important aspect of local government between the wars was the way it affected, and was affected by, the three political parties, of which the main one, in this respect, was Labour. It was not so much its two short periods of office in the period but its ineluctable success in local politics that laid the foundations for the Labour Government of 1945. As far back as the local elections of 1919 the party won Bradford and 12 London Boroughs, and achieved majorities in Durham, Glamorgan and Monmouth while gaining a significant number of votes in other areas. Several days after Labour's historic victory in the East Fulham by-election in 1933, in the municipal elections on 1 November, they gained control of 200 boroughs, and in the following March the LCC also fell to Labour so that by this time Labour's debacle of 1931 was well on the way to being reversed. A measure of the confidence of Labour, on the one hand, and the LCC on the other, is the Waterloo Bridge incident soon after the electoral victory in March 1934. As the bridge was unable to cope with the increase in traffic the council wished to demolish it and build a new one but the Government, wanting only a reconstruction, refused a parliamentary grant for a new one. Under the leadership of Herbert Morrison, the LCC demolished the bridge and built a new one without the help of any national funds. As always, the Tories, in their pragmatic way, kept abreast of the growing importance of local government as an agent of the national government with the corresponding increase in status that this conferred. Both parties developed the democratic concept of the caucus, imported from the United States by Joseph Chamberlain, whose mother was American, and which eventually led to annual party conferences, and the like, attended by 'representatives' of the

Conservative Party and 'delegates' of the Labour Party. The difference is important for Burke correctly enunciated that the duty of a Member of Parliament was not to act in the narrow interest of his local constituency but in the wider interest of the national constituency, which is the reason why Conservative MPs are able to support, for example, the abolition of capital punishment, when it is manifestly against the beliefs of their Conservative constituents, at least. On the other hand, the 'delegate' theory is that power comes from below which is the reason why the Labour Party and Labour Governments have continually to resort to 'fudging' issues when this particular aspect of idealism conflicts with common sense and responsible behaviour. As has been seen, Labour governments have much more difficulty in dealing with local government extremism than Conservative governments. In the case of the Liberal Party it was a story of decline. Whereas, in the nineteenth-century days of municipalization, the Liberals, inspired by Chamberlain in Birmingham, were the dominant force in the days of comparatively independent local government, it was their failure between the wars to play a significant part in the new situation whereby local government applied the policies of central government, that ensured the Party's decline nationally. Local activists were divided and discouraged by the bitter disputes between their leaders after Lloyd George replaced Asquith in 1916 and by the electoral consequences that followed. Also, of great significance locally, where the Liberal Non-Conformist element had been so important, was the successful way in which Salisbury and Balfour had reformed education (pp. 201–2), including to the comparative satisfaction of the Non-Conformist elements, in spite of their initial opposition to the reforms (pp. 197–8). The demoralized Liberal councillors were short of money and increasingly called themselves Independents and voted with the Conservatives.

> By 1930 local elections were being conducted openly on a party basis and the two-party system triumphed in local politics even though there were still three parties at Westminster.[1]

However, the pre-war planners of Civil Defence requirements were aware that 'Mr Mayor', his aldermen and councillors, and his conscientious officers, could not be entrusted with the responsibilities of a wartime emergency. Thus:

---

[1] *England, 1914–1945*, by A.J.P. Taylor, p. 266.

In 1937 a sub-committee of the Committee of Imperial Defence (the Warren Fisher Committee) recommended the immediate institution of 'a revised administrative organization which would include not only the existing headquarters of staff in London, but the formation of 13 areas outside London, each with its own headquarters staff. This change is necessary in peacetime for the purpose of the effective examination of local authority schemes, and in war a regional system of administration will be an essential element in the wartime organization.[1]

In fact, the skeleton regional organization set up at the time of the 1926 General Strike had been retained so that on 1 November 1937 the first regional office was opened at Leeds with a second one at Birmingham the next day. By mid-1938, there were offices at Edinburgh, Liverpool, Newcastle-upon-Tyne, Nottingham, Reading, Bristol, Glasgow, Cambridge and Cardiff and following the Munich crisis a list of Civil Commissioners, who would become Regional Commissioners in time of war, was made, and later finalized and published in April 1939. The instructions to the Commissioners said:

The Commissioners would act as the Representatives of His Majesty's Government in their Regions with the responsibility of seeing that effect was given to the Government's 'measures for civil defence' . . . But circumstances might arise which would necessitate the Commissioners taking emergency action on the Government's behalf beyond the power entrusted to Departmental representatives, and without consultation with the Ministry concerned.

Fortunately, in the absence of a German invasion, the Regional Commissioners were never called upon to use these executive powers, but in view of the administrative chaos following the bombing in 1940 of West Ham, Stepney and Southampton and later of Plymouth, the powers of the Commissioners were increased, and in conjunction with the Regional Boards, set up in January 1940 to deal with production, they became the main figures of an enormous regional system, co-ordinating the activities of the regional offices set up by the Ministries in London. Following a crisis such as a heavy bombing the regional authorities would act at once without consulting the central government, while the creation of instruments such as the Emergency Hospital Service and the National Fire Service

---

[1] *Britain in the Century of Total War*, by Arthur Marwick, p. 280. Further facts and figures in this chapter are attributable to this authority.

was only done by cutting across the functions of the local authorities. There were two other striking features about the Regional Commission, the first being that their headquarters remained a secret throughout the war and the second being that in spite of requests to the contrary, they were never individually given any written confirmation of their extensive powers. The consequences were, on the one hand, that while 'Mr Mayor' went about his business, visibly but ineffectually, the war was being run by the Ministries and the Regional Commissioners and, on the other hand, this was done on an entirely 'de facto' basis. Significantly, Herbert Morrison, the Minister of Home Security, a man nurtured on and steeped in local government, was completely opposed to formalizing the Commissioners' powers for this would represent a threat to the established authority of local government. Thus, in spite of much talk of and a spate of literature on the reform of local government at the end of the war, the vested interests of local government were insurmountable, so that the Commissioners were abolished at the end of the war although many government departments retained their regional offices. This was the only good thing that came out of the radical wartime reorganization of local government which reverted to its conservative and pre-war self, looking back to 1894 and 1888 and even to 1835. The opportunity to create an elective regional government was lost – probably for ever.

In dealing with post-war local government the first requirement is to recapitulate, in detail, the structure and functions of the various local authorities at that time making up our local government which, in spite of the 'reforms' of the Local Government Act of 1972 (put into force in 1974), will appear to be familiar today.

The County Borough

The number had increased from 74 when Marriott wrote in 1910 to 83, and the average population was around 100,000, of which 20 were less than 70,000 and 18 were above 200,000. Typical of local government, in 1888 many smaller towns pressed for County Borough status and some succeeded in their quest, while those which did not objected to giving up particular services which accounts for the fact that some quite small towns ran their own schools until the 1944 Act.

The County Borough, as the name implies, had the powers of a County and a Borough and it was a 'single tier' authority which provided the full range of local government services within its boundaries: namely police, education, public assistance, welfare,

261

public health, housing, slum clearance, roads, town and country planning in addition to local transport, and gas and electricity. Whereas a citizen living in a County Borough found that all his services were provided by his County Borough Council, the citizen in a Borough, or in an Urban District found that some of his services were rendered by the Borough or Urban District Council and others by the County Council while if he lived in a Rural District they could be provided by the County Council, the Rural District Council and the Parish Council.

The Administrative County

These remained at 62, the historic 52 shires, with the exclusion of the County Boroughs, and the sub-division of the larger ones. Yorkshire was divided into three – East, West and North Ridings; Lincolnshire into three – Holland, Kesteven and Lindsey; Suffolk and Sussex into two – West and East parts; Cambridgeshire into two – Cambridgeshire and the Isle of Ely; Northamptonshire into two – Northamptonshire and the Soke of Peterborough; and Hampshire into two – Hampshire and the Isle of Wight.

There was a remarkable divergence in the size of populations in the Counties, with Lancashire and Rutland having populations of 2,000,000 and 18,000 respectively. There were as many as 13 Counties with populations of less than 100,000 but around one-third were between 100,000 and 300,000 which was about the average size.

The 'two tier' County Councils administered highways, education, welfare services under the National Health Scheme and the care of the aged, infirm, deaf, dumb, blind and of orphans and children lacking parental care, under the National Assistance Act. They also had a number of licensing functions and joined with the Quarter Sessions in appointing a Standing Joint Committee, the Police Authority outside the County Boroughs.

The Borough

There were 309 Municipal or non-County Boroughs, 35 of which had populations between 5,000 and 10,000 and 63 with populations below 5,000, and of these latter, 21 had even less than 2,500 – mostly the ancient Boroughs of pre-Industrial Revolution days. On the other hand, as many as 11 of the non-County Boroughs had populations between 100,000 and 200,000, the usual range being from 20,000 to 70,000.

The Boroughs, like the Urban Districts, Rural Districts and Parish Councils, were not subordinate to the County Councils but each, within the County area, was independently responsible for its particular range of functions, although in the case of some services the County Councils delegated certain responsibilities to the Borough or District Councils or used them as local executive agents.

The Boroughs and the Urban Districts, which differed in the constitution of their Councils but had mainly similar functions, ran the greater number of 'communal' services, such as sewerage and sewage disposal, refuse collection and disposal, lighting and cleansing of streets, regulative public health, building regulations, parks, gardens, allotments, and the like. Although the cost of classified roads was borne by the County and of trunk roads by the Ministry of Transport, the larger Boroughs and Urban Districts carried out maintenance work, repairs and improvements and all the Borough and District Councils controlled their own district roads. Like the County Boroughs, many of the Boroughs and Urban Districts also provided public utility services such as water supply and street transport. As we have seen, some which were above a certain population, also provided until 1945 the elementary education and the maternity and child welfare services, as well as having their own police forces, but after 1945 all these functions reverted to the County.

The Urban District Council

Of the 572 Urban Districts, two had populations of between 100,000 and 200,000 and were large enough to be County Boroughs and to drop out of the Administrative County, but as many as 299 had less than 10,000 of which 149 were under 5,000, with around 100 between 2,500 and 5,000 and as many as 49 being below 2,500. With such bewildering variations in the size of population served by similar councils, owing to the fact that the census of 1902 was the determining factor, English local government could not be accused of being dull and uniform. In fact, from the time of the critical report in 1947 of the Local Government Boundary Commission, there were continual complaints about the many anomalies in local government which were 'fobbed-off' by both Labour and Conservative Governments. A good example is from Macmillan's time as Minister: 'A fundamental alteration of the existing structure could be justified only if it had shown itself to be incapable of maintaining present-day needs. That is not the situation.' Functions have been dealt with under Boroughs, above.

263

The Rural District Council

Of the 475 Rural Districts, five covered areas over 200,000 acres, greater than the individual areas of six County Councils. Populations did not exceed 80,000 to 90,000, with 116 being between 20,000 and 70,000, with 209 between 10,000 and 20,000 and with 149 being under 10,000. As with the Boroughs and the Urban Districts there was great variety.

The Rural District Councils' powers were similar to those of the Urban Districts although the amenities provided in the country were different from those in the towns. In cases when villages expanded sufficiently it was necessary for the Rural Districts to acquire Urban powers. Finally, all Boroughs, Urban District and Rural District Councils were housing authorities.

The Parish

There were 7,000 Parishes with Councils and about 4,100 Parishes were governed by meetings only. The fate of Parish Councils has been discussed on page 249–50.

The London County Council

The population of Metropolitan London, that is to say, the area of the London County Council, was almost 4½ million. The division of functions between the LCC and the 29 Metropolitan Boroughs was similar, but not identical, to that between the Counties and Municipal Boroughs and Urban Districts. A number of services which in the provinces would be provided by these Councils, and not the County, were in the hands of the LCC, such as trunk sewers and housing, or of ad hoc bodies such as the Metropolitan Water Board and the London Passenger Transport Board. Thus, in spite of their large populations, the Metropolitan Boroughs were responsible for a narrower range of functions than most Municipal Boroughs and Urban District Councils.[1]

As we have seen in Chapter 6 on 'The Mixed Economy' (p. 84), there was a vast increase in the role of the State after 1945 as a result of nationalization, the Welfare State and the re-distribution of wealth, with a corresponding explosion in the demand for services.

---

[1] *The English Local Government System*, by J.H. Warren, pp. 37–9. Further facts and figures in this chapter are attributable to this authority.

The machinery of the unreformed local government was under continual pressure in attempting to cope with these demands, for, in many ways, its inadequacy was inherent. The most satisfactory of the local authority institutions was the County Borough which was a 'compendious' or comprehensive unit exercising a variety of functions and the sole authority in a compact geographical area. Unlike the ad hoc authority, which has only one function, the County Borough is in the position to co-ordinate and rationalize its activities although the former is in a similar position in a system of regional government while the latter is, after all, restricted by and to its own territory, as we shall see. On the other hand, the traditional concept of distinguishing between town and country and its 'second-tier' subordinate authorities, became increasingly irrelevant as the population moved from town centres to the new suburbs and, indeed, from the country to the cities and their suburbs, thus leading to the creation of a number of small authorities of uneconomic size and inadequate resources. Besides, the very concept of a 'two-tier' authority was fraught with difficulties of which the fact that the Boroughs and Districts collected the rates for the County services as well as their own, was the least. Furthermore, the attempt in the Counties to divide functions in the same service between different authorities led to the inevitable problems of divided responsibility and the difficulties of co-operation, in spite of the best of intentions, difficulties which were exacerbated by the artificial and often unsuitable boundaries of the historic counties and the county towns in relation to their ever-changing urban and rural communities. There were also other problems that were inherent in any system of local government, but especially that in England. First, there was the retention of existing forms even after a reform of the original structure. For example, after the Municipal Corporations Act of 1835 the pre-Industrial Revolution towns, with their ancient charters and corporations, were retained even though they were mostly unsuitable. Another example is the reform of 1888 which retained the old Shires or Counties, so beloved of the JPs, and which established Councils in the manner of the existing Municipal Corporations, thus killing off the newer ad hoc authorities which had so much promise. Secondly, the granting of additional powers to an existing authority has proved to be difficult in practice as, for example, when Education was transferred to County Boroughs and Counties in 1902. In the latter case it was agreed that Boroughs with a population of over 10,000, and Urban Districts with over 20,000 could be responsible for elementary education, but there were considerable difficulties when the 'eleven-plus' system replaced the old division between elementary and secondary education at the age of 14 so that the 1944 Education Act made the County Boroughs and Counties solely responsible for all public education. Finally, the lack of machinery capable of adapting quickly and effectively the Local Authorities' status, boundaries and functions to changing conditions of population and development, caused incalculable problems in, for example, the fields of police, maternity and child welfare, as well as education. It was little wonder that central government increasingly by-passed the local authorities.

The development that finally put the system under insuperable pressure and exposed the inadequacy even of the County Boroughs, was the growth of the conurbations, as industry expanded, in such cities as Liverpool, Manchester and Birmingham where it was increasingly difficult to tell where one town ended and another began. In such circumstances, there were so many councils involved that it became a major problem to organize activities such as the police, transport and road-building, while the provision of a modern and efficient fire and ambulance services, and the like, required a centralized system such as that appertaining during the war, with the Regional Commissioners. But the largest conurbation of all was London which had grown to about 8 million people in its built-up area, expanding far beyond the area of the London County Council, so that Greater London included parts of Surrey, Essex, Hertfordshire, Kent and all of Middlesex. Reform could be postponed no longer so that in 1957 the Conservative Government appointed a Royal Commission on Local Government in London, and by the Local Government Act of 1958 set up a number of Commissions to study specific areas, especially the problems of the major English conurbations, namely the West Midlands, south-east Lancashire, Merseyside, the West Riding and Tyneside. In 1963, the London Government Act, strongly opposed by the Labour Opposition, (owing to the fact that it weakened Labour Representation on the peripheral county councils), contained the major recommendations of the London Commission, namely the amalgamation of the LCC and Middlesex County Council to form the Greater London Council, which was inaugurated in April 1965, with the new Labour Government in office (p. 434). The GLC assumed important functions for London as a whole and the Act also established the very important 32 London Boroughs which became responsible for the remaining local government services, except for education, where, as a concession to Labour wishes, it remained as a separate entity, the Inner London Education Authority, which was identical to the old LCC Education Authority – thus ensuring the educational sacrifice of thousands of unfortunate London children. The details are as follows:

> *The Greater London Council* covered an area of about 600 square miles, containing 8 million people.[1] Responsible for development plan for Greater London; fire, police and ambulance services; main roads and transport; refuse disposal. Also shared powers in housing, open spaces, sewerage and drainage where these functions cut across or involved several boroughs.

> *32 London Boroughs* (plus the City), each with an elected Council. Responsible for housing, health, welfare, libraries, non-major roads, education (except for Inner London Education Authority area, which had special GLC committee and representatives of each IL Borough Council), and local planning.[2]

Although three of the local Commissions under the 1958 Act had presented reports by 1961, the Government failed to put in place the East Midlands Commission's recommendation that the small county of Rutland should be merged with its neighbour, Leicestershire, owing to the strength of local opposition.[3] From being a source of strength, the English tradition of local independence had become a weakness in that it enabled obscurantist and petty-minded people to reject reform by hiding behind the bogus notions of local requirements and local accountability which could, more fittingly, be dealt with by the Parish Councils.

On the other hand, there are some commentators who have great faith in our system of local government. Ian Budge and David McKay say:

> In this context it is scarcely possible to overestimate the importance of local government. Both elected local councillors and local officials are a key source of help to individuals with problems. At its simplest, local government is closer to the people and more aware of their needs than central government whether in the guise of Parliament or the executive, though constituency MPs often

---

[1] It was abolished in 1989 and its functions were divided among the London Boroughs.
[2] *British Politics*, by Philip Gabriel and Andrew Maslen, p. 212.
[3] The merger did eventually take place but Rutland will be demerged from Leicestershire in April 1997 under the proposals from the recent Local Government Commission. There is no need for historic geographical boundaries to act as administrative straitjackets. The postcode, Rutland, and its historic boundaries on the map, could be retained, but its administrative units could be part of a much larger area.

stimulate local action. The often neglected role of local authorities in tailoring administration to personal needs must be underlined – it is an important facet of representative democracy and crucial in maintaining its popular support. In addition to this representative role, local authorities also carry out the bulk of the country's administrative business. They implement the great bulk of central decisions and their attitude is crucial in determining whether or not the policies will be effective. They are not mere agents of the centre; they also negotiate with it in many areas on a basis of near equality. Local government has thus to be examined as a major act in national policy-making.[1]

Budge and McKay argue that far from Britain being a unitary state where Parliament, executive and civil service decide policy throughout the land and apply it uniformly, the reality is that it is fragmented and, far from decisions being made and applied from the centre, Britain's main governmental characteristic is that of 'sub-central decision-making'.[2] Examples of fragmentation, apart from the confrontational aspect of the British political system, are the differing views within the two main political parties ('drys' and 'wets', on the one hand, and 'right' and 'left', on the other), the conflicting interests of government departments and the fact that although it can be argued that the British Prime Minister is, politically and constitutionally, relatively the most powerful leader in the world, administratively he is in something of a vacuum, the Cabinet Office being small and with limited resources.

As for Britain being a 'centreless society', from the beginning, as we have seen, and as Budge and McKay say:

> The administrative style of British government has always been to entrust the implementation of most policies to other people – local notables serving as Justices of the Peace until the late nineteenth century, local authorities, and, in a few policy areas, interest groups. Such devolution limits the degree of control that central government enjoys.[3]

Indeed, it has been necessary, from time to time, for England to protect and maintain her unitary form of government by taming the 'overmighty subjects', as Henry I did in the twelfth century (pp. 15–16) and as Margaret Thatcher did in her attempts to contain and control the high-spending Labour councils. She has been accused of

---

[1] *The Changing British Political System*, by Ian Budge and David McKay, p. 114.
[2] Ibid., Chapter 6, also pp. 38–40.
[3] Ibid, p. 39.

increasing central authority against the traditional Local Authorities but in view of the virtual breakdown of traditional relationships and assumptions her actions were inevitable and justifiable. Thus, in regard to Budge and McKay, in spite of the interest and stimulation of their detailed arguments, in the last resort, they are merely indulging in special pleading, in intricate and detailed descriptions of truisms while they totally fail to recognize the significance of 'consensus politics', which is mentioned only once, and is wrongly dismissed as being no longer relevant 'by the early 1980s',[1] whereas we have the best ever example of the consensus in the U-turn by the Labour Party when Kinnock finally accepted that the electorate would never accept rampant socialism, a belief which has been carried very much further by Tony Blair. It is the consensus that, paradoxically, has a strong centralizing or centripetal effect on the many centrifugal forces, including adversarial politics, in the British political and governmental system. The truth is that the conclusion Budge and McKay draw from their 'nit-picking' and pessimistic description of the latter, that it is out-dated and wholly unfitted and unable to deliver the goods, is special pleading. What they have described, admittedly brilliantly from the 'nuts and bolts' point of view, is probably the most complex and sophisticated political and governmental system in the world. They have correctly pointed out how it is changing beyond recognition but whereas they wrongly portray this as a weakness it is, in fact, its greatest strength. Their exasperation at the confrontation between the Conservative and Labour Parties is a superficial judgment which entirely misses the brilliant way in which the electorate has shown its determination to reject full-blooded socialism – acting through what can conveniently be called 'the consensus'. Furthermore, they dismiss Britain as a 'centreless society'[2] but rather they should wonder at its sophistication (which they describe so well) and its recognition that life in today's world is not simple but exceedingly complicated. They say that 'the case would be very different if policy debates were simply about agreed goals,[3] but this would imply doing away with the party system and having independent MPs who, in theory, would form a government which would agree on specific goals – but this is wishful thinking in the extreme. The British party system is probably the most effective way in the world for doing precisely this.

---

[1]*The Changing British Political System*, by Ian Budge and David McKay, p. 39.
[2]Ibid, p. 115.
[3]Ibid, p. 51.

As has already been indicated, Britain's comparative economic failure is not the result of political factors, for politically England (Britain) is a great success story, but it is the result of deeper and more complex historical and social causes, attention to which has already been drawn. Also, our comparative industrial failure has been largely offset by our strength in the commercial, financial, trading and service fields which is reflected in our high position in the actual standard of living league (p. 94–5). Besides, in regard to the oft-repeated criticism of the decline of Britain's industrial base in the 1980s, this is a long-term trend in any case, and Margaret Thatcher was able to achieve record growth in productivity and in the economy, in the period, by better utilizing previously unprofitable and under-utilized resources.[1] After the war, the continued attempt to prop up manufacturing industry by protection and subsidies guaranteed a low rate of economic growth, for it deprived the potentially dynamic parts of the economy of resources. Another extremely important factor is the decision of the British people, who, before the war were so disciplined and conscientious, to change their character and gradually to embark on a spending spree, characterized by the consumer society, the Welfare State and a low capacity for saving, compared with, for example, the Japanese people. Is this yet another example of the English capacity to oscillate between the conservative and the radical? In any event, on the economic front, the alternatives are not attractive. Extreme socialist or communist, collectivist economies can only work by denying individual political and economic freedom while they are inherently incapable of wealth creation and distribution. The mild collectivism and command economy associated with corporatism and the European Community, which Budge and McKay seem to favour, suffer, to an extent, from the same defects. The last word should be with Marwick, who says:

> None the less, individualism and resistance to the encroachment of the State upon society remained stronger in Britain than in continental countries with their long history of 'étatiste' despotisms, whether monarchical or revolutionary.[2]

---

[1] In a review published in September (*The Key to Higher Living Standards,* by Walter Eltis, Centre for Policy Studies), Professor Walter Eltis argues, and provides chapter and verse, that since 1979 Britain has achieved a virtual productivity miracle. We have significantly narrowed the gap between ourselves and the economies of the United States, Germany and France. In regard to real living standards, these have been transformed, both in absolute terms and also relative to other major industrial economies.

[2] *Britain in the Century of Total War,* by Arthur Marwick, p. 28.

14

The Law

Marwick states correctly:

> Of all British social institutions, the established church very definitely not excluded, the legal systems of England and Scotland were the least touched by two total wars . . . To an even greater degree than is the case with the principles of government, the law emanates from the mists of antiquity . . .[1]

In Chapter 1 (pp. 11–24) the origins of our governmental and legal systems have been described. In primitive societies there is no distinction between governmental and legal functions but we have seen that in England this was developing as early as the twelfth century, although the King retained his residual legal authority until it was abolished in 1641. However, it reappeared again after 1660 and it cannot truly be said to have been abolished until the passing of the Crown Proceedings Act of 1947 (p. 282). The classic analysis of the origins of our legal administration is that it rested on two principles, first, that the King is the source or fount of all justice and, secondly, that 'the suitors are the judges'. At first sight, this dichotomy is contradictory but it has blended into the system that we know for the administration of justice in a primitive society is necessarily mainly local. Thus arose the importance of the local courts of the Shire and the Hundred in which 'communal' courts' justice is practically 'folk right' for it was administered by the freemen themselves and in technical terms, the 'suitors are the judges'. But against this, two forces began to operate, the centralizing authority of the Crown, on the one hand and, on the other, the more immediate authority of the local territorial magnate – feudal justice. But between these two, in justice as in government, there was more antagonism than between royal and communal justice. Hence the stern insistence of William the Conqueror's successors, notably Henry I and Henry II, upon the

---

[1] *Britain in the Century of Total War*, by Arthur Marwick, p. 404.

attendance of the tenants-in-chief at the Shire Courts and upon the rights of the sheriff as against the 'franchises' of the barons.[1] This latter expression leads to another train of thought. It is difficult for the modern mind to comprehend the fact that in the earlier period, the King's Court was one of a number of courts, including the Anglo-Saxon courts of the County and the Hundred and the feudal courts. Although these last were not intended to exercise criminal jurisdiction, in practice they dealt with minor offences. It is also important that the King's Court (Curia Regis) did not think of itself as conducting litigation as a public service, but as mainly being involved in the non-litigious task of undertaking the government of the realm – legislating, administrating and judging. As we have seen, the main incentive and driving force in the matter of litigation were the Anglo-Saxon communal courts where 'the suitors are the judges'. However, it is significant that the King did not regard himself as the sole dispenser of justice and that the right to hold a court and to take the profit from the levying of fines, and the like, arose from the 'franchise' which he granted the baron, in the same way as he granted him his property – private justice as opposed to public justice. As we know, owing to the fact that it offered better justice, the King's Court, in the course of the twelfth and thirteenth centuries, took the place of the other courts with the creation of Courts of the King's Bench, Common Pleas and Exchequer and of itinerant justices and the assizes, together with the development of the jury system, and of the Common Law (p. 17). Thus, by the fourteenth century the old Curia Regis had acquired two separate functions, the King's Court which was a judicial institution, and the King's Council which was the assembly, sometimes large and sometimes small, the smaller consisting of virtually permanent advisers and officials through which he carried on his government while the larger became the House of Lords, as we have seen (pp. 19–20).[2]

By the reign of Edward I (1272–1307) each of the three historic courts had its own staff of judges, while William I's fact-finding itinerant commissioners had become the itinerant justices visiting each country three or four times a year for their Assizes and dealing with serious crime, the lesser offences being sent to the local sheriff and

---

[1]*English Political Institutions*, by J.A.R. Marriott, pp. 301–2. Further facts and figures in this chapter are attributable to this authority.
[2]*The Machinery of Justice in England*, by R.M. Jackson, pp. 1–3. Further facts and figures in this chapter are attributable to this authority.

later the Justices of the Peace so that criminal trials were mainly held in the county where the crime was committed. On the other hand, although civil cases were held in local courts where the sum in question was small, important cases went to one of the Common Law Courts at Westminster. Since as early as 1285 it was provided that an action could be begun at one of the Common Law Courts at Westminster with the actual hearing being held in the County by the itinerant justice and the formal judgment being carried out at Westminster. Although in practice the itinerant justices at the Assizes were judges it was possible to nominate an experienced pleader to act as an Assize Court judge at any time when no judge should be available. In all, the Assize Courts were an agreeable compromise between legal centralization and decentralization.

However, then, as now, the Common Law exhibited some weaknesses and deficiencies and as the King in Council had not relinquished entirely his judicial function, he was able to redress inequalities in the operation of his courts and to correct the errors of his judges, which led to the creation of the specialized court of the Chancellor or Chancery (the Lord Chancellor being the Keeper of the King's Conscience) as well as, eventually, to the supreme appellate jurisdiction of the House of Lords. Whereas in the thirteenth century there was a flexibility about the law, with the dominance of the Westminster courts from the fourteenth century it came to be uniform, narrow and technical and the flexible 'justice' applied by the earlier judges was replaced by 'justice according to the law' which could lead to 'inequitable' results. Thus the Court of Chancery, with its guiding principle of 'conscience', by the sixteenth century, had gradually evolved a system of 'equity' to correct the 'inequities' of the Common Law Courts (p. 21). This was especially necessary in the administration of criminal justice in the fifteenth century when a litigant's Common Law remedies might be denied due to the presence of 'over-mighty subjects' whose machinations had probably been exaggerated, but it was, nevertheless, the necessity to have a court strong enough to deal with these powerful offenders that led to the creation of the Court of the Star Chamber in the sixteenth century, as has already been mentioned on page 21, as well as other courts connected with it. This was essentially a judicial development emanating from the King's Council while, at the same time, his regular councillors and attendants formed a separate council, to be known later as the Privy Council. When the Court of the Star Chamber and all the prerogative Council Courts connected with it were abolished in 1641, the Court of Chancery survived. Unfortunately, the beneficial Court of Requests (p. 21) was also abolished.

273

By the end of the seventeenth century our legal system comprised the three Common Law Courts, the Assizes, the Court of Chancery and Justices' of the Peace Quarter Sessions (p. 21–2). The victory of the Common Lawyers was almost complete – except for the Ecclesiastical Courts and the Court of Admiralty. Then, as for centuries after, their domination of the House of Commons ensured the abolition of the Conciliar Courts in 1641, while they also prevented any extension of Ecclesiastical Courts and took over the commercial work previously done in the Court of Admiralty. Further, the original division of functions between the King's Bench, Common Pleas and Exchequer was ingeniously allowed to lapse with the result that the King's Bench became the most important of the Common Law Courts. The Common Law completed its overwhelming victory by emasculating the Court of Chancery in its own image. It was invaded by the Common Lawyers so that the old concept of 'conscience' gradually disappeared from its collective consciousness and although the pretence of 'equity' was maintained in Chancery Courts, they lost their flexibility when confronted with the legal steamroller of the rule and case-dominated Common Law. By the early seventeenth century, the Lord Chancellors were trained in the same way as Common Lawyers and by the eighteenth century their courts were conducted in a similar fashion with the emphasis on rules deriving from previous decisions – case law. In fact, they were barely distinguishable and by the nineteenth century 'equity' was merely another set of rules 'which could be invoked to supplement the deficiencies of Common Law or to ease the clumsy workings of Common Law actions and remedies.'[1] Then, as now, the Common Law system was notable for its independence and independence of judgment, but also for its built-in inflexibility and difficulty, if not failure, to deal with new situations and problems. By Tudor times, statutes were cast in the form that still appertains, apart from the explanatory preambles, and the victory of Parliament over the Stuarts ensured that the Common Law judges accepted the dominance of Parliament and Statute Law, although as late as the eighteenth century it was suggested that judges might disregard a statute that contravened natural or divine law. Furthermore, they were still obsessed with the law built up from precedents and there was so much case law concerning the older statutes that they usually thought in terms of this and not the statute. Also, this attitude was fostered by the fact that, until the 1832 Reform Act, the statutes played a

---

[1]*The Machinery of Justice in England*, by R.M. Jackson, p. 6.

comparatively insignificant part. However, as the nineteenth century progressed this ceased to be so and since 1918, and even more so since 1945, the growth of Statute Law has been stratospheric, aided and abetted by a similar increase in Orders in Council, delegated legislation and quasi-judicial authority, about which more will be said later.

Nevertheless, the Common Law is still very much associated with the English legal system and traditions and is contrasted with the system and traditions of the Roman Law as practised in Continental Europe. Whereas our Common Law has been passed on to our colonies and ex-colonies, that is to say, the English-speaking world (including the United States), in places such as Canada and South Africa, where the French and Dutch systems were already in place respectively, Roman Law was the greater influence. In the British Isles, the English system has formed the basis of Welsh and Irish law, although the Irish Free State has a separate system as a result of its political history, while that of Ulster is a part of the English system. On the other hand, owing to its long association with France and Spain in the years before the Act of Union in 1707, Scotland has a separate system much influenced by Roman Law. The Roman Law dates from Justinian, Emperor of the Eastern Roman Empire based on Constantinople, in the sixth century AD, for although he and his successors failed in his ambition to reunite his inheritance with the old Western Empire owing to the continued invasions of the 'barbarian hordes', his legal reforms were outstandingly successful. By getting his lawyers to gather together all the numerous laws which had come into being under Roman rule for the previous thousand years, Justinian's vast body of laws represented the administrative experience of the most successful rulers of the ancient world. The emphasis was on codification. Almost every situation arising in social life, in business transactions or in legal proceedings had been dealt with by Roman judges, and the collection of their decisions, known as Justinian's Digest, became the foundation of what has become known as the Romanesque or Roman Law.[1] Because of its tradition of codification, Roman Law is much easier to transfer than English or Common Law which does not exist in any concise form, so that Far Eastern countries, such as Japan, and South American countries have turned towards the former when modernizing their laws. That is not to say that there are not points of contact between the two traditions, especially from the time of the nineteenth-century codes of

---

[1] *Ancient Times, A History of the Early World*, by J.H. Breasted, pp. 774–5.

France and Germany. For example, case law is an integral part of the machinery of French courts. However, the utmost importance of case law and the supremacy of Statute Law, on the one hand, has led to an entirely different legal and political tradition than the practice of codifying law for every eventuality, on the other.

We have already seen (pp. 241–2) that by the sixteenth century there had been an increase in the responsibilities of the Justices of the Peace whose members now represented boroughs as well as counties following the granting of charters by the Kings to towns which became formally independent in their counties. In particular, the justices were dealing with petty offences which were not of sufficient importance to go before the Quarter Sessions, on a summary basis, as and when it suited them, as described above, together with their administrative functions supervising the constables, Surveyors of Highways, Overseers of the Poor, and the like. Finally, they were charged with holding preliminary enquiries in order to bring before the King's justices those who were suspected of crime. This led to the summoning of a 'grand jury' whereby not less than 12, nor more than 23 men of substance, usually Justices of the Peace, deliberating in secret, received the bills of indictment against the accused persons, and heard the 'charge' or address by the visiting judge, before finding against them 'a true bill' or 'no true bill', as the case may be. In the former case, the accused 'stood indicted' and the trial proper would commence before an ordinary trial or 'petty-jury', the descendant of the early Norman juries of sworn witnesses to facts and which had become judges of the facts from the sworn testimony of the witnesses – and from that only. Grand juries, which could be said to date from Ethelred II's time (p. 16), were abolished in 1933 but the jury system survives – in an emasculated form.

Apropos the jury system, Marriott makes an interesting comment. He says:

> In the persistence of the jury system we have a further illustration of a characteristic English trait to which attention has already been directed; a certain mistrust of 'expert' or 'professional' opinion; a desire to associate laymen with experts, amateurs with professionals. We have seen it in the harmonious co-operation of Cabinet Ministers and Civil Servants; of Town Councillors and Town Clerks; of stipendiary and unpaid magistrates. Most remarkable of all, perhaps, is the association of the 'learned' judge and the unlearned jury.[1]

---

[1] *English Political Institutions*, by J.A.R. Marriott, p. 305.

In other words, in the nineteenth century the cult of the amateur was elevated into a way of life and a way of government. The country was run by country gentlemen with a classical education with the help of subordinate 'professionals' in the form of civil servants. As has already been noted, this was an excellent system for running an empire but not for surviving industrially in an increasingly technical age, especially when the self-made industrialists were succeeded by their graduate sons. It was this reason, as well as the fact that we were first in the field, that led to our technological deficiencies in the last quarter of the nineteenth century.

Because of the uncodified or unwritten nature of the English legal system, it is especially difficult for the non-specialist or 'man in the street' to understand it, except vaguely, even after he has had recourse to it. As with so many other subjects, it is difficult, if not impossible, to attain an understanding without some knowledge of its history, which this chapter has attempted to cover briefly. It remains to deal with four aspects of the law and their ramifications, knowledge of which are essential for an understanding on the subject.

1. The Rule of Law

'The Rule of Law' is traditionally regarded as the foundation of the English constitution, namely that the 'legality and impartiality' of English institutions arises from the fact of the predominance or supremacy of law in England. As we shall see, these notions were famously erected into a principle by A.V. Dicey in his book *Law of the Constitution*, in 1885, but since the 1930s it has become a minor industry among legal historians to decry Dicey and to say that 'the rule of law' is virtually meaningless. For example, Jackson says:

> It is a pity that such a high-sounding phrase, suggestive of a decent international and social order, should have acquired too many meanings to be of much use.[1]

Nevertheless, the fact remains that the expression is still used continuously by politicians and statesmen, among others, in both this country and those English-speaking counties which adopted the English legal system so that it behoves us to try to understand its meaning and, more important, its significance. Undoubtedly, Dicey was very much a child of his time and his views have been largely

---

[1] *The Machinery of Justice in England*, by R.M. Jackson, p. 17.

outdated by the march of time, in regard to their practical application and relevance, but the censorious critics have committed the sin of 'throwing the baby out with the bathwater'. In the same way as the popularity of a painting such as 'The Mona Lisa' or the works of Shakespeare do not depend on the opinions of experts, but on 'popular' appreciation throughout the ages, so, too, the tortuous reasoning of legal academics has not managed to kill the 'popular' espousal of Dicey's 'rule of law'.

Dicey's three propositions were as follows:

(1) That no man is punishable or can be lawfully made to suffer in body or goods except for a distinct breach of the law established in the ordinary legal manner before the ordinary courts of the land.

(2) That not only is no man above the law but (what is a different thing) that here every man whatever be his rank or condition is subject to the ordinary law of the realm and amenable to the jurisdiction of the ordinary tribunals.

(3) That with us the law of the Constitution, the rules in which foreign countries naturally form part of a constitutional code, are not the source but the consequence of the rights of individuals as defined and enforced by the courts.[1]

E.C.S Wade, the editor of the Ninth Edition (1939), in which he includes a weighty introduction and appendix, sums up the above propositions succinctly, as follows:

(1) In England no man can be made to suffer punishment or to pay damages for any conduct not definitely forbidden by law.

(2) Every man's legal rights or liabilities are almost invariably determined by the ordinary courts of the land.

(3) Each man's individual rights are far less the result of our constitution than the basis on which the constitution is founded.[2]

Wade's criticism of Dicey is scholarly, unbiased and constructive after which he allows some meaning in Dicey's doctrine which is, in my view:

---

[1] *Law of the Constitution*, by A.V. Dicey (Ninth Edition), pp. 188–96.
[2] Ibid., Introduction, p. Ixxvii. Further facts and figures in this chapter are attributable to Wade's comments.

a. The independence of the judiciary.

b. A man can do whatever he chooses to do provided that he does not break the law. This is the fundamental difference from the Continental Roman Law countries with their written constitutions and tradition of codes of law to deal with every eventuality, which are necessarily more restrictive than the classic liberal English tradition of complete freedom (legal and political) within the law. The point does not need labouring that these different traditions account for our failure to identify with the collectivist and bureaucratic inclinations of the European Union, as has already been pointed out on page 68.

c. Whatever legal privileges may be enjoyed by civil servants, and the like, once they exceed those privileges they are legally liable in the manner of any ordinary man, while in regard to any crimes or civil offences which they might commit as private individuals, they are equally liable.

The criticisms of Dicey are two-fold; first, technical and secondly, historical. They are both bound up with the whole subject of Administrative Law which will be dealt with more fully later in this chapter and only partially here.

The Technical Criticism of Dicey's 'Rule of Law'

The classic view of the functions of the State was that it was responsible for the maintenance of law and order and of the armed forces, the conduct of foreign affairs and of the colonies and the levying of taxes. Apart from foreign affairs and the forces, officers of the government had little in the way of discretionary powers which were mainly vested in the courts, remembering that local administration was enforced for centuries by Justices of the Peace exercising their legal powers. In retrospect, it can be seen that from the time of the Elizabethan Poor Law, the seeds were being sown for the wholesale provision of services by public authorities, empowered by statute (Administrative Law as opposed to Common Law) which has become so much a feature of the twentieth century. However, even by the middle of the nineteenth century the existence of the Boards of Guardians, Highway Boards and local Boards of Health denoted the development of a system of administrative regulation which had been further expanded by 1870 by the activities of such bodies as School Boards, turnpike (roads and canals) trustees, gas, water and railway companies, while the Factory and Mines Acts, and the like, amounted to a system of public inspection of private industries – administrative control compared with legal control. After 1870, as we have seen, this development escalated as the old ideals of 'laissez-faire' lost their hold.

> Had he chosen to examine the existing scope of administrative law he would have been forced to enumerate, even in 1885, a long list of statutes which permitted the exercise of discretionary powers which could not be called in question by the courts. Abuse and excess only could be checked. In particular, the Public Health Act, 1875, afforded many examples of such powers.[1]

From legislation such as this, there evolved such practices as the compulsory acquisition of land by public authorities, which could not be justified under the Common Law, and the establishment of administrative tribunals by Parliament which do not administer the Common Law or follow the procedure of a court of law.

That Dicey recognized the existence of Administrative Law is attested by the fact that in 1915 he wrote an article, 'The Development of Administrative Law in England'. In 1914, in the introduction to *Law and Opinion*, he wrote that:

> by 1900, the doctrine of 'laissez-faire', in spite of the large elements of truth which it contains, had more or less lost its hold upon the English people.[2]

He pointed to the progress of collectivism in the years 1906–13, citing such important sources of Administrative Law as the Old Age Pensions Act, 1908, the National Health Insurance Act, 1911, the Coal Mines (Regulation) Act, 1908, and the Coal Mines (Minimum Wage) Act, 1912, together with the Finance (1909–10) Act, and other examples. He noted that the National Health Insurance Act had greatly increased the legislative and judicial authority of the government or of officials closely connected with the Government of the day, and admitted that the Insurance Act had created in England a system bearing a marked resemblance to the Administrative Law of France; and further that such law 'had some distinct merits'. Nevertheless, Dicey was a child of his time and in spite of the fact that he acknowledged the growth of 'collectivism' he thought that it was undesirable, while he refused to countenance the break-up of the

---

[1] *Law of the Constitution*, by A.V. Dicey, Introduction, p. Ixxviii.
[2] Ibid, Introduction, pp. Ixxxvii–Ixxxviii.

Common Law into Civil Law and Administrative Law. It was for this reason, as well as for the fact that he wrongly associated it with the pre-1641 Court of the Star Chamber that Dicey was so critical of the French system of having separate administrative courts – 'Droit Administratif'.

It was for the same reason that he made the technical error of failing, or refusing, to accept the fact that the law had given special immunities and privileges to public authorities and servants, as against the ordinary citizen. In doing so he was merely endorsing the judicial opinion of his day and since, which, first, has insisted on the judges' independence of the executive, as late as 1932 refusing to accept the status of servants of the Crown under the Order in Council of that year reducing the salaries of civil servants. Secondly,

> True to the Common Law tradition, they have adhered to the principle that every governmental act must be capable of being justified by rules of Common or statute law. In general this principle has led them to assume the defence of private rights invaded by public authority. The task has not been easy ... However strongly the judges may insist on the principle that all government must be carried on according to the law, the law itself does not enable them everywhere to impose the same measure of control on public authorities as on the ordinary citizen.[1]

In the first instance, and not mentioned by Dicey, there were the rights and immunities which the Crown and its servants (i.e. the government ministers and civil servants) held, not by statute, but by virtue of the Royal Prerogative.

> ... The prerogative powers are, in the words of Dicey, quoted in the House of Lords, 'the residue of discretionary or arbitrary authority, which at any given time is legally left in the hands of the Crown'. They consist of the powers which the courts recognize as remaining to the King after the revolutions and subject to the statutes which Parliament has passed under the supremacy which it has successfully claimed since 1688.[2]

The Common Law maxim was that 'the King could do no wrong' owing to the fact that as the courts were his courts no proceedings

---

[1]*Constitutional History of Modern Britain, 1485–1937*, by D.L. Keir, pp. 515–16. Further facts and figures in this chapter are attributable to this great authority.
[2]*The Law and the Constitution*, by W. Ivor Jennings, p. 179. Further facts and figures in this chapter are attributable to this authority.

could be brought against the King exercising his legal powers through one or some of his servants (i.e. civil servants), they enjoyed special privileges in regard to legal proceedings. For example, in civil actions, the Crown could only be proceeded against by its own consent, but in practice this was usually done by an historic proceeding known as 'petition of right', and although significant privileges remained in the power of the Crown in practice, petition of right proceedings were usually not dissimilar from those of the ordinary courts. It will be noted that I have been writing in the past tense for most of the consequences of the Common Law maxim that 'the King can do no wrong' have been eliminated by comparatively recent legislation, namely the Crown Proceedings Act of 1947. This provides that:

> The Crown shall be subject to all those liabilities in tort to which, if it were a private person of full age and capacity, it would be subject . . .

Nevertheless,

> It is still true that the law applying to the Crown and its servants is different from the law applying to private persons, even in respect of civil liability.[1]

On the other hand, and, secondly, there are those public authorities, such as the local authorities, whose privileges and immunities are not derived from the Crown but from statutes. For example, statutes such as the Constables' Protection Act, 1751, and the Justices' Protection Act, 1848, give necessary protection for acts done 'bona-fide' but in excess of legal authority, while the Public Authorities Protection Act, 1893 penalizes, with heavy costs, unsuccessful actions against them as well as giving them a very favourable statute of limitations, any remedy against the authority being inapplicable after as short a period as one year. The object was to prevent one generation of ratepayers from being saddled with the obligations of another. Nevertheless, Jennings finally and grudgingly, in this respect, sums up in Dicey's favour. He says:

> It is clear, therefore, that by 'equality before the law' and 'obedience to the law' Dicey was not referring to that part of the law which gives powers to and imposes duties upon public authorities. What he was considering – and subsequent chapters

---

[1] *The Law and the Constitution*, by W. Ivor Jennings, p. 204.

make this clear – was that if a public officer commits a tort he will be liable for it in the ordinary civil courts. I have explained that normally, and subject to qualifications, this is true.[1]

This was even more true after 1947. Although Dicey was not concerned with it, as we have noted, and as Jennings has confirmed, the greatest problem for the maintenance of judicial control of public authorities under the Common Law, was statutes conferring sub-legislative powers to the executive that were so broadly drawn that ministers could legislate much as they pleased. In many cases the words in the statutes seemed specifically to exclude judicial review under the 'intra vires' rule that the legislation must be within the meaning of the statute by which it was authorized. For example, the statute could state that the subordinate legislation was to 'have effect as though enacted in this Act', or its making was to be 'conclusive evidence that the requirements of this Act have been complied with'. In such cases, Common Law review has ceased to be applicable. This brings up the whole question of delegated legislation, and discretionary and quasi-judicial authority, and will be dealt with in the section on Administrative Law. It is worth noting at this stage that there are no such problems with local authorities which are statutory bodies subject to a minister. A local authority is not given a general authority to develop a service as it pleases, a fact which is enforced by government departments exercising their statutory powers of control. Similarly, Independent Statutory Authorities, the old nationalized industries, the BBC, and the like, are limited to the statutory powers embodied in their charters, which is quite a constitutional achievement in view of the facts that the Postmaster General only has limited powers of control and that parliamentary control is limited by the fact that there are no responsible ministers to answer questions.

The Historical Criticism of Dicey's 'Rule of Law'

Although not entirely, this mainly concerns my first definition of Dicey's doctrine – the independence of the judiciary – which is implicit in so much of what he wrote in *Law of the Constitution* and which is stated explicitly in pages 409–410 in the ninth edition. In their interpretation of Dicey, the legal academics are too legalistic, as one would expect. For example, in belittling the traditional view as to

---

[1] *The Law and the Constitution*, by W. Ivor Jennings, p. 296. (See ante pp. 204–10).

the difference – and superiority – between the Common Law and Roman Law, Jackson states:

> Among suggested differences is the part that case law plays in the common law, but the Romanesque systems make considerable use of precedent. French case law is voluminous and essential to the working of their courts. Again, jury trial has been singled out, but jury trial has spread widely in the Romanesque system. The 'rule of law' is often instanced. If this means merely public order and civil liberties, we can claim no monopoly: if it means the constitutional position of our Parliaments and courts, it does not exist in the United States: if it means that the powers of government are derived from law, then it is characteristic of every state.[1]

Speaking of the doctrine of judicial precept and judicial independence, even the admirable Wade, says:

> In fact this amounts to little more than saying that English law reflects the prevailing opinion in favour of our particular form of government . . . We may deplore the political philosophy of such states, but it is no help to an understanding of legal principles of our own constitution to claim the rule of law – as a legal rule – as a unique feature of the British constitution. It is, as so viewed, merely a manifestation of our political system which we may believe rightly or wrongly, to be superior to that of our neighbours.[2]

On the other hand, Dicey, and constitutional historians such as Marriott (who was admittedly a similar generation to Dicey), point out that whereas we had established the sovereignty of Parliament, the independence of the judiciary and the 'rule of law' by the end of the seventeenth century, on the Continent the eighteenth century was the classic Age of Absolutism. The main historical landmarks were: the dismissal of Lord Chief Justice Coke (1616), the arbitrary imprisonment of Sir Thomas Darnel and others (1627), the Petition of Right (1628), the abolition of the Prerogative Courts (1641), the Habeas Corpus Act (1679), the Bill of Rights (1689) and the Act of Settlement (1701). The legal historians say that it might have gone either way and that if the case for the Prerogative and the Stuarts

---

[1] *The Machinery of Justice in England*, by R.M. Jackson, p. 17.
[2] *Law of the Constitution*, by A.V. Dicey, Introduction, pp. xciii–xciv.

had won against Parliament, then our legal and constitutional structure would be entirely different. This is certainly true for, as we have seen, the doctrine of the Prerogative has a long and proud tradition and is still by no means dead (for example, it must be the only reason for British governments' ruthless insistence on various aspects of secrecy) and it was enunciated with great skill by Coke's rival, Bacon, whose judges made arbitrary judgments in the ordinary courts, let alone the conciliar courts, on the pretext of 'matter of state', and in contradiction to the Common Law. But whatever the semantic arguments of lawyers the historian must not only take account of, but base his judgments on, what actually happened and what were the consequences of those happenings, namely the supremacy of the Common Law and the independence of the judiciary, as explained on page 66 and the constitutional settlement as explained on pages 67–8. He is also conscious of the fact that the victory of the Common Law, and the Common Law lawyers, so overwhelmingly represented in Parliament, was complete and although this produced the invaluable bonus of legal and political freedom for the English, and later, the British, it also produced the legal conservatism (embodied by Dicey) which has prevented us from establishing a coherent and independent system of Administrative Law in the footsteps of the Tudor conciliar courts.

It has already been remarked that although Dicey was aware of the growth of 'collectivism' he was not happy about it (p. 280). Jennings is especially critical of Dicey in this respect:

> The 'rule of law' in this sense means that public authorities ought not to have wide powers; that is that the 'collectivism' which has infused the policies of all Governments since Disraeli's is an undesirable principle. The 'rule of law' in this sense is a rule of action for Whigs and may be ignored by others.[1]

All this means to the historian is that, like Dicey, Jennings was a child of his time for is his book not dedicated to one, Harold J. Laski? Even by the end of the nineteenth century Liberal thinkers like T.H. Green and Bosanquet were enunciating a philosophy that was substituting the classic Liberal emphasis on the individual for the collectivist principle that the individual's economic survival in a well-organised state was more important than theories about legal

---

[1] *The Law and the Constitution*, by W. Ivor Jennings, p. 292.

and political freedom. They were influenced by the German philosophical idealism (collectivist) compared to the traditional English empirical philosophy (individualist). Also, Jennings would have been influenced by the strong reaction by the historians of his day against 'the Whig interpretation of history', namely that the political revolution and settlement of 1689 had led to a situation that was perfect and which could not be improved upon. Both these propositions were untenable, of course, but although the inevitable and natural reaction against them is intellectually interesting and significant, it does not detract one whit from their supreme importance. The same applies to Jennings's criticism of Dicey such as that on the latter's third proposition (p. 278), which can be described as tortuously legalistic, but which nevertheless has been neatly summarised:

> By this is meant that the legal right of the subject, e.g. his freedom of action and speech, are secured not by guaranteed rights proclaimed in a formal code but by the operation of the ordinary remedies of private law against those who unlawfully interfere with his liberty of action, whether they be private citizens or officials. A person libelled may sue his defamer. Free access to courts of justice is an efficient guarantee against wrongdoers.[1]

Dicey is here referring not to the mass of rights derived from statutes, e.g. pensions, insurance or free education, but to the fundamental political freedoms − 'the common law of the constitution' − freedom of the person, freedom of speech, freedom of association. On the contrary, we have the interpretation according to Jennings:

> Lastly, 'the constitution is the result of the ordinary law of the land,' says Dicey. It is equally true that the law of the land is the result of the Constitution. The fundamental principle of the law is the power of Parliament, which came by a political movement and which was then recognized as law. In this sense the law determines the Constitution, though the Constitution determines the law. Law and constitution cannot be separated.[2]

If Dicey is tortuously legalistic, Jennings is doubly so as well as being inexcusably tendentious.

---

[1] *Constitutional Law*, by E.C.S. Wade and G. Godfrey Phillips, (Fourth Edition, New Impression, 1953), p. 50.
[2] *The Law and the Constitution*, by W. Ivor Jennings, p. 297.

2. Administrative Law

The above section, The Technical Criticism of Dicey's 'Rule of Law', (pp. 279–83) serves as an introduction to the question of Administrative Law in this country. On the point of definition, Maitland, writing in 1908 says:

> Constitutional law deals with structure, administrative law deals with function. If this idea were pursued, then constitutional law would tell us how a King comes to be a King, and how he can cease to be King, how a man comes to be a peer of the realm, when, where and how men are elected to the House of Commons, how parliament is summoned, prorogued, dissolved, how men become privy councillors, secretaries of state, judges, justices of the peace, aldermen, poor law guardians – for constitutional law deals not only with the structure of the sovereign body, but also with the structure of inferior bodies possessing legal powers of central or local government. But if we ask what can these bodies and these officers do, what are their functions, then, according to the general idea, we should be sent to administrative law.[1]

On the other hand, Jennings says, in Britain:

> The only fundamental law is that Parliament is supreme. The rest of the law comes from legislation or from those parts of judge-made law which have not been abolished by legislation. Strictly speaking, therefore, there is no constitutional law at all in Great Britain; there is only the arbitrary power of Parliament.[2]

As we have seen, owing to social and political developments in England since the end of the First World War, Administrative Law has become a significant and important branch of the law relating to the civil service, local government, nationalized industries and the legal powers which these authorities exercise. That is to say, special powers are placed in the hands of administrative authorities. By the same token, the individual now needs greater protection from the administration, and the administrators, than from his fellow citizens. However, unlike England, most Continental legal systems make a clear distinction between public and private responsibility and accordingly provide separate administrative courts, notably the 'Droit Administratif' in France.

---

[1] *The Constitutional History of England*, by F.W. Maitland, pp. 533–4.
[2] *The Law and the Constitution*, by W. Ivor Jennings, p. 64.

Dicey's criticism of the '*Droit Administratif*' was due to the fact of its separation between Civil Law and Administrative Law the consequence of which was that it offended the second of his three propositions that comprised 'the Rule of Law', (to repeat) that 'every man, whatever be his rank or condition, is subject to the ordinary law of the realm and amenable to the jurisdiction of the ordinary tribunals.'[1] In contrast, Dicey said that in France:

> Officials are, or have been, in their official capacity to some extent exempted from the ordinary law of the land, protected from the jurisdiction of the ordinary tribunals, and subject in certain respects only to official law administered by official bodies.[2]

Dicey's conclusions idealized the English system and made the French system seem unchanged from the days when:

> In 1717 Voltaire was sent to the Bastille for a poem which he had not written, of which he did not know the author, and with the sentiments of which he did not agree.[3]

However, although the '*Conseil d'Etat*', the superior administrative body, derives many of its qualities from the pre-1789 era, and its Roman Law traditions, it was refashioned by the Revolutionary statesmen (later embodied in the Napoleonic constitution) in such a way as to nullify the control of the judicial authority over the administration, which had been abused, by providing that the latter authorities should be controlled only by higher administrative authorities, in accordance with the French concept of the 'separation of powers' which was, and is, rejected by the English system. At this time, Dicey's strictures could be justified, but from around 1815 when machinery was developed for enabling the citizen to bring his complaints to the attention of the '*Conseil d'Etat*', which after the Revolution of 1848 was recognized as a Court, a fact which was embodied in the law in 1872 which established a special court, the '*Tribunal des Conflicts*', whose function was and is to establish whether a case brought before a civil court should be heard in an administrative court and, indeed, to determine whether either kind of court has jurisdiction. Thus, although in the body of his book, Dicey continued to fulminate against the '*Conseil d'Etat*', and all its works,

---

[1]*Law of the Constitution*, by A.V. Dicey (Third Edition), p. 193.
[2]Ibid, p. 193.
[3]Ibid, p. 193.

in the later editions he inserted two qualifications to his criticism of the French system (p. 288), namely, 'or have been' and 'to some extent' which indicate that, on further reflection, he acknowledged the reforms of the *'Conseil d'Etat'* in the course of the nineteenth century. Indeed, by this time, it had become a court in every sense of the word, with its judges holding office, in fact, during good behaviour and deciding legal questions according to rules of law, and thus building up a system of precedents in what may be called the English tradition. Although it was originally created to protect the administration against the civil courts, thus depriving private persons of the right of action against it, it now provides exactly the opposite function, protecting the citizens against excessive and illegal acts of the State and its subordinate authorities. As has been said:

> The jurisdiction is divided, however, between the civil courts and the administrative courts. If the wrong committed by the administrative officer is not committed in the course of his public employment, an ordinary civil action may be brought against him to the civil courts, and the measure of his liability is determined by the ordinary civil law. If on the other hand, the act or neglect may be impugned to his employment, the administrative court alone is competent, the remedy is against the administration and not the officer, and the principles of liability are rather more stringent against the administration.[1]

Thus the *'Conseil d'Etat'* has achieved for France a solution of the major political problem of the day – the reconciliation of the powers of the executive with the rights of the subject and the rule of law – by the recognition of the absolute autonomy of the executive which is the essence of the French administrative law. But as Dicey correctly stated, such recognition was repugnant to our Common Law principles or prejudices. The consequence is that through insisting on maintaining a theoretically universal 'rule of law' we have preserved only the fiction of a formal legalism and control has been maintained with difficulty, and not effectively, by ad hoc methods including the multiplication of specialized tribunals.

As we have seen (pp. 282–3), the phenomenon of delegated legislation has increasingly reduced the powers of the High Court effectively to control the adminstration, while in practice it has been necessary to empower the latter by statute, to act as and when it considers action necessary. That is to say, the administration has

---

[1] *The Law and the Constitution*, by W. Ivor Jennings, p. 213.

'discretionary' powers, similar to those once exercised by the Crown as part of the Prerogative – but founded on statute. This involves the questions of legality, on the one hand, and expediency, on the other, the latter being determined in terms of public advantage – what used to be called 'matter of state'. On the contrary, action taken by an administrative authority in the public interest may threaten the individual's rights and the property rights of the private individual so that the public authority, in exercising its 'discretionary' powers, is, in effect, in the position of a judge, deciding between the respective interests of the community and the individual citizen. These 'quasi-judicial' powers have been expressly conferred by many statutes on public bodies which are not, in any meaningful sense, courts of justice. They offend the first principle in that they are judges in their own cause and might be tempted to put the public interest, as they interpret it, before the rights of the individual. Again, they determine their own procedure which could be inimical to the rights of individuals and which could lead to arbitrary and capricious decisions, not subject to scrutiny, public or otherwise.[1] On the other hand, they have the great advantage of technical familiarity and competence, compared with a court of justice, while their procedure is quick and inexpensive – the greatest boon of all in comparison with the slow and expensive procedure of the civil courts. The growth of quasi-judicial powers such as those of the ministries responsible for town and country planning, health, National Insurance, employment, rents, immigration, education, and the like, has created an extensive administrative jurisdiction in modern Britain, exercising functions similar to those of the earlier conciliar courts. In the absence of the legal dualism practised on the Continent, here the ordinary courts endeavour to ascertain that the administrative jurisdiction is exercised, as much as possible, in a judicial spirit and as if the administrative bodies were, in fact, courts. How is this done?

The judicial control of the administrative authorities is carried out in three ways. First, the courts hear appeals from the decisions of the authorities. For example, the income-tax payer may appeal to the High Court via the General or Special Commissioners of the Inland Revenue. County courts hear appeals from Council Tax payers regarding their assessments and from property owners against demolition orders. The justices in petty sessions hear many appeals under the Public Health Acts as well as such matters as the

---

[1]However, since our period, judicial powers in reviewing delegated legislation have been strengthened. See ANISMINIC v the Foreign Compensation Commission, 1969.

290

apportionment of charges for making up streets. There are, however, limitations to the effectiveness of the rights of appeal to the courts for, in the first place, the administrative function is usually given to the administrative authority for the good reason that some expert technical knowledge is necessary, in comparison with the cumbersome legalism of the courts and it can only be justified where there is the possibility of a miscarriage of justice. This can arise when the authority has an interest in the case, which is often so, when there is the possibility of corruption, as in local authority grants of building permission, or when there is questionable political influence. In such cases, the need for recourse to a court is obvious but there is still the question as to whether judicial or administrative techniques are more suitable, for the latter could lead to an appeal to a higher administrative authority such as an administrative tribunal or an administrator. The court procedure will be expensive and long drawn-out in comparison, although it must be said that, other things being equal, the public prefers to put their case to professional judges rather than special tribunals. The conclusion can only be that in retaining the ascendancy of the Common Law and in not accepting a duality of laws, we have made life harder for everybody – the public, the administrators and the judges.

The second form of control is to apply the test of 'ultra vires' by the issue of the medieval prerogative writs which, typically, have been modernized by replacing them by orders obtained by a more simple procedure of application to the Queen's Bench Division of the High Court, while injunctions and declarations of illegality are also issued, in order to prevent an administrative authority from committing an illegal act or to enforce the performance of a legal duty. In particular, the writ of mandamus[1] compelled a public authority to perform any duty imposed on it by statute; the writ of prohibition prevented a public authority from exceeding its jurisdiction on the grounds that it had no statutory or Common Law power to carry out a particular form of administrative adjudication; the writ of certiorari reversed a decision of a public authority on the ground that it had no legal power to take the decision; the writ of quo warranto contested the assumption of office by a public authority which was not justifiable by law. Thus these writs enabled the courts to control the administrative authorities by defining the limits of their powers and by issuing orders to prevent any such excess of powers, as well as by

---

[1]Although these historic writs have been abolished since our period they remain of indirect relevance.

enforcing them to do their duty. They also required the authorities to give the subject an opportunity of stating his case, they demanded that no person whose private interests were affected by a decision should be involved in making it, as well as that no decision should depend on extraneous considerations. Although the prerogative writs came to be used to restrain inferior Common Law courts their adaptation to restrain public authorities exercising semi-judicial powers had been comparatively successful, although it could have been criticized as an ad hoc solution. Certainly, the courts have assumed that if it is intended to prevent such interference with public authorities, there should be an express statutory prohibition, as indeed there is in certain modern legislation such as that concerning housing and town and country planning. Nevertheless, the courts resist any such attempts to deprive them of their jurisdiction but, in the last resort, they are limited to the confines of Acts of Parliament. Judges are powerless to alter oppressive legislation where, in a democracy such as ours, the remedy is in the hands of the people by way of the ballot-box.

The third form of control comprises the application of ordinary remedies for proceedings as a result of an unlawful act by an administrative authority, or its officers, thus injuring a private individual or another public authority. As we have seen, owing to the immunities applying to a legal entity known as 'the Crown' the law in this respect has been unsatisfactory, but the situation has been improved significantly by the Crown Proceedings Act of 1947 (p. 282). One reason why Dicey's interpretation of the English legal system in regard to its relationship with the administrative authorities was unrealistic was that he did not include the special prerogatives of the Crown, the prerogative writs and other remedies, as well as the important fact that there was usually a statutory remedy wherever a public authority was in a position to interfere with private rights. Another important point is that in England, as in France, the law as to remedies is a small part of Administrative Law which is mainly concerned with the organization and powers of administrative authorities, which is why, under the influence of Dicey, who was so intent on showing that we had no Administrative Law in the former sense, the myth arose that England had no Administrative Law. In 1930, a Lord Chief Justice stated that 'there is not here any system of administrative law, such as is to be found on the Continent'.[1]

It is therefore not surprising that at about this time it was

---

[1]*Introduction to The English Constitution*, by Sir Maurice Amos (1930), p. vi.

recognized that the control of public authorities was far from satisfactory and a Committee on Ministers' Powers was formed which reported in 1932. The words of a preliminary report are significant:

> The most distinctive indication of the change of outlook of the government in this country in recent years has been its growing preoccupation, irrespective of party, with the management of the life of the people. A study of the Statute Book will show how profoundly the conception of the function of government has altered. Parliament finds itself increasingly engaged in legislation which has for its conscious aim the regulation of the day-to-day affairs of the community, and now intervenes in matters formerly thought to be entirely outside its scope. This new orientation has its dangers as well as its merits. Between liberty and government there is an age-long conflict. It is of vital importance that the new policy, while truly promoting liberty by securing better conditions of life for the people of this country, should not, in its zeal for interference, deprive them of their initiative and independence which are the nations most valuable assets.[1]

The Committee recommended that ministerial tribunals should be set up, that reports on which decisions are made should be published and that people affected by decisions should be informed of the reasons whereby they are made. Nevertheless, it rejected any separation between ordinary and administrative jurisdiction or any system of appeal from ministerial decisions to the courts of law, although it admitted the need for recourse to an Appeal Tribunal in exceptional circumstances. In other words, the matter was left comparatively unchanged. As Keir says:

> There the problem remains. In the modern State an extended executive able to make, enforce and interpret law, has come into being under imperfect parliamentary and judicial control. The principle of the separation of powers has been violated. Considerations of 'policy and government', as they would have been called in the seventeenth century, have been accorded a larger place in the constitution than they have held for two hundred years. To many critics, the process is disquieting. It seems to threaten a more fundamental breach in the continuity of our constitutional history than has ever been effected in any previous

---

[1] 'Report of the Committee on Finance and Industry', Part 1, Chap. 1, para 8, p. 415 (Cmd.3897, 1931), cited 'Report of Committee on Ministers Powers', 1932, (Cmd.4060).

age. It may in reply be suggested that the danger has been exaggerated. Numerous as are the statutes giving sub-legislative powers, no statute has yet created a general as distinct from a particular power to govern. All such powers are held by a tenure revocable at the will of parliament. The number of instances in which quasi-judicial powers include the right to judge in matters of law as well as on the questions of fact to which administrative action relates is limited, and their existence is looked on askance.[1]

This section can only be concluded by giving more consideration to the extraordinarily successful alternative system, the French '*Conseil d'Etat*'. If it has any bias it is towards the subject while its jurisdiction is centralized and universalized as was once the case in the King's Court in England. Every administrative act may be examined and sanctioned or annulled as the case may be while a full appeal ('*appel*') may be made to it as of right from the judgment of any administrative tribunal, even if that tribunal is specifically empowered to make final judgment by means of a '*recours en cessation*', an appeal upon a point of law or of form. The *Conseil* will annul the administrative exercise of a non-discretionary power if the administrative order is '*insuffisament motivé*', that is to say, if it does not accurately and sufficiently describe the grounds of the order. In the case of a discretionary power, the *Conseil* does not require a statement of the grounds in the actual order but, if the order is questioned, the *Conseil* requires the ministry to state its reasons which are passed on to the plaintiff following which the *Conseil* will inquire into their sufficiency. If the ministry fails to answer it can be put '*en demeure*' (in arrears) and in the event of further refusal the *Conseil* will make its judgment on the grounds that every relevant claim made by the plaintiff is correct. Furthermore, even when the Ministry exercises a discretionary power on what is 'prima facie' a sufficient reason, the *Conseil* may quash the order if it is, or appears to be, based upon a '*fait matériellement inexact*', which provides extensive scope for review. It compares drastically with the virtually arbitrary powers enjoyed under certain circumstances by authorities such as our ministries concerned with town and country planning, and the like, not to mention the worst examples of delegated legislation.

It is, however, important to appreciate that in spite of the popular notion, the *Conseil* is not exclusively a court, although admittedly this

---

[1] *The Constitutional History of Modern Britain, 1485–1937*, by D.L. Keir (Third Edition, 1946), p. 520.

is numerically preponderant, and that of its five sections only one exercises judicial business – '*la section du contentieux*'. The main function of the *Conseil*, as an institution, is to advise the government and the executive, not in the mode of a critic but as an expert collaborator of the administration in the broadest sense, attempting to prevent situations which it may have to redress '*au contentieux*'. The remarkable thing is that the advice of any of the four administrative sections does not bind the judicial section for, as a court, this section may find that the action advised by another section is unlawful. The *Conseil*, especially the '*section du contentieux*', is detached from the day-to-day involvement of actual administration although it has an unrivalled knowledge of public affairs upon which it is consulted by government. It is this combination of detachment with an intimate concern with and knowledge of administration that is the secret of the *Conseil*'s success. The main criticism of the *Conseil* is the problem that has arisen owing to its own success, namely that the demand for its services grew so much that there were inordinate delays between the filing of a petition and the judgment thereon, which has led to devolution by strengthening the inferior administrative tribunals, such as the '*conseils de préfecture*', and by a system of inspection and circuits in order to reduce some of its duties as a court of first instance. In 1953 '*conseils de préfecture*' were renamed Administrative Tribunals and empowered to hear general law cases of administrative disputes with the possibility of appeal to the '*Conseil d'Etat*'. The latter remained, however, the court of first and last resort for certain specified cases of particular importance.[1] Another problem of success is that the more cases there are the more difficult it is to ensure that the execution of the *Conseil*'s decisions are carried out satisfactorily. Nevertheless, as has been said, the '*Conseil d'Etat*' has been brilliantly successful in France and it is no exaggeration to say that it is the envy of the world.

Indeed, instead of chasing rainbows such as a Bill of Rights, political and administrative reformers should concentrate on incorporating some of the ideas and practices of the *Conseil* into our own system. For obvious reasons, there is no question of copying,

---

[1]An important reform in 1987 instituted an intermediate jurisdictional tier between the Administrative Tribunals and the '*Conseil d'Etat*', in the shape of five Administrative Appeal Courts sitting in Paris, Lyon, Nantes, Nancy and Bordeaux, and presided over by a '*Conseil d'Etat*'. The '*Conseil d'Etat*' has thus retained its competence as the court of first and last resort for petitions against orders and regulations issued by ministers and major administrative authorities.

wholesale, the French system. For example, as with the French judiciary, in general, the *Conseil*, including its judicial section is an hierarchy mostly selected by examination at an early age, in conformity with the Roman Law tradition whereby a lawyer must choose at an early age whether he is going to practise before the courts as an advocate or whether he is going on the bench as a judge. Under this system, the judiciary is part of the administrative hierarchy but although the judiciary, in general, and the *Conseil*, in particular, are independent of the government, it does mean that the judiciary and the lawyers are separate professions. On the other hand, the English tradition is that the legal profession is virtually an autonomous body with the likelihood of the best and the most successful practitioners being elevated to the judiciary, on an independent basis from the government, as we have noted, and enjoying considerable prestige both within the profession and in the world at large. (I say this in spite of the fact that recent pronouncements and decisions by judges have caused great disquiet.) However, in view of the English genius for pragmatism and compromise it should be possible to mould a form of Administrative Law and courts onto the English system, the seeds of which can, perhaps, be seen by the way in which a group of judges in the Divisional Court of Queen's Bench, who specialize in Administrative Law, handle appeals from the decisions of tribunals with an impressive expertise. English lawyers, both barristers and solicitors, have long specialized in various fields such as criminal, commercial, family, property and patent so that an administrative bar is a feasible proposition. Although, alone, this would still be tied to the cumbersome and expensive Common Law courts, there could be scope for integrating it with a vastly expanded Ombudsman organization. The very existence of the Ombudsman is one more example of the ad hoc manner in which the English legal system has had, perforce, to admit its inadequacy in dealing with the conflicting interests of central and local government, on the one hand, and the individual citizen, on the other hand. Surely, it is only a question of time before the question that was fudged by the 1932 Committee on Ministers' Powers is answered positively.

There could be no more fitting conclusion to this section than to refer to the Crichel Down affair. In 1949 the Ministry of Agriculture took over the responsibility for 725 acres of land at Crichel Down in Dorset, which had originally been purchased by the Air Ministry in 1937 under a requisitioning procedure. Unfortunately, the land was sold by the Ministry to a relative of one of its civil servants in spite of the fact that a Commander Marten, heir of one of the previous owners, had been endeavouring to repurchase the property. The public inquiry which followed reported in 1954 that the ministry's civil servants had shown 'a most regrettable attitude of hostility' to Commander Marten and that:

> In present times the interests of the private citizen are affected to a great extent by the actions of Civil Servants. It is the more necessary that Civil Servants should bear constantly in mind that the citizen has the right to expect, not only that his affairs will be dealt with effectively and expeditiously, but also that his personal feelings, no less than his rights as an individual, will be sympathetically and fairly considered.[1]

The affair is also notable for the fact that the resignation in 1954, after the report, of Sir Thomas Dugdale, the Minister of Agriculture, was the last example of the exercise of this extreme form of ministerial responsibility whereby the minister resigns in spite of the fact that he had had no knowledge of or anything personally to do with the affair.

3. The Courts

There is a fundamental distinction between the role of the courts in an unwritten unitary constitution such as in England/Britain and a written federal constitution such as in the USA. As we know, the judiciary in England has rendered itself completely independent of both the executive and the legislature but, in the last resort, the judiciary, although distinct from the legislature, is inferior to it for the legal powers of Parliament are unlimited. In theory, it can abolish the Monarchy and the House of Lords by a majority of a single vote, after due process.[2] On the other hand, in the United States, its

---

[1]'Report Arising Out of Crichel Down', P.P., 1953–4, X, Cmd.9220.

[2]The repercussions of the European Union's European Court of Justice pose the threat of a fundamental constitutional change whereupon the House of Lords, for the first time in history, becomes a constitutional court. In March 1994, in the Equal Opportunities Commission (EOC) Case, it ruled that aspects of the Employment Protection (Consolidation) Act 1978 were incompatible with European Community Law and in December 1994, the Employment Secretary, Michael Portillo, finally and reluctantly conceded that all workers employed for 8 to 16 hours a week (part-time workers), must be eligible for similar redundancy payments for those working full time.

Again, in response to Spanish fishermen in the 1980s registering dozens of boats as British so as to have access to British quotas, and thus get round the fish quotas set

written constitution is above the ordinary law and the judges of the Supreme Court have the authority and the duty, embodied in the Constitution, to interpret the law of the Constitution and to determine the legality of laws passed by the legislature. In a legal sense, the judges are superior to both the legislature and the executive. On the contrary, in the absence of a written constitution, English judges are confined merely to interpreting the law, not that this should be dismissed as of little consequence owing to the powerful part played by the Common Law. By the same token, although, essentially, the judicial and administrative functions do not differ (the difference between interpreting the law and exercising a discretion being difficult to define at the margin) in a written constitution it is necessary to make a distinction, and this is usually done by establishing a supreme court on the one hand, and, by

---

for them by Brussels, the Marine Shipping Act was passed in 1988 so as to disqualify the Spanish who, in turn, appealed to the European Court of Justice. In 1991 the unelected Court ruled the Act passed by our elected Parliament illegal whereupon the Spanish fishermen sued so that in addition to the £2.4 billion which we pay annually to Brussels (much of which goes to the Spanish Fishing Industry) it appears as though we shall be paying them £35 million pounds 'compensation'.

Dicey's concept of the sovereignty of Parliament is further shattered by the fact that the European Court of Justice in Luxembourg may rule that the legislation of member states violates Community Law. The same would apply if the British Government were to accept the desire of other members of the Council of Europe to make the acceptance of petitions to the European Court of Human Rights, in remote Strasbourg, mandatory. Also in December 1994, the Commission in Strasbourg condemned the process by which a Minister of the Crown, at his executive discretion and on the advice of the parole board, can continue to keep in custody those who murdered when they were juveniles. In particular, the Home Secretary, Michael Howard, will oppose any attempt by the Court, if it adopts the Commission's findings, to release the boy killers of James Bulger immediately after they have served their recommended minimum sentence of 15 years or even earlier. Earlier in the year (1994) the Commission ruled that the rights of the former Guinness Chief, Ernest Saunders, were infringed in the Department of Trade and Industry investigation into the 1985 Distillers takeover. If the Court confirms the findings, he, and his co-defendants, could sue for an estimated £1 million. The Human Rights Court has ruled against Britain in 30 of 52 claims since 1950. Our Governments have too readily in the past accepted its judgments. I have selected only a few of the judgments emanating from these unrepresentative courts, which being steeped in the Roman Law tradition, are completely foreign to our legal inheritance. It is unthinkable that in the long run, or for that matter, the short run, we can allow such an inferior system to replace the much more mature and flexible one which we have developed over a thousand years.

legislation, inferior courts, on the other hand, whose judicial powers are defined and limited. But in England, such a distinction is unnecessary and meaningless. As Jennings says:

> The truth is that no distinction can be drawn according to function and the judicial function does not exist as something clear and definite. We can only say that certain courts are courts because they have always been called courts. They are the High Court, the Court of Appeal, the House of Lords, the Judicial Committee of the Privy Council, the County Courts, the Courts of Quarter and Petty Sessions and certain local courts. What they do, in the main, is to administer civil and criminal law. But, . . . they exercise certain functions in regard to administrative law.[1]

The constitution of the United Stated, and similar written constitutions, embody the principle of 'the separation of powers' which the French writer, Montesquieu, in the *L'Esprit des Lois*, (p. 68), attributed as the main reason why the English political system avoided the despotisms that were so common in the rest of Europe, whereby heads of state exercised absolute power, untrammelled by judicial or legislative restraint. Of course, the English system did not fit this definition as the executive was and is a part of the legislature but Montesquieu was struck with the impressive fact that the English judiciary enjoyed complete independence from the executive. The founding fathers of the United States were influenced by the prevailing intellectual ideas of their day but they were much more so by their determination to ensure that, unlike George III, their President's powers should be separate from and limited by the separate powers of the legislature and the judiciary. Thus we have the paradox that the United States's constitution, with an insignificant number of amendments, is in an eighteenth-century time warp, retaining the eighteenth-century 'spoils' system, and all, whereas the English 'constitution', with its ability to change by 'convention', has been continuously updated. Even written constitutions of comparatively recent origins soon begin to appear dated. One has only to think of the entirely unsatisfactory French Constitution, with its excessive Presidential powers (shades of De Gaulle!) and its correspondingly weak Parliament and Prime Minister. It is unbelievable that there are staunch advocates of a written constitution for Britain.

On page 274, I have dealt with the development of the English legal system and courts in the eighteenth century. In view of the fact

---

[1] *The Law and the Constitution*, by W. Ivor Jennings, p. 225.

that I have been critical of their conservatism it should be noted that in the middle and last quarter of the nineteenth century there were major reforms that led to a significant simplification of the system. This initially took place in the field of civil jurisdiction, namely the creation of County Courts under the Act of 1846 in order to satisfy the demand for local courts to deal with small civil cases in view of the decline of the old local courts and the excessive centralization of the Common Law courts which were consequently costly and dilatory. This was the time when the reforming and rationalizing ideas of Jeremy Bentham were a powerful force but it must be said that the Scottish and Whig Lord Chancellor, Lord Brougham, succeeded in getting the Act through Parliament in spite of the opposition of most of the legal profession. The first thing to be said about the new courts is that they were completely distinct from the historic Courts of Shire or County for in good rationalist spirit they were not based on the geographic counties, but they were organized for convenience and not tradition, an outlook which would have been extremely beneficial in the field of local government. For County Court purposes England was divided into around 500 districts in each of which a court was held every month and the districts were grouped into circuits to each of which a judge was appointed by the Lord Chancellor. There were about 50 such judges so that each judge was responsible for about ten districts, they usually sat without a jury and were competent to try claims that did not exceed £50. The new courts were exceedingly popular for they were comparatively prompt, efficient and cheap and their jurisdiction was considerably enlarged by statute in 1905. Although plaintiffs could elect as to whether to proceed in a County or High Court, for the above reasons they usually chose the former, while the right of appeal to the High Court and on to the House of Lords was seldom used owing to the satisfaction given by the County Courts.

Although further changes have been made they remain broadly the same as they were originally conceived. For example, in line with their initial concept, the Lord Chancellor has used his power to alter the number and boundaries of county court districts, and places where courts are held in such a way as to discontinue them at places where there was a small requirement, and to concentrate them where they were in greater demand and more convenient. The result has been a reduction in the number of courts to around 340 in England and Wales by 1977[1], by which time in the Metropolitan districts the

---

[1]Today (1996) the figure is around 270.

300

demand was so great that the courts were virtually in constant session with some courts having two or three judges, while in less heavily populated districts there was a single judge or even a part-time judge. Although it is beyond our period, the Courts Act of 1971 altered the original organization and meaning of 'circuits' being exclusively served by County Court judges, as such. The Act divided England and Wales into six circuits in which, apart from the very serious cases to be taken by the High Court judges, the remainder were to be dealt with by Circuit judges or Recorders, including the County Courts. The Circuit judge was a new-style judge with a wide discretion, and the new-style Recorder is not to be confused with his predecessor who sat only in borough Quarter Sessions. The result of the new structure has been to concentrate legal work into fewer centres, as has already been noted. The County Courts Act, 1984, governs the general jurisdiction and procedures, currently.

In regard to jurisdiction, there has been continual pressure to extend this (for it can only be done by statute) in view of dissatisfaction with High Court procedures and costs. However, apart from the usual legal conservatism, this has been resisted because of a serious conflict of interests between solicitors and members of the Bar – barristers. Unusually, solicitors have a right of audience in county courts which are spread around the country, like solicitors, whereas the Bar has a virtual monopoly of advocacy in the higher courts which, like the barristers, are based in London and a few large cities. Consequently, attempts to increase county jurisdiction has been supported by solicitors and opposed by the Bar. This has been especially so in the case of divorce jurisdiction where it was hypocritically argued that divorce was too important to be relegated to County Courts, and solicitors, so that the Bar kept it in their purlieu by using County Court judges in a fabricated High Court setting. However, by the Matrimonial Causes Act of 1967 the County Courts were given jurisdiction in undefended divorce while the liberal Divorce Reform Act of 1969 recast divorce law so that it was to be based on breakdown of marriage instead of on matrimonial offences. Last year's Divorce Bill (1996) took the final politically correct step of establishing "no fault" divorce (p. 313, note 4). There has been a corresponding increase of County Court jurisdiction in other fields. The 'County Court Practice' for 1974 named 64 subjects and those dealt with by County Courts, comprise: Recovery of Income Tax, Bankruptcy, Family Provision, Matrimonial Home and Property, Recovery of Land, Rent Acts, Landlord and Tenant, Matrimonial cases, Hire Purchase Acts and Attachment of Earnings in relation to the enforcement of debts. As in divorce, there was the conflict of interests between the High Court and County Courts over ordinary actions of contract and tort and, over the years, the High Court has had to agree to a more reasonable division of work between it and the County Courts, which was embodied in the County Courts Act of 1955. This Act fixed the general limit of County Court jurisdiction at £400, and it was increased to £600 in 1966 while the previous legislation was consolidated in the County Courts Act of 1959. It was recommended in 1968 that the level of claims should be increased to £1,000 but by the Administration of Justice Act it was raised only to £750, which was no change in view of the effect of inflation. The Act did, however, make a breakthrough by empowering the specific sum to be increased by Order in Council, with no upper limit – a good example of delegated legislation. This was done in 1974 to increase the sum to £1,000. The current limits on County Court actions in contract and tort are £5,000 under the 1984 Act.[1]

In the course of the nineteenth century further superior courts were founded – or refounded. In 1857 the old jurisdiction of the Ecclesiastical Court over testamentary and matrimonial causes were abolished and transferred to the newly created Court of Probate and Court of Divorce, together with some new powers such as that of completely dissolving a marriage. The proceedings for bankruptcy were strengthened while ineffectual attempts were made to improve the very complicated and inefficient system of appeal courts. However, there was the major problem that there were too many superior courts with a confusion of jurisdictions and procedures and with poor co-ordination. In spite of the domination of Chancery ('equity') by Common Law ('law'), by the eighteenth century (p. 274), there remained a dual and confusing legal system with Chancery procedure, inherited from the old Ecclesiastical Courts, and rules of obligations and remedies, differing from the Common Law so that in order to obtain full justice it was sometimes necessary to go to two courts.

Thus a complete reorganization and simplification was made of the superior Civil Courts by the Judicature Acts of 1873–75 by which the eight superior Courts of First Instance (courts numbered 1–8 in the table on page 304) together with the four appellate courts were abolished. In their place was established a Supreme Court of Judicature divided into The High Court and The Court of Appeal

---

[1]The trend for the monopoly of barristers to be gradually eroded culminated in the Courts and Legal Services Act, 1990, under which solicitors have the right of access to the Higher Courts.

(see table). The jurisdiction of the above eight courts was conferred on the High Court and that of the four appeal courts, upon the Court of Appeal, after modifications and additions. The High Court consisted of five divisions and Assizes (see table) but in 1881 three of the Divisions (as indicated in the table) were amalgamated thus leaving the Queen's Bench, Chancery, Probate, Divorce and Admiralty Divisions, and the Assize Courts. The Court of Admiralty has a record extending to the fourteenth century while by the Tudor times it dealt with all forms of commercial disputes, including maritime, but by the eighteenth century the Common Law Courts had taken over from it all disputes except purely maritime. The Judicature Acts therefore formally ended the separation of 'law' and 'equity' as the High Court inherited the jurisdiction of both – but their rules were not amalgamated for it was provided that both sets of rules should apply, although, in the event of conflict, equity must prevail. As Maitland stated:

> To each of these divisions certain business is specially assigned . . . But this distribution of business is an utterly different thing from the old distinction between courts of law and equity. Any division can now deal thoroughly with every action; it can recognize all rights whether they be of the kind known as 'legal', or of the kind known as 'equitable'; it can given whatever relief English law (including 'equity') has for the litigants.[1]

In regard to the use of juries, it was provided that questions of fact could be referred to a jury with the leave of a judge in the case of the Chancery Division, but in those of the other two it was at the instance of either party. However, even as early as this time, jury actions were rare, except in the Queen's Bench Division, and even there they were tending to become less frequent. It is extremely interesting and pertinent, considering that he was writing in 1910, that Maitland should have said that,

> Trial by jury in civil cases is becoming less and less common. Very usually both parties are willing that all questions whether of law or fact shall be disposed of by the judge.[2]

---

[1] *The Constitutional History of England*, by F.W. Maitland, p. 472.
[2] Ibid, p. 472.

Table 1

Reorganisation of the Superior Courts of Law in the Nineteenth Century

Superior Courts in the Nineteenth Century prior to the Judicature Act 1873

1 The High Court of Chancery

2 Court of Queen's Bench

3 Court of Common Pleas at Westminster

4 Court of Exchequer

5 High Court of Admiralty

6 Court of Probate

7 Court for Divorce and Matrimonial Causes

8 Assize Courts

9 Exchequer Chamber
(common law appeals)

10 Lords Justices in Chancery
(Chancery appeals)

11 Appellate jurisdiction of
Privy Council in Lunacy &
from High Court of Admiralty

12 Other appellate jurisdiction

SUPREME COURT OF JUDICATURE
Judicature Acts 1873–75

THE HIGH COURT
(Justices of the High Court)

Chancery Division

Queen's Bench Division

Common Pleas Division   } – After 1881, Queen's Bench Division

Exchequer Division

Probate Divorce and Admiralty Division

Assizes

THE COURT OF APPEAL
(Lords Justices of Appeal)

HOUSE OF LORDS. Final Court of Appeal for Great Britain and (now Northern) Ireland. (Lords of Appeal in Ordinary). Appellate Jurisdiction Act, 1876.[1]

[1]*The Machinery of Justice in England*, by R.M. Jackson. p. 8

On the question of appeal, in certain cases there was a right to appeal to the High Court from inferior courts while from the High Court, including Courts of Assize, there was an appeal in almost every case to the new Court of Appeal. This consisted of the 'ex-officio' judges; the Lord Chancellor, the Lord Chief Justice and the President of the Probate, Divorce and Admiralty Division; six permanent judges; the Master of the Rolls and five Lords Justice of Appeal. Also the Appellate Jurisdiction Act of 1876 introduced four salaried professional judges, Lords of Appeal in Ordinary (the 'Law Lords'), for the House of Lords so that it became an adequate final court in its judicial capacity. The four 'Law Lords' were also appointed to the Judicial Committee of the Privy Council which had been deprived of all jurisdiction in England in 1641, except that it remained the supreme Court of Appeal for Admiralty cases and for all the King's overseas dominions, which latter had become significant with the advent of the Second British Empire. Thus the composition of the Judicial Committee of the Privy Council was virtually identical with that of the House of Lords sitting in a judicial capacity. But there is a difference in procedure. Whereas a judgment of the House of Lords is a quasi-legislative act where a vote is taken, the Judicial Committee, as a Committee of the Privy Council, 'advises' the Crown and it is the Queen in Council by whom the Order, giving the judgment, is formally made. Although, like the House of Lords, the judgments of the Judicial Committee do not need to be unanimous, the convention is that it does not give multiple judgments. However, while the latter is bound by its own decisions, the former is not.

So far we have been dealing with the 'civil' courts which are concerned with the rights and disputes of citizens – 'private law'. It is now necessary to deal with the 'criminal' courts which are concerned with offences against the Crown, or the State, in other words, with crime – 'public law'. Both legal systems were subject to a major reform by the Courts Act of 1971, which is beyond our period, but, nevertheless, it is now necessary to describe the development of the criminal courts up to that date, as has already been done regarding the civil courts. Jurisdiction over serious crime had been in the hands of the King's judges since at least the fourteenth century and it was carried out mainly in the counties where the offences were committed, by itinerant judges under the commission of assize (p. 16), and the name 'assizes' became associated with this court where itinerant judges dealt with both civil and criminal cases. The creation and rise of 'justices of the peace', during the same period, to deal with lesser crime, has already been described (pp. 21–2) as also has their increase

305

in responsibilities by the sixteenth century (pp. 241–2), so that by the nineteenth century they were dealing with non-indictable crime, 'petty offences which were not of sufficient importance to go before the Quarter Sessions, on a summary basis' (p. 276). In regard to the more serious indictable crime, they were responsible for the summoning of a 'grand jury' and where 'a true bill' was found 'the accused "stood indicted" and the trial proper would commence before an ordinary trial or "petty jury"' (p. 276) at Quarter Sessions, while the more serious cases were sent on to the Assizes. After the abolition of Grand Juries in 1933 persons have been sent for trial direct from the preliminary inquiry by the justices – the committal hearing in magistrates' courts under the terms of the 1933 Administration of Justices Act in order to ensure that no one stood trial at a higher court unless a strong prima facie case was established. However, by the middle of the nineteenth century, with the creation of an efficient police force, it was no longer necessary for the justices to 'get up' a case so that the police became responsible for deciding, on a judicial basis, whether the prosecution has produced sufficient evidence for the accused to be sent for trial at Assizes or Quarter Sessions.[1]

The close relationship of local justice with local government has resulted in the mayors of boroughs and the chairman of county and district councils, as well as other local dignitaries, becoming Justices of the Peace, 'ex-officio'. The number of petty offences that the Justices of the Peace were dealing with on a statutory and summary basis (trial without jury before two justices or one stipendiary magistrate) grew rapidly during the eighteenth and nineteenth centuries and in 1848 a statute was passed regulating the procedure of these courts which came to be known as Petty Sessions and from which there was generally an appeal to the Quarter Sessions, and from both to the High Court of Justice. In the larger boroughs, after 1835, lay magistrates were superseded by professional barristers, appointed by the Home Secretary, and known as 'stipendiary magistrates' or 'police magistrates'. Such was the difficulty of law enforcement in the metropolis that this development had been initiated there following a statute in 1792 authorizing the

---

[1]In February 1994, it was announced by the Home Secretary that the committal hearings in the magistrates' courts were to be abolished. In future, cases would go straight to the Crown Court. Instead of a committal hearing JPs would study the papers in a case and give a written ruling whether it should proceed to the higher courts.

appointment of metropolitan police magistrates. The use of the word 'police' in connection with magistrates was unfortunate, especially in view of the fact that the expression 'police court' came into use, for the correct form was Court of Summary Jurisdiction, which included Petty Sessions and special sessions known as Juvenile and Matrimonial Courts. Accordingly, the Justices of the Peace Act, 1949 instituted the Magistrates Court which was and is a court of summary jurisdiction or of preliminary trial by examining justice or justices and, as with its predecessors, its main work is dealing with the lesser offences. A further Justice of the Peace Act was enacted in 1979. As there were and are many more magistrates courts than stipendiary magistrates, they have been normally associated with lay magistrates, while they also hear civil matters such as certain local tax, matrimonial and affiliation cases. There were also a few remaining administrative functions, namely the granting of liquor and betting licences, and historic functions, including the granting of summonses, warrants for arrest and search, while the taking of declarations and witnessing documents are performed out of court.

In regard to the superior criminal courts, although there was continuous tinkering with the system, there was no fundamental change until the reorganization of 1971 which bears comparison with that a hundred years previously. The traditional pattern continued of the Assize judges going on Circuits to visit the counties two, three and four times a year in the cases of Manchester, Leeds and Liverpool. As always, London was a special case and in 1834 the Central Criminal Court (the Old Bailey) was established. The biggest change was in Quarter Sessions. In those boroughs which, by virtue of a Royal Grant, had their own Quarter Sessions the Municipal Corporation Act of 1835 provided that they should be presided over by a Recorder, a barrister appointed by the Crown. As we have seen, the Local Government Act of 1888 deprived the County Quarter Sessions of nearly all their administrative functions following the establishment of elected County Councils, so that they became basically courts for the trial of indictable offences. The allocation of indictable cases between Assizes and Quarter Sessions changed significantly in the course of the nineteenth century. The convention was that Quarter Sessions could not try cases that were subject to the death penalty, but whereas at the beginning of the century this applied to hundreds of offences, after the enlightened legislation between Peel's time and 1861, it was virtually confined to 'treason, murder, piracy with violence and setting fire to dockyards and arsenals'. This greatly increased the jurisdiction of Quarter Sessions and the rule became that they could not try offences where there would be a maximum life imprisonment on a first conviction, except burglary. Again, the earlier simple distinction between petty 'non-indictable' offences and serious 'indictable' ones, requiring trial before a jury at Assizes or Quarter Sessions, did not stand the test of time. It was found that some so-called 'indictable' offences were too trivial to warrant a jury trial while some 'non-indictable', summary offences, needed to be tried in a higher court by jury. These anomalies followed from the traditional classification of criminal offences as treasons, felonies and misdemeanours as the distinction between felonies and misdemeanours was notoriously unclear. The distinction was abolished by the Criminal Law Act of 1967 following the recommendation of the Criminal Law Revision Committee in 1965.

From 1945 there was a continuous effort to reform the higher criminal courts without weakening their traditional form. This culminated in the Royal Commission on Assizes and Quarter Sessions in 1967 the chairman of which was the redoubtable Lord Beeching, Chairman of the British Railway Board, and which reported in 1969. Its main recommendation, that there should be only one higher criminal court for trying criminal cases, the new Crown Court, which would be separate from the High Court, was embodied in the Courts Act of 1971. The recommendation followed from the fact that the County Quarter Sessions exhibited many anomalies. For example, on the first day of sessions as many as 20 or more justices would appear on the Bench so that the Justices of Peace Act, 1949 limited the number to a maximum of 9. There was also the problem resulting from the fact that as the county justices elected their own chairman, he was often a layman of the 'country gentleman' type, remembering that since 1835 the Borough Quarter Sessions had their Recorders. Although there was legislation in 1938 to try to remedy this defect, the legislation was ambiguous but eventually virtually all the counties had legally qualified chairmen which was statutorily enforced in 1962. However, the main post-war problem was the rapid increase in the volume of work. Between 1938 and 1959 criminal cases dealt with by Assizes and Quarter Sessions had doubled and trebled respectively but as priority was given to these, civil cases suffered massive delays which were accentuated by antiquated court procedures, with the result that prisons were seriously overcrowded by men waiting to be tried. As the problem was especially bad in south Lancashire, two new Crown Courts were established in 1956 by statute at Liverpool and Manchester respectively. However, the problem remained intense in the rest of the country and a Home Office enquiry published in 1960 showed that at the magistrates' courts most of the cases were heard within eight weeks but at Assizes and Quarter Sessions many had to wait for three or four months, or even longer. Unfortunately, a committee appointed in 1958 to investigate the problem did not recommend the extension of the Crown Court system that was working so well in south Lancashire, and which was to be applied nationally in 1971, but merely proposed tinkering with the existing organization of Assizes and Quarter Sessions. The Criminal Justice Administration Act of 1962 provided for five more High Court judges, but this improvement in the Circuit system was still tarnished by the continuous use of obsolete practices, such as the necessity for the attendance in court of a High Sheriff even though this was a mere formality. However, the Lord Chancellor was given new powers regarding the sittings of courts, the fixing of remunerations and changes in jurisdiction so as to improve the flexibility of the system. Also, the creation of Greater London in 1963 (pp. 266–7) led to a significant increase in courts in the London area. Whereas the Old Bailey or Central Criminal Court had been the Assize Court for the heavy population of London since 1834, the area was enlarged to coincide with that of Greater London in 1964. The Administration of London Act, 1964 divided Greater London into five commission areas – Inner London and four for outer London – each area being treated as any other county with its own justices, Quarter Sessions, officers and administrative system, but with the important addition of a further pool of justices on which they could draw. The Old Bailey had four sittings a year, of about three months' duration, so that it was virtually a continuous court, while it also acted as Quarter Sessions for the historic City of London. As in any other Assize Court, its judges sat by virtue of a commission which included the Lord Mayor of the City of London and the City Aldermen, but in reality it was exercised by a judge of the Queen's Bench Division, the Recorder of the City of London, the Common Sergeant and specially appointed additional judges. As these all sat separately there were a number of courts sitting simultaneously.

In spite of the improvements initiated by the Criminal Justice Administration Act of 1962, and those following the London Government Act of 1963, the increase in the number of criminal cases, with the escalation in the use of legal aid, led to intolerable delays in awaiting trial and unacceptable consequences on civil legislation.

The main causes of the inadequacy of the judicial system was that it was tied to the areas of local government, that is, to counties, boroughs and London. There were 60 towns where Assizes were held, 93 borough Quarter Sessions, 80 County Quarter Sessions, together with the Old Bailey and 5 Quarter Sessions for Greater London. In many instances two Quarter Sessions sat in the same town, one for the county and one for the borough. There was virtually no recognition of the principle of organizing a service for efficiency and the convenience of the public. Other services had long had a head office, regional offices and an operational level of offices sited so as to be convenient and accessible to people within an appropriate 'catchment area', but the system of justice was rooted in history and in so far as it was ever intelligently planned it was devised for travel on horseback. The tie with counties and boroughs was almost inevitable before the middle of the nineteenth century because the central government had virtually no provincial or regional organization . . . By the middle of the last century, with improved communications and increasingly efficient central government departments, there was no longer any necessity for relying on local authorities. When county courts were established in 1846 they were organized for convenience, ignoring traditional units, with a central administration under the Lord Chancellor. The taking over of the administration and cost of local prisons in 1877 was the first 'nationalising' by transferring a service from local to central government. Transfers of poor law, hospitals and other services in the period after the 1939–45 war involved political controversy but that has died down and these matters are commonly seen as problems of organisation. The Beeching Commission was a most suitable body to tackle the problem of the organisation of the higher courts. It is a pity that it was not done years ago but those in authority were averse to change that went beyond nibbling; by 1970 there was something of a crash programme to get a new system working before there was a great break-down.[1]

The result was the Courts Act of 1971 which introduced a new system for trying criminal cases on indictment, namely the establishment of one higher criminal court, the Crown Court, separate from the High Court. The appeal system in criminal cases had recently been reformed. Astonishingly, there was no such system in the more serious criminal cases until 1907, before which there were several obscure procedures including one called the Court for Crown Cases Reserved, established by a statute in 1848 – applying only to a conviction and not an acquittal – but this required the consent of a judge or chairman of Quarter Sessions. It was following a grotesque miscarriage of justice that the Court of Criminal Appeal was set up

---

[1] *The Machinery of Justice in England*, by R.M. Jackson, pp. 193–4.

310

in 1907 to hear appeals from the higher criminal courts of Assizes and Quarter Sessions. It, in turn, was abolished in 1966, its jurisdiction being taken over by the Court of Appeal with its two divisions, civil and criminal.

Although it is not a criminal court, the Coroner's Court has a connection with criminal proceedings. Unlike the County Courts that were founded in 1846 the Coroner's Court descends from the old county courts because at its inception in 1194 it was elected by the county with the object of protecting the Crown's fiscal rights. This applied in the case of violent death which could benefit the Crown financially because of fines, the seizure of the chattels of a convicted person, and the like, so that the holding of inquests on sudden deaths became the greater part of the work of coroners, which was redefined by the Coroners (Amendment) Act, 1926. The Coroner's Court is a fact-finding institution, without the capacity to try any civil or criminal issue even though it is a court of law.

As has been mentioned, the Scottish legal system has been much influenced by the Continental Roman Law, (p. 275). For example, in Scotland, there is no equivalent of the traditional English public preliminary hearing in the Magistrate's Court, which latter has been criticized as unnecessary and prejudicial to the defendant (see footnote p. 306). Also, in Scotland, in common with Roman Law countries, such as France, and unlike England, criminal proceedings may not be initiated by the police but by the appropriate Public Prosecutor – the Lord Advocate (at the highest level), or the Justices of the Peace Fiscal or Burgh Prosecutors.

> The lowest civil courts are the Burgh (or police) courts presided over by local councillors serving as magistrates, or, in the counties, Justices of the Peace Courts. The Sheriff Courts have both civil (corresponding in this respect to County Courts in England and Wales) and criminal jurisdiction. At the top of the criminal system is the High Court of Judiciary, and at the top of the civil system is the Court of Session.[1]

Unlike the public inquiry in the Coroner's Court in England, on a sudden or unusual death, in Scotland the matter is dealt with in private by the Procurator Fiscal.

It remains to consider the part played in the legal system by the judges. That they have retained their independence from the executive, as promulgated by the Bill of Rights in 1689, is beyond

---

[1] *Britain in the Century of Total War*, by Arthur Marwick, p. 406.

any doubt. Also, in common with other professions, but even more so, lawyers enjoy a striking degree of independence in that through their elected councils they are completely self-governing. There is the paradox that although they do not enjoy the power of 'judicial review', like judges who wield this political authority where there is a written constitution, in a more subtle sense, they certainly have more day-to-day political influence than if they were guarding a written constitution. A good example is the many discretionary powers exercised by the judges including tribunals, control over local authority by-laws, planning law, and even when parliamentary Acts:

> empower ministers to make detailed regulations roughly in conformity with a (very often vague) general intention. This ministerial discretionary power is entirely subject to control by the courts, with the effect that though an Act may not be overruled, most of the steps necessary to make the Act 'do' anything can be.[1]

On the face of it, Statutory Law (Acts of Parliament) is a straightforward, black and white concept, but there is much more to it. By their decisions and attitudes the judges can influence Parliament to legislate for a particular purpose whilst, by the same token, their interpretation of a particular statute is often as important, if not more important, than the statute itself. Then there is the important fact that Civil Law is mainly derived from Common Law, or 'judge-made' law. Budge and McKay summarize:

> The most important aspects of law that involve a judge's private ideology in his legal decisions:
>
> 1. The interpretation of statutes where they are unclear.
>
> 2. The inclusion within statutes of concepts which call for judges to decide an essentially unknowable thing; i.e. what a reasonable man would do, or whether a minister 'is satisfied that' or whether (more rarely) something is 'in the public interest'.
>
> 3. Statutes that require the judge himself to use discretion with little in the way of guide lines. Typically these are family law cases where the judge must decide himself what is in the interest of the child.[2]

---

[1]*The Changing British Political System*, by Ian Budge and David McKay, p. 167.
[2]Ibid, p. 175.

312

In addition, 'Parliament is far too busy and preoccupied to monitor what judges are doing in their vast areas of discretionary power over our lives',[1] while the Law Commissions for England and Scotland exercise considerable direct and indirect influence by virtue of their technical revisions of law which are generally approved by Parliament.[2] In their eccentric way, Budge and McKay use the above penetrating and true analysis to justify their thesis regarding the 'fragmentation' of British government. 'In many respects, the courts are yet another 'alternative government' with extensive areas of independent decision-making.'[3] As in the case of local government and the other examples of 'fragmentation' that they quote, this is yet another manifestation of the maturity, and indeed the complexity, of English political institutions and does not detract from the reality of its unitary nature, notwithstanding that this needs to be enforced, and reinforced, from time to time.[4]

4. Law and Order and the Police

As we have seen, there was no effective system of police until the force established in the Metropolis by Sir Robert Peel in 1829 was reproduced in the reformed Municipal Borough Councils after 1835 (p. 243).

> It was a disgraceful condition of things, and had many evil consequences. But the wonder is that society held together at all without the protection of a strong civic force trained to control mob violence and to detect theft and crime. That we dispensed so long with a proper police force is a testimony to the average honesty of our ancestors and to the value of the old Poor Law, in spite of all its defects.[5]

---

[1]Ibid., p. 169.

[2]The proposal to abolish committal hearings in the magistrates' courts (as noted on p. 306) follows a recommendation in 1993 by the Royal Commission on Criminal Justice.

[3]*The Changing British Political System*, by Ian Budge and David McKay, p. 159.

[4]A case in point is the recent tendency of the English Law Commission to espouse politically-correct ideas, such as the 1996 Divorce Bill, whereby 'fault' is no longer applicable, the only reason for divorce being breakdown of the marriage; thus, at a stroke, debasing the glorious institution of marriage to no more than a civil contract. This has led to a great weight of criticism, and the conservative forces in our society have been alerted to this undesirable development.

[5]*Illustrated English Social History*, (Volume 2), by G.M. Trevelyan, p. 89. Further facts and figures in this chapter are attributable to this authority.

Work was provided either in Houses of Correction or by Justices of the Peace for able-bodied men in the parishes. As Trevelyan further comments,

> We shall have occasion in later chapters to consider the serious faults of Poor Law administration in the Eighteenth century. Some of them resulted from the decline of the control exercised by the Privy Council over local magistrates and parishes, a decay of a much-needed central authority which was the heavy price paid for Parliamentary government and constitutional freedom. But the Poor Law had taken such firm root in the days of Royal Prerogative that it survived as custom of the country in Parliamentary times.[1]

Without anything like it on the Continent, where absolute monarchies continued to prevail, there was the depredation of unrelieved unemployment and poverty, especially in old age, manifested in armies of beggars who were prime revolutionary material, as well as being a constant threat to the maintenance of law and order.

> That is one reason why there was never anything like the French Revolution in our country, and why through all our political, religious and social feuds from the Seventeenth to the Nineteenth Centuries the quiet and orderly habits of the people, even in times of distress, continued upon the whole as a national characteristic.[2]

Another reason, as pointed out on page 25, was the absence of the worst excesses of absentee landlordism in England. Thirdly, what might have been the disastrous neglect of the people by the comfortable and self-satisfied Established Church of the eighteenth century, was obviated by the work of the Dissenters in the early part of the century, and by John Wesley, who lived and died as a Tory parson, from the middle of the century. Both had to contend with the fact that the almost entirely rurally-based Church of England had neglected the inhabitants of both the earlier and the later towns where it was common for people to know only of the word 'Christ' as a swear word, while Wesley and his Methodist followers, such as George Whitfield, also covered large tracts of the countryside, where the people were introduced to a Christ whose dynamic message of

---

[1]*Illustrated English Social History*, (Volume 2), by G.M. Trevelyan, p. 88.
[2]Ibid., p. 89.

love and hope could be better conveyed in the open fields and in the highways and byways, than in the beautiful yet socially stratified village churches. The great French historian, Elie Halevy, has stated that it was the influence of Evangelicalism on the British aristocracy in the nineteenth century which enabled the country to surmount the worst excesses of the industrial revolution and the revolutionary forces that plagued the other countries of Europe – except Belgium.

However, as always, the line between an orderly and a disorderly England was a narrow one while it remained, and remains, a land of bewildering contrasts. A narrow and repressive government, as between the French Revolution of 1789 and the death of Castlereagh in 1822, can ensure the maintenance of law and order but, at the same time, brutalize the people, while too tolerant government, such as the permissive governments of the 1960s and 1970s, can unleash anti-social forces which always reside a little below the surface unless they are suppressed. In the same way as the Abolition of Slavery in 1833 soon disillusioned the liberal believers in the idea of the 'noble savage' our more recent social reformers have no answer as to how to control the very much more aggressive and dangerous elements for which they are responsible – except to spend more and more money on enlarging the police force which, by definition, is not the answer to the problem. The historic contrasts in London afford a good example of the eternal truth that beneath what appears to be a calm and orderly surface in society there is an underlying vein of unpredictable violence which only the most purblind of rulers will ignore.

> Two miles away from the Parliament at Westminster and the Queen's Court at St James's lay the centre of the greatest city in the world, less amenable to the jurisdiction of Court and Parliament than any other portion of English soil. London was governed by her own freely elected magistrates; policed, in so far as she was policed at all, by her own constables; guarded by her own militia; and rendered formidable to the neighbouring seat of government by the largest and least manageable mob in the island.[1]

With more than a tenth of the population of England, London overshadowed her nearest rivals, Bristol and Norwich, while she was the *entrepot* for the English towns and villages from which she drew her requirements, such as food, raw materials and coal, and supplied them with her own manufactured luxury goods as well as foreign

---

[1] *Illustrated English Social History*, (Volume 3), by G.M. Trevelyan, p. 39.

products arising from the dominance of the Port of London in trade with the East Indies, Europe, the Mediterranean, Africa and America. It is difficult to envisage in our day that the City proper, within its ancient walls, which survived to the end of the eighteenth century and which is now deserted at night, was the most densely populated area in England. It was still the place of residence as well as of trade for its wealthy citizens, although by this time the grandees had left their ancestral palaces in the City and the Strand (one of the City's limits) for what later came to be known as the West End.

This is not surprising in view of the appalling and filthy living conditions of the mass of dockers and unskilled and casual labourers, both within and just beyond the City limits, with overcrowding and lack of sanitation, in spite of the rebuilding after the Great Fire in 1666. As a consequence the death rate was far greater than the birth rate and the population only increased because of immigration from the country, a problem which became worse as gin-drinking began to overtake the drinking of ale. As has already been intimated, the ignorance of the unskilled workers was almost total, for their lack of knowledge of the gospels was merely a reflection of their general educational neglect. This led to the foundation of Charity Schools by public subscription and to Parliament in 1711 providing the funds to build 50 new churches in the towns so that the Established Church moved in tardily where the Dissenters had already established their own chapels. However, London remained notable for the existence of a large criminal element – thieves, highwaymen and harlots – with violence and theft being commonplace. In the evenings, the criminals had the place to themselves except for the fact that gangs of the younger gentry also roamed the streets in search of adventure. The magistrates and the constables completely failed to combat this lawlessness except for the remarkable Fielding brothers (the novelist Henry Fielding and his blind brother, Sir John), magistrates, who in the middle of the century set up their famous operation in Bow Street. Nevertheless, Londoners remained excitable and quarrelsome so that there was always a danger that what began as a legitimate political protest would be transformed by the 'mob' into a frightening riot. Such an event were the Gordon Riots in 1780 when an orgy of thieving and arson led to the burning of seventy houses and four gaols by the London mob and which would have been even worse if the weather had not been particularly still. But we must not forget that London was, and is, a city of contrasts. It included a large number of clerks, managers, shopkeepers and middlemen as well as those engaged in manufacturing, and the skilled work of finishing processes in the luxury trades, including the Huguenot silk manufacturers who had settled in Spitalfields after their expulsion from France for their Calvinist beliefs towards the end of the seventeenth century. Its role as the financial centre of the country was established by the foundation of the Bank of England in 1694 (by a Scotsman, William Paterson) and by the flowering of the joint-stock principle and of the later Stock Exchange by the activities of the businessmen in the City coffeehouses. By this time, political, religious and financial pamphleteering was well established and the growth of interest in science was recognized by Charles II when he founded the Royal Society. Interest in literature was broadened by the down-to-earth writings of Steele and Addison and the imaginative work of Defoe, while a new type of stage entertainment appeared in the form of opera. As Trevelyan concludes: '. . . the capital contained, alongside the most brutal ignorance, an immense and varied stock of skill and intellect.'[1]

In dealing with the background to the question of law and order we move on a century or more and to the wider national sphere, in country and town, and we note the fact that as a result of the French Revolution the Tory Party became reactionary and opposed to all reform, political and religious, and denounced all reformers as Jacobins, including the leader of the Whigs, Charles James Fox (Fox the Younger. 1749–1806) who supported the revolution and the writing of the republican and revolutionary Thomas Paine, whose book, *The Rights of Man*, (1791–92), was suppressed by the Government. It was a time of the hardening of the English party system, for those Whigs who had been hostile to George III but who could not condone revolution left Fox and supported the Government which Pitt had led since 1783, and who can thus be said to have broken with his reforming past and who ceased to enjoy a great measure of his previous independence from both Whig and Tory influences. The fact that Pitt was head of such a reactionary government indicated the extent to which both the rulers and the people felt threatened by revolutionary forces both at home and abroad, although he remained essentially a reformer for he resigned in 1801 when the King vetoed his Bill for Catholic Emancipation, which would have allowed Irish Catholics to sit in the newly created British/ Irish Parliament at Westminster following the Act of Union in 1800.[2]

---

[1] *Illustrated English Social History*, (Volume 3), by G.M. Trevelyan, p. 41.
[2] Pitt became Prime Minister again in 1804 for only he had the capability to form the Third Coalition against Napoleon, but the decisive defeat of the Austrian army at Ulm and Austerlitz in 1805 led to his premature death in 1806, in spite of the glorious victory of Trafalgar in October, 1805.

However, as a young man, Pitt had witnessed the Gordon Riots in 1780 where the mob was every bit as violent as that which took the Bastille in 1789, the difference being that whereas Louis XVI was cowardly and ineffectual, George III saved the situation in London by his personal courage and leadership. It is an excellent example of my contention that the forces of violence must be ruthlessly contained by governments and that the line between the maintenance of law and the outbreak of violence is a narrow one, which is not the same thing as saying that governments should not condone liberal reform or be illiberal and reactionary. The latter was the case when the Combination Acts of 1799–1800 described trade unions as a restraint on trade and on free-bargaining, and made them illegal and their members liable to imprisonment. The earlier factories had inevitably led to the formation of locally-based trade unions for the purpose of raising wages by combined action, while their leaders tended to be radicals inspired by the writings of Thomas Paine and supporters of the French Revolution, but the brutal suppression of the trade unions led to great embitterment among the factory workers. On the other hand, from the Government's point of view, it is significant that the Combination Acts were introduced by William Wilberforce who, with Lord Shaftesbury, was the most famous of the Evangelicals or Humanitarians owing to the fact that he devoted his life to the freeing of negroes from slavery.

Following Trafalgar, Napoleon enforced an economic blockade of England by the Berlin Decrees of 1806, known as the Continental System, to which England replied by Orders in Council declaring a blockade of all ports that enforced the Continental System. However, well before this time the war led to the elimination of the supply of foreign corn which was becoming necessary owing to the rapid growth in population as a result of greatly improved medical facilities, leading to a sharp reduction in the death rate. For example, between 1801 and 1831 the population of England, Wales and Scotland increased from 11 to 16½ million. Between 1792, the year before war with France began, and 1812, when Napoleon invaded Moscow, wheat rose from 43 shillings a quarter to 126 shillings, with the consequence that the poor in town and country suffered severe hardship from the unprecedented sharp increase in the price of bread. Hardest hit, though, were the agricultural labourers in southern England. Not only were they not in a position to combine to improve their position, like the factory workers, but rural wages in the northern counties were higher than those in the south, owing to the need to compete against the neighbouring factories and mines. Also, the enclosures of the open fields and common lands, and the decline of cottage industries, affected the southern labourers more than those in the north. In fact, it was to avert the threat of starvation that in 1795 the magistrates of Berkshire met at Speenhamland, near Newbury, to follow the ancient custom of fixing a minimum wage for the county in accordance with the price of bread but, instead, they took the fatal decision to draw up a scale, or dole, to be paid from the poor rate – a certain sum a head for the labourer and each member of his family, the amount to vary with the price of bread. What became known as the Speenhamland system was adopted by the magistrates throughout the southern counties, especially, with the result that the labourers affected, the most numerous class in England, were pauperized by being perpetually dependent on parish relief. What was applied as a temporary wartime measure, lasted until 1834 (p. 243) virtually 20 years after the war ended. The obverse was that the large landowners, who were enjoying unexampled prosperity as a result of the high price of corn, had their wage bills subsidized by the smaller contributors to the parish rates, including the small farmer, whose decline had been delayed by the high price of corn but who nevertheless did not benefit from Speenhamland, as he and his family worked their own land and did not employ labour. One can scarcely envisage a situation more socially and morally unjust, let alone inimical to the maintenance of law and order, especially as the coming of peace in 1815 led to no relief.

For a quarter of a century the war had caused unexampled suffering at home. As wars go, it was not a particularly bloody one from the British point of view, for, as usual, there was no conscription (unlike the Continental armies), except for the press-ganging of the navy, and Wellington's famous victories were won by a comparatively small professional army at a cost of around 50,000 lives, comparatively less than those of Marlborough's campaigns a century earlier. As Wellington said: 'The Battle of Waterloo was won on the playing fields of Eton'. On the other hand, after visiting the poorest parts of Turkey, Byron stated that he had never seen such squalor as in England. But the suffering was not confined to the labouring classes for the introduction of Pitt's income tax in 1797 and the exceptionally high parish rates were vexatious, to say the least. Much more serious were the effects of the Continental System and Orders in Council on trade and manufacturing. For example, the output of cotton and wool mills exceeded sales so that bankruptcies took place and workmen were sacked, while it was a bankrupt, broken and deranged trader, John Bellingham, who assassinated the Prime Minister, Spencer Perceval, in 1812, a unique occurrence, for assassination is not in our tradition. It was also the British Navy's insistence on searching neutral ships that led to the abortive war with the United States between 1812 and 1815. As has already been noted, the exception was the landowners and farmers. As Byron wrote:

See those inglorious Cincinnati swarm,
Farmers of war, dictators of the farm;
Their ploughshare was the sword in hireling hands,
Their fields manured by the gore of other lands;
Safe in their barns, these Sabine tillers sent
Their brethren out to battle. Why? for rent!
Year after year they voted cent for cent,
Blood, sweat, and tear-wrung millions – why? for rent!!
They roar'd, they dined, they drank, they swore they meant
To die for England, – why then live? for rent!

('The Age of Bronze', 1823)

However, booms always come to an end and this one was no exception. With Napoleon's retreat from German lands in 1813 the Continental System came to an end and foreign corn poured into Britain, following which its price collapsed and thousands of farmers went bankrupt. This was an eventuality that the Tory, landed interest was not prepared to accept so that, with its predominance in Parliament, it passed the Corn Laws in 1815 which stipulated that no foreign corn should enter Britain unless the home price was 80 shillings a quarter – a starvation level! The result was that the price of a four-pound loaf rose from an 'average' price of tenpence to one and tuppence (with the price being higher in some places), compared to a pound and eight shillings a week which was the most that would be earned by factory labourers and agricultural labourers, respectively. Furthermore, the Speenhamland system broke down for in most places the rates were so high that it was impracticable to raise them any higher. With starvation the only alternative the desperate agricultural labourer turned to poaching to keep his family alive, but whereas the plentiful rabbits, hares, birds and fishes cost the landowners nothing, and could easily be spared, the Tory Government passed a new Game Law in 1816 which enacted seven years transportation for the minor offence of poaching, or even being caught with poaching equipment. In addition, the landowners virtually declared war on the poachers by planting killer spring guns and mantraps in their woodlands. As few ever returned home from the convict settlements the poachers were increasingly prepared to kill gamekeepers rather than be taken. Thus the landowners had brutalized the previously quiescent agricultural labourer so that the capacity for mob violence was no longer confined to London and the towns. Even after the end of the reactionary excesses of the Tory Government in 1822 (see p. 324) there was the infamous incident of the Tolpuddle 'Martyrs' in 1834 when starving labourers in Dorset paraded to demand a wage of half-a-crown a day. For their 'riotous' behaviour three of the leaders were hanged and four hundred and twenty were transported to Australia as convicts. The fact that these latter were later pardoned and returned to their suffering families only adds to the culpability of the perpetrators of this crime for it is those responsible for the original conviction who should have been transported! As an American observer wrote in 1830:

> The term pauper as used in England and more particularly in agricultural districts, embraces that numerous class of society who depend for subsistence solely upon the labour of their hands.[1]

This state of affairs compares most unfavourably with that a century or so previously.

> The observant eyes of Defoe, as he rode through Queen Anne's England, had been pleased by the harmony of the economic and social fabric. It was shattered now, giving place to a chaos of rival interests, town against country, rich against poor.[2]

Defoe would have felt the same about the English village in Walpole's time as Prime Minister (1721–42) where the majority of Englishmen lived in a truly integrated society, with different grades of property, craftsmanship and wealth but where the poorer were sustained in times of bad harvests by the cottage industries, mainly spinning and weaving. It was accepted that the English villager was more prosperous and independent than any Continental peasant. A century after Defoe, another horseman, William Cobbett, on his 'Rural Rides', (1830), noted starkly the decline of the rural poor, as has been described here, and launched an inspired crusade against their oppressors. The village harmony of a century earlier had been replaced by resentment, and even hostility, between the farmer and the cottager and, what would have been previously unheard-of, the latter was reflected by rick-burning through the operations of 'Captain Swing'. (It has been pointed out by later historians that, despite his sufferings, the English labourer of this period was not

---

[1]Quoted in *Illustrated English Social History*, (Volume 2), by G.M. Trevelyan, p. 7.
[2]Ibid., p. 3.

subject to the kind of social pressures and conflict to which his Continental brother was subjected. No doubt life was not uniformly black for the southern agricultural labourer but historical revisions, although interesting, should not detract from the truth of Trevelyan's broad picture.)

Similarly, the situation in the towns had deteriorated markedly by the middle of the Napoleonic wars and unemployment, low wages and hunger were endemic in the towns of Nottinghamshire, Yorkshire and Lancashire. As the industrialists economized by introducing or adding more machinery, 'Captain Ludd' organized machine-breaking in the Midlands (1811–12) as well as demanding that existing laws, some dating back to Elizabeth, should be applied for the regulation of wages and hours, which had at least been recognized, if erroneously, by the rural magistrates, but in 1813 the new Liverpool Government, predictably, repealed the statutes giving magistrates power to enforce minimum wages. Although Liverpool was Prime Minister between 1812–27 the strongest influence and effective leader in his Cabinet was Castlereagh, between 1812 and his death in 1822.[1] Whereas Castlereagh carried on Pitt's work of organizing the coalition which finally defeated Napoleon and, with Metternich, was mainly responsible for the statesmanlike and moderate Treaty of Vienna in 1815, at home he was completely reactionary, especially when the no-nonsense Duke of Wellington joined the Government in 1818 after his brilliant military exploits. After the war, which was followed by a slump in Britain and Europe, the workers of the industrial North, many trained to speak in the Dissenting chapels which were looked down upon by the Anglican middle classes, vented their radicalism in an orgy of public meetings. The only forces for reform were outside Parliament the main one of which was Jeremy Bentham, with his Utilitarian movement, who criticized the archaic legal system which had made a God of Common Law, as we have seen, and who demanded parliamentary reform, a cry which was taken up by the radical orators. Unfortunately, to the Tory Government this demand was tantamount to revolution in spite of the fact that a great number of constituencies consisted of 'rotten' and 'pocket' boroughs where there were only a handful of voters.

In 1816–17 there were Radical meetings throughout the north, an

---

[1]If Margaret Thatcher had remained in power and contested successfully the 1992 election, she would have been the longest continuous-serving Prime Minister since Lord Liverpool instead of merely that for the twentieth century.

'insurrection' in Derbyshire and dangerous riots in London. The extremely radical traditionalist, Cobbett, in the eyes of the authorities, was fomenting trouble and a new development was the outbreak of unlicensed assemblies to practise drill and the use of arms, not for defensive purposes, but to be used against an oppressive government. This latter was in a cleft stick because there was no effective police force and juries mainly refused to convict those apprehended as the penalties were so severe. It thus resorted to its last desperate resource, and in 1817 suspended the Habeas Corpus Act so that it was able to imprison arbitrarily the main speakers and troublemakers and gain a brief respite, but when it was restored, a year later, the speakers immediately continued their agitation, including Cobbett, who returned from the United States where he had fled. In 1819 a large mass meeting was held at St Peter's Fields at Manchester where 'Orator' Hunt and other Radicals spoke. The local magistrates took the ill-fated decision to send troops to arrest Hunt and when they found their way impeded, drew their swords and charged, killing and injuring many people in the process – many more, in fact, than historians have recorded. Because this infamous and uncharacteristic act was perpetrated by dragoons who had won the praises of the nation at Waterloo, it was bitterly described as the Charge of Peterloo. Its results were entirely negative. The radicals became increasingly hostile, the Whigs in Parliament, whose opposition had been ineffectual, embarked on the course which led to their coming to power in 1830 and, most important, there was a reaction and a repulsion by the mass of sober-thinking Englishmen against anti-Jacobin Toryism. Nevertheless, this did not prevent Castlereagh from passing the Six Acts in 1819 by which there were to be no assemblies for drill and no political meeting without permission from the magistrates, while there was to be a penal stamp duty on pamphlet literature and justices were to be enabled to search for arms. In other words, there was the complete cessation of free speech and one had to go back to the Rye House Plot of 1683 for a comparable reaction by the Government. The only reason why it worked as well as it did was that, in spite of the fact that by 1820 one third of the population lived in towns (and by 1850 one half), the factory districts in Lancashire and other northern areas where Radicalism was strongest, were still occupied by a comparatively small minority of the population, for the great majority of the English working class were still employed in the old pursuits of agriculture, pre-Industrial Revolution industry, domestic service or as seamen. Then there was the Cato Street Conspiracy in 1820 when Arthur Thistlewood and a group of Radicals planned to assassinate the cabinet 'en bloc'. However, the plan misfired and the conspirators were apprehended, but not before Thistlewood had killed a man and escaped. He was captured next day and executed soon after. The incident reveals the tensions of the day and the unpopularity of the Government which increased immeasurably when the unpopular Prince Regent ascended the throne in 1820 and involved the Government in his unsuccessful attempt to gain a divorce against his popular wife, Caroline of Brunswick. The fact that the Bill for this purpose was defeated in Parliament shows that the Whigs were getting their act together. The final act was that the strain proved to be far too much even for such a strong character as Castlereagh, for in 1822 his mind gave way, he committed suicide and the volatile Londoners jeered and gloated at his funeral cortège. Lord Sidmouth, who had been his Home Secretary and ally in his reactionary legislation, resigned and although Lord Liverpool remained Premier, the real leaders of the Government became the promoted Tory reformers – Canning as Foreign Secretary, Peel as Home Secretary and Huskisson as President of the Board of Trade.

Thus was initiated a new era for the Tory Party as well as a new era for England as the three new Tory leaders continued the work of reforming English institutions that had been begun by Pitt after the War of American Independence but from which he had been distracted by the French Revolution. Each of these three great men played a crucial part. George Canning, far the best equipped as a politician and a human being, took Castlereagh's place as effective leader of the ministry and was mainly responsible for the new spirit of toleration that led to the repeal of the hated Combination Acts in 1824. The trade unions immediately abused their new freedom and the demand arose for the old restrictions to be reimposed, but the new 1825 Act applied certain restrictions while it confirmed the main reforms and was the basis of our trade union liberty and law. As Foreign Secretary, Canning was one of our greatest. In an age when there was far too little liberalism at home he initiated Britain's nineteenth century tradition and reputation for supporting liberal movement abroad, yet, at the same time, championing Britain's interests – as he did in securing freedom from Turkey for Greece and for the Spanish colonies in South America. William Huskisson was a master of detail and a disciple of Pitt, and who for 20 years had studied the ruinous effects of bureaucratic restrictions and duties on commerce and trade imposed during war and by the much older Navigation Acts. Like Walpole before him in 1721 and Pitt, after 1782, Huskisson set about the task of reforming the situation with the result that by 1824 prosperity had returned. Even though the boom peaked out temporarily it is one of the many examples provided by history of the fruitlessness of international trade restrictions, not only in regard to the growth of international trade and wealth but to that of the country or countries imposing the restrictions. (The difficulties faced by the organization of the General Agreement on Tariffs and Trade [GATT] of 1947 in promoting international free trade in the post-war world makes one despair for the future when one considers the inward-looking economic predilections of the European Union and, indeed, years of negotiations between the two institutions to free agricultural trade have virtually broken down, due to the intransigence of the vested interests behind the Common Agricultural policy, especially those of France.)

However, we have yet to deal with the third and, from the point of view of our present discussion, most important member of the three leaders of the Government, Sir Robert Peel. Peel was a baronet and the son of a wealthy Midlands manufacturer who was public-spirited enough to agitate for the improvement of conditions in the factories for children, especially of the pauper apprentices. His son inherited his orderly and business-like mind and devoted his life to the pursuance of the public interest. In both respects he could be said to be the true inheritor of Pitt, and as soon as he became Home Secretary he immersed himself in solving the problem of crime and disorder – more of which anon. In the meantime, it is necessary to deal briefly with the outcome of the brilliant Tory reforming ministry which, as might be expected, drew much of its support in and out of Parliament from the Whigs and Radicals. In fact, its real opposition sat on Tory benches and Lord Liverpool's main and extremely useful function was to prevent an irreconcilable clash between the two sections of the Party. When Liverpool had a paralytic stroke early in 1827 Canning succeeded him as Prime Minister with the support of a number of the Whigs. Peel was no reactionary but he was much more of a rigid Tory than Canning and Huskisson so that, together with Wellington, he resigned with four other Tories. Unfortunately, future years of greatness were denied to Canning when he died after only five months in office and his ineffectual successor, Lord Goderich (1827–28), was succeeded by Wellington, with the support of Peel, both of whom were opposed to Catholic Emancipation and Parliamentary Reform, two of the three main questions of the day. The third question, the Corn Law, was largely mitigated by Huskisson before he left the Government after quarrelling with its leaders. His Sliding Scale of 1828 substituted an import duty, which was to vary inversely with the market price, in place of an outright prohibition and thus alleviated the worst suffering under the original system. Wellington's and Peel's policy was confounded by Daniel O'Connell and the people of County Clare, in Ireland, who elected him to Parliament with a large majority in 1828, but he could not, as a Catholic, take the requisite oath which would enable him to take his seat. The Irish Catholics were ready to take up arms if the oath was not waived and although for the greater part the Tories were against concession their leaders, Wellington and Peel, realistically and reluctantly passed the Catholic Emancipation Act in 1829, with Whig votes. From this time on the demand for Parliamentary Reform was insurmountable, especially as, in France, the failure of the Bourbon, Charles X, to make concessions to popular demands, led to the rising in Paris in 1830 and to his dethronement. With the accession of the Whig, William IV, in 1830 in place of the Tory, George IV, later in the year, and with the Canningite Tories voting with the Whigs, Wellington lost his majority and had to resign. The Whig aristocrats, under Lord Grey (1830–34), took over and passed the First Reform Bill in 1832. It was the end of the Tory ascendancy which had prevailed since the French Revolution. The fact that Peel had played such a major part in the Tory Party before 1830 and was to be the virtual founder of the modern Conservative Party in the following years (the name Conservative first appeared in 1831), gives more than a clue to his essential greatness and to his importance in our history. We have yet to deal in detail with his unique contribution in our history of Law and Order and the Police.

I say unique, advisedly, and I have given this comparatively long introduction to the question of law and order which had been a problem since the Middle Ages because Peel's work in combatting it was the point in our history when, in retrospect, it can be seen that it was not necessarily or entirely insoluble. In other words, from his day the problem of law and order was never the same and had entered its modern phase even though it might be argued that this is far worse than that which preceded it – but this brings up the wider and more complex question that I asked in the first sentence of Chapter 5. To recapitulate; for many years the main causes of crime were, apparently, ignorance, appalling living conditions and the ease with which offenders escaped justice. The first two of these causes have been transformed by improvements in education and in the standard of living, which leads to the belief that the vast section of society which does not have innate criminal predilections can be increased by means of these and other improvements in society, but that there will always be a hard-core criminal element owing to the 'imperfectibility' of man. Peel, and his successors, were concerned with the third cause.

The eighteenth century was notorious for the fact that it attempted to prevent crime by enacting ferocious punishments for trivial offences. The death penalty was imposed for over 200 'crimes' including not only horse and sheep stealing and poaching but stealing in a shop to the value of five shillings and stealing anything, such as even a handkerchief, from an individual's person. As we have seen, the eighteenth century was also an age of great contrasts and along with the age of savage punishments went the age of humanitarianism so that juries refused to convict even though they knew that the prisoner was guilty. The Benthamites were also highly critical of the fact that attempted murder was still only lightly punished and that owing to the illogical and over-elaborate chaos of the Common Law it was easy for a real criminal to escape punishment on purely technical grounds. The situation appertaining was that five out of six thieves arrested could avoid conviction in this manner while the unlucky one would be hanged – *'pour encourager les autres'* – as the eighteenth-century expression went. Justice for its own sake, did not enter the equation. Peel immediately set about remedying this unsatisfactory state of affairs because he had understanding and vision enough to accept the Benthamite criticism that if crime was excessive the law and its administration must be largely to blame and, above all, the punishment must be made to fit the crime, and then to be exacted. Thus, he embarked on the historic achievement of reforming the savage criminal code that he inherited, reducing the number of capital offences by a hundred, in the first instance, by carrying four Bills through Parliament in 1823 to that effect. Among other beneficial consequences, this had the inestimable result of significantly reducing the incentive to murder by, for example, the starving poachers and, accordingly, a very important step was taken to alleviate the brutalization of society.

Peel's second great achievement was to improve markedly the possibility of arrest for, as we have stated before, there was no effective police force in the country so that in the event of trouble, the only recourse was to call out the troops, as in the cases of the Gordon Riots and Peterloo when, invariably, and especially in the latter case, the problem was seriously aggravated. This was due also to the unpopularity of the 'Redcoats' who had no barracks but who were billeted in alehouses where they lived and quarrelled in sordid conditions, with the dregs of society. To digress, another aspect of the brutal nature of life in the 'Age of Elegance' was that of the press-ganged sailors whose food was scarce and foul, pay inadequate and irregular, health provision non-existent and discipline unbelievably severe, enforced by the whip, there being one example of a soldier receiving 30,000 lashes in 16 years – and surviving to tell the tale.

> These were the men who by sea and land won England her empire and defended her trade and secured her wealth and happiness at home, and such was their reward.[1]

Perhaps the main reason for not forming a proper police force for so long was the refusal to bear the expense, in the form of increased rates, as was the case in so many reforms making life more tolerable, especially in the towns. However, the clear-headed Peel obviously regarded as intolerable the policing of the towns by a few decrepit watchmen and of the countryside by the parish beadle and the magistrates' servants, supplemented by special constables called upon, at the last moment, in times of crises. Thus, as already mentioned in the first sentence of this section (p. 313), he completed his work for establishing law and order by the creation of the Metropolitan Police in 1829 – in his second term of office, under Wellington – to take the place of the watchmen and the Bow Street runners. It was this 'new force' that saved London during the Reform Bill troubles in 1831, unlike Bristol and other towns which suffered from the riotous Radical mobs. The blue-coated 'Peelers' or 'Bobbies' were an immediate success, mainly because their top hats (later changed to helmets) and staves emphasized their civilian character, unlike their Continental equivalents which, with their employment of steel and gunpowder, were effectively an adjunct of the army. As we have seen, Peel's police were gradually introduced throughout the country and by 1856 every county and borough had to have a police force, partly local, partly national in its administration, discipline and finance. Riot, and fear of riot, ceased to play such an important part in English life.

> The days of the inefficient Watchman of the Dogberry and Verges type were gone by for ever; person and property were well guarded at last without any sacrifice of freedom, and mobs and meetings could be dealt with, punctually and quietly, without calling on armed forces as at Peterloo.[2]

Emphasis has been placed on the dichotomy in the eighteenth century of the complete lack of a general social conscience, leading to

---

[1] *Illustrated English Social History*, (Volume 3), by G.M. Trevelyan, p. 55.
[2] Ibid, p. 68.

the existence of inhuman conditions and situations as well as to the all-pervading brutality, alongside the flowering of the spirit of humanitarianism and philanthropy in individuals. A good example was the appalling mortality of poor infants, especially bastard children, thousands of whom were abandoned; of the remainder who became a charge on the parish, only a few lived to be apprenticed. The sailor, Captain Coram, could not bear the sight of these deserted children lying dying on the roadside while passers-by took absolutely no notice, so that he obtained a charter to build a Foundling Hospital in London 1745 which existed until the early twentieth century, which saved many infant lives and brought up and apprenticed many deserted children to trades. Even more important, was the work of Jonas Hanway who, in the early days of George III, who acceded in 1760, finally succeeded in obtaining an Act of Parliament which compelled the London parishes to move their 'parish infants' out of the deadly workhouses into the much more salacious country cottages. A parallel development was the earliest advocacy of prison reform which, indirectly, was much more important in regard to Law and Order and the Police. English prisons were in a scandalous state for the whole of the century for, again, owing to the reluctance to spend money, they were farmed out to completely undesirable characters by the local authorities instead of employing properly-paid public officials. As early as 1729 the humanitarian, General Oglethorpe, who was particularly concerned by the cruelties in debtors' prisons, had persuaded Parliament to enquire into the scandals at the Fleet and Marshalsea, where the gaolers tortured debtors to death in the pointless endeavour to extract money from men who, by definition, did not possess any. Although some of the worst abuses were curbed there was little, if any, overall improvement. Thus, John Howard was to begin his life's work in 1773 in an unsuccessful attempt to persuade the justices of Bedfordshire and the adjoining counties to pay regular salaries to the gaolers instead of fees extorted from the prisoners. But Howard was to have a long and 'uphill' struggle for the 'public' of the day were just not interested in what went on in these sordid and cruel institutions, while they were still eager viewers, including respectable personages such as parsons, of public hangings. However, in two important respects, as well as in regard to the general concept of the Rule of Law, at least until the inception of the Code Napoleon and, in spite of all its faults as pointed out by Bentham, English justice was probably the best in the world, as Blackstone claimed in his monumental *Commentaries on the Law of England* in 1765. They were: first, the prisoner in political cases had the opportunity to

329

defend himself, following the practices established since the Revolution of 1688–89, as embodied in the Treason Law of 1695; secondly, torture was not allowed in order to obtain confessions although, as we have seen, it was used as a punishment, especially in the army and the navy. When penal reform did finally take place Peel was its instrument, for it was due to his support that the Gaols Act was passed in 1823. The Bill, which defined and consolidated prison law, from as far back as the reign of Edward III, and enacted the improvement of prison discipline, was also a great reforming Act for it introduced 'most of the principles of enlightened prison administration advocated by a generation of penal reformers'.[1] In all, it 'was a landmark in the history of penal legislation'.[2] It remains to link the study of law and order, on the one hand, with the study of the police, on the other, by turning to the earlier legal and judicial contacts of the latter with those who had been apprehended or arrested.

This linkage was noted on pages 306 as follows:

> After the abolition of the Grand Juries in 1933 persons have been sent for trial direct from the preliminary enquiry by the justices – the committal hearings in magistrates' courts under the terms of the 1933 Administration of Justices Act in order to ensure that no one stood trial at a higher court unless a strong prima facie case was established. However, by the middle of the nineteenth century, with the creation of an efficient police force, it was no longer necessary for the justices to 'get up' a case so that the police became responsible for deciding, on a judicial basis, whether the prosecution had produced sufficient evidence for the accused to be sent for trial at Assizes and Quarter Sessions.

In other words, it was the police who became the prosecution and 'got up' the case and it was at this point that English (and Welsh) practice departed from that in Scotland where it was and is the responsibility of a judicial officer (p. 311), or for that matter from European countries (a member of the judiciary such as the '*juge d'instruction* in France'), other western democracies (an independent civilian officer) or the United States (an elected politician in the form of the District Attorney). However, when 'the police' (before 1986)[3]

---

[1]*The Life of Sir Robert Peel to 1830*, by Norman Gash, pp. 315–16.
[2]Ibid., p. 315.
[3]See page 332 for the creation of the Crown Prosecution Service in 1986 which took over from the police the decision regarding prosecution in England and Wales.

prosecuted, the legal position was that they were merely exercising the right open to any member of the public to institute criminal proceedings. Usually, these latter were agreeable to leave the conduct of criminal proceedings to the police so that most prosecutions became 'police prosecutions', the police determined that a criminal charge should be made and unless the complainant conducted his own case, a police officer became the prosecutor. Over the years, there was controversy and criticism by the legal profession of 'police advocacy' so that, following the recommendation of the Royal Commission on the Police in 1962, most police officers were increasingly confined to presenting the simpler cases in which all that was necessary was to get the case before the court. This situation was a vast improvement on that in the middle of the nineteenth century when often there was no preparation of a prosecution, and at the trial court the clerk merely gave a copy of the indictment of the accused, and the deposition to a barrister, who attempted to conduct the case with these briefest of instructions or, even worse, there was no barrister and the judge conducted the case from the deposition.

Nevertheless, until recently, there was no uniform system except in the comparatively few serious cases sent to the Director of Public Prosecutions. The DPP dates back to 1879. He is appointed by the Home Secretary, and although he is not involved with criminal investigation which is carried out by the police, he occupies a central position in the administration of criminal justice. His main functions are:

1. He gives advice if he thinks it right to do so to those who apply, whether to government departments, police or others. He may give advice orally.

2. The police must report to him certain offences that are specified in the Regulations; there is quite a substantial list, which includes many offences because they are serious or because they are difficult. When there has been an investigation of a complaint against a police officer, unless the chief officer is satisfied that no criminal offence has been committed, he must send the papers to the Director.

3. The Director prosecutes:

   a. In murder and in all offences punishable with death.[1]
   b. In cases referred to him by government departments, if he

---

[1] Or comparable punishment following the abolition of the death penalty.

thinks there should be a prosecution. The Home Secretary can require him to prosecute.

c. In any case which appears to him to be of importance or difficulty or which for any other reason requires his intervention.[1]

Again, until recently, the prosecuting solicitor advised, but the decision to prosecute was taken by the Chief Constable which was unsatisfactory because it led to regional and unpredictable differences in policy, apart from the general question as to whether the chief constable was the right person or authority to have the responsibility of exercising this 'judicial' discretion. Although it is beyond the scope of this section and book, mention must be made of the extremely important creation in October 1986, of the independent Crown Prosecution Service throughout England and Wales which has taken the decision regarding prosecution out of the hands of the police. It is based in areas, each with a Chief Crown Prosecutor and a legally trained staff of civil servants, all under the control of the Director of Public Prosecutions. Thus, in this respect England (and Wales) has come into line with Scotland and the rest of the world. Similarly, the lack of uniformity of police practice was dealt with by the Police and Criminal Evidence Act of 1984 which was:

> The biggest reform in police power this century . . . The Act's main value lies in codifying what are basically the best practices from the past and applying them uniformly across the land.[2]

Thus, although the police no longer make the decision regarding the prosecution they are still concerned with their historic function of the investigation of crime which involves the controversial subject of interrogation. On the one hand, the police must be permitted to ask questions but, on the other hand, they do not have the overriding authority to compel a person to answer. Although a witness may be compelled to attend a court for the purpose of answering questions he can refuse to do so before proceedings actually commence. Also, the police may ask a person to go to a police station to help them and be questioned by them for many hours, but they have no power to detain a person for questioning. In point of fact, most of the problems with interrogation have not arisen in the case of potential

---

[1] *The Machinery of Justice in England*, by R.M. Jackson, p. 220.
[2] *The Changing British Political System*, by Ian Budge and David McKay, p. 197. Further facts and figures in this chapter are attributable to this authority.

witnesses or potential suspects but in those of definite suspects and those who have become 'accused', for it is at this stage that an individual's liberty is most threatened as British subjects have not had statutory protection from intimidation by the police. For example, statements made by him are not 'admissible in evidence' at the trial unless they accord with 'judicial requirements'. Again:

> It is a rule of evidence that a confession is inadmissible if it is given 'involuntarily' (a statement is said to be involuntary if it is obtained from the suspect by 'fear of prejudice or hope of advantage exercised or held out by a person in authority'). The same rule applied to statements which amount to rather less than full-scale confessions (and which are known as 'verbals' or 'admissions'). It is needless to add that 'prejudice' includes acts of physical violence.[1]

As in the case of chief constables deciding on whether or not to prosecute the problem was that police interrogators were being asked to act in a 'judicial' capacity, something for which they had not been trained so that guidance was asked of 12 judges in 1912 who produced what were called the 'Judges Rules' with a view to ensuring that statements to the police were of a voluntary nature. They were subject to much modification since but until they were replaced recently they dealt with three stages or situations[2]:

> The first is when a police officer is trying to discover whether or by whom an offence has been committed. He can ask questions of anyone, whether suspected or not, and whether or not the person has been arrested, provided that he has not been charged with an offence. The second stage is that, as soon as a police officer has evidence providing reasonable grounds for suspecting a person, he must caution him. The police can continue to interrogate the suspect but records must be kept. The third stage is that he is formally charged with an offence, when he must again be cautioned and he may not then be asked further questions though there are exceptions.[3]

In the very nature of things there was much that could be criticized in the Rules. They had no binding force, were vague, could be

---

[1] *The Protection of Liberty*, by I.N. Stevens and D.D.K. Yardley, p. 22.

[2] Contemporary problems regarding the rules of evidence are illustrated by the three notorious IRA judgments that have been quashed in the course of 1991–92 – the Birmingham Six, the Guildford Four and the Maguire Seven.

[3] *The Machinery of Justice in England*, by R.M. Jackson, pp. 232–3.

interpreted in different ways and therefore could the more easily be disregarded. The necessity to caution a man before interrogation and if he wants to give evidence in court, and the inability to question the accused, are unnecessarily legalistic for they are based on the adversarial nature of English criminal trials where, for example, a judge cannot interrogate the accused, unlike courts based on the Roman Law precept where the judge quite literally presides from beginning to end. In other words, the judges imposed the same restrictions on the police as they did on themselves, which was not very sensible for their functions were entirely different, the former being observers and literally judges and the latter having the positive responsibility of apprehending a suspect or suspects. For the police's activities to be restricted by the question of 'admissibility of evidence' in a criminal trial is unsatisfactory for it amounts to a 'trial within a trial', especially in view of the fact that this can be done better by a separate enquiry which has been made easier by the 1964 Police Act. It would have been much more satisfactory for the police to have been subject to statutory requirements. Again, proposals that police interrogations should be made in the company of the suspect's solicitor or some independent solicitor, and for electronic monitoring and the like, are practicable when the interrogation is held in the police station but these and other proposals are impractical when police on patrol make their investigations as, indeed, is the whole question of statements in these circumstances when police officers' notes are written subsequently from memory.[1] On the general issue of compliance with the Rules, Budge and McKay (1989) state categorically that they 'were very widely disregarded'[2] but an earlier and more considered view would appear to be that of Jackson (1977):

> There has been controversy over whether the Rules are generally observed, whether the police could do their work adequately if they kept to the strict letter of the rules, and as to what (if anything) ought to be done about it. The Royal Commission on the Police[3] carefully avoided saying whether police do use guile and other inducements in order to obtain confessions (which some responsible and well-informed witnesses thought did happen from time to time) and contented themselves with the conclusion that 'Practices of this kind, if they exist (and evidence about them is

---

[1] Some police forces are currently experimenting with the tape-recording of interviews/enquiries by beat officers.

[2] *The Changing British Political System*, by Ian Budge and David McKay p. 197.

[3] 'The Royal Commission on the Police', 1962.

difficult to obtain and substantiate) must be unhesitatingly condemned.'[1] I had occasion to go through much material, and I agree with those who regard abuses by the police as being isolated instances.[2]

However, the important bipartisan Police and Criminal Evidence Act of 1984 (p. 332) did much more than codify and apply uniformly the best police practices.

> The Judges Rules are now replaced either by clauses in the Act itself, or by elaborate Codes of Practice for police officers attached to the Act. A breach of one of these codes will now automatically constitute a disciplinary offence by a police officer in a way that ignoring Judges Rules never could be. In general the rights of suspects will now be on a much surer footing.[3]

It remains to discuss the more general question of police evidence in court. A good example is when a magistrate has to make the decision as to whether to remand a person awaiting trial in custody or release him on bail. As the former is a denial of the principle of the presumption of innocence before the proving of guilt, it behoves the magistrate to make a careful balance between the freedom of the individual, on the one hand, and the public interest, on the other. It is to be noted that the Bail Act of 1976 refers to 'a general right to bail of accused persons', thus indicating that the bail is to be refused only in exceptional cases.[4] In view of the fact that the police will inevitably be much more familiar with the case than the magistrate, in practice he will depend heavily on police statements regarding their estimate of the person's future behaviour and the seriousness of the crime. A most important point is the familiarity of the police with the magistrate's court which is in stark contrast with the typical defendant, especially if he is representing himself. In the case of a summary trial, after the prosecution's case has been put, usually by a police constable, the defendant is invited to ask questions which he invariably takes as an opportunity to state his own case, whereupon

---

[1]Ibid., Final Report, Cmmd. 1728 (1962) para. 370.
[2]*The Machinery of Justice in England*, by R.M. Jackson, p. 233.
[3]*The Changing British Political System*, by Ian Budge and David McKay p. 197.
[4]It is noted that in the 1994 Criminal Justice Bill the presumption is in favour of bail. This is in spite of the fact of increasing evidence of persistent offenders being granted bail and committing further crimes while on bail. It is to be hoped that the magistrates take good note of these 'exceptional cases' and act accordingly.

he is immediately stopped by the presiding magistrate or clerk and told that he must confine himself to questions or cross-examination which is tantamount to denying him a hearing because the art of cross-examination is a skill acquired by barristers after years of practice. The scene is repeated after every witness has given his evidence, and when the defendant is finally told that he can make a statement or give evidence he usually feels that he is at a great disadvantage. The Magistrates' Courts Act of 1952 did something to redress the balance but the fact remains that the police do enjoy a special status in magistrates' courts, based on the fact that they are well known to the magistrates, and vice versa, as well as to their familiarity with the procedure. On page 306–7 I have dealt with the historical reasons for the unfortunate use of the word 'police' in connection with magistrates and magistrates' courts or, more correctly, Courts of Summary Jurisdiction. Whereas magistrates' courts must, of course, be strictly independent of any police influence it has been difficult to preserve this independence from the point of view of appearance. For example, before the war, prosecuting chief constables sometimes sat alongside the clerk, in front of the magistrates' bench, thus appearing to be a court official. Although this and similar misleading practices no longer occur, senior police officers continued to act as if they were in charge of the court in their attitude to a defendant or witness. Finally, appearances perpetually deceive where many local authorities have built their courts as part of a police station, leading inevitably to the thought, if not the actual terminology, of a 'police court'.

Also, rightly or wrongly, there is the presumption that the police are honest public servants, whereas defendants have a vested interest in being untruthful, if they are guilty; the cynic would say the presumption is 'guilty until proved innocent'! On the question of police honesty, Jackson states:

> I do not mean to suggest that police veracity is no lower and no higher than that of the average citizen. It is rare for a Crown Court or High Court Judge to show unswerving faith in the police, for their professional experience has taught them that a desire to get convictions and an internal 'esprit de corps' may well result in untrue or biased evidence. It is sometimes clear that police evidence may be substantially true but inaccurate in detail.[1]

---

[1] *The Machinery of Justice in England*, by R.M. Jackson, p. 279.

In the 1920s people's confidence in the police was rudely jolted by the notorious Savidge Case concerning the relationship between a Miss Savidge and a senior Labour politician, Sir Leo Chiozza Money. In this case, the lady in question was badly treated but the subsequent enquiry concluded that bribery of police by prostitutes 'must inevitably occur',[1] while confidence was further eroded in the next year by the Report of the Royal Commission on Police Powers.[2] The year 1958 was notable for the number of prosecutions of police officers, including the Chief Constable of Brighton, and in our period there were further inquiries, mainly that on the Sheffield Police in 1963 and on the Metropolitan Police in 1964. Following the 1962 Royal Commission on the Police, the 1964 Police Act (p. 334) strengthened the remedies available against police conduct by those aggrieved, and increased the responsibility, and therefore the involvement of the Home Secretary, apropos the chief constables. But there remained the weakness that there was no independent body in dealing with complaints against the police, a proposal that was rejected by the Royal Commission on the grounds that it would weaken the authority of the chief constables. After our period there was a compromise solution embodied in the Police Act of 1976 which created two new bodies, an independent Police Complaints Board and a Disciplinary Tribunal, which latter consists of a chief constable as chairman and two members of the independent Police Complaints Board.

> All this is most complicated though it is the result of prolonged discussion, and it has to be realized that there are substantial difficulties in combining an adequate control by senior officers over the members of a disciplined force with sufficient recognition of the rights and susceptibilities of members of the public, some of whom are antagonistic to the police and not averse to disturbing the public order.[3]

Jackson's conclusion sums up an inherent problem that will not be solved merely by organizational changes.

We have already dealt with the first of the two historic responsibilities of the police service – the detection and control of crime. The second – the maintenance of public order – is much more controversial as it has political overtones, which is why the Peterloo

---

[1]'Report on Street Offences', Cmd.3231 (1928), para. 59.
[2]Cmd.3297 (1929).
[3]*The Machinery of Justice in England*, by R.M. Jackson, p. 281.

Massacre was so important at the time and as a landmark in this particular aspect of our history. In regard to public order two great traditions apply. The first is that since the days of Peel it has been understood that the police should not act as agents of the government but that they should uphold the law with impartiality – in the manner of the judges since 1649. For example, during the General Strike of 1926 the Home Secretary was at pains to prevent the police from doing anything that would make the police appear to be an agent of the government against the unions. To stray beyond our period, even as late as the 'Winter of Discontent' in 1978–79 the police were not willing to apprehend pickets who were breaking the law, on grounds of impartiality – but this leads to the comment that either the law was wrong or the police were wrong not to enforce the law. As long as the law remained on the statute book it was the duty of the police to enforce it, because it is the Members of Parliament, not the police, who are our lawmakers. Although Budge and McKay imply that the tradition of police impartiality was breached by the Thatcher Government which thrust them 'into the front line of potentially explosive disputes (like strikes and riots)',[1] the police were pursuing their historic task of upholding the law in the riots of 1981 and 1985, the Wapping Newspaper dispute in 1986–87 and, especially, the miners' strike in 1984–85.[2] Budge and McKay also say:

> While police officers in command positions have at least in the past sought to avoid protecting the government per se, they have had a totally different attitude to the idea of upholding the law. This they have seen as sacrosanct, however little they think of the politicians who create it. It is this notion of the law as an absolute which must be upheld and protected, which justifies the absence of political control . . . The image of impartiality in upholding the pure law that the police believe they have is of practical value to them. Police officers are well aware that they can only uphold the law with at least the passive acceptance of the population; and such acceptance, so the argument goes, is dependent on the image of impartiality.[3]

---

[1] *The Changing British Political System*, by Ian Budge and David McKay p. 192.
[2] Although it is well beyond our present period, it should be said that in view of the fact that Scargill was manifestly breaking the law as well as challenging the authority of the Government, it was right to oppose his pretensions by the use of the police and not the army.
[3] *The Changing British Political System*, by Ian Budge and David McKay p. 192. However, on occasion, the courts have held that the police cannot be forced to enforce the law (e.g. against prostitution) and they retain a broad discretion.

On the other hand, in other European countries the police tradition of impartiality does not exist as, for example, in France where they are under the direct orders of the Minister of the Interior to intervene as he, and the government, see fit. The second great British tradition regarding public order, since Peterloo, of course, is that soldiers should not be used against civilians. There are necessary exceptions (which prove the tradition) such as the placing of troops at Heathrow, and similar venues, and the occasional use of the SAS such as the relieving of the seige of the Iranian Embassy in London in 1980 (both examples after our period, of course). However, neither of these occurrences can remotely be described as using troops against civilians, for they are more properly protecting and helping civilians as they have done on the numerous occasions when, usually due to strikes, they have been called in to run public services in fire-fighting, refuse collection, transport, electricity and docking. The greatest exception is Northern Ireland but it is not really an exception as British troops have been on a war footing there since 1968.

Whereas other European countries' police forces are not impartial in their attitude to governments, unlike Britain, there is little or no difference between the police and the military or army. As Budge and McKay say:

> Comparisons between France, Germany and Britain underline a rather important point; under its military budget France fields 76,400 gendarmes, equivalent to 33 per cent of its non-conscript troops, while the German Bundes Grenz Polizei, again part of the military budget, is 20,000 strong. These parliamentary[1] forces, trained and armed as soldiers, do not exist in Britain – which into the bargain has a police service with no great capacity, training or resources for the use of extreme violence in a systematic way. (Apart from the fact that all French Police are armed, there is also the CRS *Compagnies Républicaines de Sécurité*, which numbers around 13,500.) Nor are France and Germany unusual; most countries have some form of disciplined armed force they can call upon to deal with major disturbances without having to go all the way to using the regular military. But Britain, which traditionally does not trust the government to dispose of coercion (hence the localization and autonomy of ordinary police), has never had such a force. Consequently, when situations occur beyond the scope of the police, the army has to be used.[2]

---

[1]Or should it be said, 'paramilitary'?
[2]*The Changing British Political System*, by Ian Budge and David McKay pp. 194–5.

Northern Ireland is an excellent example. And this is as it should be. Budge and McKay's excellent analysis brings out the essential differences between the Continental countries, steeped in the Roman Law, and England with her Common Law traditions. As always, the former is much more straightforward and practicable while the latter is subtle and complex but, by the same token, it ensures much greater respect and guarantee of the rights and freedom of the individual. Fascist dictatorships of the right and the left all begin from the former position. Typically, the legal position in England regarding the use of troops to control civilians is not straightforward but 'subtle and complex'. The well-known 1714 Riot Act which required a magistrate to read a proclamation ('reading the riot act'), thereby making the rioters guilty of a felony, was repealed in 1967 by the Criminal Law Act under Section Three of which it became lawful to use force such as is 'reasonable' to suppress a riot, but the definition of 'reasonable' is, again, 'subtle and complex'. For example, military law requires the presence of a magistrate to initiate the act of suppression but this is not so in the case of common or statute law which, as in so much else in the English situation, leaves the soldier or officer or, for that matter, the government in exactly the same position as the ordinary citizen. That is to say, they can do anything provided that they uphold and do not break the law. Again, Northern Ireland is a good example. Although the rights of the army there have been strengthened by emergency powers, soldiers who shoot to kill are still liable to be charged for murder or manslaughter. Finally and although it is well beyond our period, mention must be made of the third of the great major statutory changes during 1984–86 – the Public Order Act of 1986 – which

> is the most far-reaching legislative overhaul of criminal law dealing with public disorder since the 1936 Act was passed in the face of fascist and communist clashes on London streets.[1] Until the passage of the 1986 Public Order Act, . . . the powers of the police rested on a combination of a relatively old statute, the 1936 Public Order Act, and a host of rather ill-defined common-law powers developed in an ad-hoc manner over the years. The new Act does not seriously pretend to alter powers in any dramatic way, but does seek to make them much clearer, and better designed to fit the realities of street police work in a highly conflictful situation. It is sorely needed, and though not popular with the political left and

---

[1] *The Changing British Political System*, by Ian Budge and David McKay p. 184.

340

civil libertarians, may prove as much in the interests of protesters in the future as of the police.[1]

It remains to deal with the 'constitutional' and 'political' situation of the police in Britain in the context of its historic development and not so much in comparison with its European counterparts. As we have seen in Chapter 13 on Local Government, after the 1888 Act each county had its own force, local control being

> committed to a Standing Joint Committee of Justices of the Quarter Sessions and County Councillors. However, boroughs with populations of 10,000 or more at the time of the 1881 census were permitted to retain separate police forces, controlled by their own Watch Committees (p. 248).

The Metropolitan Police Force, which was responsible for the Greater London Area, retained its separate identity and was directly controlled by the Home Secretary while the City of London also had its own force under a commissioner appointed by the City. Thus there was the inevitable establishment by the police of the tradition of local autonomy and comparative independence from central political authority which applied in so many other directions in English life, with all its strengths and weaknesses. It must be noted though, that the one exception, the Metropolitan Police, was Peel's original foundation so that the local emphasis, in this case, was not necessarily inevitable. Elsewhere, there has been a significant degree of indirect control by central government by its determination of the extent of grants from the Exchequer, by the need of the local forces to satisfy the Home Office inspectors as to their efficiency, and by their comparative dependence on government departments for technical information and expertise (p. 254). Nevertheless, as Budge and McKay state:

> The constitutional position of the police in Britain has been in one sense simple with only one important Act governing them; but in another it has been extremely complex; they have no clearly defined role, and the mechanisms of political control over them are few and ill understood.[2]

That Act was the 1964 Police Act which put into effect the recommendations of the 1962 Royal Commission on the Police. We

---

[1]*The Changing British Political System*, by Ian Budge and David McKay p. 196.
[2]Ibid, p. 184.

have already noted (pp. 334 and 337) the important changes introduced by the Act, including the matter of bringing complaints against the police. However, owing to the 1888 dispensation to boroughs with populations of 10,000 or more there were by this time over 150 separate forces in England and Wales, outside London, and some of them were extremely small, in numbers and area, as well as being notably individualistic. The Commissioners decided that this nineteenth-century pattern could not provide the organization and specialization required for the twentieth century and, having rejected a minority report for nationalization, the Act gave the Home Secretary the power to amalgamate the local forces, which had far-reaching practical consequences in regard to the number and size of forces, besides increasing the uniformity of operation and highlighting the question of political control. By 1969, amalgamations under the Home Secretary, Roy Jenkins, had reduced provincial police forces to 45 although the Royal Commission had recommended the optimum size of a force of about 500 officers, which compares with the West Midlands Constabulary, with about 7,255 officers (1996). Further reorganization took place under the local Government Act of 1972, after which there were 41 police forces outside London.[1] In place of the previous variety of Police Authorities, these became uniform, comprising two-thirds members of the local authorities and one-third magistrates, while they continued to be 'local' in that their areas consisted mainly of the large counties or boroughs. However, the introduction of combined areas, such as the Thames Valley Police, cut across old local authority boundaries, which was all to the good in that it reduced the capacity for local introspection and 'fuddy-duddiness' and struck a blow for realism in that policing, like everything else, should be organized to take account of areas of population and not lines on an ancient map. It is inevitable that under the pre-1964 system the police should have had a much greater rapport with the old and smaller local police authority than under its larger successor. This arises not only because of the elimination of the historic boundary links, in many cases, but also because many of the councillors, especially in Labour-controlled

---

[1] In December 1996 there were 39 in England (including the 2 London forces and the RUC), 4 in Wales and 8 in Scotland. The prospect is that there will be further significant reductions, one proposal being to as few as 13 forces in England and Wales, with boundaries to match those of Crown Prosecution Service areas which are due to be reduced from 31 to 13.

inner-city areas, regard themselves not as a police authority but as an anti-police authority – although this was only an unwelcome cloud on the horizon in 1964.

The important Police and Criminal Evidence Act of 1984 has already been mentioned (p. 332). Budge and McKay comment further:

> Far-reaching though the 1984 Act may prove to be, it does not affect the general constitutional position of the police, the structure of the service, or the all-important role of the chief constable. One reason the 1984 act is important is that even if it changes little of substance, it at least gives a statutory backing to what has been largely a common-law matter to date. Even now the law on policing is scattered in hundreds of precedents, by-laws, and conventions accredited over time.[1]

Thus, I have left till last a discussion of the role of the chief constable for, in spite of their loss of prosecution powers in 1986 (p. 332), they are the all-important links between the local police forces and the central authority, and are the key to understanding the complex constitutional and political powers and responsibilities of the British police. For it is the chief constables,[2] and the chief constables only, who, by tradition and Common Law and, since 1964, by statute, have a connection with the political factors – the Home Secretary (and the Scottish, Welsh and Northern Ireland Secretaries within their regions) and the Police Authorities. He also has complete and undisputed control of all officers in his force as well as full responsibility for all operational, administrative, disciplinary, and other such matters, in that force. With the exception of the Commissioner of the Metropolitan Police he cannot be given an order on any such matters by any political authority, while in the former case the Home Secretary rarely exercises his authority over his Commissioner. Conversely, the Chief Constable, alone, is 'responsible' to his Police Authority although only in administration, not in operational terms. On page 342 I discussed the changes of the 1964 Act on the size and nature of Police Authorities, and I would not agree with those who think that the new authorities are too large, or that they should have the power to intervene in 'operational'

---

[1]*The Changing British Political System*, by Ian Budge and David McKay p. 184.
[2]The Chief Constables of the police forces outside London, the Commissioners of the Metropolitan and City of London Police Forces and the head of the Royal Ulster Constabulary in Northern Ireland.

matters and to dismiss a chief constable.[1] The combination of small Police Authorities wielding those enlarged powers would reduce British policing to chaos although I shall qualify this statement when I discuss the alternative of a national police force at the end of the chapter.

The chief constables have considerable powers. In what sense, and how, are they accountable constitutionally and politically? As always, the answer is 'subtle and complex'. Both the Home Secretary and the Police Authorities can call upon the chef constables to report upon developments in their commands, while each chief constable is required to report about his force to his Authority every year, although this is at his discretion so that he sometimes refuses to divulge information expressly required by the Authority. On the other hand, only the Home Secretary (or the regional Secretaries) may call for reports on 'operational' matters, and as he is responsible to Parliament there is no question of withholding information from him so that he always succeeds and, the Police Authorities to a lesser extent, in learning about what happened in a particular chief constable's area, after the event. Thus, in regard to the latter, the 1964 Act is not working as well as the Royal Commission intended and, where it does work, it is mainly due to the exercise of left-wing political bias. But the main point about the chief constables' accountability is that there is really no one responsible, and no machinery, for preventing one of their number from pursuing a particular course of action – apart from the Home Secretary's power of dismissing a grossly inefficient chief constable, in extreme circumstances. As in the case of the police constable, the soldier or even the ordinary citizen, a chief constable can do anything provided he does not break the law and if and when he does that, like them, he will be subject to due legal process. This leaves the chief constables with the extremely important discretionary power of deciding how to use limited resources 'operationally', unlike France where directions would be given by the Ministry of the Interior, and unlike the situation which, it is contended, should exist in this country, where it should be the responsibility of a person or persons responsible to Parliament. As in the case of the second great discretionary power recently withdrawn from the chief constables – the decision to prosecute (p. 332) – there is the unanswerable criticism that different chief constables will have different priorities in regard to the choice of 'operations' against particular aspects of

---

[1] *The Production of Liberty*, by M. Stevens & D.C.M. Yardley, pp. 65–6.

crime. Although there has been an increasing amount of informal co-operation through the non-accountable Association of Chief Police Officers, leading to a greater measure of uniformity, in practice it remains impracticable, repugnant and unacceptable that, in the last resort, 'operations' against crime should be different in different parts of the country – not necessarily because of genuine differences in criminality, but because of differences in the personalities and precepts of the various chief constables. We conclude by discussing the alternative of a national police force.

Not all police forces are territorially or locally organized. The British Transport Police, the Atomic Energy Authority's Police, the police forces operating in former dock areas operate throughout the United Kingdom, as also does the civilian police force guarding Ministry of Defence establishments, and, more crucially, the security service and the Special Branch of the Metropolitan Police which operates within local forces throughout the United Kingdom. This last-named is an excellent example of a typically ad hoc British solution to a problem, the problem being that the central control of the police, in the interest of efficiency, is incompatible with the traditions of the political independence and impartiality of the police. All the above-named forces are centrally controlled although the degree of political control is 'subtle and complex'. It has already been stated (p. 342) that the 1962 Royal Commission rejected a minority report for nationalization. This was the work of A.L. Goodhart, an extremely distinguished academic commentator on English Law, who was born in the United States and who, although a well-known Anglophile, was possibly less susceptible to the English prejudice in favour of a locally-based and politically independent police force.[1] His solution was a national police force, directly under Parliamentary control. The single police force would be the responsibility of the Home Secretary, or some similar government minister, in the same way as the Metropolitan Police and it would, undoubtedly, have worked as well. However, the complaints of the vested interests, especially the chief constables, were deafening:

This was, and still is, opposed as being too dangerous an instrument. One chief constable recoiled in horror at what he saw as a massive force of 120,000 men under the control of one super-chief

---

[1]A.L. Goodhart: Professor of Jurisprudence, Oxford University (1931–51), Master of University College, Oxford (1951–63). His especial interest was the Common Law.

constable. His argument was that the power of a chief constable was much too great to put such a force in any one man's hands.[1]

But unlike the chief constables who did, and still have, considerable political control and independence, the proposed super-chief constable, or chairman of a committee, or whatever, would have neither.

The point is that only by making the central state directly command the police force can it be politically controlled.[2]

Although it is not usually presented in this way, it can be argued that the current structure of the police service is a compromise between efficiency, supposedly served by amalgamations and greater size, and the need to keep the police independent of the central government.[3]

However, if the police force were national, centrally controlled, and responsible to Parliament, it would be possible to have smaller and more numerous local police forces and Police Authorities, if that were so desired.[4]

---

[1]*The Changing British Political System*, by Ian Budge and David McKay p. 188.
[2]Ibid p. 188.
[3]Ibid p. 188.
[4]Sadly, the Government's Police and Magistrates Bill, published in December 1993, proposing that the Home Secretary should appoint the chairman of the police authorities and half of their 16 members, was bitterly and successfully attacked in the House of Lords by 'Backwoodsmen', led by Lord Whitelaw and other senior Tory ex-ministers. Fortunately, the sensible proposal that the Home Secretary 'may by order determine objectives for the policing of the areas of all police authorities' was not abandoned in response to these and other romantic manifestations of the backward-looking obsession with local control that has been such a millstone around our national neck – and was included in the Act of Parliament in 1994. Another manifestation of this problem, in the course of the Criminal Justice and Public Order Act, 1994, was the Lords' rejection of the Home Secretary's proposal to establish five secure units to which the hard core of young offenders, aged 12 to 14, should be sent, on the grounds that the magistrates should have the option of placing these young criminals in existing local authority institutions, from which they have absconded regularly in the past. The opposition was led by the dank Lord Carr, an ineffectual Home Secretary in the Heath Government but, again, it is good to be able to note that the eventual Act made provision for the new secure units while the local authority and other institutions could only be used if the former were not available.

15

Social, 1945–64

In Chapter 1 (p. 26), I make the point that 'pre-war Britain was an entirely 'class-ridden society' and give some details of the inequalities as between the predominant working class and the rest of the community. Elsewhere, as in Chapter 6 on Education, the monumental neglect of the working class until 1870 is noted while Chapter 7 on Housing indicates the problem posed by the 'throwing-up' of towns in the industrial revolution and the rapid growth in population in the matter of providing satisfactory accommodation for the masses. I also say in Chapter 1 (p. 26) that 'wars usher in great social changes', and on p. 25 I attribute the successful transformation from the pre-war situation to the 'social revolution' of the 'Swinging Sixties' to the 'complex mixture of the conservative and radical' which 'has been and is an enormously potent force in English Society'. It is now necessary to analyze that 'revolution' more deeply, especially in view of the opening remarks in Chapter 5, but it should be noted that it is not strictly relevant until the period after 1964 although, as we shall see, its seeds were undoubtedly sown in the previous period – as is to be expected. Perhaps the best way of appreciating the extent of the change that has taken place, before examining its beginnings, is to describe the social situation before and immediately after the war. The distinguished investigative journalist, Graham Turner, did this in a series of brilliant articles in the *Daily Mail* in June 1990 and much of the following descriptions (although not all) are quoted from these articles.

The eminent Oxford Sociologist, Professor A.H. Halsey, himself from a working-class family, says that before the 1939 war and, indeed for ten years after, the working class was not only large (manual workers and their families consisting of about 75 per cent of the population) but it was also, for the most part, quite extraordinarily decorous, disciplined and high-minded. Most families did not know anyone who was divorced and looked on it as a scandalous indulgence peculiar to film stars and aristocrats. Reg Parkin, a retired mill worker from Macclesfield in Cheshire said:

Before the war there were very few members of the working class who were in any way unrespectable – just a little clique who got drunk, used bad language and had fights. People like that were rare exceptions in those days. Nobody would have anything to do with them. Things could hardly be more different now.

Professor Halsey states that the moral standards preached in church and chapel were regarded as the norm and Reg Parkin agreed:

Almost every family had been brought up with a religious streak. It began at school where you said the Lord's Prayer, the Catechism and the Ten Commandments quite regularly. If you had nothing to do with Church, you were definitely the odd one out.

A Durham miner recalled that anyone in his pit village who did not go to confirmation class was considered a distinct oddity. Old and young alike shared a remarkable deference to their elders, and to those set in authority over them, as the Catechism enjoined: 'To submit myself to all thy governors, teachers, spiritual pastors and masters: to order myself lowly and reverently to my betters'. 'The local bobby would give you a thump behind the earhole for minor things like raiding orchards,' said Eric Haigh, who began life as a bobbin lad in a Macclesfield silk mill, 'and if you complained to your parents, you got another one from them. If you told your parents that you'd had the cane at school, they said: "serve you damn well right".' In those days, he added, teachers were people who commanded respect. 'I can remember my first headmaster, Mr Simpson, walking to school in his bowler hat, bow-tie and stand-up collar. If you were late, even by a few minutes, you got the stick.' 'Working-class people looked up to the middle-class,' said Reg Parkin. 'A lot of that went back to mill life. You had to call the owner "Sir" – it was always "Sir". If you got into his bad books, you'd not got a job, and you clung to your job because you knew that, if you didn't do it well, there was always someone else who would.' Women would still curtsy when they met members of a family who owned a good deal of property. Because of the emphasis on religious teachings, such as respect and obedience, the young found themselves faced by an apparently unbreachable United Adult Front, the power of which was reinforced by the fact that, for children, it was an all but moneyless world. Children were expected to work for such money as they were given. Elizabeth Booth, brought up in Barnsley, got one old penny for scrubbing the floors of the outside toilets which served their row of mill cottages, tuppence if she scoured the pans as well. The possession of a push-bike was what most working-class children coveted, but few could afford the 6d down payment and 6d a week thereafter until the whole £2.10s was paid off. With the average wage not more than £2.0.0 per week the reason for this shortage of money was painfully simple. Some families were so poor that they could not afford a Sunday joint and the working-class diet, in general, was extremely plain. 'Bread and jam was the main thing,' said Les Denison, son of a Durham miner, 'but Sunday was special because then my old man always had bacon and eggs, and he'd usually cut off the rind and give it to us. Sunday was also the one day we had a pint of fresh milk, which meant we could have rice pudding – a real treat.' Clothes were often the cast-offs of older children or the local middle class. The lack of cash certainly discouraged any inclination toward sexual precocity and even after the war there was no great kudos to be gained from advanced sexual activity.

Astonishingly, many of the old working class do not look back on the straightened circumstances of the pre-war years with sourness or complaint – quite the reverse. 'It never struck us that we were poor if we had enough,' said Eric Haigh. 'Wages never altered, you weren't going in for rises ever year, but, prices didn't change much either, so we didn't spend all our time thinking about money as we do now.' Except in the South-East where new light industries were beginning to flourish by the middle of the 1930s, very few rose out of the working class. 'There was no way up or out,' said Les Denison. 'If you passed for grammar school before the war you had to be paid for – and one of the big disgraces was to pass out and then find that your parents couldn't afford to kit you out. Quite a few passed but very few were able to go.' So why was there not more widespread bitterness and, indeed, social upheaval? It was not only that the working class had low expectations. There were also consolations which today's working class no longer enjoy. It was, Professor Halsey points out, an ordered world with 'a very stable horizon of moral expectations', a very secure family life and a strong sense of comradeship. 'The area you lived in was one big family,' said Les Denison. 'When my mother was having kids, the old woman down the street was always ready to help. The tradesmen, too, knew of your poverty, so the butcher would give you bacon and beef bones for soup, and you would always get stale cakes and broken biscuits from the baker. You never heard of break-ins. I can't remember our door ever being locked.' Despite all the deprivations, furthermore, there was also very little violence, apart from the occasional fight outside pubs or dance halls, and even then conducted only with fists

349

– never boots, knives or bottles. It was, says Professor Halsey, 'the most peaceable domestic period in our history. You could walk the streets of working-class districts in complete safety, by day or by night.' 'Women,' said Derek Clark, an educational psychologist whose father was a Yorkshire miner, 'ran the community and enforced their standards. Sex was carefully regulated by them, and any woman who strayed became the butt of opprobrium by the local women, not the men. Nowadays, people think nothing very terrible can happen to them. If they lose their job, they'll go on the dole, they'll survive somehow.' Before the war, by contrast, there was no handout, very little in the way of unemployment pay, and a family could easily lurch into the chasm of joblessness and penury. Because the working class accounted for the vast bulk of the population, it was not as it is today, a derided underclass. Because of the lack of opportunity it was not being constantly denuded of its more talented members. Even the working-class heroes, such as the top footballers, remained members of the working class and did not change their style of life, which was inevitable in view of their low wages. However, the point is that they were not ashamed of being working class and had no wish to cease to be so. Very few of the working class owned their own homes, and their possessions were so modest that there was no comparison of material things and no concept of their being status symbols. Their minds were focused on the elementary things – food, warmth and shelter – and they were doing very well if they achieved these. The comparisons that were made were about behaviour rather than material things. They felt morally superior to the idle rich and despised them as much as they despised the idle poor. Les Denison said that he felt sorry for today's working class, that all their values were based on money, there was no community spirit as he had known it and there had been a massive decline in moral standards. He'd hated the degradation of having to sleep five in a bed when he was a boy but, taking all that into account, he'd come to the conclusion that they'd had more than the working-class youngsters of today.

The lower middle class comprised about 10–15 per cent of the population and were completely and utterly divorced from the working class. When he was a boy in the 1930s, the lower-middle-class Kingsley Amis said the working class had been 'unimaginable, though they were known to exist' and they spoke in what his parents called 'bad' accents. His parents made sure that he never came into contact with these 'roughs' so that he was sent to a private primary school, no doubt at some financial sacrifice to his parents. Another scion of the lower middle class, Jack Mason, who was 80 in 1990 and who worked with Thomas Cook, said, 'We had no contact at all with the working class. They just didn't talk the same language as us. After all, you couldn't imagine a chap who'd left school at fourteen, which they usually did, joining our local amateur dramatic society, the Beckenham Players. If he had, he'd have found himself pretty isolated. Although we regarded the working class as jolly nice chaps, we didn't mix with them.' Mason's father was in charge of the strongroom at Thomas Cook until he retired in 1935 on an ex-gratia pension of £2.10s a week but, like Amis's father, he was regarded as part of the lower middle class by virtue of having a white-collar job. Mason's parents sent him to a dame school, with the modest fees of £4.0.0 a term, and then to Beckenham and Penge Grammar for £5.0.0 a term where many of the scholarship boys from the local council schools could not afford to have the school blazer. Mason and all his friends followed their fathers into white-collar jobs in the City or the West End. Between their world – the world of clerks, (with bowler hats as they grew more senior), state school teachers and junior managers – and that of the working class was fixed a narrow but, they believed, unbridgeable gulf as was evidenced by the fact that manual workers always seemed to have scarves around their necks. The former also spoke with what Professor Halsey calls 'cleaned-up local accents', while when they had reached a position of any responsibility at work they expected to be addressed as 'Mister'. This was and is the great 'giveaway' for the lower middle class for the upper class in those years addressed each other by their surnames from preparatory school days and for the rest of their lives. Similarly, the lower middles were very conscious of and dependent on the increased status conferred by even the slightest visible manifestation, such as the superior facilities of the senior staff restaurant compared to the junior staff restaurant. In the case of Jack Mason, by the time war broke out he was earning £200 a year, which sounds modest enough but there was often a considerable differential between the salaries of the lower middle class and the wages of the manual worker. A man who made gas meters in London counted himself lucky if he earned £2.10s a week before the war, while a clerk on the railway could expect to receive five guineas. And, whereas skilled workers at the MG car plant at Abingdon, Oxfordshire, were earning only £2.14s.6d for a 48-hour week, Sydney Hancock, a primary school teacher in Staffordshire, collected £366.0.0 a year, or just £7.0.0 a week. This says much about the complete change in the social status between such teachers then and now but, unfortunately, even if this differential were restored, present-day state-school teachers, as a class, have forfeited the status they once enjoyed as a result of the unacceptable behaviour of their union activists, individually and collectively, not to mention their way of dress.

The lower middle-class were also proud to be able to keep the woman of the house in the house which, however, was inevitable, as the majority of white-collar jobs were closed to married women. When Sydney Hancock married his wife, Hannah, who was also a teacher, she had to resign. So did Jack Mason's first wife, who worked for Shell, while the same rule applied throughout the Civil Service. Given that the birth rate among them was low, that left a great many educated and intelligent women running distinctly modest households. The result was, to put it mildly, they left nothing to chance in the way they brought up their offspring. For instance, some did not allow their children to read comics because they were 'rather vulgar', while pantomimes were not considered appropriate because, like comics, 'they were a bit trashy' although it was in order to take them to plays like *Toad of Toad Hall*. Their dedication to their offspring's welfare was all the keener because they usually had domestic help of some kind. This was seldom of the living-in variety which was generally restricted to those rising into the middle ranks of the bourgeoisie, but those who indulged in this luxury had to pay only around 10s. a week. Much more common was the mother's help who came in once a week and who wore her own pinafore rather than any kind of uniform. The social life of the lower middle class had a veneer of gentility which is why today, elderly people of this class appear almost to be upper middle class. Such books as they had in their homes – a set of Dickens or volumes with titles like *With Buller in Natal* – were often displayed in the 'lounge' as signs of cultural status, although Arthur Mee's *Children's Encyclopedia* could be bought for the enlightenment of their children. Their holidays, usually two weeks and paid, compared with the working class's one week and unpaid, were spent in places well away from the madding, red-faced throngs of Blackpool, Brighton and Southend. Usually, even after the war, lower-middle-class families would either provide their own food or stay in a boarding house, seldom hotels.

Before the war, by no means all the lower middle class owned their own homes, although a modest terrace house in Staffordshire could be purchase for around £325.0.0 cash, the purchaser probably intending to live in it for the rest of his life, and without a thought of selling it in the future so as to realize a profit. Nor did most have motor cars, even though many could afford them, which is why the semi-detached villas of the period had no garages. When they did buy cars they were very much a long-term investment. As a class, they were quite exceptionally parsimonious, often because they needed to be, as when the history master at a grammar school in Cheshire had to sell a pre-war suit to pay the maternity bills of £4.10s for his son born in 1948, the year before the National Health Service was set up (sic). Ladies fastidiously kept household account books and there was little spare money for indulgences such as buying Christmas presents or alcohol, which was usually confined to a bottle of ginger wine at Christmas. Although family meals were formal and sacrosanct rituals the food was unimaginative and the rations were spartan. Even after the war, material ambitions were still modest. 'Fitted kitchens were not de rigueur in those days,' said a former grammar school teacher who was paid £435.0.0 a year in 1946. 'I never thought I was underpaid and there was very little grumbling about salaries in the staff room. By today's standards you could call it respectable poverty.' When I gave up my princely salary of around £600.0.0 a year at Shrewsbury School to work in the City in 1957, in the early 1960s a very senior office manager, (of over 30 years' experience), was only receiving around £700.0.0 a year and resisted my efforts to persuade him to ask for more. In the mind of one, Stella Weaver, however, the years before and just after the war were a wonderfully tranquil and peaceful time. Hostilities between the generations had still not broken out. 'We never dreamt of any of the teenage problems there are today. None of my friends ever went against their parents, family life was terrific, and it was wonderful to get home for toast and tea with mother in the lamplight and the firelight. There was a wonderful sense of security – and so much leisure.' Certainly, middle-class morality was a different world from today's standards. Premarital and extra-marital sexual intercourse did not enter into the scheme of things, while abortion and illegitimacy were virtually unheard of. In fact, in spite of our present consumerist and materialistic society it is only the existence of middle-class standards, in the last resort, which provides the backbone for our moral survival. As A.J.P. Taylor said, the middle class 'sets the standard of the community . . . is its conscience and does its routine work'. It is for this reason that I have devoted more space to it than to the other classes.

Before the war, the upper middle class provided the leadership for, in their minds, they were born to rule, or at least command, and felt vastly superior to the working class and the lower middle class. It is significant that stockbrokers were not acceptable at London's prestigious White's Club. On the other hand, Public School masters were allowed in as honorary members, of which I have had personal experience with the Shropshire 'county set' on my £600.0.0 a year! Much more than even the lower middle class, the working class and its institution (such as the pubs), was very largely a *'terra incognita'* into which the upper middle class seldom, if ever, ventured. It was certainly a small and select band accounting for only between 3 or 4 per cent of the population, consisting largely of the older professions – clerics, doctors, lawyers, university professors, senior civil servants and officers in the services. To be accepted one had to be 'pukka' – and this was not a question of money, the income range being from £400.0.0 to £40,000.0.0 a year. They were united by a common purpose, 'a moral commitment to see that bridges were built, patients cured, the hungry fed, in short to make sure that civilization continued'. One of my sixth-form pupils, in the mid-fifties, whose father was a regular army brigadier and who subsequently became a stockbroker (following in his mother's family's footsteps) told me that his ambition was 'to serve the Empire'! Seen from working-class eyes, the upper middle class were very lofty creatures indeed. For example, upper-middle-class vicars seldom, if ever, invited lower-middle-class parishioners to the vicarage while they fraternized (on Christian name terms) with their social equals. The same applies to doctors of that ilk while they all regarded themselves as superior to the 'decadent' aristocracy. The hallmark of the upper middle class was the presence of several live-in servants. Even those with comparatively modest incomes could afford them. When Douglas Henchley joined the army as a lieutenant in 1937, his salary was £400.0.0. On that he and his wife were able to rent a five-bedroom house (at £2.10s a week) and employ a live-in maid for 12s 6d, not to mention an aptly named Mrs Lillywhite to do all the laundry, 'except the smalls', and a man to clean Henchley's belt and buttons. Servants banished much of the drudgery from the bourgeois life while the burden for upper-middle-class women was lightened further by shopping by telephone, followed by free delivery, which indeed continued for at least ten years after the war – certainly in Shrewsbury. However, the presence of servants meant that the upper middle class had to lead orderly lives, on the surface at least, and great care was taken not to exploit or hurt the servants (by being late for meals, and the like), and to set them a good example.

And, most important, none of this meant great consumerism for, like the lower middle class, the uppers led comparatively frugal lives. They were completely non-materialistic. Christmas presents were to be modest and practical and young people were taught that money was to be saved, not spent. Anything remotely approaching conspicuous expenditure was considered 'bad form'. All of which goes to explain that the largest and mass spenders in the age of affluence have been those ex-members of the working class who have

354

suddenly and uniquely found themselves with ample money to spare and who were innocent of middle-class traditions in regard to spending and saving. For example, the modern fetish about wanting desperately to have a car with a recent registration number is foreign to the traditional middle-class way of thinking, as also, for that matter, is the whole concept of the modern consumer society. This, together with the permissiveness introduced by Roy Jenkins in his years as Home Secretary and the tragedy of the comprehensive schools gives the clue to the answer to my first question at the beginning of Chapter 5. For holidays, most of the upper middle class considered those abroad as too extravagant – and too hot, if not morally weakening – and went for brisk, healthy and educational walking tours in Britain. Grouse shooting and fishing in Scotland are survivors of this tradition in our age of package holidays and sun worship. Even though the upper middle class may have permitted themselves few material indulgences, they had infinitely more leisure than their hard-pressed modern equivalents. For the ladies, there was time for bridge and tennis parties, to join sketching and painting circles and time to order great lists of books from circulation libraries, and time, above all, to spend with their children for whom they were usually 'always available'. The men, too, enjoyed much greater leisure and were able to make full and uninhibited use of such institutions as the West End Clubs, as the hours of work were much shorter than now, and there was considerably less pressure and stress. In the City, and elsewhere, this civilized situation continued until the 1960s. But, above all, the distinguishing feature of this class was that no one ever talked about money which, together with excessive spending, was anathema to them. And no one chose a career to make money which accounts for the widely different status of the City before and after the war. Before the war, the expression 'something in the City' was a meaningful slight. The financial independence of the upper middle class derived from generations of financial prudence and saving providing private incomes which, in a non-inflationary age, did not have to be very large to be extremely helpful.

Eddie Sackville-West told a wonderful story about his aunt who, soon after World War II had broken out, stretched out her hand and switched on the light, saying to him, 'Let that be a lesson to you, Eddie. We must learn how to do things ourselves now.' The period between the wars was a hard one economically for the upper class or aristocracy as a result of low farm rents and extremely depressed agricultural land prices. Nevertheless, those who survived (130 big houses were pulled down) enjoyed a plethora of servants both in manor houses and big houses such as the Marquess of Salisbury's

Hatfield House. The servants rose at 5.30 a.m., so that by the time the family and guests came down for breakfast at nine, all the housework would have been done, and for the rest of the long day they would continue to provide for every household and personal need. Perhaps the most burdensome task which the lady of the house was required to undertake, apart from going through the day's menus with the cook, was to resolve below-stairs crises. It was a small price to pay. Meanwhile, other servants – in the form of nannies, nursery maids and governesses – spared the upper-class lady from having to look after her own children. 'In the 1920s and 1930s, you hardly ever saw your parents,' said James Lees-Milne. 'They expected us to lead a separate life. We were even kept out of their part of the garden. The only time of the day when you were allowed to be with them was at tea, when you'd be dressed up in your Sunday clothes, brought down from the nursery, where you spent most of your time and had your meals, and asked to recite something to them. To this day I can still hear my father's groan of boredom from behind the *Morning Post* as we made our appearance.' At some houses, like Hatfield, there was a more liberal regime. 'When children became old enough to behave, say four or five,' said Lord Salisbury, 'they were allowed to come down to dining-room lunch and sat at a large round table in the corner which was called "The Pig's Table"!': hardly the deification of the young! But, on the other hand, very much better than the American-inspired modern concept of completely spoiling children by large overdoses of 'understanding'! Taken in conjunction with the spartan nature of pre- and immediate post-war Eton, where most upper-class boys went, their upbringing was literally spartan in that the boys of this ancient republic were brought up communally, almost from birth, in a kibbutz-like environment. Meanwhile, the girls usually acquired their education in less arduous ways, through governesses and travel, going to Paris to learn French and to Munich for German.

Having delegated their domestic responsibilities, including their children, so comprehensively, members of the upper classes were free to do exactly as they liked, except that they took very seriously such traditional responsibilities as being Lord Lieutenant of the County, chairman of the county council and colonel of the local yeomanry – sometimes as in the case of Lord Digby's father, fulfilling all three functions. Apart from that their lives were one long holiday. The casinos took them to France – Monte Carlo or Menton every other year – and then they went to Scotland in August 'to kill things', as Lord Grimond remarked drily. Lord Digby said that his father would 'do something sporting at least four days of the week. He'd hunt three days, he always shot in Scotland for a month and we had a river in the West of Ireland, so he spent a lot of time fishing over there. Sport was really a religion.' The young began to hunt at around the age of nine and the main punishment for being naughty was not to be allowed to hunt. The upper class were often aggressively lowbrow. 'If you mentioned Shakespeare to my father, it was like red rag to a bull,' said James Lees-Milne. Regular churchgoing was still taken for granted, either because it was 'the thing to do' or from a sense of duty and, in the case of Mrs Lees-Milne's parents, in spite of the fact that they both had long-term lovers. 'There were lots of parties in the years before the war,' said Lord Salisbury. 'Four or five big house parties here at Hatfield in the spring and summer, two or three more in the autumn – and we'd stay in the half a dozen different friends' houses during the course of the year. Then there was Scotland and the Highland balls. It was really a very full life.' The young went away almost every weekend in the summer, there were Hunt Balls in the autumn and during the Season there were coming-out parties the whole time. Ineffectual charity work was their main contribution towards the welfare of the community. It was very much a closed circle. It was made up, in Lord Salisbury's view, of 'the bulk of the peerage plus county families who'd lived in the local manor houses for several generations, the Archbishop of Canterbury and all the diocesan bishops ex-officio and army officers who qualified by their birth. All of them,' he added, 'either knew the other people personally or knew people who knew them.' Then, as now, this select band shared one common characteristic, a quiet and impermeable self-confidence and felt no need to show off and abhorred nouveaux riches City types who did, and whose offspring were given a hard time at Eton by their sons. It followed that their other chief characteristic was a deliberately unostentatious style of life; simple creature comforts, other than servants, were often hard to come by. 'There was no electric light in this house until 1930,' said Sir Charles Mott-Radcliffe of his Norfolk manor house and 'only one bathroom and no central heating at all. It really was bitterly cold.' However, as mentioned above, in the years between the wars, the lives of many upper-class families were clouded by intense financial problems. They would have been astonished by the quite remarkable and unexpected renaissance in the fortunes of their class since the war, mainly due to the escalation in the price of land.

Marwick makes a pertinent comment on the obvious profound changes in our society since the pre- and immediate post-war period, as follows:

The social and geographical statistics of the 1950's when compared with those of the Edwardian period, express both the great transformations associated with the two world wars, and the unchanging elements in Britain's modern history.[1]

In point of fact, profound as were the changes within society after 1939, the greatest alteration in the old class structure took place during World War I. High taxation, imposed before 1914 but greatly increased during and at the end of the war, did lead to extensive sales of property by the aristocratic landed class as well as to their need to increase income by the sale of outlying holdings, a practice established since the turn of the century.

But their great landed empires were curtailed and their feudal dominance over the countryside was almost at an end, as their own tenants took the opportunity presented by the land sales to set themselves up as owner-farmers.[2]

The outcome was the transference of political power from the great landowners to businessmen which

was symbolized by the passing over of Lord Curzon in favour of the 'countrified businessman', Stanley Baldwin, for the Prime Ministership in 1922 (sic, 1923), and by the establishment in the same year of the influential 1922 Committee of Conservative back-benchers, most of them businessmen.[3]

The other important feature at this time was the strengthening of the salaried class, notably the professions, the civil servants and clerical administrators, the managerial class and women.

In 1911 less than 1.7 million were included under this heading, while in 1921 the figure was over 2.7 millions, an increase from 12 per cent to 22 per cent of the occupied population.[4]

However, whereas after 1919 there was a pervasive feeling of disillusionment by the mass of the people, the point has been made

---

[1] *Britain in the Century of Total War*, by Arthur Marwick, p. 383. Further facts and figures in this chapter are attributable to this authority.
[2] Ibid., p. 168.
[3] Ibid., p. 169.
[4] Ibid., p. 170.

several times that this was certainly not true after 1945. A.J.P. Taylor's often-quoted expression that, 'In the Second World War the British people came of age' (p. 42) sums it up. He also said that it 'was a people's war in the most literal sense'.[1] By 1942 national unity had reached previously unrealized heights. For the first time, following the mass circulation newspaper phenomenon, the masses read a daily newspaper and the *Daily Mirror* headed the circulation list, but unlike its two great rivals, the *Daily Mail* and the *Daily Express*, it was not founded by a wealthy proprietor, for it was the creation of the ordinary people on its staff. Also, the fighting men were much more integrated with the community than they were in the First World War. Many, especially the navy and the air force, and the army awaiting the invasion of France, were stationed at home and had much in common with civilians in the Home Guard, civil defence and on the receiving end of Hitler's bombs. Even the servicemen overseas were linked with home by the short-wave radio by listening to Churchill's speeches, *ITMA* ('It's that Man Again') and, on a more intellectual level, from 1941, *The Brain's Trust* which was a precursor of an increased communal intellectual and cultural activity which took place during the war. But there was an important material reason for this satisfactory state of affairs. Most people were much better off and had a security which had previously been unknown.

> While the true cost of living had risen in 1942 by 42 per cent since 1938, average weekly earnings were 65 per cent higher, and the disproportion increased thereafter – in 1944 the cost of living was 50 per cent higher than in 1938 and weekly earnings were 81½ per cent higher. Broadly speaking, the entire population settled at the standard of the skilled artisan. This was a comedown for the wealthier classes: no private motoring or foreign travel, few domestic servants or none, far fewer clothes and these less smart.[2]

Although, as we have seen, the most fundamental weakening of the old class system took place during and after the First World War, there was a much wider redistribution of incomes (both ways) between 1939 and 1945 as a result of severely increased taxation, rationing, an effective nutrition policy and higher wages (see above). Furthermore, and most unusually, the post-war Labour Government

---

[3] *English History, 1914–1945*, by A.J.P. Taylor, p. 549. Further facts and figures in this chapter are attributable to this authority.
[2] *Ibid.*, p. 550.

continued the policy of redistribution by retaining the high wartime levels of taxation.

> Between 1938 and 1949 there was a fourfold increase in taxation: in 1938 7,000 persons had had net incomes of over £6,000 per annum: in 1947–8 there were only 70 such incomes.[1]

Furthermore, a decisive factor in determining the structure of post-war British society was the Labour Government's insistence on the principle of universality in the application of the Welfare State. Free medicine, family allowances, pensions, insurance benefits and, up to a point, subsidized housing, were offered to both rich and poor or, one should say, to poor and rich – for the point was that there was no distinction: the poor were entitled to the same as the rich and the rich were entitled to the same as the poor. Apart from the question of practicability, the principle amounted to a social revolution. In the same way as in the First World War the aristocracy were humbled financially, politically and socially, in the Second World War the middle class were similarly humbled financially and socially. However, in both cases this did not, of course, become immediately apparent either to themselves or to the world at large for, as Marwick says, there was the dichotomy of 'the great transformations associated with the two world wars and the unchanging elements in Britain's modern history'. (p. 358)[2] As always in our history there was the combination of the radical and the conservative influences.

For the nation, as a whole, immediate post-war life was a continuation of wartime conditions and scarcities, manifested by rationing and austerity. The greatest hardship was probably in the field of housing, in the chapter on which the virtual cessation of building during the war is described on page 232, while the repair of bomb-damaged houses was not effectively put in hand until 1943. However, as we have seen above, the average wartime diet was better than that of pre-war, while this remained true even in 1947 when owing to worldwide food shortages, the ending of Lend-Lease and an economic crisis, bread rationing was introduced for the first time. By 1950, before the Welfare State could have had much influence, there was evidence of the impressive improvement in the health of the nation, which was perhaps the most welcome legacy of the war.

---

[1] *Britain in the Century of Total War*, by Arthur Marwick, p. 360.
[2] However, as early as 1946 Terence Rattigan's play, *The Winslow Boy*, celebrated the courage of the upper class in the face of bureaucracy and the post-war situation.

In the last of his three social surveys of York, Seebohm Rowntree discovered that post-war children in all sections of the community were taller and heavier than in 1936. In 1950 infant mortality fell below 30 per cent for the first time in British history, though rates continued to be higher among low-income than among high-income groups. Even the birthrate began to show an upward movement . . .[1]

By the mid-fifties there was detected the new phenomenon of 'affluence' – the great increase in the number of people enjoying high living standards – which is explained by the following facts:

Average weekly earnings of male manual workers over twenty-one, £3.10s.11d in 1938, £6.2s.8d in 1946, £8.8s.6d in 1951 and £11.7s.10d in 1955, reached £13.16s.6d in 1959 and £18.8s.10d in 1964. Average wages in real terms rose by 20 per cent between 1951 and 1958, and by another 30 per cent by 1964.[2]

At the same time there was the infiltration of the ideas and practices of the great American consumer society which was reinforced by the 30,000 American airmen who were based in Britain after 1952, following the onset of the Cold War, which was foreign to the traditions of all classes in Britain but which proved to be a highly infectious concept. From personal experience, I remember being forcibly struck by my first contact with American packaged consumerism on my wartime journey from New Zealand to Britain in 1943. It was a revelation to me. As we shall see, there were other influences, but it was the spread of affluence which, more than anything, led to the weakening of class barriers and to a sharp increase in the mobility between classes, notably an increase in the size of the middle class or, more realistically, a reduction in that of the working class. The pre-war trend of relatively fewer people being involved in directly producing goods and relatively more in professional, technical and clerical occupations (p. 358) was intensified during the war. The outcome was the estimate that the middle class in 1954 comprised 30.4 per cent of the population. Apart from transforming society, it was the 'phenomenon of "affluence"', as well as the increasing cost of the Welfare State, that was one of the main causes of Britain's post-war balance of payments problems. Whereas before the war Britain, with its wealth in the hands of a tiny

---

[1] *Britain in the Century of Total War*, by Arthur Marwick, p. 360.
[2] Ibid., p. 418.

minority of the population, was able to finance its imperial and world commitments by putting 'guns' before 'butter' (p. 28), by the mid-fifties this policy had broken down. Before the war, Britain's comparative lack of natural resources was not a problem because of the system of imperial trade (manufactured goods in return for food and raw materials) and because of the low level of consumption of the people. However, the marked rise in the material standards following the advent of the 'affluent society' led inevitably to a significant increase in imports, and the attempt to pay for them by increasing exports led to a further increase in imports – of raw materials. The problem is still one of the main concerns of British governments and it can only be solved by substantially increasing the productivity of British industry. Only Margaret Thatcher, in the 1980s, has succeeded in doing this.[1]

In his book, *The Affluent Society*, (1958), Professor J.K. Galbraith was drawing attention to the existence of private affluence and public squalor in the United States. On similar lines, in Britain in the late 1950s and early 1960s, the criticism of academics such as Richard Titmus, and novelists and playwrights, was directed towards the existence of pockets of poverty in the midst of the prevailing 'affluence', although it must be said that even poverty is relative and, thankfully, conditions which are presently regarded as unacceptable are a vast improvement on conditions a generation or so earlier. This is heresy to the 'poverty lobby', and politicians only utter it at their peril, but it is true nevertheless. The Galbraithian criticism did apply in Britain however, especially in the fields of housing and the Health Service. The former aspect should cause no surprise in view of the opening and closing remarks in Chapter 7 on Housing, the wartime housing situation (already quoted) and its post-war history dealt with on pages 233–8. As mentioned on page 131, in practice the Conservatives then, as now, had a much better record in the NHS than did Labour which presided over a service which was desperately short of accommodation and staff.

> Each year since 1945 less hospital construction had been undertaken than in each year in the decade before the Second World War; two-thirds of the hospitals still in use had been built

---

[1]Professor Walter Eltis has recently (September 1996) published a review (The Key to Higher Living Standards, Centre for Policy Studies) claiming that since 1979 Britain has achieved what is tantamount to a productivity miracle. It has also been one of the main economic consequences of our departure from the Exchange Rate Mechanism in September 1992.

in the nineteenth century. At the same time as half a million people awaited hospital places, over 10,000 beds lay empty due to shortage of staff.[1]

In 1962 the Macmillan Government inaugurated a much needed ten-year hospital building programme and Enoch Powell, as Minister of Health, from 1960–63, improved the staff situation by employing the new immigrants (p. 167). In regard to affluence, at the other end of the scale, whereas many of those who fell below the poverty line, especially the old, failed to take up their entitlements, the middle classes were quick to take advantage of the extensive social services offered, especially in education and health, so that whereas the traditional middle-class would never ever enjoy the superior financial and social status which they had before the war they were significant beneficiaries of the Welfare State, although it was claimed at the time that the social benefits, on the one hand, and taxation, on the other, were virtually equal, in monetary terms, in the case of the 'average' person. A further important factor is that this period was comparatively beneficial to the middle classes in that there was no escalation of inflation, a situation which was going to deteriorate after 1964. Directly and indirectly, they were also helped by the reawakening of the Stock Market following the Conservatives' elimination of controls in the early 1950s. By now, as we have seen, the middle class was extended by the entry of those who had previously been working class and lower middle class, and we can see the ramifications of this dynamic development in two particular fields – education and housing. In the first case, as well as taking full advantage of the state system they also sent their children to the private fee-paying sector. At Shrewsbury School, for example, which would be typical, in the 1950s the percentage of new boys whose fathers did not attend public school was as high as 40–50 per cent. Equally significant was the fact that by 1950, 30 per cent of the population owned, or were buying, their own houses.

Although we shall soon be dealing with more subtle post-war social changes and developments it was the rising tide of affluence that is associated with the intensification of social problems which went along with it – and has continued to do so ever since.

By 1958 a great increase in crime in the population at large was apparent, but it was most significant in the 17–21 and 14–17 age-groups, where crime rates reached the highest ever known; among

---

[1]*Britain in the Century of Total War*, by Arthur Marwick, pp. 435–6.

the 8–14 group too, there was a rise from 924 criminal offences per 100,000 in 1955 to 1,176 per 100,000 in 1958.[1] Within the same time-span the Christian Economic and Social Research Foundation detected a sharp increase in drunkenness among under 21's. Insobriety in all age-groups in the late Fifties was about 40 per cent above the average for the 1930's, which represented a relapse to the worst conditions of the mid-1920's.[2]

Also, from the late 1950s there was a sharp increase in cases of venereal disease, of road accidents and of cancer which was the cause of one out of every five deaths. The following comments of the Committee on Children and Young Persons cannot be bettered:

> During the past fifty years there has been a tremendous material, social and moral revolution in addition to the upheaval of two world wars. While life in so many ways has become easier and more secure, the whole future of mankind may seem frighteningly uncertain. Everyday life may be less of a struggle, boredom and lack of challenge more a danger, but the fundamental insecurity remains with little that the individual can do about it. The material revolution is plain to see. At one and the same time it has provided more desirable objects, greater opportunity for acquiring them illegally, and considerable chances of immunity from the undesirable consequences of so doing. It is not always so clearly recognized what a complete change there has been in social and personal relationships (between classes, between the sexes and between individuals) and also in the basic assumptions which regulate behaviour. These major changes in the cultural background may well have replaced the disturbances of war as factors which contribute in themselves to instability within the family.[3]

And yet, compared with what came after, in the 'Swinging Sixties', the 1950s period is remarkable, at least superficially, for its continuity from the pre-war years. What lay behind the superficiality? Before addressing this interesting question, it is worth noting that immigration from the new Commonwealth was not significant until around 1960 (p. 167) so that this particular development cannot have any bearing on social changes in the 1950s.

---

[1]'Report of Committee on Children and Young Persons', 1960. Quoted in, *Britain in the Century of Total War*, by Arthur Marwick, p. 442.
[2]*Britain in the Century of Total War*, by Arthur Marwick, pp. 442–3.
[3]'Report of Committee on Children and Young Persons', 1960. Quoted in, *Britain in the Century of Total War*, by Arthur Marwick, p. 442.

Because of its pre-war morality and social attitudes as embodied, among other things, in marked class differences in speech and dress, the 1950s seem completely remote to us today. Yet these years created much that produced our present way of life and, more to the point, sowed the seeds for the revolution of the mid-sixties which is generally regarded as the dynamic turning point in post-war British social history. It is too often forgotten, or overlooked, that rock music started in this period with the advent of 'Rock Around the Clock' in 1955 and 'Let's Twist Again' in 1961, while in the early 1960s the Beatles (their first LP was in 1963), followed by the Rolling Stones, transformed the pop music scene as also did Mary Quant, in the field of fashion, around 1964, with her introduction of the mini-skirt. Apart from the pubs, night life was entirely geared towards the rich by virtue of cost and the rigorous dress codes but in the mid-fifties the theatre people were behind the opening of two West End Clubs, Gerry's and Buckstone, which were cheap and casual with, of course, no dress code. Hélène Cordet opened The Saddle Room, the first discotheque in London in 1961 and thereby established the spiritual home of the 'Swinging Sixties', where the long-haired priestesses gyrated in their mini-skirts. It was in the 1950s that the Italians pioneered the concept of popular restaurants for the masses, which was an essential part of the sixties' social revolution. Mention has already been made (p. 359) of 'an increased communal intellectual and cultural activity which took place during the war' for as well as the *Brain's Trust* there were the Council for the Encouragement of Music and the Arts, and Dame Myra Hess's lunchtime concerts at the National Gallery. This trend continued after the war as when the BBC took over the Henry Wood Promenade Concerts, thus popularizing them as well as saving them from closure. Even now, they evoke a delightfully nostalgic post-war atmosphere in spite of their increasing informality. The creation of the Third Programme in 1946 was another way in which the still paternalistic BBC furthered intellectual and cultural standards. In opera and ballet Benjamin Britten and Margot Fonteyn, respectively, won international recognition while in 1947 the success of the Van Gogh exhibition at the Tate Gallery is attested by the fact that it had 12,000 visitors a day. Art sales, which had prospered during the war, continued to do well in addition to establishing an English painting style, distinct from Continental influences. That most ambitious of post-war cultural developments, the Edinburgh International Festival of Music and Drama, was founded in 1947. However, the culmination of all this cultural activity was the Festival of Britain in 1951, which was 'post-war Britain's first great exercise in cultural paternalism, its repercussions have influenced public arts policy for decades'.[1]

In the field of communication the wartime habit of newspaper reading (p. 359) continued apace with the circulation of national and provincial daily newspapers increasing by 50 per cent between 1937 and 1947, and although it was no doubt initially due to wartime shortages the size of the newspapers was severely reduced thereby helping to pioneer the modern trend of sacrificing quality to quantity, in the sense of the number of newspapers as opposed to their size. From its beginning, with Northcliffe and Beaverbrook, the English popular press was unique in the world for its 'sensationalism', which was and is all the more dangerous owing to the national dominance of London. Compared to newspapers published in London, those published in New York, Paris, Bonn, Madrid or Rome are as much local as national newspapers. Another habit which was encouraged by wartime conditions was the reading of books and this also continued after the war so that in 1950 an international Gallup Poll showed that the British read many more books than any other nation which was also a tribute to the wartime cultural renaissance, which we have noticed, as well as to such negative causes as the blackout and restricted opportunities for entertainment. However, as always, 'culture' was confined to the articulate minority, and the popular culture was expressed on the football terraces and in the pubs, and especially, as an antidote to post-war austerity and poor housing conditions, the cinemas, attendance of which peaked-out at 1,635 millions in 1946.

> Central Office of Information inquiries conducted in March and October 1946 revealed that 32 per cent of the adult population went to the cinema at least once a week, that 13 per cent went more than once, and that only 24 per cent did not go at all. Among children of school age, 65 per cent went to the cinema once a week or more, and only 5 per cent did not go at all.[2]

In other words, the cinema played a similar part in the lives of the people, especially the children's, as does television today – and this fearsome instrument of mass culture and entertainment had its roots in the 1950s when it ran alongside radio, which was thriving on

---

[1] Richard Morrison, *The Times*, 27/4/91. Further facts and figures are attributable to Richard Morrison's article, 'A far from Merrie England'.
[2] *Britain in the Century of Total War*, by Arthur Marwick, p. 362.

producing programmes such as *The Goon Show*, the quintessence of British humour.

It was in the 1951 election that the parties, with some trepidation, first made television broadcasts. However, it was the televising of the Coronation in 1953 which was the initial impetus leading to the popularization of television, for many people bought television sets for this event specifically and immediately became addicts. Commercial television followed soon after and Granada's *Coronation Street* became part of the national consciousness, disregarding class and status, as did later programmes such as *Steptoe and Son* in these earlier pristine days of television innocence. In November 1953 a White Paper proposed to establish a new public corporation, the Independent Television Authority (in the manner of the BBC), to control sponsored television. The Television Bill, which had been opposed by the Labour Opposition, was published in March 1954, with strong emphasis on government control of the ITA, and commercial television commenced in September 1955. There was also strong opposition to this particular and vulgar manifestation of private enterprise among the conservative forces of society. I remember initially and ineffectually attempting to prevent my young family from watching it, but the forces arraigned against me were insuperable. By 1954 there were 3.5 million television licences in Britain and in 1958 Granada Television broadcast candidates and scenes from the Rochdale by-election campaign after preliminary discussions on the legal problem of possible infringement of the election laws; the BBC took up such reporting thereafter. By 1959 there were 10 million television licences in Britain and Aneurin Bevan called for the televising of Parliament. The 1959 General Election was known as the 'television election' (p. 410). The other aspect of today's mass culture, the package holiday, was also pioneered in the 1950s by Butlin's holiday camps which were tailor-made for the masses – another social revolution, in fact. Finally, Harold Macmillan is associated with the introduction of Premium Savings Bonds in 1956 and the Betting and Gaming Act of 1960, both of which represented a breakout from the bonds imposed by Victorian evangelicalism. The former was a restoration of the institution of public lottery which had thrived in the eighteenth century, and the latter was a brave attempt to restore respect for the law by legalizing street betting shops, gambling houses and bingo. However, this had an unfortunate by-product in that the legalizing of West End gambling clubs left them vulnerable to criminal 'protection' rackets and provided the notorious Kray brothers with their biggest opportunity, for they soon established supremacy in this endeavour, against all-comers.

367

Our understanding of the 1950s has been recently enhanced by the televising of H.E. Bates's, *The Darling Buds of May*. The paradox is that this idealized version of English village life, in the period, where the sun always shines, coincided with the 'decade of Suez and McCarthy, bleak Samuel Beckett plays and Stockhausen's ghastly electric music, grey architecture, rationing and tight-lipped prudishness'.[1] But Bates was drawing on the deeply ingrained English tradition of a romantic conception of village life – fresh-cheeked maidens with high bosoms, besporting themselves around the maypole and besmocked men of the soil viewing them from the thatched-roofed village pub nestling close to the beautifully spired medieval church – both the centres of village life. The medievalists say that 'Merrie England' was at its height in the twelfth century but as we have seen (p. 321), the English rural scene was comparatively unspoiled until the middle of the eighteenth century, and although we note its subsequent decline, the English genius for reconciling change and tradition means that Bates's Larkin family, although drawing on large quantities of writers' licence, is by no means improbable. In my view, the wisest political remark ever made was Adam Smith's dictum: 'There is an awful lot of ruin in a nation.' This applied especially to post-war Britain. But whereas Marwick bemoans the 'deadweight of "gradualism"'[2] in our peacetime history, as ruinously resisting change (and as I also have in some particular respects, such as local government), on the whole, I welcome it because it is combined, paradoxically, with the capacity for change. Nowhere is this illustrated better than in *The Darling Buds of May*. As Richard Morrison says:

> The cockney working-class hero, out-witting his social superiors, entered British culture. Little people began to shout for their rights. In one Ealing comedy after another, downtrodden underlings suddenly uttered bulldog snarls against those accustomed to giving orders.[3]

The sensuality and sexuality also exhibited by Bates's heroes and heroines, innocently and unselfconsciously, anticipated the permissive society of the 1960s which was also captured in the lines of the contemporary poet, Philip Larkin:

---

[1]'A far from Merrie England', *The Times*, 27/4/91, by Richard Morrison.
[2]*Britain in the Century of Total War*, by Arthur Marwick, p. 462.
[3]'A far from Merrie England', *The Times*, 27/4/91, by Richard Morrison.

Sexual intercourse began
In nineteen sixty-three
(which was rather late for me)
Between the end of the *Chatterly* ban
And the Beatles first L.P.[1]

Similarly, 'Pop' Larkin and his family could not remotely be classed as rebels, in the 1960s sense, for, in the end, they accepted, without reservation, the social conventions and class divisions of their day.

There were, however, rebels at the time. Although the expression 'Angry Young Man', was first used as the title of L. Paul's book in 1951, in 1957 a symposium of 'Angry Young Men' expressed in 'Declaration' their opposition to consumer values and Establishment complacency, a view which was mirrored in a significant literary outburst. Plays such as John Osborne's *Look Back in Anger* (1956) and novels such as Kingsley Amis's *Lucky Jim* (1956) and John Braine's *Room at the Top* (1957), known as 'Kitchen Sink' drama in the first case, and which broke decisively away from the vapid, drawing-room comedies of the Noel Coward era, rubbed the noses of the public in the bleak and unromantic problems of everyday working-class life. The publisher of *Declaration* was Ken Tynan, the controversial London theatre critic and 'the luvvie to end all luvvies'. In his declaration, Tynan eulogizes downward social mobility as opposed to the Victorian ideal of upward social mobility and self-improvement, and he linked it with socialism and sexual liberation. In 1960, Tynan was the first journalist to use the four-letter word in one of his articles without being prosecuted, while in 1965 he actually said it on a BBC late night programme. In 1969 his nude review, *Oh Calcutta*, was a world-wide success. More down-to-earth prophets were Richard Hoggart and Raymond Williams who published books in 1957 and 1958 respectively, praising the virtues of the working class and making their behaviour appear attractive. That there was a demand for the new 'Kitchen Sink' drama was not surprising in view of the fact that the middle and upper classes were also traditionally repelled by consumer values, as well as to their capacity to absorb and respond to social change – that wonderful English tolerance and liberalism (with a small 'l' of course) which can be so frustrating to those of us who are dedicated to maintaining traditions and traditional values. This is also the main reason why the rebels

---

[1] 'A far from Merrie England', *The Times*, 27/4/91, by Richard Morrison.

incurred the displeasure of their Continental contemporaries, whose attitude was much more akin to that of the egregious Dr Jonathan Miller who declared:

> The ranks are drawn up and the air resounds with the armourer's hammer. When the battle is joined, one can only hope that blood will be drawn.[1]

Instead, by 1961 the middle-class intellectuals had created the safety valve of the satire industry in the form of *Beyond the Fringe* and *Private Eye*. A by-product was the television programme, *That Was the Week that Was*, but it was significant that in 1963 Hugh Carleton-Green, the BBC Director General, opaquely announced that it would end because 'the political content of the programme will be difficult to maintain'. It was probably more to the point that a general election was imminent, together with the prospects for the renewal of the BBC's charter. In the field of morals and morality, the Wolfenden Report of 1957 recommended the legalization of homosexuality[2], while the saga of D.H. Lawrence's *Lady Chatterly's Lover*, when the decision of Penguin Books to print an unexpurgated paperback, led to the sensational court case in October 1960 which not only failed in its purpose but afforded the utmost publicity for the book itself – four-letter words and all – and was an historic watershed for this particular liberal cause. At the end of the period, in 1963, the Bishop of Woolwich's 'Honest to God' asked questions about the literal truth of the Bible which had previously been kept well 'under wraps', in spite of the implications of Darwin's nineteenth-century theory of evolution. Thus, the Sixties' social revolution went on to make history by decisively broadening the basis of our society but, unfortunately, like most revolutions it went to

---

[1] Quoted by Christopher Booker in the *Sunday Telegraph*, 16/6/92. He also gave us the glad tidings that Dr Miller had announced that he was to abandon 'mean, peevish, little Britain' to work abroad.

[2] A private member's Bill to this effect was introduced in 1966 by the Conservative MP, Humphrey Berkeley, but his constituents were so incensed that he lost his seat in the ensuing surprise General Election, which also put paid to his Bill, although a new one was introduced and passed in 1967. Together with the abolition of the death penalty and 'reforms' in the laws on abortion, race relations, divorce and the right to vote, marry and enter into financial dealings at the age of eighteen, this ushered in the so-called 'permissive society'. The Labour philosophy of the time was summed up by Roy Jenkins, Home Secretary, from 1965 to 1967, in his alleged statement: 'the permissive society is the civilized society' – or words to that effect.

seed. Christopher Booker's book *Neophiliacs*, written in 1969, described this process as 'the fantasy world into which so many people were drawn in the Fifties and Sixties by their mania for any new thing, however meaningless'.[1] More specifically, it was hijacked by the liberal establishment, on the one hand, and our most unfortunate and unwelcome post-war creation, the tattooed and mindless working-class thug, on the other. The only thing which could have stopped the latter in his tracks was corporal punishment which was abolished as a court sentence (except in the Isle of Man) by the Criminal Justice Act of 1948.[2] The link between the two was Roy Jenkins, and all that he stood for, and the relentless rise in personal wealth in spite of continued economic crises, together with the introduction of the comprehensive system of education and the 'progressive' prejudices that went with it.

It remains to consider the effects of the Sixties revolution on the Establishment which by no means went unscathed and which is well illustrated by the abolition of the distinction between 'Gentlemen' and 'Players' in 1962 by the MCC, perhaps the most formidable of all Establishments. The superficial reason for this decision was that it was out of keeping with the times that the 'Gentlemen' should have 'Mr' in front of their names, be called 'Sir' by the professionals, enjoy separate dressing rooms and travel first class on trains while the professionals travelled third. The basic reason was the diminishing number of talented cricketers with private (unearned) incomes. Nevertheless, the paradoxical result has been that in a world in which all cricketers are now professional, the game has gradually declined owing to the absence of its gifted amateurs for, as Orwell has pointed out, cricket is 'one of the very few games in which the amateur can excel over the professional'.[3] Even more important, the abolitionists, in their haste to abolish the remnants of class distinction and elitism, overlooked the all-important fact that English county cricket could not successfully support 200 or more professional cricketers. It would have been much better, from every point of view, to have carried on

---

[1] Quoted by Christopher Booker in the *Sunday Telegraph*, 19/5/91.

[2] It is still on the statute in the Isle of Man but is subject to strict guidelines.

[3] 'We can't afford to lose our amateurs', The *Sunday Telegraph*, 14/4/91, by Geoffrey Wheatcroft. The whole sad story has culminated in the humiliating defeat of England by Zimbabwe in the Christmas and New Year Tests in 1996–7. Until the time of writing this note I have neither heard nor read one commentator who has admitted that the two amateur fast bowlers (both farmers) who destroyed us were infinitely more talented than our opening bowlers.

as before and simply abolish the social distinctions which had become meaningless, even though there would have been the problem of maintaining the supply of amateurs. In his excellent article, Geoffrey Wheatcroft describes the outcome as 'the law of unintended consequences'.[1] He also states:

> It was appropriate that cricketing amateurs disappeared at the beginning of the 1960's, the decade in which the country fell for a particular illusion of modernity and grew too big for its boots. Cities were pulled down and were hideously rebuilt, the poor were decanted into tower blocks, new universities sprouted everywhere. This would have been bad enough if we could have afforded these foibles or follies, but we could not; and the expansion of the Sixties has been at the heart of our problems ever since. Similarly, the abolition of the amateur cricketer was carried out in a mood of naive optimism. The question had been debated in the wrong terms.[2]

It is significant that the governments of the 1960s were presided over by 'the two Harolds' who took to the prevailing philosophy like 'ducks to water' so that the policies of their governments were barely distinguishable. Chapters 6 and 7, on 'The Mixed Economy' and 'Full Employment', respectively, describe Macmillan's obsession with indicative planning and the 'ill-fated' corporatism (p. 82) which were applied even more rigorously by Wilson, with even more disastrous results. Both were guilty of entering Christopher Booker's 'fantasy world' by proceeding on the basis of completely unrealistic economic growth targets which failed to take into account that Britain was no longer in a position to compete against Japanese large-scale industry and that her strength was in smaller-scale operations, facts which were appreciated after 1979. Wilson was also naively attached to the idea that Britain's economic problems could be solved at will by somehow utilizing the fruits of science and technology as was summed up in his memorable phrase, 'the white heat of the technological revolution'. Macmillan did not think of this but if he had the idea would have appealed to him equally. Above all, both were up to their eyes in the culture which was responsible for the creation of shameful, architectural monstrosities throughout Britain. In London, and elsewhere, working-class 'villages', where people had

---

[1]'We can't afford to lose our amateurs', The *Sunday Telegraph*, 14/4/91, by Geoffrey Wheatcroft.
[2]Ibid.

lived in their sparse but homely back-to-back houses for generations, using the local pub as a social centre, were replaced by cheerless tower and other blocks which simply tore the soul out of their way of life and from which they have never recovered. Whereas the old houses could have been modernized to form even more agreeable communities, they were destroyed to create these monstrosities which inevitably became universities of crime and 'hell-holes' for the majority of law-abiding citizens. High-rise hotels and office blocks were built in London and other cities by both governments, usually against the provisions of local by-laws, and without any thought or attention to the safeguards that would be enforced in a city such as Paris to protect its visual appearance and character. Then there were the violations of the planners who relocated industry and people from city centres to outer districts, thus creating wastelands in the old centre and unnecessary communications problems in the new locations. As Sir Desmond Pitcher, of Littlewoods and Liverpool, who has been associated with the recent regeneration of Merseyside, has said: 'The heart was torn out of the city by moving industry and people to places such as Skelmersdale.' When I used to take boxing teams from Shrewsbury School to its 'Mission' in Scotland Road in the early 1950s, this area of Liverpool was grim – a veritable eye-opener – but it had plenty of heart – and soul. Similarly, Manchester was destroyed in the 1960s and 1970s, probably even more than Liverpool, as Nicholas Pevsner, the distinguished architectural critic, acknowledged by saying that when he visited Manchester in 1969 he 'walked through areas of total desolation'. The outcome is modern Moss Side and Salford, high-rise estates and forbidding 'no-go' areas which are symbolic of the tragic heritage bequeathed to us by the 'idealists' of the 1960s.

16

Political, 1945–64

At the end of Chapter 5 (p. 77) I set out the aspects of the post-war consensus that were to be the subjects of the following chapters. Chapters 6–10, inclusive, are necessarily confined to the period 1945–64, but Chapters 11–13, inclusive, are, in effect, brief histories of their particular subjects while Chapter 14, on Law, can be regarded as a brief history when taken in conjunction with the relevant parts in Chapter 1 and in Chapter 13 on Local Government. However, they all end at 1964 and do not deal with the more narrow 'political' situation. On the other hand, Chapter 5 is concerned with the political situation leading to the General Election of 1945. It therefore remains to cover the 'politics' of the remaining years until 1964 and this shall be done by each section dealing with the political events and trends leading up to each particular general election. As indicated on page 72 an analysis of each election is necessary in order to emphasize the fact that our electoral system succeeds where other more mathematically precise ones do not, in reflecting the wishes and needs of the people.

The General Election of 1950

As early as 1941 the Conservatives set up the Post-war Problems Committee under the leadership of Butler and Maxwell-Fyfe and this became the Advisory Committee on Policy and Political Education in 1945. During the war Churchill discouraged party political activity, party because of his preoccupation with his monumental task, and partly on principle, so that what little was done was mainly due to backbench activity and through unofficial groups such as the Tory Reform Group, led by Quintin Hogg and Lord Hitchingbroke, which played an important part in persuading Conservative ministers to accept the Beveridge Report. Although the electoral defeat of 1945 was a severe setback to Churchill he did not galvanize himself into an inspired Opposition leader but continued to wear his mantle as a world statesman, as we have seen. Insofar as he was interested in

374

home affairs and party policy (we have already noted the significant extent of political consensus after 1945) he clung to the Disraelian ideals of a 'Tory Democracy'; that is to say, 'a paternalist but magnanimous state that would intervene to protect the underprivileged members of society . . .'[1]

Nevertheless, all-important changes were made in these post-war years to both Conservative Party policy and organization. Owing to wartime neglect, the 1945 election showed that the latter had lost its pre-war superiority to the Labour Party and the immediate need was to remedy the situation. To do this Churchill made the inspired move of appointing Lord Woolton as Chairman of the party in 1946. When he displayed his impressive skills as an administrator in his wartime role as Minister of Food, Woolton was a true member of the National Government as he did not join the Conservative Party until 1945. However, his success in increasing the party membership and finances was quite outstanding for by 1950 there were as many as 575 full-time local agents in England and Wales alone, around twice the number employed by the Labour Party in the whole of Great Britain. Paradoxically, the 1948 rule forbidding candidates to donate more than £25 per annum to party funds led to a strengthening of both the former as well as party organization. The rule followed the report on the party machinery by the Maxwell-Fyfe Committee which stated that:

> The organization of the party was weakest in places where a wealthy candidate had made it unnecessary for the members to trouble to collect small subscriptions.

In 1949 Lord Woolton initiated a major expansion of the Young Conservatives which was to become the largest youth organization in the world (and, probably and unofficially, the largest marriage bureau) and by far and away ahead of its rivals in the other two parties – a veritable political greenhouse. Owing to Lord Woolton's efforts the Conservatives regained their old reputation for superior organization, in the way of soliciting postal votes and the like, which paid practical dividends in winning seats that would otherwise have been lost. On the whole, the Conservative Party has retained this advantage and has only looked like losing it when in recent years it has been tempted to succumb to the American importation of slick

---

[1]*Post-War Britain*, by Alan Sked and Chris Cook, pp. 77–8. Further facts and figures in this chapter are attributable to this authority.

election campaigns run by advertising and media men. Neil Kinnock must rue the day when he failed to resist this enticing temptation although Tony Blair's New Labour would seem to have made more successful use of modern techniques, but much more important are his personal gifts of presentation.

In regard to policy, Lord Woolton's dynamism in the field of organization was mirrored by R.A. Butler, who became Chairman of the Conservative Research Department in 1945 where he was assisted by brilliant young men, including future ministers, Reginald Maudling, Enoch Powell and Iain Macleod. He was also supported by the more established Conservative intellectuals, namely Oliver Lyttleton, David Maxwell-Fyfe, Harold Macmillan and Anthony Eden. The establishment of the Committee on Policy and Political Eduction, again with Butler as chairman, and the Conservative Political Centre provided for the dissemination of policy and ideas to the local party organizations, as well as for the reverse process whereby local views were sent back to Butler and his scions at Smith Square. From the latter emanated the 'One Nation' group of 1950, followed by the Bow Group, both outlets of dynamic, radical and Young Conservative ideas. The importance of this development cannot be exaggerated for, in its own field, it was just as great a change as confining candidates to £25 donations.

Meanwhile, on the wider front, an Industrial Policy Committee produced the party's 'Industrial Charter' in 1947 which, in Butler's words, was

> an assurance that, in the interests of efficiency, full employment and social security, modern Conservatism would maintain strong central guidance over the operation of the economy.[1]

This was the embodiment of the post-war consensus (and Butler was essentially a consensus man) and, with a view to the forthcoming election, similar statements were made on agriculture, the Empire, Scotland and Wales after Eden had skilfully and successfully presented the Industrial Charter to the annual party conference in 1947, thereby overcoming possible objections by Churchill or the more traditional party activists at the conference. However, as well as undertaking to maintain and extend the social services, the party also committed itself to encouraging private enterprise by reductions in taxation, and the like, thus laying the post-war foundations for the

---

[1] Quoted in *Post-War Britain*, by Alan Sked and Chris Cook, p. 80.

economic credibility of Conservative governments (in spite of the problems of 'Stop-Go'), whereas Labour was to become labelled as the party of high taxation and economic failure. In December 1947, the Gallup poll gave the Conservatives 50.5 per cent, Labour 38 per cent and the Liberals 9 per cent.

A general election had to be held by July 1950 at the latest and the Labour Government needed a recovery in the economy and ideally the ending of rationing and controls. In the latter respect, Harold Wilson, the young President of the Board of Trade, did excellent work from 1948, abolishing the rationing of potatoes, bread, jam, footwear and reducing that of clothes in that year, as well as the elimination of 20,000 licences, to be followed by another 900,000 in 1949 – a 'bonfire of controls', in his words – thereby ending all clothes and textile rationing while the petrol ration was doubled for the summer. Only meat remained scarce. The economic recovery of 1948, under Cripps's guidance, the continued dollar deficit leading to the devaluation of 1949 and heralding the post-war weakness of the British economy, have been dealt with on pages 91–3. Although both the Government and the Opposition had, in practice, reached a consensus in regard to the question of nationalization it was this that came to the fore in the months leading to the election. In the Labour publication of April 1949, 'Labour Believes in Britain', there were concessions to the left, including a major extension of public ownership and the introduction of equal pay for women. The bill for the nationalization of iron and steel was given its third reading in May, to the accompaniment of intense Opposition hostility, but in order to allay the opposition of the House of Lords to the Parliament Act (reducing the Lords' veto from two years to one year) p. 80 the Government undertook not to proceed with the former bill until after the election. However, this did not prevent (indeed, it could be said that it encouraged) the outbreak of an intense anti-nationalization campaign by the steelmakers, aided and abetted by the insurance companies (which established 400 anti-nationalization committees throughout the country) and the cement and sugar industries, including the invention of the unforgettable 'Mr Cube' by Tate & Lyle.

Wisely, Lord Woolton ensured that the Conservative Party did not join in this full-frontal attack on nationalization for there was much ammunition that it could usefully deploy, the lead being given by Churchill. He said that:

Socialism with its vast network of regulations and restrictions and its incompetent planning and purchasing by Whitehall officials,

377

(was) proving itself every day to be a dangerous and costly fallacy.[1]

Coming so soon after the groundnuts farce (pp. 81–2) these words must have struck home forcibly. He said further:

> Every major industry which the Socialists have nationalized, without exception, has passed from the profitable or self-supporting side of the balance sheet to the loss-making, debit side . . .[2]

Furthermore, the post-war euphoria for economic planning was now being attacked by distinguished academics. In 1948, Professor John Jewkes of Manchester University, published his *Ordeal by Planning* which attacked socialist controls and called for an untrammelled market economy. More philosophically, Thomas Wilson, an Oxford economist, in his *Modern Capitalism and Economic Progress*, argued that private capitalism was the best guarantee of individual liberties, thus supporting Churchill's controversial speech in September 1949, the main import of which was that Socialism and Communism were intimately connected. The same can be said of George Orwell's novel, *1984*, written, of course, in 1948 which, at least on the face of it, gave a frightening picture of the consequences of Communist rule.

Having established its credentials as a believer in the Welfare State, the Conservative Party was now appearing to be the moderate party in view of the venomous statements made by some of its leading opponents, such as Bevan stating that Tories were 'lower than vermin', Shinwell saying that he 'didn't give a tinker's cuss' except for organized labour, Bessie Braddock declaiming: 'I don't care two hoots at any time if the other side is not alright; I don't care if they starve to death.' Less venomous yet more frightening was Hartley Shawcross's boast: 'We are the masters now.' In the cold-war atmosphere of the time Labour's tendency towards extremism was emphasized by the fact that between 1949 and 1950 five MPs were expelled from the Parliamentary Labour Party for 'fellow-travelling'. As Churchill emphasized in his significant statement in 1952 (p. 152) there was a consensus on foreign policy and defence (as well as on social services) so that the real critics of Ernest Bevin's foreign policy were within the Labour Party, dating from the issue of 'Keep Left' in 1947, written by Michael Foot, Richard Crossman and Ian Mikado, calling for a

---

[1] Quoted in *Post-War Britain*, by Alan Sked and Chris Cook, p. 83.
[2] Ibid., p. 83.

socialist foreign policy separate from both those of the United States and the Soviet Union. In January 1950 the group published a second pamphlet, 'Keeping Left', which reluctantly accepted the American Alliance. On the eve of the election, in February 1950, Churchill caught the Government off its balance by proposing 'another talk with Soviet Russia at the highest level' in 'a supreme effort' to end the 'hatred and manoeuvres of the cold war'. Although Bevin dismissed this as an election stunt, once again Churchill had successfully portrayed himself as a world statesman among mere politicians.

A Conservative election document was published in July 1949, before Attlee had announced in October that there would be no autumn election. 'The Right Road for Britain' argued for the retention of economic controls until the trade gap was closed but looked for an eventual partnership of capital and labour under the guidance rather than the control of the state. Significantly, at the Conservative Party annual conference in October Churchill admitted that as far as the existing nationalization measures were concerned, 'it is physically impossible to undo much that has been done.' (The climate of opinion had certainly changed by 1979.) Nevertheless, by the end of that month the Gallup poll showed 45 per cent Labour, 39 per cent Conservative and 12 per cent Liberal support. In January 1950, 'Keeping Left' had also attacked the wage restraint policy and the two major party election manifestos appeared. Although there was little enthusiasm among the leadership for nationalization, the left was strong enough in the Labour Party for its, 'Let Us Win Through With Labour', to list the cement, chemical and sugar refining and manufacturing industries for public ownership, a choice which at the time seemed rather arbitrary and curious, thus further diminishing respect for the concept of nationalization. The Conservative's, 'This is the Road', called for 'a true property-owning democracy' and promised the Scotland Office Cabinet Status. In all, by removing the prospect that if they were returned to power the Tories would dismantle the Welfare State (although they made the valid point that the government should not be regarded as a bottomless financial pit) they were in a position of strength to benefit from the various causes of dissatisfaction occasioned by any Labour government in power. At the end of the month, at an emergency Liberal conference in London, Clement Davies had declared that Liberals had high hopes of emerging from the election stronger than for two generations. In October 1948 their statement, 'Programme for Britain', called for proportional representation, home rule for Scotland and Wales and ownership for all through profit-sharing and co-partnership. In early February their manifesto, 'No Easy Way', claimed that the Liberals were the only party free of class conflict. Yet, as we have seen in Chapter 2, whether or not there was any merit in the claim, this was making a virtue of a necessity, as the fundamental reason for their loss of power was the failure to capture working-class support at a crucial time. The General Election of February 23 1950 took place under different conditions from the previous one, following the Representation of People Act in 1949, which abolished the university and business premises' franchises as well as that of the City of London as a separate constituency, thus reducing the number of MPs from 640 to 625. However, the evening-up of the numerical size of the constituencies, in order to eliminate the large anomalies in 1945, led to the creation of 17 new constituencies. The result was as follows:

Party	Votes Gained	Percentage of Vote	Average Vote per MP	Number of MPs
Conservative	12,502,567	43.5	41,955	298
Labour	13,266,592	46.1	42,116	315
Liberal	2,621,548	9.1	291,283	9
Communist	91,746	0.3	—	—
Others	290,218	1.0		3
	28,772,671	100.0		625

Source: Derived from D. Butler and A. Sloman, *British Political Facts, 1900–75.*

The electorate had proved to be extremely interested: the poll was 10½ per cent up on that of 1945 and at 84 per cent the heaviest recorded in British history. This meant that nearly 4 million more voters than last time had turned out on polling day. The results of the election were somewhat paradoxical: Labour had received more votes than at any other time in its history, but it had also seen its overall majority reduced to only five. The Liberal and Communist parties had lost further ground, despite increased numbers of candidates. Finally, the Conservative Party had failed to win the election although it had gained an extra 2 million votes. There had been a swing to the Tories of 3.3 per cent, a swing which was most marked in the suburbs of the south. Labour had frightened the middle classes in the suburbs of the home counties and the north as well, although it survived this loss of popularity because it could count on enthusiastic working-class support. Both parties, in fact, could see in the election results some form of moral victory: the

Conservatives on account of their impressive gain in seats, Labour on account of its unprecedented number of votes. It was the Labour Party, however, which had won the victory which mattered. For the Liberal and Communist Parties there was simply no consolation. 319 out of 475 Liberal candidates lost their deposits, while their parliamentary representation was cut from eleven to nine. Ninety-seven out of 100 Communist candidates lost their deposits and not a single one this time was elected. Needless to say, the electoral system once more held back the Liberals. It took only 42,000 votes to elect a Labour or Conservative MP, while to elect a Liberal member, on the other hand, required almost 300,000 votes.[1]

The General Election of 1951

In retrospect, Hugh Gaitskell said, referring to the new Labour Government, with its narrow majority of five:

> Most of us who were in the 1945–50 Parliament knew that we just about had as much as we could conceivably digest in those five years.[2]

In an otherwise uncontroversial King's Speech in March, the Government included the promised nationalization of iron and steel which passed into public ownership in February 1951. But the Government leaders were aged. Cripps and Bevin were destined to retire before the next election because of ill health and Dalton, Morrison and Attlee were also coming to the end of their political careers. It was necessary to resort to bringing sick MPs to the House of Commons on stretchers. On 29 March, the Government suffered its first Commons defeat when it decided to adjourn the fuel and power debate, by 283 to 257 votes, but Attlee refused to resign on grounds that the defeat was not serious. Nevertheless, there were some, even if superficial, grounds for optimism in the economy, and elsewhere, as we noted on page 377 and in more detail on page 93. The recovery in the economy since 1948 and the 1949 devaluation had led to the aforementioned extraordinary increase in exports and, following the significant easing in controls, the Government planned to celebrate its post-war achievements by organizing the Festival of Britain to be held on the centenary of the Great Exhibition of 1851. However, as Harold Macmillan replied with one word, 'Events', when asked what most

---

[1] *Post-War Britain*, by Alan Sked and Chris Cook, pp. 85–6.
[2] Ibid., p. 87.

worried him as Prime Minister, the inherent weakness of this Labour Government was ruthlessly exposed by a series of 'events' overseas, the first and most fatal of which was the Korean War.

This is dealt with in Chapter 10, Foreign and Defence Policy, (pp. 146–7), while the disastrous financial and economic consequences are recorded in Chapter 7, Full Employment (p. 96), notably the balance of payments crisis in the summer of 1951 as a result of 'the pronounced rise in world commodity prices following the Korean War, which was exacerbated by the 1949 devaluation . . .' But it was the political 'fallout' of Gaitskell's controversial 'Tory-like' budget of April 1951 which will capture the headlines of history when the financial crisis has been sidelined. On 3 April Bevan had warned that he 'will never be a member of a government which makes charges on the National Health Service', the budget was presented on the 10th and Bevan resigned in protest as Minister of Labour on the 21st, followed by Harold Wilson, as President of the Board of Trade, on the 23rd, on the grounds that the economy could not bear the level of rearmament which the Government was proposing (a view with which Churchill effectively concurred as Prime Minister in December) (p. 97), and by John Freeman, a junior minister. On the 26th, a private meeting of 15 Labour MPs, including Bevan and Wilson, founded the 'Bevanite' grouping as the successor to 'Keep Left' and they proceeded to launch a left-wing revolt against the Government's foreign and defence policy. In June the 'Tribune' group published, 'One Way Only', by Bevan and Wilson, calling for a reorientation of foreign policy to support colonial liberation movements and for reduced armaments. This was a substantial nail in the Government's coffin and it only needed Dr Mussedeq's nationalization of British oil assets in Iran which, in turn, encouraged Egyptian intransigence regarding the Suez Canal, to nail it down completely. Morrison's failure to surmount the unfortunate sequence of events in the Middle East is described in Chapter 10 (pp. 150–1) and although Egypt's abrogation of the 1936 treaty with Britain did not take place until two days after the General Election of 25 October, by this time the Government had lost the will to govern for it was called on 19 September. More and more was being left to the senior civil servants as was evinced in Douglas Jay's memorable remark that 'the man in Whitehall "knew best"', and also in the words of Richard Crossman: 'In 1951 the Attlee government quietly expired in the arms of the Whitehall Establishment.'[1] However, it must be said that Attlee's governments

---

[1]*Post-War Britain*, by Alan Sked and Chris Cook, p. 98.

took the moderate course of pursuing 'a programme designed to consolidate and strengthen the social cohesion engendered by the war',[1] thus becoming 'a respectable and natural party of government'.[2] By the same token, by its moderation, the Conservative Party had helped to create the consensus that has been described. In the 1950s and 1960s both parties had to come to terms with the fact that it was increasingly difficult, if not impossible, for Britain to play the part of a world power, which was intrinsically linked with the major problem of her flawed economy.

In September, the Conservative election manifesto, written by Churchill, called for a stable government and promised the denationalization of steel and the construction of 300,000 houses a year, which Labour castigated as pure electioneering and which Bevan said was 'impractical and dishonest'. However, it had been called for at the party conferences in 1950 and 1951 (p. 236) in the former of which Churchill also envisaged a 'growing association of Tory democracy with the trade unions', which heralded his fraternal policy towards them when he formed the next government. It was followed by the Labour manifesto which made no new public ownership proposals and called for peace and full employment – the counsel of perfection! In early October the Liberal manifesto called for national unity and the ending of party and class strife – another council of perfection! Throughout 1950 Churchill and the Conservatives had made gestures towards an alliance with the Liberals, even considering proportional representation, which made a great deal of sense, considering the fact that in the two great break-ups of the Liberal Party, 1886 and after 1916, the Conservatives took over not only the vast majority of its personnel but also of its policies and traditions. The Liberals thus condemned themselves to being a fringe party in every sense of the word, a situation which was confirmed when the Alliance, consisting of the combined Liberal Party and Labour's 1981 dynamic offshoot, the Social Democratic Party, was killed off by David Steel after the 1989 General Election.

In the event, the election was fought on superficial party rivalries concerning war and the economy. In regard to the former, there was not only the Korean War but also the emergency in Malaya and the threatening situations in Iran and Egypt. In Korea, the British feared that 'the US would use the atom bomb and cause a world war' (p. 147), although this had been largely overcome by President Truman's dismissal of General MacArthur in April 1951 after he had openly

---

[1]*Post-War Britain*, by Alan Sked and Chris Cook, p. 100.
[2]Ibid., p. 101.

defied the President in calling for an extension of the war to China. Nevertheless, Labour condemned the Tories, in general, and Churchill, in particular, as warmongers. Michael Foot stated that:

> The threat of world war under Tory rule was the 'main issue' of the election campaign and the proposition 'Churchill and MacArthur = Atomic War' was bandied about irresponsibly by many Labour candidates.[1]

There was also the infamous headline in the *Daily Mirror* on election day – 'Whose Finger on the Trigger' – which led to an historic libel suit. On the economic front, Labour also employed scare tactics by dredging up horror stories of pre-war unemployment under the Tories. The eternal Michael Foot

> warned against 'the mass unemployment which we always have under the Tories' and Harold Wilson averred that 'mass unemployment which would most surely follow a return of the Tories to power would lay the country open to the evils of Communism'.[2]

Apart from their more positive policies on house-building and tax reductions, the Conservatives repaid the complaint by pointing out the instability of socialist mis-management of the economy and failure to support the nation's interests. Churchill was in a very strong position to criticize Morrison's tenuous grasp on foreign policy, not to mention the threat posed by the views of Bevan and his 'Bevanite' colleagues. The Conservatives led in the opinion polls throughout the campaign although it was reduced to a lead of only 2.5 per cent by polling day on 25 October.

The result was as follows:

Party	Votes Gained	Percentage of Vote	Average Vote per MP	Number of MPs
Conservative	13,717,538	48.0	42,731	321
Labour	13,948,605	48.8	47,283	295
Liberal	730,556	2.5	121,759	6
Communist	21,640	0.1	—	—
Others	177,329	0.6		3
	28,595,668	100.0		625

Source: Derived from D. Butler and A. Sloman, *British Political Facts, 1900–75*.

---

[1]*Post-War Britain*, by Alan Sked and Chris Cook, p. 98.
[2]Ibid., p. 99.

Once again the election had attracted enormous interest, an interest which was demonstrated by a poll of 82 per cent. Despite Labour's slight lead in votes, there had been a swing against it in the country which gave the Conservative Party a majority in the House of Commons. Two factors were instrumental in producing this. In the first place, Labour tended to accumulate its votes in large majorities in safe constituencies. Secondly, the comparative lack of Liberal candidates undoubtedly helped the Conservatives. 475 Liberal candidates in 1950 had secured more than 2.5 million votes and over 9 per cent of the poll. In 1951 only 109 Liberal candidates presented themselves and took less than 3 per cent of the poll with less than three quarters of a million votes. The majority of former Liberal voters, it was estimated, therefore, had this time voted for the Conservative Party.

For the Liberals themselves, the election was an unmitigated disaster: their representation in Parliament was reduced from nine MP's to six; their plight was surpassed only by that of the Communist Party which received a derisory 0.07 per cent of the poll. Once again, the results could be claimed a moral victory for both the major parties. The Labour Party, though defeated, had won more votes than ever before and for the third time since the war had secured more votes in an election than the Conservative Party.[1]

The General Election of 1955

When he became the peacetime Prime Minister for the first and only time Winston Churchill was 77, having already had two strokes, while he was to have two more before his retirement in 1955. Thus during this period he was only a shadow of his former self, not only physically but also mentally. An apocryphal joke at the time summed it up when Churchill, referring to a junior member of the Government, was alleged to have growled: 'Who's that young man?' It was for this reason that Anthony Eden's appointment to the all-important position of Foreign Secretary was so significant, for like everyone else, Churchill regarded him as his natural successor, although he could well have had a premonition that he was not strong enough for the task, which is probably one reason why he was loathe to retire. Inevitably, the average age of the Cabinet was 60 years, for it consisted largely of his wartime colleagues and his aristocratic and upper-class friends such as Lords Woolton, Charwell and Leathers, and David Maxwell-Fyfe as Home Secretary. Men

---

[1] *Post-War Britain*, by Alan Sked and Chris Cook, pp. 99–100.

such as Beaverbrook and Bracken were not in the Cabinet but they nevertheless wielded great political influence. Churchill regarded his peacetime Cabinet as an extension of his wartime one, not only in relation to personnel but also to attitudes and organization. For example, his meritorious 'overlords' experiment between 1951 and 1953 had the object of reducing the size of the Cabinet by including several ministries under super-ministers or 'overlords'. For example, Lord Charwell, as Paymaster-General, was to co-ordinate scientific research and development, Lord Woolton as Lord President of the Council was concerned with food and agriculture and Lord Leathers with Transport, Fuel and Power, thus permitting the Minsters of Agriculture and Fisheries, Food, Transport and Civil Aviation, and Fuel and Power, to be excluded from the Cabinet. Unfortunately, the experiment did not succeed because all the 'overlords' sat in the House of Lords. But it must not be thought that Churchill's Government was entirely conservative or backward-looking because it manifested the other historic English precept of radicalism, namely the appointments of R.A. Butler as Chancellor of the Exchequer, and Harold Macmillan as Minister of Housing. Both were regarded as leaders of the radical Conservatism which had emerged with Lord Woolton's post-war reorganization of the party. By the same token, Iain Macleod, Enoch Powell and Edward Heath attained their first government appointments during this administration, that of the first as Minister of Health in May 1952 being especially important. Neither should it be forgotten that Churchill was, above all, unconventional and capable of radical ideas (p. 45). This was well summed-up in his policy, at the time, of 'houses and meat and not getting scuppered' which showed his early appreciation of the post-war consumer society and the need for the Conservative Party to adapt. Above all, it cannot be denied that Churchill's immense stature as premier contributed greatly to a national feeling of well-being, especially after the death of that good and popular man, George VI, in February 1952, and his succession by the youthful, beautiful and exciting Princess Elizabeth. Even before her coronation in 1953 people were talking of 'a second Elizabethan age' which the conquering of Everest did nothing to dispel. This is not idle chatter, for in my own case, it was at this time, inspired by this aspiration, as well as by a long and thought-provoking journey to the Temple of Delphi in Greece, that I realized I was beginning to become envious of the boys whom I was sending out into the world, and decided to leave the comfortable and secure womb of Shrewsbury School with a view to fighting my way to a much less comfortable and secure place in the Palace of Westminster – for by this time I realized I was a political animal, so that there was really 'no alternative'.

As with all post-war British governments, the economy was the first and greatest of its problems (p. 96), and it only remains to reiterate the main points regarding the era of 'Butskellism', which was characterized initially by a 12 per cent recovery in terms of trade, exactly offsetting the 12 per cent deterioration under the unfortunate Gaitskell. This, combined with the problems created by 'fixing' sterling against the dollar and attempting to maintain the 'sterling area', was the background to 'stop-go', and to the fixation of governments in the 1950s and 1960s as to the level of sterling rather than to that of employment. Retrospectively, we can appreciate the hopelessness of fine-tuning in view of the impossibility of detecting the underlying trends in the economy, and that by far the most important factors are those beyond the government's control, such as the state of world trade and changes in the terms of trade. This was not appreciated until 1979 after which the emphasis was on 'good housekeeping' (no overspending) and the creation of a strong financial and economic structure through the control of the money supply, afforced by supply-side incentives. Be that as it may, the strength of the British economy between 1952 and 1955 enabled the Government to abolish what remained of wartime rationing, controls and restrictions while there was an increase in the standard of living and a boom on the Stock Exchange. As has also already been noted, iron and steel and road haulage were denationalized and, in spite of signs of overheating in the economy, in 1955 'Butler presented a frankly electioneering budget to emphasize the prosperity that Conservative rule has brought' (p. 99). It would be acceptable to say that this was the first of the post-war Tories' unsuccessful 'dashes for growth'. The unacceptable and daftest thing is to say:

> Butler can be judged as the first of the Tory Chancellors who, in Samuel Brittan's words, were not merely 'innocent of economic complexities, but . . . did not even have the practical financial flair that one might reasonably expect from a party with business links'.[1]

On the other hand, whatever the long-term merits of his house-building achievement no such criticism could have been made of the effectiveness of Harold Macmillan as Minister of Housing and Local

---

[1] *Post-War Britain*, by Alan Sked and Chris Cook, p. 105.

Government, until he became Minister of Defence in October 1954. It is set out on pages 236–8 and served to create a favourable image for the Government and, as we have seen, to consolidate greatly Macmillan's position in the Conservative hierarchy. Indeed, it was he who was largely responsible for finally persuading Churchill to retire. In regard to the Welfare State, of which the main Conservative criticism was that its financial demands were apparently limitless, three Government reports – on national insurance, old age pensions and the National Health Service – led to an increase in the rate of benefit applying to pensions and national assistance, and to the restoration of the principle of a common basic weekly rate for pensions and other benefits, while there was an increase in both contributions and Exchequer supplements. The Guillebaud Committee's favourable report on the NHS was accepted, Gaitskell's controversial imposts were retained and a prescription charge of two shillings was applied. Thus by 1955 Churchill's statement of 1952 that 'on social services, foreign affairs and defence, nine tenths of the people agreed on what had been done and what would be done' (p. 152), had been amply demonstrated in the case of the social services. He could well have included in his statement the post-war acceptance of the trade unions as an estate of the realm and, as we have seen on pages 112–13, in this case his zeal was somewhat excessive as was well summarized by Anthony Crosland in his comment in 1956 (p. 114).

In spite of superficial differences, the same was even more true in the fields of defence and foreign affairs, whether it was the development and production of the atomic bomb in 1952 and the hydrogen bomb in 1955, the retreat from Empire, the Atlantic Alliance or the pursuance of Britain's worldwide interests and responsibilities. This has been set out in Chapter 10 on Foreign and Defence Policy (pp. 151–2) where great emphasis is made on 'the outstanding part played by the Foreign Secretary, Anthony Eden' (p. 152). It is impossible to emphasize the extent of Eden's dominance, both nationally and internationally, in the period of the Churchill Government. First, he was the main force in settling the questions of German rearmament and European defence following the Russian threat posed by the Korean War, culminating in the Paris Agreements in May 1955. 'It was one of the great post-war diplomatic watershed . . . (and) it was Eden's greatest diplomatic achievement and the high point of his political life . . .' (p. 155–6). In taking over the negotiations for the formation of the European Defence Community from Attlee and Bevin, he and Churchill disappointed the European federalists by maintaining the former's

388

policy of 'all care and no responsibility'; that is to say, they would do everything to encourage the ideal of a united Europe except actually joining it (p. 154). It was the Korean War that led to 'some strains in the "special relationship"' (p. 147) both under the Labour and Conservative governments and when Eden played a leading part in security a moderate settlement in 1953 (p. 157) it has been seen that this was resented by Dulles 'whose ambition was to "roll back the communist world Empire"' (p. 157), and who went on to regard the British relationship as detrimental to American interests when France failed to ratify the Pleven Plan in 1954 (p. 155). This development was, of course, to prove to be disastrous both for Britain and for Eden, personally. In the meantime, he had apparently settled the Middle Eastern problems in Iran and Egypt brilliantly, in comparison with Morrison's efforts (pp. 156–7). Eden's further 'diplomatic triumph' in negotiating the 1954 partition of, Vietnam and Vietnamese peace settlement, was again prophetic for the future as Dulles refused to sign the agreements (p. 157). 'In the meantime and following the Geneva Conference, Eden took part in a frenzy of diplomatic activity with a view to strengthening world peace and security' (p. 158). In 1955 he arranged Britain's membership of SEATO, organized by Dulles, but when the latter called a meeting of its non-Asian members Eden 'objected forcibly' and the meeting was postponed. When Britain joined CENTO it was Dulles's turn to rebuff him, for the United States refused to join as it 'resented the British presence in the Middle East' (p. 158). In spite of 'the writing on the wall' Eden's period as Foreign Secretary during the Churchill Government was, and must still be, regarded as an outstanding success.

The nature of the post-war consensus, and of our political consensus, in general, is discussed in Chapter 5, pages 74–6). It is a blinding glimpse of the obvious to say it does not mean that there is no disagreement among the parties. And when there is agreement there are important differences in emphasis,

> on welfare, for example, it was a question of the level of benefits and range of entitlements; on the retreat from empire, a question of pace and timing; on public ownership, a question of the extent of state regulation. No Labour government seriously entertained ideas of widespread public ownership and no Conservative one until 1979 had tried to dismantle the nationalized sector.[1]

---

[1] *Consensus Politics from Attlee to Thatcher*, by Dennis Kavanagh & Peter Morris, p. 13.

In the months prior to the 1950 General Election, on the subject of nationalization, Churchill's statement when the controversy over the Iron and Steel Bill was at its height in the early part of 1949 (p. 377-8) was highly critical of the whole concept but, later in the year, in a more conciliatory fashion, as we have already noted (p. 379), he said, 'it is physically impossible to undo much that has been done.' Consensus also does not mean that there is no disagreement within the parties. Both parties 'contained wings which dissented from the ruling orthodoxy.'[1] The Conservative right:

> called for more individualistic and free market policies, lower direct taxation and reduced State spending. They opposed the retreat from empire and were critical of the country's obvious subordinate relationship with the United States.[2]

A good example of this is the attitude of the right wing to Eden's constructive negotiations with Egypt as to the gradual withdrawal of British troops from the Suez Canal Zone (p. 156-7). In December 1953 he suspended these negotiations in order to defuse a revolt of 41 Conservatives, the 'Suez Group', but in July 1954 their leader, Captain Waterhouse, announced that the group would vote against any withdrawal of British troops from the Canal Zone, which it proceeded to do when the agreement was approved later in the month by the Commons by 257 to 26 votes – another example of the working of the consensus. In the case of the Labour Party the dissent came from the left which 'advocated unilateral nuclear disarmament, major extensions to public ownership and a harsher climate for private business and wealth'.[3] Another important factor is that both parties are prisoners of their histories in the sense that they are virtual coalitions. The Conservatives' absorption of dissenting Liberals, over the years, has been a great source of strength, making it, like the old Church of England, an all-embracing party, which follows from the nineteenth-century observation of A.V. Dicey that 'the Conservative and Liberal Parties divided on differences which are "important but not fundamental"'.[4] In spite of its shorter history, the Labour Party consists of a number of coalitions which are both a

---

[1] *Consensus Politics from Attlee to Thatcher*, by Dennis Kavanagh & Peter Morris, p. 14.
[2] Ibid., p. 14.
[3] Ibid., p. 14.
[4] Ibid., p. 13.

source of strength and weakness – or divisiveness. First, there is the manifest difference between the Party before and after 1931 which has been explained in Chapter 3. Secondly, there is the difference between the middle-class Fabian intellectuals and the working-class pragmatists, who have been historically associated with the trade unions but, as we have seen, these have not always been pragmatic since 1931. Thirdly, there is the difference between the social democrats and the extreme left wing which, in the last resort, has been to override or dispense with the authority of Parliament which led to the breakaway by the Social Democratic Party in 1981.

The dissenters in each party usually grow stronger and become more vociferous after an electoral defeat but, as we have seen above, this is inherently more so in the case of the Labour Party. As has been noted on page 84:

> As always, after an electoral defeat the left wing moved further left and demanded more and more nationalization, the right wing and the leadership did not reject nationalization in principle but were disillusioned with it in practice while there emerged a third group, called the revisionists, who regarded it as irrelevant in achieving the ideal of socialism which was equality.

These last were to have an important, yet indefinable, effect on Labour Party thinking in the coming years, but it was the hectic and dynamic opposition of the 'Bevanites' in foreign affairs as well as on social and economic issues to official party policy which was the feature of the years between 1951 and 1955. It was the classic period of the Labour Party being torn by internal strife and compared unfavourably with a successful Conservative Government which had not encountered problems with the economy or in foreign affairs which Labour had predicted and in the face of which the party would have adopted a more unified stance. It was in the defence debate in March 1952 that the Bevanites first struck. The defence programme was, of course, largely that of the previous Labour Government and to which Bevan and Wilson had already made their well-known objections. The official Opposition policy was to accept the programme but to abstain from voting on the grounds of no confidence in the Government's ability to implement it. However, 57 Bevanites voted against the Bill and the consternation was such that the Standing Orders of the Parliamentary Labour Party were reimposed, having been suspended since 1945, in order to prevent further Bevanite revolts, by the threat of withdrawing the party whip or expelling recalcitrant members. Nevertheless, exactly a year later

Attlee was still having to avert a Bevanite revolt on the question of national service by asking for it to be reviewed annually, a request which was eventually rejected. Also, the Bevanites carried their revolt into the annual party conferences and influenced the proceedings, such as in September 1952 when a resolution asked for a list of 'key and major industries' to be taken into public ownership which, as we have seen, was against the policy of the leadership. It was at this conference that the Bevanites won six of the seven constituency seats on the party's National Executive Committee: Bevan, Driberg, Wilson, Mikado, Crossman and Castle taking the places of Dalton, Morrison, Shinwell, Callaghan and Gaitskell – the first time that the NEC majority did not consist of the official party leadership. In order to enable Morrison to sit on the NEC the post of the Deputy Leadership of the Labour Party was created. Indeed, it was in the NEC that the Bevanites wielded their greatest influence, for to carry motions at conferences they needed the trade union block votes and these were not usually forthcoming as Arthur Deakin, Bevin's successor, was of the old pragmatist school and followed the official party line.

In November 1952 the Parliamentary Labour Party voted by 188 to 51 to disband all unofficial groups within the party in a move aimed at the Bevanite Tribune Group which dissolved itself accordingly. This enabled Bevan to attempt to influence the party from the inside so that he challenged Morrison for the Deputy Leadership, but lost by 194 to 92 votes. It also led to his being elected to the Shadow Cabinet so that his pamphlet, 'In Place of Fear', presenting the Labour Party as the party against both poverty and property, had that much more authority. However, we have already noted the threatened Bevanite revolt over national service in March 1953, while in June they attacked the Government for linking the Kenyan Nationalists with the Mau Mau insurrection following the conviction of Jomo Kenyatta, a nationalist leader. The establishment of the Central African Federation, connecting Northern and Southern Rhodesia and Nyasaland, was against the wishes of the African leaders and the precepts of the Bevanites. It was in defence of these views that Bevan resigned from the Shadow Cabinet in April 1954 in protest at Labour's support of SEATO which, together with the later CENTO, he attacked as a means of defeating national liberation movements. Significantly, for the future, Harold Wilson exhibited his skilful political footwork by taking his place in the Shadow Cabinet. In July, Tribune published, 'It Need Not Happen', arguing against German rearmament as a threat to European peace, and in answer to the Labour Party's, 'In Defence of Europe', in June, which supported it, within the projected European Defence Community. The Bevanites had also been persistent critics of NATO but in spite of his continued opposition to party policy, or really because of it, Bevan opposed Gaitskell in the election for party Treasurer in September, which he lost by 4.3 million to 2 million votes, thus confirming the latter's emergence as the favourite of the union leaders in place of Morrison. Following his defeat, Bevan launched a furious attack on the Labour leadership and made an apparently veiled reference to Gaitskell as 'a desiccated calculating machine unmoved by human suffering'. He had not forgotten Gaitskell's dismissal of the Bevanites in October 1952, as 'a group of frustrated journalists', and as Gaitskell went on to say that a sixth of the constituency delegates (the source of the Bevanite support) were either Communists, or Communist-inspired, they could draw their own conclusions as to where he placed them in this line-up. Bevan continued his opposition. In March 1955, following a Defence White Paper, Churchill argued in the Commons defence debate in support of the manufacture of the hydrogen bomb on the grounds of its deterrent effect, and Attlee agreed with Churchill 'that deterrence, by the possession of the thermonuclear weapon, is the best way of preventing another war', a self-evident and proven truth, if ever there was one. The disbelieving Bevan not only attacked Churchill and Eden but criticized Attlee's lack of leadership, and led 62 MPs in abstaining from the Labour amendment although he was careful not to endorse a unilateralist position. Two weeks later the PLP agreed by 141 to 112 votes to withdraw the whip from Bevan, but as an election was imminent the Labour NEC agreed narrowly (by 14 to 13 votes) not to expel him from the party and Attlee asked him for assurances on his future conduct. Significantly, the NEC called on the Government to develop the hydrogen bomb in order to consolidate British independence.

Churchill was over 80 years old and had suffered his fourth stroke, the third being in April 1953 when he took over the duties of the Foreign Secretary when Eden became ill, an early indication of the latter's lack of stamina. Churchill's stroke was kept secret and Lord Salisbury became acting Foreign Secretary. It was becoming increasingly difficult to conceal his mental and physical deterioration from the outside world while his colleagues found him increasingly difficult to work with. However, he clung to office in his eternal hope of meeting the Soviet leaders at a summit which would secure world peace, and which would be the climax of his unique career and statesmanship. But this was not to be for Stalin's death in 1953 was followed by a weakening in the Russian leadership, Bulganin having succeeded Malenkov in February 1955, so that in April Churchill retired. Eden became Prime Minister and Macmillan, who influenced Churchill in his decision, succeeded him as Foreign Secretary. A general election was called for 26 May in what were decidedly favourable conditions for the Conservative Government, which had been apparently successful on virtually every front. In spite of 'stop-go' and threats of inflation through excessive wage claims and settlements, the economy appeared to be thriving with everyone's standard of living rising. In November 1954 Butler felt confident enough to predict that it would double in the next quarter century and in his famous, or infamous, pre-election budget he prematurely pre-empted some of that prosperity. The trade unions were getting so much of their own way that there was no trouble on that front. Wartime restrictions and rationing had been finally abolished. The Welfare State had not been threatened and it could be argued that it had even been improved. Macmillan's house-building achievement was regarded as a minor miracle. Finally, the new and glamorous Prime Minister, in his role as Foreign Secretary had appeared to make the job look easy and to create the impression that Britain was still a world power as she had been before the war. Lord Woolton's post-war drive to increase the party membership had been brilliantly successful for by the end of 1953, it had reached a record of 2,805,832. He retired with honour, as Conservative Party Chairman, in June 1955. The Government had won every by-election since 1951, and in 1953 South Sunderland had been won from Labour, while the 1955 municipal elections had been favourable to it, as also were the opinion polls.

The Government could look forward to the election with confidence, but this was certainly not the case with the Labour Party. This need not have been necessarily so for after their electoral defeat in 1951, the Labour Opposition made big gains in the municipal elections in May 1952. After that, however, it was downhill all the way and, as has been chronicled here, after years of Bevanite opposition, by 1955 the party appeared to be fundamentally divided on the main issues, especially that of defence. To make matters worse, Labour's electoral prospects were harmed by a series of strikes in the weeks prior to the election by printers, miners, footplatemen and, the most serious, dockers. Even the latest Boundary Commission's readjustments of the constituency boundaries, by increasing the number of seats from 625 to 630 worked against Labour who voted against the proposals when they were approved by the Commons in January 1955. The fact that at end-1952 the Labour Party membership was 6,108,000, with the TUC membership at

8,020,000, was not particularly relevant in view of the increasing evidence of the false impression given by the retention of the 'contracting-out' principle as opposed to that of 'contracting-in'. What was more relevant was that between 1951 and 1954 the circulation of the *Daily Worker* had fallen from 185,000 to 87,000. In June 1953, Labour's 'Challenge to Britain', was mainly concerned with the proposal to abolish grammar schools (p. 218) but it also called for the renationalization of steel and road transport. The party's election manifesto, 'Forward With Labour', reiterated the promise to renationalize steel, but its vagueness emphasized the serious division within its ranks. It stated that a Labour Government would 'start new public enterprises . . . where necessary', and that its defence and foreign policy would not be conducted in a 'party spirit', so that its main suggestion was to call for a summit to deal with international problems – a case of Clement Attlee attempting to out-Churchill Churchill, not to mention Anthony Eden. At the Liberal Party Assembly in May 1952, Clement Davies made the superficial observation that the swing of policies between the two parties was bringing democracy into dispute but, on a more practical level, the reorganization of the party was confirmed, with paid organizers in more manageable constituencies. Following their previous dialogue, their April 1953 Party Assembly presented a programme of electoral reform to Churchill who rejected it for the present Parliament thus leaving the door slightly open. But this was also the period of the 'woolly-minded' Liberals so that the 1953 Assembly adopted, against the Executive's wishes, a policy enforcing compulsory co-ownership upon all limited liability companies. More to the point was the 1954 Assembly's specific reference to the Crichel Down affair (pp. 296–7) in calling for increased civil liberties for the individual against the state. Also, by 1955 the earlier party reorganization, together with the unpopularity of the Labour Party, was having a beneficial effect on the Liberal Party whose membership doubled in 1954, while at the end of that year they were placed second in a by-election at Inverness. In spite of their mere six Members of Parliament, this was probably the first of the many post-war Liberal outbreaks of euphoria that they were on the point of providing a non-socialist alternative to the Conservative Party. However, their election manifesto, 'Crisis Unresolved', offering a defence of the 'fundamental freedoms' against tyranny, although worthy, was not such as to capture the popular imagination. The much more earthbound Conservative manifesto 'United for Peace and Progress', reiterated Butler's assertion of the prospect of the doubling of living standards within 25 years – under a Conservative Government.

The election was therefore in every sense a quiet one. Eden quietly impressed the electorate and Labour quietly suppressed its division. The result was a foregone conclusion in a way in which few British general elections have been. The turnout figures reflected this, dropping from 82.5 to 76.7 per cent. The votes recorded for the three main parties were:

Party	Votes Gained	Percentage of Vote	Average Vote per MP	Number of MPs
Conservative	13,286,569	49.7	38,624	344
Labour	12,404,970	46.4	44,783	277
Liberal	722,405	2.7	120,401	6
Others	346,554	1.2		3
	26,760,498	100.0		630

Source: Derived from D. Butler and A. Sloman, *British Political Facts, 1900–75.*

The Conservatives thus emerged with an overall majority of no less than sixty seats and were the first party in a century to increase their majority in Parliament as a result of a general election. The Tory vote, it is true, had dropped by almost half a million, but the Labour Party vote had fallen by more than a million and a half. The marginal voter, it seemed, was happy to let the Conservatives carry on. For the Liberal Party the election once again offered little comfort. No seats were lost, it is true, but the party had been looking forward to an increase rather than a fall in its vote and if its share of the poll had increased, the increase – from 2.5 to 2.7 per cent of the poll – was totally insignificant. Much the same could be said in general about the party's role in British politics.[1]

The General Election of 1959

Following his apparently effortless success as an international diplomat and, in conjunction with his aristocratic good looks and charm, no man has ever succeeded to the premiership with more going for him than Anthony Eden. Furthermore, in domestic politics he was associated with the progressive ideas, such as 'a property-owning democracy', which had become such an important part of the

---

[1] *Post-War Britain*, by Alan Sked and Chris Cook, p. 124.

post-war Conservative Party. The *Daily Telegraph* summed it up well in its comment: 'Training, knowledge and courage are in high degree the unquestionable assets of our new Prime Minister.'[1] His rapid decline and fall therefore almost take on the qualities of Greek tragedy. I say 'almost' because it cannot really be said that he exhibited the Greek sin of 'hubris', or arrogant pride, but certainly he was a god-like figure, in the manner of the Greeks, and it is no exaggeration to describe his fall as 'nemesis', that which overtook those whose excessive pride annoyed the Greek gods, who were very human in their likes and dislikes. The details have been recorded above – the economy on pages 99–101, including Butler's two budgets, the one electioneering and the other, deflationary, and his successor, Macmillan, with his deflationary budget, Eden's mounting domestic and other problems on pages 158–9 and, finally, the Suez debacle on pages 159–63.

There remains the interesting question of the manner of Eden's resignation in January 1957. On the face of it, he went to Jamaica on 23 November and on his return he was told by his doctors that, due to his failing prostate, he was in no physical condition to continue in office as he was on the point of collapse: it was apparently a matter of life or death. Inevitably, this straightforward explanation has been queried such as in the conclusion of Richard Lamb's book, published in 1987, *The Failure of Eden's Government*:

> It is more probable that Eden's colleagues, spearheaded by Macmillan, told him they would not serve under him any longer, although he himself wanted to continue.

Alan Sked and Chris Cook, in an addendum, make a similar comment:

> This at least was the official version. Eden's latest biographer, however, has suggested that Eisenhower demanded the Prime Minister's resignation and that Macmillan, Butler and Churchill dutifully helped to engineer it.[2]

Another Eden biographer, Dr David Carlton, agrees:

> Eden was dissuaded from soldering on by pressure from his colleagues and the fear that somebody would spill the beans on his

---

[1] *Post-War Britain*, by Alan Sked and Chris Cook, quoted on page 125.
[2] Ibid., p. 137.

lying to the Commons. He was afraid that if he did not go, someone, somewhere would tell the story and he would look totally dishonourable.[1]

This refers to the fact that on the day before Anthony Eden left for Jamaica, 22 November, the Government 'to general incredulity', denied any collusion with Israel while, after his return, on 20 December, he told the Commons that he had 'no foreknowledge' of the Israeli attack on Egypt, although he admitted that the Government knew of the possibility of such an attack. Dr Carlton refers to this statement as 'Eden's notorious lie to MPs' but Richard Lamb, who reviewed Keith Kyle's book, *Suez*, in the *Spectator*, rejects this view and is quoted in Mandrake's column in the *Sunday Telegraph* as saying:

> It is sometimes suggested that factors other than his health affected Eden's final decision to resign. This is unlikely . . ., if the Prime Minister had been really determined to stay, it would have been hard to see what (in the short run at least), would have stopped him.

Nevertheless, there was 'the mounting evidence of Eden's indecisiveness' (p. 161) and his lack of 'physical and mental toughness' (p. 159). In a letter to the *Sunday Telegraph* (4/8/91) Dr David Carlton says:

> . . . As early as November 23 1956, President Eisenhower's secretary wrote in her diary: 'indications are growing that Anthony Eden will not return as Prime Minister: he is off to Jamaica for a rest.' Winthorp Aldrich, US Ambassador in London, later recorded that in the aftermath of the Suez ceasefire (November 7), 'Eden soon reached the point where he was incapable of assuming responsibility and it was perfectly obvious that he'd have to be superseded.' . . . in the wake of the Suez humiliation three senior Cabinet Ministers (Butler, Macmillan and Lord Salisbury) had taken to dealing with Aldrich on a confidential basis because, in the Ambassador's words, 'it became necessary to bypass the Prime Minister and the Foreign Secretary'.[2] Another senior American diplomat . . . stated: 'it was my definite understanding that when Eden took his first trip to Jamaica (Nov. 23) there was no

---

[1]Mandrakes Column, The *Sunday Telegraph*, 7/7/91.
[2]Selwyn Lloyd.

intention that he would return as Prime Minister. It was explained
that this was an example of British finesse' . . .

There is probably much truth in the latter statement even though it
was probably meant as a cynical aside. Eden's indecisiveness and
serious ill health, his 'escape' to Jamaica and his problem with his
statement in Parliament regarding the Treaty of Sevres, with
France, in October 1956, the calls for his resignation by the
Opposition and the criticism by Dulles and Eisenhower (in that
order), would all have had the natural consequences of his offering
to tender his resignation, without being pushed into it, and his
senior colleagues would have handled the matter with 'tactful
British finesse', as the American diplomat said. However, the last
word should be left to Sir Anthony Eden. In a speech to Young
Conservatives in November 1956, he stated: 'We make no apology
and shall make no apology for the action that we and our French
allies took together.'
    In the meantime, there were several developments during the Eden
Prime Ministership that were portentous. First, there was the
resurgence of the Irish Republican Army (IRA), which had
apparently been defunct since the war, when it raided an army
training centre at Aborfield, in Berkshire, in August 1955. The
political 'fallout' was that in the following October two Ulster
Unionists took the Sinn Fein seats in the Commons. On 12
December 1956 the IRA opened a military campaign to end the
partition of Ireland, with a series of attacks on border posts and
military installations throughout Ulster, while at the end of the
month, on the 29th, Sinn Fein, the political wing of the IRA, was
declared illegal in Northern Ireland. Secondly, the great period of
imperial disengagement under the Macmillan Government was
foreshadowed when Britain agreed to grant independence to the Gold
Coast (Ghana) in September 1956, the actual event taking place in
1957. Although Cyprus was to attain independence in 1960 the inter-
racial troubles there between Greeks and Turks were such that an
inconclusive conference of foreign ministers of Britain, Greece and
Turkey was called in London in August 1955. In the following
November a state of emergency was proclaimed there and in
December, Macmillan, the Foreign Secretary, made a statement in
Parliament on the increasingly serious situation in Cyprus. In March
1956 Archbishop Makarios, the Greek Cypriot leader, was deported
to the Seychelles, and in the Commons debate on the subject,
Aneurin Bevan condemned the Government's inability to understand,
in spite of the past experience in Ireland and India, that it was

necessary to negotiate with people they may regard as seditionists or terrorists. The Macmillan Government took him at his word, after recalling Makarios in 1959, as we have seen, but the racial conflict in Cyprus continued and was resolved, as so often in history, by partition, at the hands of the Turkish invaders in 1974, which still remains the subject of United Nations surveillance and negotiations. Meanwhile, Britain retains an indirect interest through its two bases – RAF and Army – both of which remain British sovereign territory – but for how long?

There were also important developments taking place in the trade unions and the Labour Party. Following the sudden death, in May 1955, of Arthur Deakin, he was succeeded as General Secretary of the Transport and General Workers Union, in June, by his friend, and equally moderate, Jock Tiffin. When he was replaced, in May 1956, by the aggressively left-wing socialist, Frank Cousins, there was a watershed in the history of post-war trade unionism in Britain. As stated in Chapter 8, The Role of the Trade Unions, (p. 114):

> . . . from the mid-1950s a change in the relationship between the unions and the governments, and the two main parties, can be detected, . . . For example, in 1955 the first national strike for 20 years took place in the form of an extended railway strike by ASLEF while in 1957 the number of days lost through strikes (8.5 millions) was the highest since 1926.

The situation deteriorated during the first years of the Macmillan Government with the advent of militant shop stewards and the massive escalation of strikes in 1959 (pp. 114–15). As explained on page 115:

> '. . . it was also from this time that the unions became increasingly unpopular with the public . . . This was to prove to be a great disadvantage to the Labour Party in view of its close association with the unions . . .

It was undoubtedly an important factor in determining the result of the General Election of 1959.

Nevertheless, in retrospect, it can be seen that immediately after their electoral defeat in 1955 Labour began laying the foundations for their victory in 1964 and, although there were still serious internal disagreements and weaknesses, they put behind them the 'blood-letting' of their disastrous years between 1951–55. In June, the month after the 1955 election, Hugh Dalton resigned from the Shadow Cabinet, because of his age, in an attempt to defuse Morrison's leadership pretensions, which was very much in the interests of the Labour Party and which was successful. On Clement Attlee's resignation in December, Hugh Gaitskell won the first ballot for the Labour leadership outright with 157 votes, with 70 votes for Bevan and 40 for a disappointed Morrison who resigned as deputy leader. This position was filled by the 'safe and sound' James Griffiths in February 1956 who gained 141 votes against Bevan's 111. In the previous October Gaitskell, at the Party Conference, was decisively re-elected Labour Treasurer against Bevan, and soon after assuming the Party leadership he appointed Bevan Colonial spokesman, in February 1956, thus endeavouring to assuage personal and party differences. This wise move was consolidated when Bevan was finally elected Treasurer, against George Brown, at the Party Conference in October 1956. In November, Gaitskell's attack on the Government led to violent scenes in the Commons and he also appealed, in a broadcast, to Conservatives to overthrow Eden while Bevan led an anti-Government demonstration in Trafalgar Square which ended in violent clashes with the police. Perhaps, from the point of view of the future, even more important was the appointment by the Labour National Executive Council, in June 1955, of a sub-committee, under Harold Wilson, to investigate the organization of the Party. In the following October, Wilson reported that the organization was the cause of the recent election defeat, declaring that Labour 'is still at the penny farthing stage in a jet-propelled era' and he called for a nucleus of full-time agents to be sent to the marginal constituencies. Thus Wilson took the first steps in establishing his bent for public relations, based on his 'cheeky chappie' image and his flair for coining the apt but superficial phrase hinting at miraculous and painless remedies for current problems. Also important, for the future of the Labour Party, and as set out in Chapter 6, The Mixed Economy (p. 84), was the growing importance of the revisionists:

> The revisionists included men like Crosland, Healey and Jenkins and their ideas were formulated and popularized in Crosland's book, *The Future of Socialism*, published in 1956, in which he advocated greater public expenditure and a further major redistribution of wealth and income such as had already been achieved by the provisions of the Welfare State but not by nationalization and economic planning.

In the Eden period, Clement Davies announced his resignation as Liberal leader in September 1956 and he was succeeded in November by Jo Grimmond – a breath of fresh air. Finally, although in the foreign affairs field the Suez crisis dominated everything, in the period, there was one development which was of great future significance, especially for Eden's successor, namely the first proposals for a European Common Market and the British riposte of a European free trade area. Macmillan was Foreign Secretary when it was decided that Britain would not attend the inaugural meeting for the former (Chapter 10, Foreign and Defence Policy, p. 174 and he was Chancellor of the Exchequer when he and Eden suggested the latter (ditto, p. 175).

Harold Macmillan's appointment as Prime Minister on 10 January 1957 meant that each of the three political parties had a new leader. The appointment was a surprise as it had been assumed that Butler was Eden's natural successor for we have seen that he was 'acting' Prime Minister on Eden's holiday in Jamaica, and when there were rumours of his resignation in January 1956 it was probably thought that Butler would take his place. On the other hand, the lugubrious Butler was not popular with the party Establishment as he was associated with the pre-war appeasers and, unlike Macmillan, he had not been particularly loyal to Eden, although he was very popular with the post-war Tory 'intellectuals' whom he had encouraged at Central Office, and elsewhere, as we shall see. From the time that Churchill had appointed him British Minister-Resident in North Africa, in 1942, and then in the Mediterranean Area, followed by Italy, Macmillan had shown that he was a man to be reckoned with and, as we have seen, his reputation was significantly enhanced by his exploits as Churchill's Minister of Housing, and we have also seen that he was close enough to the latter to influence him in his decision finally to resign the Premiership. Similarly, he had the resilience and strength of personality to be much closer personally to Eden than Butler, and during his time as Eden's Chancellor of the Exchequer he established himself as the 'strong-man' of the Cabinet. He was undoubtedly the popular choice of the Conservative Party for the Premiership although he 'emerged', as the Queen made her appointment after consulting Churchill and Lord Salisbury, the two senior Conservative elder statesmen. His political inheritance was grim, following the Suez debacle, which was reflected in the decisive Labour lead of 48 per cent in the Gallup poll, at the end of the month, with 43 per cent for the Conservatives and 7 per cent for the Liberals. In February, Labour won the Lewisham by-election, turning a Conservative majority of 3,236 into a Labour majority of 1,110. However, from the outset, Macmillan, who had already established a public persona of Edwardian charm and elegance of presentation, combined with respect for his political abilities, exhibited supreme

402

confidence and enthusiasm which rubbed off on both the Conservative Party and the country at large. As he tackled problems on all fronts he seemed to succeed effortlessly, thus wiping out the post-Suez doubts and lack of confidence, and by the time of the 1959 General Election he was known as 'Super-Mac'. Although Butler remained as Home Secretary, he also became Leader of the House of Commons, the invaluable Lord Hailsham continued as Minister of Education, and the loyal Selwyn Lloyd as Foreign Secretary, while notable new appointments were Peter Thorneycroft as Chancellor of the Exchequer and Duncan Sandys as Minister of Defence. In fact, Macmillan retired a number of the older (1951–55) ministers of whom only four remained after March 1957 and their places were mainly taken by men who had entered Parliament after 1950. It was more than a Macmillan Cabinet: it was Macmillan's Cabinet.

Whereas Macmillan who, as early as the 1930s, had the reputation of being a radical and a reformer, had lived up to this image in his selection of his Cabinet and other ministers, in other respects it could be said that he, and the Conservative Party, had not really changed and that political power was still concentrated in the hands of a very narrow section of society.

> It is clear that the 'silent social revolution' of the past half-century has largely by-passed the leadership of the Conservative Party. Its leading strata have remained firmly fixed in the upper levels of our stratified society. Admittedly wealth rather than birth has become significant and professional men are not prominent in the hierarchy of the Conservative Party organization.[1]

Like most very successful men in public life, Macmillan was a consummate actor and he delighted in fostering his aristocratic and 'grouse-moor' image, although the facts that his wife was the daughter of the Duke of Devonshire, that his mother was American and that several generations back he was descended from Scottish crofters, are themselves tributes to the then mobility and vitality of British society. However, this particular allegation (above) was quite literally true of the leadership of the Conservative Party, bearing in mind that seven out of nineteen of Macmillan's Cabinet Ministers were related to him by marriage and that six of those Ministers were old Etonians. We now know, though, that his was the last gasp (but

---

[1]*British Political Elite*, by Guttesman, pp. 294–5. Quoted in *Britain in the Century of Total War*, by Arthur Marwick (p. 422). Further facts and figures in this chapter are attributable to this authority.

one) of 'aristocratic' government, that the last three Conservative Prime Ministers have been grammar school boys and a grammar school girl and that their cabinets have been completely non-aristocratic. Not that there is anything intrinsically wrong with having an hereditary governing class for the main criterion of any form of government, including a democracy, is: does it work efficiently and fairly? 'Popular' government can become the victim of its own excesses and be converted into a tyranny, as happened in France after 1789 and in Russia after 1917. Be that as it may, this particular allegation was certainly untrue of the organization of the Conservative Party, both centrally and locally, at the time. I know because I was there, both as a Conservative councillor, constituency officer and parliamentary candidate. True, there were still, fortunately, one or two of the old school around: 'country gents' who unquestioningly played the parts of public servants in the form of local and county councillors, JPs, and the like. But what immediately impressed me, at both levels, was the completely democratic nature of the organization and, as a result, its wide and inclusive social mixture. Also, and most important, was the part played by political discussion groups, and allied activities, in bringing people to the fore, regardless of rank and wealth, which was, of course, directly related to the reforms at Central Office after 1945. Finally, elections to office were absolutely democratic and there was a limited period of three years for tenure of office, which compared with the Labour Party where tight little groups hogged office for many years, to the dissatisfaction of other disgruntled party workers. Similarly, in the final selection of parliamentary candidates every member of the party was and is entitled to vote, an exercise in democracy the late John Smith only managed to achieve at the Labour Party Conference in 1993, but only after John Prescott, in an inspired speech, managed to persuade, by shock treatment, the assembled trade union and constituency delegates that anything less would be politically disastrous.[1] Nevertheless, at the Labour Party Conference the Trade Union block vote still counts for 70 per cent of the vote which, together with the undemocratic nature of the block vote is as unacceptable as the eighteenth-century 'rotten' and 'pocket' boroughs which were abolished by the First Reform Bill of 1832.

Macmillan's foreign and defence policy is described in Chapter 10,

---

[1] The premature death of the clear-headed and reliable John Smith on 12 May 1994 was a misfortune for both the Labour Party and the country.

404

Foreign and Defence Policy, pp. 163–83, and is summed up on pages 163–4:

> There are three interlocking strands in the foreign and defence policies of the Macmillan governments (1957–64), all a part of the post-war consensus – imperial disengagement, the development of the nuclear deterrent (the fact that it was no longer independent being a tribute to the re-building of the 'special relationship') and reluctant Europeanism giving way to the earliest attempts to come to terms with the strong tides of Europeanism flowing on the continent.

The second of these strands was by far the most important in his first administration, with which we are now dealing, but I shall deal with the other two initially. Even before Macmillan's 'Wind of Change' speech in 1960 the process of imperial disengagement had begun during Eden's Premiership, notably in the Gold Coast (p. 165) and Cyprus (p. 399–400) and the latter development was completed under Macmillan in 1960, together with the granting of independence to the Federations of Malaysia in 1957 and of the West Indies in 1958 (Chapter 10, p. 165). In June 1959 Singapore became a self-governing state, but the other imperial and colonial developments in 1959 were such as to add to the disillusionment with the 'burdens' of empire. In February, the Labour MP, John Stonehouse, was expelled from Southern Rhodesia, after calling for majority rule after a visit there, and Labour brought an unsuccessful censure motion on the subject. In March, in Hola Camp, Kenya, 11 Mau Mau detainees were beaten to death after refusing to work, and in the subsequent Commons debate on the affair, the Colonial Secretary, Alan Lennox Boyd, expressed his horror at the deaths, but asked the Opposition to place them in the context that 'the authorities had to launch a spiritual and psychological crusade' against the Mau Mau and that this was bound to provoke resistance. Nevertheless, the State of Emergency in Kenya was lifted in October. Also in March, Dr Hastings Banda and other leaders of the Nyasaland African Congress were arrested after riots where they demanded independence and the break-up of the Central African Federation of Southern Rhodesia, Northern Rhodesia and Nyasaland, established by the Churchill Government in 1953 (p. 164). The other side of the coin was the attack by Sir Roy Welensky, the Rhodesian Prime Minister, on the Labour Party's approach to majority rule, and his warning that the relationship between a future Labour Government and Rhodesia could prove impossible. The outcome was the appointment of the Monckton Commission in July, to review the constitution of the Central African Federation. In common with the other colonial Federations, it was broken up in 1963 (p. 166) under the radical Colonial Secretaryship of Iain Macleod.

The third strand of Macmillan's foreign and defence policy, 'the first proposals for a European free trade area' were foreshadowed in Eden's day (p. 175 and p. 402) and Macmillan was involved in both. However, when Macmillan assumed office,

> Events moved much faster than the British Government expected and the treaties establishing the European Economic Community and Euratom were signed in Rome in March 1957, subsequently ratified by the Six and became effective on 1 January 1958 (p. 174).

Macmillan immediately 'determined to establish a European free trade area, including the six EEC countries, a task which was made all the more difficult by the return of General de Gaulle to power in France in 1958' (p. 176). The breakdown of these negotiations and the formation of the European Free Trade Area (EFTA) after the General Election in October 1959, and culminating in January 1960, is described on page 176.

> In dealing with the second strand in the foreign and defence policies of the Macmillan Government, the development of the nuclear deterrent, we shall take note of the 'special relationship' with which it was intimately connected – the consensus of Atlanticism, in a word. Macmillan's first objective when he 'emerged' as Prime Minister on 10 January was to restore good relations with the United States . . . (p. 168).

How he set about this so successfully is related on pages 168–9 while the restructuring of British defence policy, with the appointment of Duncan Sandys as Minister of Defence, and the provisions of the 1957 White Paper on Defence, is covered on page 169. It is to be noted though that during the period of this administration the British nuclear deterrent, 'the cornerstone' of Britain's defence policy, remained independent, Britain's first thermonuclear bomb having been exploded in March 1957.

> Whereas Atlanticism and the development of the nuclear deterrent had the undivided support of the Conservative Party, it was not so easy for the Labour Party which, as we have already noted, shifted to the left after its defeat in 1951 so that, together with its further defeats in 1955 and 1959, the Labour leadership and its left wing

were split during the period over Atlanticism, defence and nuclear policy (p. 171).

The Campaign for Nuclear Disarmament (CND) was launched in February 1958 by Bertrand Russell and Canon Collins and in March 1959 the CND Aldermaston march attracted 20,000 people to Trafalgar Square. Opinion polls estimated that between a quarter and a third of the British public agreed with its aim of unilateral nuclear disarmament. In my view, this was an overestimate as it certainly did not enjoy 'popular' support, for it was confined to the typical Liberal voter (p. 1), the Labour-voting 'chattering classes' and to the very small number making up the extreme left, remembering that the 'block vote' of the TGWU entirely misrepresented the views of the majority of its members. Inevitably, the Liberal Party was the only political party that adopted it as its policy, which it did at its annual conference in September 1958. A joint Labour-TUC statement in June 1959 called for Britain to take a lead in forming a non-nuclear club of countries other than the United States and the Soviet Union, though unilateralism was rejected. In the following month, the TGWU, under the left-wing leadership of Frank Cousins, brutally rejected the idea of a non-nuclear club and voted in favour of a unilateralist defence policy. Nevertheless, neither before nor after the General Election in 1959 was there 'the 'blood-letting' of their (i.e. Labour's) disastrous years between 1951–55' (p. 400). The key, of course, was Gaitskell's wisdom in appointing Bevan to his Shadow Cabinet in February 1956, soon after he became party leader. In spite of the fact that Bevan had been opposed to the construction of the H-bomb from the time of Attlee,

> he opposed the left-wing campaign for nuclear disarmament on the grounds that it would not be right to send a Labour Foreign Secretary 'naked into the conference chamber' (p. 171).

As early as the Labour Party annual conference in October 1957 he caused consternation among the left wing when he made these views known and successfully opposed a unilateralist motion. However, he remained true to his principles for in a foreign affairs debate in April 1959 Bevan stated that a future Labour Government would stop all nuclear tests. With the October General Election in mind it could be concluded:

> The Prime Minister, indeed, could enter the election campaign with an apparently respectable record in foreign affairs. He had restored

the 'special relationship' with America; he had refashioned British defence policy in such a way as to preserve the country's great-power status; he had handled difficult problems in Commonwealth affairs with patience and not without success; he was retrieving Britain's position in Western Europe by negotiating a European Free Trade Area; and he had shown Britain's desire for peace in the world by negotiating with the Russians.[1] How fragile some of these claims were would be clear after 1959.[2]

The state of the economy that Macmillan inherited was equally challenging. It will be remembered that as Chancellor of the Exchequer in the last post-Suez days of the Eden Government it was he who had to apply to the IMF for support following the large-scale selling of sterling (p. 101). His new Chancellor of the Exchequer, Peter Thorneycroft, immediately deflated. 'The euphoria of 1952–55 gave way to a period of Conservative stagnation for two years with the annual increase in the GNP falling to under one per cent' (p. 101). Pages 101–3, in Chapter 7, Full Employment, deal with the economy, and its problems, until the general election. 'Thorneycroft, like Macmillan before him, was concerned with the inflationary implications of excessive wage increases about which he warned publicly in July . . .' (p. 101). This was also the period of the first instalment of corporatism and of Macmillan's famous utterance, 'most of our people have never had it so good.' But he added:

> Our constant concern today is – can prices be steadied while at the same time we maintain full employment in an expanding economy? Can we control inflation? This is the problem of our time. (p. 101)

It was the early days of 'the age of affluence' and what Macmillan called 'the expanding economy' was the expansion of consumer demand following persistent wage increases – too much money chasing too few goods. The only solution was to reduce significantly the amount of money in circulation and Macmillan's failure to support Thorneycroft and his two colleagues in this endeavour led to their resignations. However, the financial restrictions were continued by his successor, Heathcoat-Amory, but he relaxed them in the second half of the year and in April 1959, he introduced a tax-reducing and expansionary budget.

---

[1] p. 176.
[2] *Post-War Britain*, by Alan Sked and Chris Cook, pp. 151–2.

Labour inevitably criticized the budget for its 'electioneering' provisions and equally inevitably Macmillan called an election for October which he won overwhelmingly on a tide of Tory prosperity (p. 103).

However, as with foreign affairs and defence, the reality was somewhat less encouraging, for it was in the mid-fifties that there began the long and apparently inevitable decline in the absolute and relative performance of the British economy. The depressing statistics are set out at the end of Chapter 7, Full Employment, (p. 107).

It seemed that Labour had benefited from the Suez debacle, judging from the Gallup polls of January 1957 (p. 402), and September 1957, with Labour on 52 per cent, Conservative on 33 per cent and Liberal on 14 per cent (a 100 per cent increase!), and when they won the Lewisham by-election in February 1957, turning a Conservative majority of 3,236 into a Labour majority of 1,110, but subsequent by-elections were to show that it was the Liberals who were gaining electoral support. As Enoch Powell stated:

At no stage were the Opposition benches able to establish a decisive ascendancy over the Government in morale and debate, even when all the cards, which a Government's opponents could possibly want, had been thrust into their hands.[1]

It has already been noted that, 'the Labour leadership and its left wing were split during the period over Atlanticism, defence and nuclear policy' (p. 406–7) and that in July 1959 the TGWU 'rejected the idea of a non-nuclear club and voted in favour of a unilateralist defence policy' (p. 407) which, it was said, would give Britain 'the moral leadership of the world'. The former, more feasible concept, was official party policy, together with the suspension of nuclear tests, British control of US missile bases in Britain and the abolition of National Service. As mentioned above (pp. 407), with Bevan working alongside and in agreement with Gaitskell in the Shadow Cabinet, the left wing had lost the only leader who had the capability of 'tearing the party apart' so that the differences over nuclear policy probably did not do it much harm, although undoubtedly they did not do it much good. Much more detrimental were the adverse effects of the new-found power of militant and left wing shop-stewards in the form

---

[1]Quoted in *Post-War Britain*, by Alan Sked and Chris Cook, p. 154.

of strikes over apparently trivial matters, such as demarcation disputes and the timing of tea breaks. Chapter 8, The Role of Trade Unions (p. 115) concludes:

> . . . it was also from this time that the unions became increasingly unpopular with the public in view of the inconveniences they suffered through strikes and through disapproval of their 'bloody-minded' attitude.

Strikes had been escalating since 1955 and in 1959 they reached a peak (p. 115) which was detrimental to the Labour Party in view of its close association with the unions.

Too much has been made of the internal split of the party between the extreme unilateralist and shop-steward dominated and trade union left, the traditionalist left, who really believed in nationalization and Clause IV of the Party's constitution (which groups intermingled), and the traditionalist right which only gave 'lip-service' to these shibboleths and, finally, the revisionists (pp. 84 and 401). The hard left was gradually losing ground to the traditionalist right, which was necessary if Labour were ever to form a government again, and the revisionists were the alchemists who were doing the most to bring about this desirable state of affairs. It has been said that Hugh Gaitskell failed 'to re-establish unity within the party' and that although he was 'a courageous and honest man . . . (he) . . . lacked the necessary guile to lead a major party in Opposition.'[1] Furthermore, Gaitskell 'simply lacked the political gifts of the unflappable and theatrical Macmillan', defects which were exposed by the new election medium of television (the 1959 General Election was known as the 'television election' − (p. 367) on which Macmillan thrived and, even more so, the new Liberal leader, Jo Grimmond.[2] But all of this is either untrue or irrelevant. In regard to party unity, as I have pointed out several times, compared to the 'blood-letting' between 1951–55, the situation between 1956–59 was quiescent, in spite of the differences − all due to Gaitskell's wisdom in taking Bevan into his Shadow Cabinet and no doubt due also to his subsequent excellent handling of the fiery Welshman. One also wonders to what mythical period the failure 'to re-establish unity within the party' refers? Another way in which Gaitskell's leadership was so thoroughly beneficial to the party was that he was completely

---

[1]*Post-War Britain*, by Alan Sked and Chris Cook, p. 154.
[2]Ibid., p. 158.

in tune with the revisionists. As for the complaint that '. . . his abrasive personality did not endear him to the left. Instead, once he had made up his mind on any issue he tended to propagate his views both forcefully and eloquently, leaving his opponents within the party to come to terms with his stand unilaterally,'[1] I can think of no greater compliment to him. That is what is called leadership and it requires strength of character and conviction. Gaitskell possessed these qualities in abundance, besides which histrionic talents pale into insignificance – a fact which the Labour Party has since learned to rue. Admittedly, he made tactical errors in the election campaign. Labour's manifesto, 'Britain Belongs to You', concentrated on improving the social services and expanding the economy and, in spelling this out he gave 'hostages to fortune', promising more benefits without the need for tax increases, thus providing the Tories with excellent ammunition, such as Macmillan's 'the biggest budget leak in history' and Butler's 'a bribe a day keeps the Tories away'. But the fact that he was on the receiving end of these superficial, electoral debating points does not diminish one whit the enormous debt that the Labour Party owed and owes him.

Although, as usual, the final electoral result was disappointing, the period is one of the few in the post-war years when the Liberal Party appeared to be making a breakthrough. This resulted from the combination of an agreeable new leader, who was impressive as well as charming, and the fact that the early stirrings of the anti-nuclear movement captured the active loyalty of a significant minority. As already mentioned, it was the Liberals, and not Labour, who gained from the dramatic fall in the Conservative vote in the early by-elections, for whereas that of the latter remained static the former's rose, as at Tonbridge, as early as June 1956, while in Edinburgh South in May 1957, and Gloucester in September, the Conservatives lost as a result of the Liberal candidates taking more than 20 per cent of the vote. Although Ludovic Kennedy failed to win Rochdale[2] in February 1958 he gained second place, with nearly 18,000 votes, a precursor to the first Liberal by-election win in post-war British history, at Torrington, in March 1958, when Mark Bonham-Carter, Asquith's grandson and Jo Grimmond's brother-in-law, defeated the 'National Liberal and Conservative' candidate, by turning a majority of 9,312 into a Liberal majority of 219. As in Rochdale, the Labour vote did not reach the level attained in the 1955 election. However,

---

[1] *Post-War Britain*, by Alan Sked and Chris Cook, pp. 154–5.
[2] The Rochdale by-election was the first election to be covered by television (p. 367).

from then on the Liberal phenomenon lost its momentum and in spite of his political attractiveness, Grimmond's manifesto, 'People Count', failed to make the breakthrough that had been threatened in the earlier by-elections, although it must be noted that they more than doubled their share of the poll and had gained nearly a million extra votes without securing a net increase in seats – a hard but necessary system!

When Lord Hailsham became Chairman of the Conservative Party in September 1957 the Labour Party was still well ahead in the polls, but perhaps the change can be dated from the time in the next month when he appeared on the platform at the annual conference, wildly ringing a handbell and calling on the Conservatives to 'beat the daylights' out of the Labour Party, a stratagem which established his popularity for all time with the rank and file even though it was frowned upon by some of the party establishment. Be that as it may, the Conservatives had already embarked on a very ambitious, and expensive, publicity campaign which continued until the eve of the general election on 8 October 1959 and was intensified once the election campaign began. At the same time, business organizations spent even more money countering Labour's nationalization proposals. Evidence of the success of this campaign appeared as early as October 1958 when the Gallup poll recorded a Conservative lead at 45 per cent, with Labour at 41 per cent and the Liberals at 12 per cent, in spite of the fact that earlier in the month, at the annual party conference, Butler had resisted the popular call for tighter immigration restrictions, and the deportation of those immigrants who committed criminal offences, by appealing to 'our time-honoured tradition of hospitality'. Ominously for Labour, the Conservatives made big gains in the municipal elections in May 1959, returning to their pre-Suez strength. Their election manifesto, 'The Next Five Years', emphasized Britain's prosperity and affluence and once again, predicted a doubling in living standards. They asserted: 'Life is better with the Conservatives' and added: 'Don't let Labour ruin it'.

When the election results came in, therefore, there was a shock awaiting Labour. The Conservative Party had won another decisive victory and had increased its overall majority to 100 seats. Labour's vote had fallen by 189,000, while the Tory vote had increased by no less than 463,000. The Liberal share of the poll had doubled from 2.7 to 5.9 per cent. But although it had gained nearly an extra million votes it had secured no net increase in seats, despite the fact that it had forwarded 106 more candidates than last time. The final figures were:

Party	Votes Gained	Percentage of Vote	Average Vote per MP	Number of MPs
Conservative	13,749,830	49.4	37,671	365
Labour	12,215,538	43.8	47,347	258
Liberal	1,638,571	5.9	270,095	6
Others	125,096	0.9		1
	27,729,035	100.0		630

Source: Derived from D. Butler and A. Sloman, *British Political Facts, 1900–75.*

The election result represented a personal triumph for Harold Macmillan. He had come to power in the aftermath of Suez expecting to have to relinquish office fairly soon. Instead, he had revitalized his party and led it to its greatest post-war electoral victory. It was a truly remarkable achievement and one which seemed to be full of great political significance. Was affluence undermining the whole pattern of British voting? Would the Labour Party ever again be called upon to govern Britain? It seemed as if the Conservative Party, having won three elections in a row, each time with an increased majority, had discovered the secret of eternal power. If booms could be engineered before election dates by employing Keynsian economic methods and if the Prime Minister alone was responsible for choosing the election date, why could not an intelligent prime minister – and Macmillan was certainly that – cling on to power for ever? All these questions were posed time and time again as social scientists now turned to investigate the society which had grown up in Britain since the war.[1]

The General Election of 1964

With 'Super-Mac' presiding over the overwhelming Conservative electoral victory in 1959 it seemed that both he and the party could cling on to power for ever, especially as the election was won 'on a tide of Tory prosperity' (p. 103). However, there was to be no exception to the rule that all post-war British governments experienced their greatest difficulty with the economy. Although those in employment (the vast majority, in spite of rising unemployment)

---

[1] *Post-War Britain*, by Alan Sked and Chris Cook, pp. 158–9.

had 'never had it so good' the deterioration in the economy was well under way by 1959. Paradoxically, it was at the very time of this new-found state of 'affluence' under Conservative governments in the mid-fifties that 'The post-war expansion in industrial production as a whole and output per man halted' (p. 107), a trend which is discussed in Chapter 7, Full Employment, (p. 107), and which was not to be rectified, in regard to productivity, until after 1979. Heathcoat-Amory's pre-election budget in April 1959 was embarrassingly inflationary and was inevitably criticized by Labour for its 'electioneering' provisions (p. 103) and, equally inevitably, he was soon back on the 'Stop-Go' syndrome. His budget in April 1960 was the first instalment of another 'Stop' which was significantly reinforced in June (p. 103). The expansion in credit had resulted in a large deficit in the balance of payments which, as usual, led to another sterling crisis.

> A special problem for Britain was her poverty in natural resources, masked in the days of imperial and trading supremacy before 1914, and of low consumption after 1918, but now fully exposed. Rising material standards at home inevitably meant an increase in imports; even increased exports depended to some extent upon increased imports of the necessary raw materials upon which British manufacturing industry was based.[1]

Marwick castigates the Conservatives for not maintaining import restrictions, quoting Sir Roy Harrod, but although these are justifiable in the case of emerging economies such as Germany and France in the last quarter of the nineteenth century, in mature economies they are inflationary and lead to gross distortions, both internally and externally, reducing the creation of wealth in both spheres. It is because it is the repository and embodiment of this outdated nineteenth-century concept that the European Union is such bad news and is destined to fail. It can only get started by bending the rules and it can only work by the imposition of rigorous centralization and central control which will lead to the same economic failure as communism and socialism, not to mention the question of personal freedom.

In July 1960 Heathcoat-Amory retired to the Lords, to be succeeded by Selwyn Lloyd. Lord Home, a member of the House of Lords, became Foreign Secretary, and it was significant that Gaitskell, as Leader of the Opposition, criticized the appointment as

---

[1] *Britain in the Century of Total War*, by Arthur Marwick, p. 429.

'constitutionally objectionable'. Lord Hailsham, who had been replaced by Butler as Party Chairman, immediately after the election, became Lord President of the Council. The new Chancellor of the Exchequer was as unsuccessful as his predecessor in attempting to work the 'unworkable system' of fine tuning (pp. 98 and 387) which was evidenced by the sterling crisis of July 1961, following the large balance of payments deficit, with the usual sharp increase in Bank Rate, an appeal to the IMF and the latest desperate instalment of fine tuning, the 'pay pause' (p. 104). It was during this Chancellorship that Macmillan introduced his concept of indicative planning in the form of the National Economic Development Council (NEDC) but both this and the attempt to appease the unions by ending the 'pay pause' failed, as explained on pages 104–5. The appointment of Reginald Maudling as Chancellor of the Exchequer, following the cabinet 'reshuffle' of July 1962 (p. 105), saw the establishment of the National Incomes Commission for, as had long been predicted, the granting of wage claims far in excess of productivity was leading to a new post-war phenomenon, a sharp increase in unemployment (p. 105). However, 'although lip-service was still given to the ideal of full employment, increasingly in the 1950s and 1960s the main object was the protection of sterling from weaknesses caused by balance of payments deficits . . .' (p. 97). Maudling is mainly remembered for initiating the first of the Tories' futile 'dashes for growth' which, in this case, bequeathed the new Leader of the Opposition, the adroit Harold Wilson, with the political gift of the largest monthly trade deficit ever recorded (pp. 105–6). In January 1964, when he was no longer a member of the Government, Enoch Powell anticipated the need for the monetary discipline, introduced by Margaret Thatcher, by denouncing the NEDC and the whole idea of regulation of prices and incomes as nonsensical in a non-Communist economy.

As has already been noted (pp. 163 and 405): 'There are three interlocking strands in the foreign and defence policies of the Macmillan governments (1957–64) . . .',

The conventional view is that Macmillan's Government was overwhelmed by its problems after the election of 1959 but this was certainly not true in regard to its handling of imperial disengagement for it was in this period that attempts to restrain the ambitions of the indigenous peoples were finally abandoned, even though it was realized that with the departure of the British there would be severe problems, at the best and, at the worst, political and economic chaos. It was summed up in Macmillan's famous 'Wind of Change' speech in South Africa in 1960, which was doubly important for it struck a chord with British popular opinion, which as a result of Mau Mau atrocities, EOKA violence and the Suez debacle, was becoming disillusioned with the 'burdens' of empire. The process had already begun before 1959 . . . However, it was the advent of Iain Macleod as Colonial Secretary in October 1959, immediately after the election, (p. 165) which gave decolonization an impetus which was unstoppable.'

This remarkably successful process is described on pages 165–6 but the creation of the multi-racial Commonwealth did lead to two unwelcome developments. The first was the departure of South Africa from the Commonwealth (pp. 166–7) and the second was the problem posed by immigration, the solution to which, the ending of the principle of free entry for Commonwealth citizens, became a part of the consensus, in spite of superficial opposition (pp. 167–8). For example, Gaitskell attacked the Commonwealth Immigration Bill, in November 1961, as a 'plain anti-colour measure in practice'.

The second strand in Macmillan's foreign and defence policy was the development of the nuclear deterrent which required, first, the rebuilding of the 'special relationship', following the trauma of Suez, which is dealt with on pages 168–71. This was soon brought into full play in the Middle East by the enunciation of the 'Eisenhower Doctrine' in January 1957. Attempts to downgrade the relationship were unsuccessful, partly because Macmillan 'exercised his considerable old-world charm on the younger man' (Kennedy) and partly because, in the last resort, 'the Americans were not really prepared to ditch the 'special relationship' which was to pay them dividends in the years to come' (p. 170). The White Paper on Defence in 1957 (p. 169) with the object of cutting back Britain's massive defence expenditure (8 per cent of GNP) was only another instalment of her perpetual post-war dilemma. One facet of this problem was the development of an independent nuclear deterrent following the delivery of the British hydrogen bomb to the Vulcan bomber force in 1958, the development and cancellation of Blue Streak and of the American Skybolt, culminating in the Nassau Agreement, in December 1962, whereby American Polaris missiles were to be fitted with British nuclear warheads into British nuclear submarines (pp. 169–70). 'At the time, the Nassau Agreement was regarded as a British diplomatic triumph' and there is no cause to disagree with this judgment in spite of the fact that it did not succeed in reducing defence expenditure, that it was not truly independent and, further, that the contemporary Cuban Missile Crisis and Dean Acheson's 'memorable remark', exposed Britain's second-power status

416

(pp. 170–1). It is reading history backwards to argue that the Macmillan Government was in a state of terminal decline after 1959, regarding foreign and defence policy. It is more correct to say that Macmillan succeeded in dealing with Britain's perpetual post-war problems in these fields better than most Prime Ministers. On the other hand, pages 171 and 406–7 describe how '... the Labour leadership and its left wing were split during the period over Atlanticism, defence and nuclear policy.' Page 172 describe how Hugh Gaitskell who, 'Fortunately for the Labour Party ... had a clear head and strength of character' fought back to reverse the 1960 Labour Party Conference resolution calling for nuclear disarmament, in 1961.

This brings us to the third strand of Macmillan's foreign policy, 'the end of the period that we have called "reluctant Europeanism"' (p. 176) and it is described on pages 176–83. 'Politically, it was only natural that with the "process of imperial disengagement" Britain began to look with more interest' (p. 177) at Churchill's first 'circle' – the European. There was also encouragement by the United States, from the very beginning, for Britain to do this. More important was Britain's faltering economic performance in comparison with that of Europe, in general, and France and Germany, in particular, but it is equally important to take note of the 'coincidence theory' enunciated on pages 177–9.

> The decision to approach Europe was in many ways based on calculations of political interest and influence; but it was the supposed commercial advantages that were most important. The decline in national confidence was the real wind of change in 1960 and it, rather than any long-maturing evolution in official thinking, led to the decision to approach the EEC[1]

in July 1961 with Edward Heath in charge. This argument is reinforced by the fact that the application took place before the Cuban crisis and Acheson's speech, 15 and 17 months later, respectively. As described on pages 179–80, there was no question of a national consensus. For example, in the Commons debate in August on the decision to enter the EEC, Sir Derek Walker-Smith and his Conservative colleagues joined Labour left wingers, like Michael Foot, attacking the Government, while the former, in conjunction with Peter Walker, issued an anti-EEC pamphlet, 'A Call to Commonwealth', in June 1962. Duncan Sandys, the

---

[1] *Consensus Politics from Attlee to Thatcher*, by Dennis Kavanagh and Peter Morris, p. 105.

Commonwealth Secretary, said in the same month that disruption of the Commonwealth was too high a price to pay for EEC entry. In July 1962, 40 Conservative MPs tabled an anti-EEC motion, reminding the Government of Britain's Commonwealth commitments, although the communiqué after the Commonwealth Prime Ministers meeting in the following September was a victory for Macmillan in that it did not condemn EEC entry. Thus, with the Commonwealth to contend with as well, it was understandable that Macmillan should have proceeded cautiously and it makes nonsense of the allegation that 'the Macmillan Government's application to enter Europe had been taken "dishonestly as far as Britain was concerned"' (p. 180). The first of the two reasons for the failure of the application (p. 180–2) was the ramifications of the Common Agricultural Policy (CAP). The second reason was 'de Gaulle's pathological aversion to the "Anglo-Saxon" hegemony of the United States and Britain' (p. 176). Following the failure of the United States to amend the McMahon Act, regarding the application of thermonuclear warheads, in favour of France, this led him to veto the application in January 1963.[1] But, more realistically, he did not want to forfeit to Britain France's leadership of the EEC while, in the last resort, the political support of the French farmers was a more important factor than any gains deriving from making concessions in the CAP. In all, it is completely wrong to regard the veto as a mortal blow to the Macmillan Government which acted in accordance with its, and the country's well-established interests and principles. It is when a government ceases to do this that it finds itself in trouble which is the real reason for the problems of the Major Government, in its determination to push the Maastricht Treaty through Parliament.[2]

The decline in the fortunes of the 1959 Conservative Government, that became so pronounced in the course of 1962, was not apparent throughout 1960 and 1961. Macmillan was confident enough of his position at home to begin a month-long tour of Africa in January when he made his much reported 'Wind of Change' speech and

---

[1] Sir Edward Heath, in an article in *The Times* (1/1/94), has stated: 'I have always thought Macmillan greatly underestimated the impact of his meeting with the French president the previous December and his subsequent agreement with President Kennedy to take Polaris instead of Skybolt.'

[2] Written in June 1993. The outlook was much improved by John Major's brilliant negotiation of the Opt Out Clause for the Social Chapter but the combination of the machinations of the Commission and the foreign European Court of Justice means that it is only a question of time before the Opt Out is virtually cancelled.

inaugurated, in conjunction with his new Colonial Secretary, the brilliant handling of imperial disengagement and the successful creation of the multiracial Commonwealth. Also, throughout the period, he continued to play, what, at the time, must have appeared a not insignificant part on the world scene. In February 1960, Britain signed an agreement with the United States to build an early warning station at Fylingdales, Yorkshire, giving Britain four minutes warning of a nuclear attack, and in June the agreement with the United States to supply Skybolt missiles to Britain was announced, in return for which it was announced in November that Britain would lease a nuclear submarine base at Holy Loch, near Glasgow, to the Americans – all precursors to the Nassau Agreement of December 1962. In September, on the occasion of the famous 'shoe-banging' scene, when Macmillan was interrupted by Khrushchev as he addressed the Summit Conference at the United Nations General Assembly in New York in July 1961, he announced the decision to apply to enter the European Common Market, and in his Guildhall speech in November, he stressed the need for increasing interdependence between the three groups of the free world – the United States, the European Community and the Commonwealth. Although this revamping of Churchillian rhetoric was to fall on stony ground, it should be regarded as no less legitimate than the original utterance. Nor was there any sign of the decline to come in 1962 in the election results, both national and local. In March 1960, Labour lost the Brighouse and Spenborough by-election to the Conservatives, a Labour majority of 47 becoming a Conservative one of 666, in May the Conservatives made big gains in the municipal elections, while in December the Conservatives were ahead in the Gallup polls, at 47 per cent, compared to 37 per cent for Labour and 14 per cent for the Liberals. Accordingly, in April 1961 they made gains in the borough, county council and LCC elections.

On the other hand, the Labour Party appeared to be following its usual course of internal division and to be literally supporting 'unpopular' causes. Aneurin Bevan was unanimously elected deputy leader several weeks after the general election, but well before his death in the following July the rot had set in. The conventional interpretation is to blame Gaitskell for this, as immediately after the general election he argued at the Annual Conference in November that Clause IV of the Party Constitution, committing Labour to 'the common-ownership of the means of production, distribution and exchange' should be 'discarded as an old-fashioned shibboleth'. He said, correctly, it implied that 'nationalization' was the prime object of Labour's policy and that 'we propose to nationalize everything'

419

whereas 'we have . . . long ago come to accept . . . a mixed economy' – a prime example of a literally unpopular cause with which Labour had saddled itself and which it would need to discard if it was to have a long-term future, a fact of which Tony Blair has shown his appreciation. Instead, the proposal caused an uproar, not only among the blinkered left but also among the pragmatic right who were intent on 'papering over the cracks'. As was to be expected, the leader of the 'short-termists' was Harold Wilson, who said later: 'We were being asked to take Genesis out of the Bible. You don't have to be a fundamentalist to say that Genesis is a part of the Bible', a typically cynical and meaningless Wilson remark. In July, a week after Bevan's death, the Labour National Executive Council (NEC) decided 'not to proceed with any amendment or addition to Clause IV of the Constitution'.

However, at the end of the month the NEC supported Gaitskell's proposition as the threat of a unilateralist victory at the October Party Conference grew, by adopting a statement affirming the independence of the Parliamentary Labour Party (PLP) from all outside bodies. This was the second of the two great issues that divided the Party at the time and, inevitably, virtually all his opponents on the first issue were included among those on the second. As early as the inception of CND in February 1958 (p. 407) the Victory for Socialism (VFS) group was launched, demanding a unilateralist defence policy and increased nationalization although, at the time, Labour Party constituency secretaries were warned that the VFS was setting up a party within a party. In February 1960, Gaitskell denounced 'the small, professional anti-leadership group' in the Party, referring to the VFS group, who replied in June in the form of 15 MPs calling on him to resign because of his anti-nuclear views. It has been claimed that, at its height in 1960, 'opinion polls suggested that between one quarter and one third of the British public favoured' the CND's aims.[1] Once again, the issue that Gaitskell opposed was literally not popular, in the sense of appealing to the majority. Nevertheless, there were those who took advantage of his defeat in the unilateralist debate in the October Party Conference, notably the ambitious and not-to-be-trusted Harold Wilson, who stood against him unsuccessfully for the Party leadership in the same month, Gaitskell winning by 166 to 81 votes. This was the first time in the party's history that the existing leader had been challenged and Wilson's typically obscure excuse was that

---

[1] *Britain in the Century of Total War*, by Arthur Marwick, p. 414.

he did it 'to preserve party unity'. It was in 1960 that the scandal of ballot-rigging by the successful Communist candidate in the election for the President of the Electrical Trades Union (ETU) was uncovered, although in November 1961, in the Executive elections to the ETU, the anti-Communists won a total victory. (It was a fitting conclusion when, in September 1963, Les Cannon, one of the leaders of the anti-Communist faction, was elected ETU President.) During the period, unofficial strikes continued to plague the country. In August 1960, a TUC report on unofficial strikes condemned some shop stewards' involvement across industrial boundaries in defiance of union executives, and recommended disciplinary action against unofficial strike leaders. It was little wonder that the Government was not seriously threatened by the Labour Opposition. An important omen for the future was the publication in October 1960 of 'Victory for Sanity', by William Rodgers, calling for a campaign to be organized to support Gaitskell. Rodgers, of course, was one of the original 'Gang of Three' who broke away from the Labour Party and who, as the 'Gang of Four', formed the Social Democratic Party in 1981. For the moment, in December, the Campaign for Democratic Socialism (CDS) was adopted as the title of the pro-Gaitskell campaign launched in an attempt to counter the unilateralist victory at the Party Conference. At the other extreme, Michael Foot returned to the Commons in a by-election at Ebbw Vale caused by the death of his hero, Aneurin Bevan.

But, inevitably, the fact that they had been in power for over ten years finally caught up with the Tories by 1962. The deterioration in the economy was the main adverse factor – 'Stop-Go', sterling crises, the pay pause, rising prices and growing unemployment. More insidious is the fact that a government makes enemies every time it makes a decision leading to some action or other, while those members of the electorate who benefit often prove to have short memories. This is variously summed up as the 'boredom factor', the 'swing of the pendulum' or 'time for a change'. The feature of this period, however, was that it saw the re-emergence of the Liberal 'protest-vote', this time in its classic form. This was once again mainly due to Jo Grimmond's outstanding personality and organizing ability and to the Liberals' policy and practice of intense local involvement. It was certainly not due to their overall policies which continued to have no 'popular' appeal but only to that of a 'starry-eyed' minority. For example, at their Annual Conference in September 1960, they urged the Government to apply to join the EEC while supporting NATO, but illogically and dishonestly condemning the British manufacture of nuclear weapons. Again, in

September 1961, Grimmond called for workers to be represented on company boards, an issue which, correctly, has never raised a vestige of interest among British workers.

As it happens, the first sign of a Liberal revival, in the Paisley by-election in Scotland in April 1961, was untypical, in that the well-known Scottish Liberal candidate only failed by 2,000 votes to win a Labour seat, for one of the features of this Liberal revival was their failure to capture the Labour vote. However, in the course of the next two years British voting patterns were transformed. In the subsequent ten months the Liberals gained second place in eight by-elections in which they had been third in 1959. Although, as we have seen, the Conservatives did well in local elections in 1960 and 1961, the Liberals were quietly establishing their base locally in those years when in municipal elections, 130 and 194 respectively, were elected. On 13 March 1962, the Liberals only failed to gain the strong Conservative constituency of Blackpool North, by 973 votes, while on the following day they had a spectacular victory at Orpington, Kent, turning a Conservative majority of 14,760 into a Liberal one of 7,855, with the Conservative share of the poll falling by 22 per cent. The successful Liberal candidate was Eric Lubbock (later Lord Avebury) and as I had beaten him for a Boxing Blue at Oxford I jokingly suggested to my Area Agent at Conservative Central Office that I should oppose him (as I was on the Parliamentary Candidates' list), but it could only be a joke, for the actual candidate, Peter Goldman, was known as Central Office's leading 'back-room boy and blue-eyed boy' (rolled into one), and it was expected that on his election he would virtually move straight into a Government post. Peter Goldman was a classic instance of a man 'being in the wrong place at the wrong time', for to all intents and purposes he was never heard of again politically, until his premature death in 1987. On the same day as Orpington, the Tories were squeezed into third place by the Liberals at Middlesbrough East. On 28 March the *Daily Mail*'s National Opinion Poll made the Liberals the most popular party in the country, at 30 per cent, with Labour at 29.9 per cent. And so the Liberal revival continued. In April they gained 27 per cent of the poll at Stockton-on-Tees (Macmillan's old constituency) and 25 per cent at Derby North as well as retaining Montgomeryshire on the death of their old leader, Clement Davies, and only losing at West Derbyshire by 1,220 votes. May saw the Conservatives lose heavily to the Liberals in local government elections and in June the Conservative candidate lost his deposit at West Lothian. The Gallup Poll at the end of June afforded the Conservatives some consolation as it showed 39 per cent for Labour, 35 per cent for Conservative and 25 per cent for Liberal – but it was not to be. The final straw was the North-East Leicester by-election on 12 July when the intervention of the Liberals pushed the Conservative candidate into third place.

There are cabinet 'reshuffles' and cabinet 'reshuffles'. Surely the most famous of them all was Macmillan's on 13 July, in response to the disaster at Leicester North – that which has become known as the 'Night of the Long Knives'. In it, the Prime Minister dismissed one-third of his Cabinet – seven Cabinet Ministers – the most notable being Selwyn Lloyd, the Chancellor of the Exchequer, but he included the Lord Chancellor, the Minsters of Defence, Housing and Education, the Secretary of State for Scotland and the Minister without Portfolio. Three days later, nine non-Cabinet Ministers were also sacked. In the new Cabinet Butler remained deputy Prime Minister, though he lost the Home Office to one of the new Ministers, Henry Brooke, having given up the Party Chairmanship in the previous October to Iain Macleod when the latter became Leader of the House of Commons. The new Lord Chancellor was Lord Dilhorne (formerly Sir Reginald Manningham-Buller), Peter Thorneycroft re-emerged as Minister of Defence and Michael Noble became Secretary of State for Scotland. The most exciting of the new appointments were those of three younger men, Reginald Maudling, as Chancellor of the Exchequer, at 45 years of age, Sir Keith Joseph, as Minister of Housing, at 44 and Sir Edward Boyle, as Minister of Education, at only 38. Remembering that this was the era of corporatism and indicative planning and that the NEDC was established in February 1962, Maudling, in a letter to his Barnet constituents in June, called for Conservatives to adapt to the new conditions of the 1960s by emphasizing the need for 'national purpose'. Significantly, and although it did not do him much good, Selwyn Lloyd spoke in a similar vein in his Mansion House speech in October 1961 when he appealed for the co-operation of both sides of industry to maintain the value of sterling, and spoke of the need to set up machinery to co-ordinate the national effort and to create a sense of 'national purpose'. It is interesting and deeply significant, that this flirting with socialist planning and falling back on the typically Continental European idea of the 'Grand Vision', by a Conservative government, has been paralleled by the post-Thatcher Major Government with its acceptance of the socialistic centralized bureaucracy, represented by the unrepresentative European Commission, accompanied by meaningless talk about the need to be in the 'heart of Europe' and not to miss the 'European train', and the like. In spite of, or possibly because of, Major's protests that he wants to influence European decision-making, it is, perhaps, a sign of a Conservative Government losing its way.[1] Certainly, Macmillan's Cabinet reshuffle did not help him, as further by-elections in November still showed a decisive swing against the Government, while on 22 November, Labour won South Dorset as the result of the intervention of an anti-Common Market candidate, turning a Conservative majority of 6,693 into a Labour majority of 704.

Before dealing with the first of the 'events' which were to lead to the downfall of the Macmillan Government, the Vassall affair, it is as well to mention several developments and incidents in 1962 which although, in some cases, were not a part of the general scheme of things at the time, had a future significance. In view of future developments, it is interesting to recall that in February the IRA called off its border campaign in the face of the apathy of the Irish public, 'whose minds have been deliberately distracted from the supreme issue' of Irish unity. In April, the Committee on Security, chaired by Lord Radcliffe, pointed to the danger of Communist activity in the Civil Service unions, but recommended no changes in the security services. In July, fighting broke out in Trafalgar Square at a rally of the new National Socialist Movement as its leader, Colin Jordan, declared that 'Hitler was right' – but in this country, the extreme right has never been able to establish the same foothold as the extreme left. In July, the LCC refused to co-operate with the Government's plans for creating a Greater London Council, which culminated in the London Government Act, 1963 (Chapter 13, Local Government, pp. 266–7). The Royal Commission on the Press, chaired by Lord Shawcross, reported in September that it could find 'no acceptable legislative or fiscal way' to remove the danger of monopoly control of communications. Interestingly, in August 1960, the *Daily Herald* was sold to Odhams Press and was freed from the obligation to support Labour and the TUC. However, in March 1961, Cecil King, editor of the *Daily Mirror*, assured Labour MPs that the *Daily Herald* would 'remain a distinct paper in politics'. Yet in February 1964, the TUC sold its share of the *Daily Herald* which was to be renamed the *Sun*, to the International Publishing Corporation. We all know what a 'distinct paper in politics', the *Sun* has become. In October, Hugh Foot resigned as Britain's UN representative in

---

[1]In early February 1997, John Major's tough line to the Europeans on his determination to retain the Social Chapter and his spelling out the reasons why such a highly regulated and centralized economic system can never be successful, show signs that he is finding his way back to reality.

protest at the British Government's defence of the Southern Rhodesian Government. In other words, he was taking the 'Third World' point of view. That very astute and professional Foreign Secretary, Lord Home, had pointed out in the previous December that a crisis of confidence had arisen in the UN because of double standards. Whereas the former members wanted peaceful coexistence, they were being judged harshly in comparison with the newer, 'Third World' members, who were pro-Communist and who pursued their political aims at any price. Needless to say, Gaitskell and Wilson denounced this speech in February. The same internal political division was apparent in the Cuban crisis in October when President Kennedy initiated a total naval blockade of Cuba after the discovery of secret Soviet bases there. The 'loony' left was represented by Bertrand Russell who wrote to Khrushchev blaming the West for precipitating the crisis by its 'unjustifiable action'. The Labour NEC condemned Kennedy's action as of 'doubtful legality' which was, of course, irrelevant, while 'Hands off Cuba' demonstrations took place outside the US Embassy. In other words, the protestors were all pro 'Third World' and anti the West, the United States and Britain, whose Governments correctly supported Kennedy. The total collapse of Khrushchev, who on 25 October agreed to halt the building of missile bases and to dismantle existing bases was, and remains, a classic example of strong and intelligent leadership.

Thirty years from now it will be difficult to appreciate how some of the 'scandals' which have troubled the post-election Major Government should have assumed such an all-embracing and deeply menacing quality. The same is true, to us, of the Vassall case. Coincidental with the Cuban crisis in October, William Vassall, an Admiralty clerk, was sentenced to 18 years' imprisonment for espionage on behalf of the Russians who had been blackmailing him over his homosexual activities. There is a further parallel to today in that prior to and after the case the press had been making insinuations, including the allegation that Vassall had been protected by Government Ministers, notably Thomas Galbraith, a former Civil Lord of the Admiralty and Lord Carrington, First Lord of the Admiralty. The extent of the sense of scandal and political poison and crisis was such that the unfortunate Galbraith resigned from his new ministerial post in November, only days after which Macmillan recalled Lord Radcliffe to set up another judicial tribunal to investigate press reports of the Vassall affair. In April 1963, the Radcliffe Tribunal cleared Sir Thomas Galbraith and Lord Carrington of all suspicion and censored the press for its reporting of the Vassall case. There is an obvious parallel with the activities of today's press, but there is a difference in that Galbraith resigned, as it happens, unjustly and unnecessarily. The other difference, and the probable reason why he did resign, is that it was still assumed that the press was acting responsibly and in good faith, an assumption which can no longer be made. Even some of the so-called 'quality-press' is now guilty of the sin of the 'popular press' of pursuing sensationalism for its own sake, as opposed to the pursuit of the truth. In retrospect, it can now be seen that the change in the attitude of the press began in 1962–63, regarding the Vassall and Profumo affairs, which years, in this, as in many other respects, were a watershed.

When Macmillan said that the thing he most feared as Prime Minister was 'events' it has always been assumed that he was thinking of Vassall and the later Profumo affair but there were four 'events' which transformed his political situation, the second of which was the sudden and unexpected death of Hugh Gaitskell, at the age of 56, in January 1963, at the very time when he appeared to be succeeding in uniting the Labour Party, especially in regard to opposing Britain's entry to the European Economic Community. The new Leader of the Opposition was Harold Wilson who had been assiduously 'climbing the greasy pole' since entering Parliament in 1945 and being appointed President of the Board of Trade at the extremely young age of 31. We have seen that in November 1960, Wilson had stood unsuccessfully against Gaitskell for the Labour leadership. In the same elections, George Brown was elected deputy leader against the unilateralist, Fred Lea. Not to be daunted, two years later the persistent Wilson stood against George Brown for the deputy leadership and was beaten by 133 to 103 votes. However, in the leadership election in February, Wilson led on the first ballot with 115 votes owing to the split in the Labour right between George Brown with 88 votes and James Callaghan with 41 votes, while in the second ballot Wilson won with 144 votes to Brown's 103. Apart from the fact that the so-called left was stronger, numerically, the likeable and ebulliently brilliant but recklessly honest George Brown was no match for the clear-headed and calculating Harold Wilson. Superficially, it can be said that Gaitskell, who had lost two elections, was succeeded by a man who was to prove to be a vote and election winner, with his parliamentary and debating skills as well as those of the political operator. Also, unlike the two post-war Labour leaders, Attlee and Gaitskell, who were both firmly middle class and Old Boys of Haileybury and Winchester, respectively, Wilson, with his Yorkshire accent 'had an extraordinary ability to project a working-class and anti-establishment image which gave him credibility with

Labour voters'.[1] Yet although he was positively lower middle class he was a former Oxford don and a high-level civil servant – a veritable social and political magician! But the reality is that whatever Harold Wilson may have achieved, he did so at a terrible cost to the Labour Party, and therefore to Britain, for after he had come and gone he remained nothing more nor less than a skilful operator. What the Labour Party wanted, and wants, was a conviction politician with the courage to purge it of its left-wing extremism and sheer irrelevance and its Trade Union-based conservatism.[2] In this respect, compared to the disastrous Callaghan, Wilson was a conviction politician although his consuming interest was the short-term interests of the Labour Party. Neil Kinnock did much good work in muzzling the left wing and disciplining the Party but he was unsuccessful in persuading the Trade Union 'Draft Horse' to allow it to enter the twentieth, let alone the twenty-first, century by it becoming a one-man-one-vote party as the Conservatives have been ever since the war and as Labour, under the late John Smith, finally did as late as 1993 (p. 404). Perhaps Labour should have taken seriously the protests and pretensions of my fellow countryman, Bryan Gould, who does appear to have strong convictions, but unfortunately he did not have a sufficient foothold in either of the two strong labour power bases (the trade unions and the constituency workers), having been dependent on his patron, Neil Kinnock.[3] I have been at pains to stress, since his threat to resign from Attlee's Government on a point of principle in 1951 (p. 172), that Hugh Gaitskell was the most outstanding right-wing conviction Labour politician since the war. (Left-wing conviction Labour politicians have been, and are, a numerous breed.) It is a measure of the tragedy of his death that, if he had lived, together with his supporters in the Campaign for Democratic Socialism, he would either have turned the Labour Party into a genuine social democratic party or failing that, succeeded in forming a successful Social Democratic Party which would have taken the place of an unreformed Labour Party.

But we must return to the action of early 1963. In February, unemployment reached 878,000 (3.9 per cent) in the coldest winter since 1947. We have already seen that in January Lord Hailsham was given special responsibility for the North-East where unemployment,

---

[1] *Post-War Britain*, by Alan Sked and Chris Cook, p. 185.
[2] Since this was written Tony Blair has 'emerged'.
[3] Bryan Gould has since returned to New Zealand to continue the academic career which he had previously pursued at Oxford University.

at 7 per cent, was well above the national average (p. 105). At the end of March, an unemployment demonstration took place outside Parliament, while earlier in the month discontent with Macmillan's leadership was expressed at the Conservative Central Council which signified a complete reversal in the political atmosphere. Edward Heath, who had been prominent in the months since the application to join the EEC and in January, when de Gaulle vetoed it, was mentioned as a successor. Also in March, in the Commons defence debate Denis Healey promised that a future Labour government would discontinue Polaris, and Wilson said later that the Nassau Agreement would be 'renegotiated'. The Beeching Report on 'The Re-shaping of British Railways' called for the closure of many lines. More significant for the immediate future was the imprisonment of two reporters following their refusal to divulge the sources of their information on the Vassall affair. In April, Maudling produced his tax-reducing budget (pp. 105–6) and Macmillan, in reply to the new-found hostility to his leadership, told the 1922 Committee of Conservative backbenchers that he would lead the party at the next election – shades of John Major in 1993 and 1995!

This brings us to the third 'event' in the Macmillan Ministry, after which nothing was ever the same again – the Profumo scandal. As in the Vassall case, it combined the lethal mixture of sex and security although it was 'light years' more interesting and salacious. For months there had been rumours that John Profumo, the War Minister, had been enjoying an improper relationship with a Christine Keeler, who had also been sleeping with Captain Ivanov, a Soviet diplomat, and that much of the action had taken place at Cliveden, the Buckinghamshire mansion of the aristocratic Astors. The fuse that was eventually to cause such a massive explosion was lit by Profumo when, in March, he denied to the House of Commons that there was truth in the rumours concerning him and Christine Keeler, the Parliamentary Question having been asked largely owing to the machinations of the redoubtable Labour MP, Colonel George Wigg, who had turned himself into a veritable 'one-man MI6' – and a brilliant foil for the new Labour leader, Harold Wilson, who had put pressure on Macmillan to order the Lord Chancellor to set up an inquiry into the affair. In the meantime, Dr Stephen Ward, a society osteopath, who had rented a flat to Christine Keeler, was arrested and charged with living off immoral earnings, a travesty of justice, which is an indication of the mass hysteria of the time, fomented by press and television, alleging national immorality and decadence, led by a mythical, privileged aristocracy. Further fuel to this particular flame was provided by the 'divorce of the century' between the Duke

428

and Duchess of Argyll which culminated in 1963. Later in the year the sensitive and tragic Ward committed suicide and in September Lord Denning's report cleared Profumo of any infringement of security. However, earlier, and in order to protect himself, Ward had effectively confirmed the charges against Profumo, who had no option but to resign from the Government, in disgrace, on 5 June, and to admit that he had previously lied to the House of Commons, which provided further salacious stories for the media, led by the BBC's satirical weekly show, *That Was the Week That Was*, (p. 370). All of this was seized upon so voraciously by the public that, at the time, I remember being much more impressed by British hypocrisy than by British immorality. Profumo's confession put the spotlight firmly and extremely uncomfortably on the head of security, the Prime Minister, Harold Macmillan. As we know, Macmillan was a highly skilled and consummate politician but he had always thrived on a situation governed by what one might call, a set of political Queensberry's Rules, where gentlemanly conduct prevailed. In the absence of this scenario Macmillan had dug himself into a deep political hole because, in the first place, Profumo had not been a gentleman, both in his relationship with Christine Keeler and in his telling the lie, while, secondly, it was his gentlemanly distaste for matters concerning personal affairs that had led him to close his ears to the rumours that had been circulating for months[1] and, most fatal of all, to refrain from confronting Profumo personally. On the other hand, Harold Wilson had no such gentlemanly inhibitions for he much preferred the politics of the 'rough house' and, on 17 June, in the debate in the Commons on the Profumo affair, he attacked and exposed the Prime Minister mercilessly on the ramifications for national security of the affair and his mishandling of it. Nigel Birch, one of the three Treasury Ministers who had resigned in 1958 (p. 102), called for Macmillan to resign and he was supported by 27 Conservatives who abstained from voting. It was the beginning of the end for the Prime Minister, but Wilson had more 'shots in his locker'.

In the course of some of the investigations concerning Christine Keeler, a connection with the notorious slum landlord, Peter Rachman, who had been guilty of ruthlessly evicting tenants (thus the expression, 'Rachmanism') was established. As we have said, the 1957 Rent Act, which began the necessary process of reducing the

---

[1]In view of his wife's long-established adultery, which he bore like a gentleman, it was probably more than he could bear even to think about the situation.

suffocating grip of rent control, 'generated more heat than light' (p. 238), but in the hysterical atmosphere of the time Wilson could not resist conjuring up a picture whereby the Act had created an army of Rachmans who were exploiting the poor while the rich pursued their decadent ways. In July, Labour moved a censure motion on the Government for encouraging slum landlordism by the 1957 Rent Act, and Wilson committed his party to repealing it on coming to power. Sir Keith Joseph, the Housing Minister, correctly maintained that Rachman's activities were not typical, and set up a committee to investigate – but Wilson had maintained the political initiative. At the Transport and General Workers Union Conference in July we find Wilson platitudinously hailing the idea of an incomes' polity as 'a great adventure', in spite of recent firm evidence as to its inadequacy. However, even if, as an economist, he was aware of the truth of Enoch Powell's logical denunciation of incomes' policies (p. 415) he would not have refrained from jumping on to this particular 'bandwagon' which is, after all, the story of Harold Wilson's life. He had every incentive to maintain the political pressure, as in May the local elections had been disastrous for the Conservatives, with Labour the main beneficiary and the Liberals losing their previous electoral momentum. This trend was confirmed in the Stretford by-election in August when a Conservative majority of 14,129 was reduced to only 3,470. Soon after this he was calling for the identification of socialism with the new age of scientific planning and technology (p. 372), probably the most bogus yet most successful election gimmick of all time.

The fourth and final 'event' determining Macmillan's political life took place on 8 October when he was hurried to hospital for an operation on his prostate gland. Fatefully, he took Wilson's aphorism that 'a week is a long time in politics' too seriously for he thought his physical condition was much more serious than it was. Equally fatefully, the Conservative Party Conference had opened at Blackpool on the same day and by the time it closed, on the 12th, it had established the reputation of being the most exciting, chaotic and decisive Conservative Conference of all – unique in fact. It is a splendid example of the English capacity for radicalism and unconventionality in the midst of an otherwise prevailing conservatism and conventionality. The Conservative Party is a microcosm of this contradiction as, for example, when it indulges in the virtual worship of its leader, but is completely ruthless when it decides that that leader should go when it appears that he or she is not capable of winning the next election – much more so than the Labour Party. The saga began on 10 October when Lord Home announced Macmillan's resignation to the party representatives at the Conference, after having already told the Cabinet that he would not be a candidate for the succession, partly because he was a member of the House of Lords. In the meantime, Macmillan began the process, from his hospital, of arranging for a new Prime Minister to 'emerge' – for the last time in our history. However, the pace suddenly quickened when Lord Hailsham, who was probably Macmillan's original preferred candidate, unexpectedly announced at the conference that he had renounced his peerage to become Quintin Hogg and that he was a candidate for the leadership. Hailsham had never held one of the highest political posts, again because of his peerage and membership of the House of Lords, although as we have seen (p. 412) he had been a very popular and effective Party Chairman and was by way of being one of the two best orators in Parliament, (and, for that matter, in post-war Britain), the other being Iain Macleod. Thus, he had much to commend him but, typically, by 'throwing his hat in the ring' in such a rumbustious and undignified way he ruined his chances, within days, which, in any case, probably indicated that, in spite of his great intellectual and oratorial abilities, he did not possess prime ministerial qualities. This is borne out by the fact that, several months before, as the British leader of a joint Anglo-American team negotiating the nuclear test-ban treaty with the Russians, he had seriously upset the Americans by his emphasis on minor legalistic points to the detriment of attaining agreement on major points. The other main candidates were Butler and Maudling, but in spite of the latter's 'youth' he did not impress or, rather, because of it, he had not established a following in the Party. On the other hand, it was to be the second time in his political career that Butler had appeared to be the natural successor and the second time that he was to be rejected. He presented his reformist views of modern Conservatism to the conference but failed to arouse any enthusiasm among the representatives of the members back in the constituencies. Also, as we have already noted,

> The lugubrious Butler was not popular with the party Establishment . . . although he was very popular with the post-war Tory 'intellectuals' whom he had encouraged at Central Office, and elsewhere . . . (p. 402).

Macmillan was very much an Establishment man and would not willingly have supported Butler, who nevertheless was the choice of the majority of the Cabinet, and it was at this stage that Lord Home, whose low-profile and gentlemanly candidature was the opposite of Hailsham's, suddenly appeared to be the obvious choice.

Paradoxically, Butler's refusal to pursue his candidature aggressively, counted against him. On 18 October, the Queen visited Macmillan in hospital and Lord Home 'emerged' as the new Conservative leader. On 23 October he renounced his peerage, on 7 November he fought a by-election in the safe Scottish seat of Kinross and West Perthshire and he entered the House of Commons as Sir Alec Douglas-Home. In the meantime, Quintin Hogg was appointed Education Secretary on 23 October following the publication and acceptance by the Government of the Robbins Report, which advocated the expansion of higher education to cover all those who were qualified for it (p. 218).

Interestingly, the comparative ease with which Lords Hailsham and Home were able to renounce their titles and the membership of the House of Lords was due to the long and determined struggle of the young Labour MP, Wedgwood Benn, to renounce the title inherited, in November 1960, from his father, the first-generation Labour peer, Lord Stansgate. He immediately rejected the peerage, thus becoming known as 'the reluctant peer', and in May 1961, fought and won the Bristol South-East by-election, caused by his own elevation to the peerage, increasing the Labour majority from 5,827 to 13,044. However, the House of Commons voted by 250 to 177 not to allow Benn to take his seat because he was a member of the House of Lords. In July, the Election Court ruled Benn to be disqualified from the Commons and declared Malcolm St Clair, the defeated Conservative candidate, to be MP for Bristol South-East, which Benn criticized as showing 'the fundamentally undemocratic character of the law', and refused to compromise. This led to the passing of the Peerage Act in July 1963 which enabled peers to renounce their peerages and to stand for the House of Commons, thus complementing the Life Peerage Act of 1958. Wedgwood Benn immediately disclaimed his peerage and in August was elected Labour MP for Bristol South-East – thus making possible Hailsham's dramatic renunciation of his peerage at the Conservative Conference in the following October, as also that of Lord Home.

Sir Alec's assumption of the Premiership coincided with the assassination of President Kennedy in Dallas on 22 November, and the decision of his successor, Lyndon Johnson, in the following August, to sent United States aircraft to attack North Vietnam in retaliation for a claimed attack on a US ship by Vietnamese torpedo boats, was one of the of the great watersheds of modern world history. For years, differences had been intensifying between China and Russia and the failure of the Sino-Soviet Summit in July to resolve them resulted in the division of the Communist world into two massive 'blocs', with China, directly and indirectly, exerting pressures on South-East Asia.

432

The 'domino theory' was much more than a theory, especially in view of the fact that the recalcitrant China (and France) refused to join the United States, the Soviet Union and Britain in signing a nuclear test ban treaty in August. But, more paradoxically, Douglas-Home's Government got off to a bad start as two of the youngest and brightest members of Macmillan's Government, Iain Macleod and Enoch Powell, refused to serve under him as a protest against the 'magic circle' method of the Tory Establishment in 'evolving' a new leader and, more specifically, against their second rejection of the cerebral Butler, on this occasion, in favour of the less-than-cerebral and, superficially, at least, manifestly unsuitable, Douglas-Home. However, the complaisant Butler became Foreign Secretary and the ever-loyal Selwyn Lloyd became Leader of the House of Commons. Apart from the politics of personalities, another great handicap was the unpopularity of the Government, for the Gallup Poll showed 49 per cent support for Labour, 37 per cent for the Conservatives and 12 per cent for the Liberals. But his greatest handicap was that he was opposed by the tricky and brilliant electoral tactician, Harold Wilson, to whom the emergence of the fourteenth Earl of Home was a 'gift from the gods'. Wilson described him as 'an elegant anachronism' and, in conjunction with his outmoded manner of selection, said that he was a symbol of the Conservative failure to adapt to a competitive and technological age. On 17 February, Douglas-Home, in the BBC *Panorama* programme, said that the economy had never been stronger, but on the next day a monthly trade deficit of £120 million, the largest ever recorded (p. 106), was announced. Wilson was able to compare the Prime Minister, with his self-confessed 'matchsticks', unfavourably with his own leadership, as a professional economist, whereby the Labour Party stood for the 'white heat of the technological revolution'. This was summed up in 'Labour and the Scientific Revolution', published by the Labour Party in September 1963 and which offered:

> a new deal for the scientist and technologist in higher education, a new status for scientists in government, and a new role for government-sponsored science in industrial development.

All this meaningless verbiage was vintage Wilson but, apart from its undoubted electoral impact, it brilliantly solved several of the Labour Party's problems at a stroke, namely its traditional inability to appeal to the middle class, who could now associate it with the support of a modernized private industry, and the handicap of the unreformed left wing who interpreted it as a recipe for more nationalization and state intervention. Also, in a speech in January 1964, Wilson proposed the increased intervention of the state in the economy in order to direct investment along productive channels. Taken in conjunction with Wilson's dominance over the inexperienced Douglas-Home in the House of Commons and his even greater superiority over the television medium, it can be said that Wilson had transformed the image of the Labour Party.

On the other hand, in the same way as much, if not everything, about Wilson was superficial it would be a mistake to content oneself with a superficial judgment of Douglas-Home – and what he stood for – as there is evidence that the British public were not unresponsive to this. Although the London Government Act, creating the Greater London Council (GLC), was passed in July 1963, against strong Labour opposition (p. 266), in the first elections to the GLC, in April 1964, Labour won control with the election of 64 councillors against 36 Conservatives. Nevertheless, the Conservatives were able to check Labour gains in the Midlands in the local elections in May, while during 1964 the significant lead which Labour had accumulated in the opinion polls was gradually eroded until they were only narrowly in the lead by the summer. The trade unions remained unpopular, and when the Confederation of British Industry rejected the NEDC plans for price and profit control in March, they were speaking for a wider section of thoughtful and knowledgeable electors who were not taken in by Wilson's vague propaganda. In spite of the opposition of vested interests, the Resale Prices Act, of July, was very popular (p. 105). Above all, as with previous Tory pre-election budgets, Maudling's tax-reducing budget in April 1963 (p. 106) was well received by the public who also did not resent the increase in indirect taxes in the 1964 budget (p. 106). Nevertheless, Sir Alec was sufficiently aware of the possibility of another sterling crisis not to postpone the election beyond his chosen date of 15 October.

Also, by this time, although the Liberal Party remained full of fight under Grimmond's outstanding leadership it had failed in its quest to equate with the other two main parties. The great Liberal revival of 1962 peaked out before the winter of that year when the opinion polls showed that its support had fallen to 20 per cent, a decline which continued steadily throughout 1963, while by June 1964, it was as low as 9 per cent. Their local election results in 1963 were not discouraging, as this sector was, and is, their main strength, but this was not true of the results of by-elections where they lost their deposit at Luton in November 1963 and decreased their share of the poll at Sudbury and Woodbridge in December, a trend which continued in the series of by-elections in May 1964. The Party's national policies continued to be vague and to lack popular appeal as opposed to that of an enthusiastic and unworldly minority. For example, in the Annual Conference in September 1962, following their famous by-election victories, they attempted to make their commitment to a federal Europe more politically acceptable by stressing, illogically and impractically, that this did not necessarily mean the end of national sovereignty. Again, in September 1963, the Liberals proposed a Ministry of Expansion to overcome economic stagnation while Grimmond called for passion in politics as part of the fight against the enemy of complacency, both views expressing the impracticable and vague political notions that were current at the time. In September 1964, Grimmond called for the floating voter to support the Liberals and their manifesto, 'Think for Yourself – Vote Liberal', attempted to woo them by putting forward a radical but non-socialist programme which, as always, fell between the two main political worlds and, once again, it was confirmed that the Liberals could not retain the protest (mainly Conservative) votes that they attracted between general elections – in spite of Grimmond's brilliant efforts in the field and on television, a major reorganization of the Party in September 1962 and the provision of candidates in more than half of the constituencies for the first time since 1950.

The election campaign for the two main parties was a case of 'more of the same'. The manifestos were released in September. The Conservatives', 'Prosperity With A Purpose', pledged the maintenance of the nuclear deterrent and reminded the electorate that it was the party of economic growth as well as undertaking to review the role of the trade unions and the problem of monopolies and mergers, to reform the rating system and to build 400,000 houses a year. In the actual campaign, in the country and in the television studios, the Prime Minister, as always, was amateurish compared with the professionalism of Wilson and Grimmond, but far too much has been made of this as well as of his physical appearance and manner of speaking. Besides, he was supported by a team of able speakers of the calibre of Quintin Hogg, Edward Heath and Edward Boyle. Also there were many ordinary people in the electorate who instinctively mistrusted Wilson but who would have been impressed by Douglas-Home's patent honesty and sincerity, as well as by the fact that he was in politics in order to fulfil an inherited obligation to engage himself in public service, and not for any reason of personal aggrandizement – the everlasting justification of aristocratic government and governors. It is true that he concentrated on defence and foreign affairs, such as Labour's threat to dismantle the British nuclear deterrent, and although it is equally true that the electorate were mainly interested in the economy, they did, in the main, have a real care about the nuclear deterrent and took very seriously what he had to say about it. The Labour manifesto, 'The New Britain', called, as it had done for the last year, for a new age of scientific planning and technology and promised to create a new Ministry of Technology for that purpose, as well as the ill-fated Ministry for Economic Affairs which was to indulge in long-term economic planning, and to leave an emasculated Treasury to deal with the financial and economic minutiae – 'the best laid plans of mice and men'! There were also commitments to create a Parliamentary Commission or Ombudsman, regional planning boards, new ministries for Wales and Overseas Development, (tragically) to reorganize education in accordance with the comprehensive system (p. 218), to 'reform' taxes (!) and to repeal the 1957 Rent Act. Because of the traditional party differences on foreign affairs and defence these were confined to stating its opposition to a national nuclear deterrent, so that the manifesto concentrated on home affairs and on scientific planning as opposed to the unpopular nationalization. Thus, with what, at the time, appeared to be an exciting manifesto behind him and with the Government's record trade deficit (p. 106), Wilson embarked on a virtuoso election campaign, and although he was ably supported by the oratorial performances of his deputy, George Brown, he not only dominated those weeks personally but convincingly acted as though he was already Prime Minister. In an obvious attempt to imitate the 1960 Kennedy-Nixon televised debates in the United States, Wilson, cheekily, challenged Douglas-Home to a televised debate, but when Grimmond demanded the right to participate the idea was dropped for Grimmond was the one man who could be said to have a better television presence than Wilson.

The result was one of the closest in modern British election history and marked a political watershed.

Party	Votes Gained	Percentage of Vote	Average Vote per MP	Number of MPs
Conservative	12,001,396	43.4	39,479	304
Labour	12,205,814	44.1	38,504	317
Liberal	3,092,878	11.2	343,653	9
Others	347,905	1.3		–
	27,637,993	100.0		630

Source: Derived from D. Butler and A. Sloman, *British Political Facts, 1900–75*.

On a 77.1 per cent poll there had been a swing to Labour of 3.5 per cent, producing a working majority of four for a Labour government – the smallest since 1847. Labour had not increased its overall vote, but quite clearly, as a result of Wilson's leadership, the party faithful had turned out to see it safely home. The Labour Party's victory, therefore, was almost certainly due to the restoration of Labour's morale. The Conservative vote, on the other hand, had slumped by between 1 and 2 millions as Sir Alec's demonstrable lack of charisma had driven many normal Conservative supporters either to stay at home or to vote for the Liberals.[1]

To some extent he had also been unlucky. Just one day after polling day, news came that Khrushchev had fallen from power in Russia and that the Communist Chinese had succeeded in exploding their first atomic bomb. Had the news of these events been received a couple of weeks earlier, perhaps his emphasis on foreign affairs and defence would not have sounded so misplaced. He was also let down in the course of the campaign by his Chancellor, Reginald Maudling. The latter had described Labour's election proposals as a 'menu without prices' but had taken so long to have them costed by the Treasury that when he finally came up with a figure of £1,000 million it was already too late to influence the course of the campaign. Wilson, meanwhile, had seized the initiative and was waging an onslaught on 'stop-go', 'thirteen wasted years' and a looming deficit of £800 million, which the figures released by the Treasury for the second quarter of the year allowed him to hang around Maudling's neck with devastating political skill.

The swing to Labour was uneven. The capital swung to the left, but in the South-East and in the Midlands the Tories held their ground. Indeed, and in one at least – Smethwick – it was held that this was the result of a racialist campaign against local immigrant communities which had been run by the Conservative candidate, Peter Griffiths. There was some controversy over the exact nature of Griffiths's appeal, but when he entered the House of Commons after his election there was no doubt of the intensity of Labour's indignation at his election. Wilson condemned him as a 'parliamentary leper' and hoped that all members would treat him as one. Elsewhere in the country the swing was in favour of Labour, although the Liberals did particularly well in the Scottish Highlands. They also retained Orpington against all the predictions of the pundits and managed to win a seat from the Tories in the West Country. Their sense of political achievement, however, was marred by the fact that not only had they lost two seats, but their

---

[1] In fact, he did much better than expected.

overall performance had been frustrated by the electoral system. For having doubled their vote in the second election in a row – this time to 3 million votes – they were still rewarded with fewer than ten seats. The voting system was undoubtedly a democratic one, but it could not be described as fair.[1] Still, a new, radical premier – or so it was thought – had been elected, and Grimmond appeared to find some solace in that.[2]

---

[1] As is apparent from my arguments in Chapter 2, I disagree with this implied support for proportional representation.

[2] *Post-War Britain*, by Alan Sked and Chris Cook, pp. 194–5.